W9-CNE-493

WOMEN WHO FLY

Women Who Fly

GODDESSES, WITCHES, MYSTICS, AND OTHER AIRBORNE FEMALES

Serinity Young

OXFORD
UNIVERSITY PRESS

OXFORD

UNIVERSITY PRESS

Oxford University Press is a department of the University of Oxford. It furthers
the University's objective of excellence in research, scholarship, and education
by publishing worldwide. Oxford is a registered trade mark of Oxford University
Press in the UK and certain other countries.

Published in the United States of America by Oxford University Press
198 Madison Avenue, New York, NY 10016, United States of America.

Library of Congress Cataloging-in-Publication Data
Names: Young, Serenity, author.
Title: Women who fly : goddesses, witches, mystics, and other airborne females / Serenity Young.
Description: New York : Oxford University Press, 2018. |
Includes bibliographical references and index.
Identifiers: LCCN 2017011532 (print) | LCCN 2017052609 (ebook) | ISBN 9780190659691 (updf) |
ISBN 9780190659707 (epub) | ISBN 9780190659714 (oso) | ISBN 9780195307887 (cloth)
Subjects: LCSH: Goddesses. | Wiccans. | Women mystics. | Women. | Supernatural.
Classification: LCC BL473.5 (ebook) | LCC BL473.5 .Y685 2018 (print) | DDC 200.82—dc23
LC record available at https://lccn.loc.gov/2017011532

9 8 7 6 5 4 3 2 1
Printed by Sheridan Books, Inc., United States of America

For Rawn Harding

Flying is woman's gesture—flying in language and making it fly.
HÉLÈNE CIXOUS, "The Laugh of the Medusa"

Contents

Acknowledgments

I INITIALLY EXPLORED some of the aerial women of this book, such as swan maidens and *apsarās*, through articles I wrote for *An Encyclopedia of Archetypal Symbolism*, compiled at the Archive for Research in Archetypal Symbolism (ARAS). A few years later, I returned to ARAS to research images for this book, and I am very grateful to Ami Ronenberg for granting me access to this archive and for her assistance and insights.

In the 1980s I worked in the Oral History Department of Columbia University as a transcriber of oral histories, among which were those of the first women accepted into the United States Air Force Academy; there I later read the oral history of Hanna Reitsch. Clearly, life has presented me with opportunities, the full import of which I did not realize until this book began to take shape.

The American Museum of Natural History (AMNH), where I am a research associate, provided a stimulating environment, a formidable collection of artifacts, and access to experts in many of the world's cultural areas. Most notably, Laurel Kendall, Stanley Freed, and Robert Carneiro always provided enthusiasm and very practical advice, while the librarians at AMNH were more than helpful. Barry Landau saw me through many a computer glitch. Additionally, Laurel Kendall allowed me to audit her class, "The Korean Shaman Lens: Anthropology, Medicine, Popular Religion, and Performance," at Columbia University, which proved to be of inestimable help in sharpening my perspective on the vast geographical and historical range of all matters shamanic. Jonathan White was an enthusiastic and creative intern on this project during the summer of 2008, while the indefatigable Amanda Audette helped to move this book forward as an intern in the summer of 2014. The inestimable Linden Kawamura provided much-needed assistance with the bibliography and permissions for images, as well as with line editing in the fall of 2016 and spring of 2017. Her commitment to this project has been a crucial support. With skill and humor she corrected errors and updated references.

I am grateful to the Asian Arts Council for a grant to seek out *aspsarās, ḍākinīs,* and *yoginīs* in their native habitats in South and Southeast Asia. In India, Mary Storm, as ever, offered extremely helpful insights about South Asian images and archaeological sites along with warm hospitality, while Arundhati Banerjee of the Archaeological Survey of India once again provided helpful contacts throughout India and was unsparingly generous in sharing her knowledge of sites and artifacts. I would also like to express my appreciation to the Schoff Fund at the University Seminars at Columbia University for their help with publication. The ideas presented here have benefited from discussions in the University Seminar on Studies in South Asia.

When I presented parts of chapters 5 and 10 to of the Friends of the Saints of New York City, the members provided stimulating discussions about flying, bilocation, transvection, ascension, assumption, and so on, as well as pertinent examples of saintly and not so saintly aerial women. Sections of chapters 6 and 7 were given as lectures at the École des Hautes Études en Sciences Sociales, where I was a research scholar in the History of Science and in Archaeology, and at the Columbia University Seminar on Buddhist Studies. The many pertinent comments and suggestions I received on these occasions were most appreciated.

Christian Luczanits was generous in sharing ideas about and rare images of aerial women, while David Rosenberg, Tashi Chodron, and other staff members at the Rubin Museum of Himalayan Art were always welcoming and ready to discuss details of their exhibitions. Claudine Cohen provided excellent advice on images and walked me through prehistory, while Marian Kaplan was helpful in my initial work on Hanna Reitsch. June-Ann Greeley and Francis Tiso were particularly helpful with regard to flying mystics and discussions about the Holy Spirit as female. Claude Conyers adjusted my alignment on the topic of ballet and more generally, with his keen editorial eye, discerned the overall shape of the book at a time I was so weighted down with details that I forgot to keep looking up. James Waller provided essential editorial help that made this not only a more readable but a better book. My Oxford University Press editor Cynthia Read has the patience of a saint mixed with the requisite sense of humor that kept me on track and got me to finish.

Research librarians at both the main branch of the New York Public Library and its Performing Arts Library, as well as at Columbia University, continually amazed me with their helpfulness and erudition. Even in this age of the Internet, where would we scholars be without them? I must also thank the librarians at Queens College, the Costume Institute of the Metropolitan Museum of Art, and the Goethe Institute in New York City. Nonetheless, any errors are mine alone.

The enthusiasm of my colleagues in the Department of Classical, Middle Eastern and Asian Languages and Cultures at Queens College was a great support, as was their willingness to discuss sections of the text. I am blessed with additional friends who have a deep interest in my work and offered support both material and spiritual. This book could not have been written without them: Tim Harwood, Ralph Martin, Tina Eisenbeis, Lozang Jamspal, Gopal Sukhu, Hanna Kim, Karen Pechilis, Joel Bordeaux, Carol Anderson, Christina Stern, Andrew Martin, Marya Ursin, and Dan Potter.

WOMEN WHO FLY

Introduction

PERHAPS THE WORLD'S most famous image of a winged female is the statue of the Greek goddess of victory, Nike, also known as the Victory of Samothrace (Figure 0.1)—a centerpiece of the Louvre Museum, where it is magnificently displayed in all its glory at the top of Daru stairway, formerly the museum's main entrance.[1] It was sculpted around 220–185 BCE to commemorate victory in an unknown sea battle, and Nike is depicted at the moment of landing on the deck, her body surging with power up and through her arched and extended wings. It is one of the finest pieces of the Hellenistic Period. (More will be said about her in chapter 1.)

My adult journey with winged women began with this statue when I first entered the Louvre through its earlier entrance. Standing over eighteen feet (5.57 m) high from its base to the tip of its wings and carved out of exquisite Parian and Rhodian marble, it froze me in place, stunned with awe. Day after day I returned to sit and stare—in the early spring of 1970 there were few other visitors to disturb my contemplations—having no idea what to make of its transcendental power and beauty. As John Berger has written: "The relation between what we see and what we know is never settled . . . . [T]he knowledge, the explanation, never quite fits the sight."[2] After I returned home to the United States, the experience slowly faded from my mind, until now, these many years later, when Nike is once again paramount in my thoughts—she and, as I now know, her many sisters from around the world.

FIGURE 0.1 Victory of Samothrace (Nike), second century BCE. Marble. Photo: Michel Urtado/ Tony Querrec/Benoît Touchard. Musée du Louvre.
© Musée du Louvre, Dist. RMN-Grand Palais/Utrado, Querrec, Touchard/Art Resource, NY.

Women Who Fly: Goddesses, Witches, Mystics, and Other Airborne Females is a typology of sky-going females, an intriguing and unstudied area of the world's myths, religions, and iconography. It is a broad topic. My goal has been not to restrict this theme (or its imagery) nor to force it into the confines of any one discipline or cultural perspective, but rather to celebrate its diversity while highlighting commonalities and delineating the religious and social contexts in which it developed. Paraphrasing Christopher Hill, the paradigm itself makes it worthwhile to compare such females in the light of differing national circumstances.[3] Aerial women are surprisingly central to understanding similarities between various religious imaginations through which they carved trajectories over time.

FEMALE FLIGHT

One of the earliest stories of female flight comes from ancient China. The legendary Emperor Yao had two daughters, Nü Ying and O Huang, both of whom knew how to fly. At their father's request, they instructed the future emperor Shun (traditionally 2258–2208 BCE) in the art of flying, which he used not only to escape an immediate danger but also as an expression of his divine nature and therefore of his right to rule. His ability to fly seems to have been connected to wearing a bird suit, which is very suggestive of the feather suits that were worn by later Daoist mystics who were called "feather clothed" (see chapter 11 for further discussion of this) and the feather suits of swan maidens and some Asian fairies (chapters 4 and 5), as well as the bird suits worn by northeast Asian shamans (chapter 9). After many adventures, Shun married the sisters and became emperor.[4] In this early story, flying women are sexual beings who bestow blessings, such as sovereignty and supernatural gifts, on male heroes—a theme that is repeated in many different times and places.

As with Nü Ying and O Huang, many of these airborne women marry mortal men, transforming them into something more than they had been, but they do not always live happily ever after. Aerial women often shape-shift between human and avian forms, as with swan maidens; while in human form, however, they are vulnerable to captivity. Once captured, they sometimes live with a man for years, and even bear his children, before finally escaping back into their bird form and fleeing. At other times an aerial woman willingly accepts a man but sets a condition or taboo—one that he inevitably breaks. She then flies away. This suggests the paradoxical nature of these creaturely and sexual beings; on the one hand, they are creatively involved with humans through their reproductive powers, while on the other they reject the terrestrial realm of human beings. They are essentially birdlike, briefly nesting on the earth, but most at home in the sky. Some can confer the blessings of fertility and immortality or snatch life away. One needs to be very careful in dealing with them.

Quite often aerial females are dancers (goddesses, swan maidens, fairies, *apsarās*, and *ḍākinīs*), while some women attempt to transform themselves through dance into birdlike creatures (chapters 4 and 9), bringing the aerial to the terrestrial while intimating the human capacity to bridge the two. Then there are dance rituals (of shamans, mystics, and witches) that lead to *magical flight*,[5] a term historians of religion have coined to indicate the use of magical or religious means to achieve flight during which the soul or spirit flies while the body mostly remains on the ground.

Flying females from a wide variety of cultures are linked to sexuality, death and rebirth, or immortality. In different places and historical periods there were remarkably similar discourses about the unpredictable powers of aerial women, who could be generous or withholding, empowering or destructive. Because of their uncertain nature, the question arose as to how they could be controlled: whether by supplication or coercion. Over time, they flew through a universe of ever-increasing constraint in which similar means were used to capture and domesticate them, to turn them into handmaidens of male desire and ambition.

HEROINES, FREEDOM, AND CAPTIVITY

Supernatural women who bridge the division of earth and sky or who simply soar through space present an intense image of freedom and transcendence.[6] Yet while flight can be seen as untrammeled soaring, it can also represent fleeing from danger and/or captivity, as in tales about captured swan maidens and fairy wives. This is not to deny that several kinds of supernatural women—Valkyries, *apsarās*, *yoginīs*, and *ḍākinīs*, (chapters 3, 6, and 7)—were in the service of men, while witches were believed to fly in order to meet with and serve their horned god, or Satan (chapter 8). Even Wonder Woman is enraptured by her elusive lover and fellow aviator, Steve Trevor (chapter 12).

Sigmund Freud theorized that flying dreams express a subliminal desire for sexual power and that the feelings accompanying such an experience are repressed aspects of sexual arousal. Yet the stories in this volume tell us that, for many aerial females (such as swan maidens, fairies, and Brunhilde), having sex can mean the loss of flight, the loss of power, as sex is part of their captivity and domestication. In contradistinction, some aerial females (such as goddesses, *ḍākinīs*, some tantric practitioners, shamans, and Asian mystics) are sexual only as their desires dictate.

Flying women raise important questions about what exactly constitutes the heroic female. Traditionally in myth, folklore, and literature, the heroine is a good girl, one who knows her place in the patriarchal scheme of things and does well in the traditional female roles of passive maiden, self-sacrificing mother, or obedient and dutiful wife. In the classical tradition of ancient Greece, the main expression of female heroism is her death[7] and, to a lesser degree, giving birth. The heroine's death is decidedly female; she often dies indoors and in secrecy, not publicly, without witnesses, and by her own hand. The preferred means is that she hang herself (like Phaedra), "an act that evokes at once the adornments around a woman's neck (an erotic part of her body), the webs of deceit she traditionally weaves, and a yoke with which she is finally tamed in death."[8] Male models of heroism break free of conventional experience to enter strange realms and return with the prize of newfound knowledge, wealth, or the won princess (as evidenced by Gilgamesh, Ulysses, Aeneas, Dante, and the heroes of sleeping beauty tales, to give just a few examples). The hero returns home renewed and enriched.[9] Contrarily, women who fly want to be somewhere else to stay there; they do not want to return to conventional experience, which they view as captivity. They require us to rethink our ideas about female waywardness.

In her study of stories about the semi-legendary King Arthur, Maureen Fries has persuasively argued for a distinction between heroines, heroes, and the counter-hero:

> A heroine is recognizable by her performance of a traditionally identified, female sex-role. But any woman who, by choice, by circumstance, or even by accident, escapes definition exclusively in terms of such a traditional role is capable of heroism, as opposed to heroinism. [An example of this is when women] assume the usual male role of exploring the unknown beyond their assigned place in society; and . . . reject to various degrees the usual female role of preserving order (principally by forgoing adventure to stay at home). The[ir] adventurous paths . . . require the males who surround them to fill subordinate, non-protagonist roles in their stories. . . . [Then there is the] counter-hero [who] possesses the hero's superior power of action without possessing his or her adherence to the dominant culture or capability of renewing its values. While the hero proper transcends and yet respects the norms of the patriarchy, the counter-hero violates them in some way. For the male Arthurian counter-hero, such violation usually entails wrongful force; for the female, usually powers of magic. . . . [S]he is preternaturally alluring or preternaturally repelling, or sometimes both, . . . but her putative beauty does not as a rule complete the hero's valor, as does the heroine's. Rather, it often threatens to destroy him, because of her refusal of the usual female role.[10]

The female counter-hero is indifferent to patriarchal values; she harkens back to an earlier, non-patriarchal time and to non-patriarchal sources of knowledge.[11] For Fries, she is personified by Morgan le Fay (discussed in chapter 5)—a flying fairy sometimes said to be King Arthur's half-sister.

The female counter-heroine is the bad girl: the dark-haired one, not the blonde; sexual, not virginal; multidimensional, slippery, and cunning. In the chapters that follow, the reader is invited to rethink the shopworn categories of good and bad girls who vie for the affections of the hero. Instead, the stories presented here highlight the female longing for freedom, and center on women trying to escape constraints, whether they be physical captivity or patriarchal definitions of womanhood. These tales will resonate with any woman who has ever felt restrained or held back, who has experienced lack of opportunity or just not had enough air to breathe. These tales, in symbolic as well as overt ways, variously articulate the following things: the malaise of domesticated women that Betty Friedan famously defined as the "feminine mystique"; Carl Jung's focus on the *anima* (men's internal female guide); Freud's famous question, "What do women want?"; and modern women's suspicion that things have gone awry between women and men.

Supernatural flying women date from prehistoric times, when people postulated the radical separation of earth and sky (chapter 1). Among humankind's first religious acts was to create myths and rituals to bridge this separation. Some evidence for this can be seen in ancient carvings of women with birdlike heads (Figure 0.2), which reveal a fascination with females and flying, as well as a hint of the notion of transcendence. These bird-women are the foremothers of the supernatural and human airborne women who followed.

The desire to get beyond the mundane and the terrestrial to reach new heights of spiritual experience has been expressed in myths and the visual arts throughout the world. Flight from the captivity of earth's gravity and the mental constraints of time-bound desire are the backbone of myth-making. Women and goddesses have

FIGURE 0.2 Female figure with bird head and winglike arms, c. 3500–3400 BCE, El Ma'mariya, Upper Egypt. h: 11-1/2 inches.

Brooklyn Museum, Charles Edwin Wilbour Fund.

figured prominently in such myths, both as independent actors and as guides for men. This can be seen in the rich mythology and abundant images of the Egyptian winged goddess Isis, who resurrected her dead husband, Osiris (chapter 2), as well as in tales of swan maidens—immortal women who help mortal men transcend their brutish, impoverished state (a theme also found in fairy-bride tales). The flying Valkyries of Norse religion, like the *apsarās* of ancient India, carry slain heroes to heaven—a theme that also calls to mind the flying *yoginīs* of Tantric Hinduism and the sky-walking *ḍākinīs* of Indo-Tibetan Buddhism, who lead heroic male saints to liberation, as well as the winged goddess Nike (and her Roman counterpart, Victory), who confers success and thus immortal fame on heroes (chapter 2). Significantly, aerial women have in various cultures acted as guides to the Land of the Dead, a theme Dante utilized in his depiction of a flying St. Lucia[12] and a winged Beatrice (chapter 1),[13] because women were believed to know death in ways men could not (chapter 2).

TRANSCENDENCE AND IMMANENCE

The human desire to be in touch with the sky and sky-beings can be understood as a longing for transcendence, a word and an experience with many meanings. To transcend is to go beyond, to rise above limits, to exceed or surpass others or what has been done before, to be superior, and above all to be free from constraint.[14] Transcendence is understood to be the opposite of immanence, and in religious thinking, these opposing terms can be used to indicate that the divine is either beyond, above, and completely other or right here, among and within us.[15] This study emphasizes the oneness of immanence and transcendence in the earthly appearances of aerial/celestial females and in their ability to confer earthly (supernatural) powers or transcendence by transforming men into trans-earthly beings (immortals or liberated beings).

In many cultures the female body is depicted as personifying the human condition of mortality, mutability through aging, sensuality, desire, and earthly confinement. Ironically, "[i]n their desire for absolute transcendence and totality, men make women the repository of all bodiliness and immanence and thus efface the other [woman] as a conscious being. Masculinity in its pure form is a kind of 'bad faith of transcendence,' in which immanence and the body are denied and projected onto women, who become consciousnessless beings on whom men can assert their freedom."[16] In their flaunting of the earth's gravity and ability to shape-shift, flying females therefore challenge the masculine hold on the notion of transcendence.

SHAPE-SHIFTING

Shape-shifting, or the ability to change one's bodily form, is part of the repertoire of women who fly. There are swan maidens who can be trapped in human form if a man steals their swan suit; witches and shamans who were believed to fly by various means, including the ability to change shape; Valkyries who can appear as birds; *ḍākinīs* who change shape at will; fairies (like Morgan le Fay) who can soar or change into rock; and even Wonder Woman, who changes from dowdy, bespectacled Diana Prince into a gorgeous superhero. Shape-shifters can change others, too; certain women (like Circe) were said to have the power to turn men into beasts—a clear allusion to the similarity of animal and human nature when it comes to sexuality. Cinderella's fairy godmother could change both things (pumpkins into carriages) and beings (mice into horses, a rat and lizards into men).[17] From the male perspective, women are shape-shifters par excellence, changing from desirable, young, acquiescent women into ruthless shrews.

Shape-shifting breaches fundamental boundaries, such as those between humans and animals and between the divine and mundane realms. Shape-shifters are unnerving because they cannot be contained within the primary categories of species, suggesting other, uncanny possibilities that subvert fundamental beliefs about what it is to be human. They are indifferent to differentiation, violating the established order, including the order of gender. By changing out of their human forms, shape-shifting women shatter gendered social conceptions as well as those of species. Traditionally, women are the preservers of orderliness: they keep the cave, hut, house, or apartment separated from the dirt (nature) that drifts in from outside. The witch who turns her broom into a source of freedom rather than domestic drudgery turns the patriarchal social system upside down. Stories about seemingly domesticated captured women who change into birds and fly away not only challenge the so-called benefits women derive from patriarchal marriage, they also reveal male insecurities—and perhaps female fantasies—about the relation of gender to power and bring into question which sex actually has the greater power.[18] These stories are, after all, told primarily about women, not men, and they mostly arose in vigorously bi-gendered societies, even those that acknowledged a third sex (chapter 9).

Terrifying in their physical fluidity, shape-shifters are perversions of nature, belonging to the category of the monstrous-feminine, which goes beyond shape-shifters to include women with both animal and human features: the Gorgons, Sirens, Furies, and sphinxes of Greco-Roman mythology, demonesses of all times, and that most unnatural of females, Athena. Athena's non-womb birth from the head of Zeus qualifies her for the monstrous-feminine; an armed and armored woman, she maintains an acceptable place in the patriarchal order by helping men kill a rich assortment of female monsters (chapter 2). Also included in this category are the demanding, shape-shifting, and terrifying Indo-Tibetan ḍākinīs, who dance naked except for their ornaments of human skulls and bones, as well as the European witches who rejected Christianity and its ideas about womanhood and sexuality. Even sainted medieval women are perverted by their aerial feats (chapter 10).

The monstrous-feminine is never domestic; its members are paradigms of female inconstancy.[19] As Barbara Creed points out, the very phrase "monstrous-feminine" "emphasizes the importance of gender in the construction of her monstrosity."[20] Their power to both arouse and terrify lies in their difference—that of gender and biology.

Women Who Fly is a history of religious and social ideas about aerial females as expressed in legends, myths, rituals, sacred narratives, and artistic productions. It is also about symbolic uses of women in mythology, religion, and society that have shaped, and continue to shape, our social and psychological reality. It focuses on three clusters of religious traditions and folk beliefs that have the most vivid airborne females: the ancient Near Eastern and European cluster (chapters 2 to 5); the Asian cluster (chapters 6, 7, and 11); and the Shamanic cluster (chapter 9), which is rich in rituals that propel the shamaness to the heavens through drumming, songs, and costumes with winglike arms, feathers, and celestial imagery. A fourth cluster, that of the Judeo-Christian-Islamic traditions, is relevant because of the ways in which these traditions problematized both flying and women, a theme embodied in depictions of angels and fairies (chapter 5), male suspicions about the somatic experiences of female Christian mystics (chapter 10), and the persecution of witches who were believed to fly to witches' sabbaths (chapter 8). Where relevant, other religious traditions are referred to as well. The last chapter compares the lives of two great aviators, the American Amelia Earhart and the German Hanna Reitsch. Close in age but quite different in character, both were used as propagandistic tools of the state that foreshadowed and then prevailed during World War II. These two women and other female aviators, as well as the popular comic book character Wonder Woman, who was created during World War II, are the last of the aerial women hovering over male warriors.

In the spirit of friendly redundancy, dates are repeated and there are many cross-references for readers who may want to read the chapters in a different order.

One question lingered in my mind as I researched this book: why is a "flighty" woman a bad thing, connoting superficiality, instability, unreliability, and silliness?

Flighty also means swift, quick, whimsical, and humorous. So why does the phrase not conjure imaginative, free, creative women who think and live outside the box, especially the box of patriarchy? To "let fly" at someone is to attack, as did aerial warrior women such as the Valkyries and the winged goddesses of war and love. Thus, a flighty woman might just as well be an enraged, courageous woman. But, as will be shown, neither "enraged" nor "courageous" was an approved adjective for women unless they were under the control of patriarchal forces.

1

Earth, Sky, Women, and Immortality

FROM TIME IMMEMORIAL PEOPLE all over the world have perceived the universe as divided into distinct but integrated realms. One of the most common depictions has been a threefold division of underworld, earth, and heaven.[1] Earth is the everyday world of nature and human beings; the underworld that of the dead and spirits; and heaven the realm of the gods and ancestors. Among the first religious acts of our earliest earthbound forebears was the creation of rituals they believed would connect them to the sky realm, and they placed great esteem on those individuals—priest-kings, shamans, oracles, and the like—who could seemingly contact the heavens through such rituals.[2] This was not a one-way transmission; they also envisioned supernatural sky beings who could visit the earth: goddesses, magical beasts, demons, and so on. There is evidence that women were perceived as intermediary beings who could move between realms;[3] women, so to speak, had one foot in the mundane world and the other in heavenly and underworld realms that brought new life, death, and regeneration.

EARTH, SKY, AND BIRDS

A middle space both separates and connects earth and heaven. Birds, with their ability to travel freely through this space, were often seen as messengers of the

divine. Humans attempted to utilize this space through the rising smoke of cremation fires, as well as through burnt offerings made to ancestors and celestial
beings.[4] One dramatic example that combines birds and sacred smoke comes from
ancient India, where brick fire altars in the shape of birds were constructed.[5] In
commenting on why the fire altar has this shape, Frits Staal reminds us that in
Indian belief "fire, as well as Soma," two vital components for communion with
the divine, "were fetched from heaven by a bird,"[6] referring to *Rig Veda* IV.26 and
27. *Soma* is an elixir prepared for and consumed at Vedic rituals that may have had
hallucinogenic properties to aid participants in accessing the gods. Fire, of course,
is essential for the burnt sacrifices that carry offerings to the gods. As early as
1,000 BCE, such an altar (Figure 1.1) was prepared with the help of both human and
supernatural women for one of the most elaborate Indian rituals, the *Agnicayana*
("laying of the fire[-altar]"), which took more than a year to construct and required
more than one thousand bricks.[7] The ritual itself lasted for fourteen days. The time
and effort put into this ritual speaks for its importance to those performing it.
According to the *Śatapatha Brāhmaṇa* (c. eighth century BCE), its correct performance leads to immortality:

> "What is done here in (the building of) the altar, whereby the Sacrificer con-
> quers recurring death?" Well, he who builds an altar becomes the deity Agni;
> and Agni (the fire), indeed, is the immortal (element).[8]

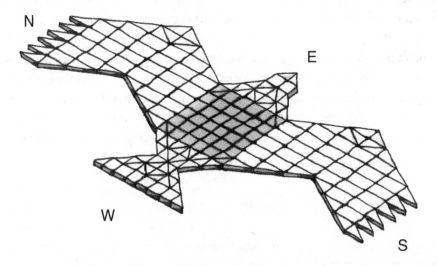

FIGURE 1.1 Bird-shaped fire altar of the Agnicayana, drawn by Linden Kawamura after Staal's
description.

During the *Agnicayana,* the sacrificer's wife molded the first brick to be used in the altar's construction, as well as the pot in which the new fire would be kindled before being brought to the completed altar.[9] The officiating priest recited mantras calling on goddesses and protectresses such as the women "with uncut wings." The mythic landscape of the ritual was thus overpopulated with femininity, a rather unusual situation in Vedic ritual.[10] Through the ritual the sacrificers were transformed into birds, and therefore they were forbidden to eat birds; this would have been tantamount to cannibalism: "For he who builds the altar of fire assumes a bird's form."[11] Similarly, during another ancient Indian ritual, a husband and wife mounted a symbolic pillar, spread their arms like wings, and cried out: "We have come to heaven, to the gods; we have become immortal."[12] The transformation of the sacrificer into a bird is even more explicit in the *Pañcaviṃśa Brāhmaṇa* (5.3.5), which says, "The sacrificer, having become a bird, soars to the world of heaven," and "Those who know have wings" (14.1.13).[13] Another Vedic ritual involved the *hotṛ* priests riding in a swing (a simulation of flying) called the "ship bound for heaven," while the sacrificer was called "the bird flying to heaven," and "the girls who danced around the fire were . . . birds flying to heaven."[14]

Such sacrifices emphasize the sky as the pathway between the human and divine. The Greek playwright Aristophanes (c. 448–388 BCE) turned this understanding to satiric advantage in his comedy *The Birds*, in which two Athenian men persuade birds to build an enormous aerial wall so that none of the sacrifices offered to the gods would reach them. The gods are thus starved into submission and the two Athenians rule in their place.[15]

Nature itself intimates an atmospheric connection between earth and sky, most beautifully in mountain peaks shrouded in clouds that blur the boundaries of earth and sky, and in rainbows that suggest a path between heaven and earth. Tibetan Buddhism utilizes the latter in the rainbow-colored dress of the sky-going *ḍākinīs* and in the concept of the rainbow body, the spiritually transformed body that dissolves into space at death. In the Judeo-Christian-Islamic tradition, a rainbow is a reminder and a sign of God's covenant with humanity that he will never again destroy them as he did in the Flood (Gen. 9:1–17). More violently, nature terrifies with thunder and lightning strikes that were believed to establish sacred spaces; coming directly from heaven, the spot burned by lightning was marked off from the mundane realm. Similarly, comets crossed the sky and meteors fell to earth—events that were thought to be rich with meaning.[16] The sky, its beings, and its phenomena were perceived as mighty forces that needed to be appeased, pacified, and engaged.

Material evidence for human interest in the sky and its phenomena dates back to the Middle Paleolithic (c. 50,000 years ago), when stones were engraved with groups of stars or constellations.[17] Later evidence comes from about 28,000 BCE, when construction was started on Stonehenge; from 12,000 BCE in central France, where notations of the phases of the moon were engraved on cave walls; from 4000 BCE in the Euphrates Valley, where constellations of the stars were drawn and labeled on clay tablets; and from the Nebra sky disc (Figure 1.2) in present-day Germany, circa 1600 BCE.[18] Cognitively, we are remarkably similar to our Cro-Magnon ancestors, who also lived in symbolized religious worlds, buried their dead, and drew or carved images that displayed a belief in the possibility of shape-shifting from human to animal and back again.[19] They were keen observers of nature's cycles and they experienced themselves as part of it.[20]

The orderly procession of the sun, moon, and planets against the comparatively stationary background of fixed stars that form the constellations provided a sense of cosmic order that was missing on earth, with its unpredictable climate, dangerous animals, and unreliable food resources. From prehistoric times, interest in sky phenomena indicated the wish to establish a relationship with the forces of the sky, and to interpret the will of the deities who resided there. This interest eventually led to empirical rules about forecasting the weather, knowing when to

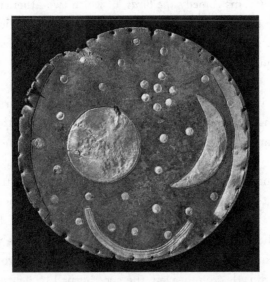

FIGURE 1.2 Nebra sky disc, c. 1600 BCE. Bronze with blue-green patina and gold inlay. The disc shows the sun and the crescent moon against a background of stars, emphasizing the seven Pleiades. The golden arc on the right represents the movements of the sun, while the lower arc represents a celestial ship that might carry the sun or the moon.

Halle State Museum of Prehistory. Courtesy of the State Office for Heritage Management and Archaeology Saxony-Anhalt. Photograph by Juraj Lipták.

plant, and how to locate oneself on the sea or in the desert. These practices became a "science" that received its fullest development in the astrological theories of the ancient world.[21]

MAGICAL FLIGHT, ASCENSION, AND ASSUMPTION

The early human urge to make offerings to or interpret messages from the celestial realm was accompanied by the urge to physically ascend to the heavens. Along with interpreting the divine messages of birds or sending earthly gifts skyward through smoke, people longed to travel skyward themselves. Some of the earliest known human stories are about making such a journey, and quite early in history we find rituals designed to recall and duplicate descents of the gods that had opened a path between heaven and earth, or to enact human ascents through ropes, ladders, mountains, or trees or by imitating the flight of birds.[22] Vivid examples of this have been found among shamanic practitioners (see chapter 9) and in the funeral rites of Roman emperors, discussed below. Less ritualized but equally intense experiences of flying up to heaven have been reported by mystics from all parts of the world (see chapters 10 and 11).

The human desire to break through earthly restraints took many forms. It could be achieved through dreams or ecstatic experiences; by ascending a mountain, tree, ladder, or ritual pole; through self-cultivation, asceticism, or spiritual discipline; or through rituals. Multiple terms exist for the varieties of aerial experience, including magical flight, transvection, bilocation, ascension, assumption, and apotheosis. Magical flight can refer either to actual bodily flight or to spiritual flight. Examples of both have been described in many religious traditions and in folk tales from around the world, making magical flight one of the earliest religious beliefs.[23] Transvection refers to being carried through the air by another entity, for example a witch, a devil, or a Valkyrie or *apsarā* carrying a dead warrior to heaven. An example of bilocation occurs when Circe instantaneously transverses space to arrive at the coast ahead of Odysseus and his men, after having been left behind by them (*Odyssey* ch. 7). Terms such as "ascension" and "assumption" usually refer to after-death experiences of rising up to heaven by various means. Well-known examples are the Ascension of Christ and the Assumption of Mary, so frequently depicted in Christian iconography.[24] Within this category, we must also include Muḥammad's Night Journey, sometimes referred to as a dream, in which he ascended to paradise on a winged horse with a woman's face (Figure 4.3, p. 90).[25] Islam, like Judaism, prohibits idol worship and consequently forbids any representation of humans, God, or angels. Shi'a Islam, however, allows images, though the image of Muḥammad's Night Journey is still controversial, and the Prophet's face is often veiled in other depictions.[26]

Other connections between ascension and death appear in biographies of Tibetan Tantric adepts who, when death approaches, are believed to rise into the sky and dissolve into space (see chapters 7 and 11). A similar notion is expressed by an above-ground grave of a Siberian shaman, as shown in Figure 1.3; its platform has collapsed, but four bird-topped posts remain attached to the coffin.[27] They are probably divers, birds important to living Evenk shamans during their spiritual flights to other worlds and in their afterlife journeys as well. Apotheosis refers to the deification of human beings upon death, a privilege usually, but not always, reserved for rulers (see Apotheosis section in this chapter and chapter 2). Magical flight, transvection, ascension, assumption, and apotheosis can lead to immortality, a boon granted by many different aerial females.

After-death examples of flight are not simply a desire to escape death; at the core of religious belief is the *denial* of death and the promise of renewal, rebirth, immortality, or salvation.[28]

FIGURE 1.3 Above-ground grave of a Siberian Shaman. Its platform has collapsed. Note the carved birds attached by poles to the top of the coffin.

Photograph Waldemar Jochelson, c. 1897. Courtesy of the Division of Anthropology, American Museum of Natural History.

DREAMS, WOMEN, AND FLYING

Since the beginning of time dreams have enabled people to glimpse the permeability of the universe, to breach the solid walls of their dwellings, or to fly through the heavens as they traveled to sacred places, changed shape, talked with long-dead loved ones, experienced sexual pleasure, and faced terrors. Freed from their bodies and mundane consciousness, they comprehended the incomprehensible. Like long-lost travelers they returned to a world ruled by physical definitions of time and space and were left to ponder their dream experiences and imagine possibilities beyond their waking life.

Dreams about flying have been recorded from the earliest times and from all over the world.[29] They are a universal experience that has provoked imitation both literal (aviators) and metaphorical (shamans) and has inspired the religious imagination. Even our word "nightmare" is derived from the Old English *maere*, a word referring to a female spirit, demon, or monster who comes to a sleeper and creates a sensation of suffocation[30]—which reminds us that such dreams can be terrifying—while "hag-ridden" means to be "afflicted by nightmares," with "hag" referring to a female evil spirit or a nightmare.[31] As negative as these terms are, they introduce a distinctly feminine element into the dreaming experience.

Whether they were terrifying nightmares or visions of hope and freedom, to the ancient mind dreams appeared to come from beyond the physical body, from realms outside mundane experience, and they were thus highly valued. From earliest times to the present, dreaming has provided access to an otherworldly realm deeply connected to women[32] that reflects ancient beliefs about aerial females and the beyond.

Although most of the dreams that have been preserved are those of men, history tells us that some of the earliest dream interpreters were women. In the ancient Sumerian story "Dumuzi's Dream" (c. 2000 BCE), it is Dumuzi's sister Geshtinanna who correctly interprets his dream.[33] Similarly, Gilgamesh's mother, Ninsun, interprets his dreams,[34] but this text marks a shift: after Gilgamesh meets and falls in love with the wild man Enkidu, it is Enkidu who interprets his own and Gilgamesh's dreams,[35] albeit incorrectly. Similarly, the Bible emphasizes male dream interpreters such as Joseph and Daniel (Gen. 40:8–14 and 41:15–33, Dan. 2:25–45, etc.). This gendered disjuncture suggests there is something of value at stake in dream interpretation—most obviously the ability to interpret otherworldly or divine discourse, an awesome power indeed—with ramifications in both the human and divine worlds.[36] Yet it is Penelope who makes possibly the most famous speech about dreams in antiquity, saying that false dreams comes through gates of ivory and true dreams through gates of horn (*Odyssey* 19.560–569). It is women who possess knowledge of dreams and of realms beyond the earthly experience.

In ancient China it was not uncommon to include a prophetic dream as part of the historical explanation for someone's rise to power, even if that person was a woman, as in the case of the childless Empress Deng (81–121 CE), who successfully ruled China despite the coming of age of the young emperor chosen by her. As a child she dreamed of flying:

> She has risen to the sky, which is perfectly blue, and is touching it with her hand. Her hand finds something described as "shaped like the nipple on a bronze bell" which she immediately puts into her mouth and begins to suck on for nourishment. When she told her parents, they consulted a dream interpreter who said, "Yao [a legendary emperor] dreamt that he climbed up to the sky, and Tang dreamt that he rose to the sky and licked it. Both cases foreshadowed their becoming sage kings. The dream is unspeakably auspicious."[37]

In early medieval Europe, women claiming to be witches who flew to witches' sabbaths were believed just to be dreaming (see chapter 8). At least one Sicilian witch confessed to the Spanish Inquisition that sometimes flying to a witches' sabbath seemed to be a dream because afterward she awoke in her bed.[38]

In addition to individuals who had dreams in which they flew, flying women were the subject of dreams and nightmares: Valkyries, witches, succubi, and *ḍākinīs* all make meaningful appearances in dreams. The ancient and medieval worlds have left us many erotic images (Figure 1.4) of beautiful or monstrous winged women who, so to speak, rape sleeping men, causing them to ejaculate. Intriguing inversions of erotic women invading male dreams are described in Greek magical papyri (second century BCE to fifth century CE), in which spells are cast and amulets made in order to invade someone's dream life. The vast majority of the papyri concern male manipulation of female dreamers with the aim of arousing sexual desire in a sleeping woman. In imagery reeking of female bondage and humiliation, the man projects all his erotic fantasies onto the passive (sleeping) object of his desire.[39] These spells were frequently carved on metal and deposited into graves because it was believed that the dead could enact or effect them; they are thus a concrete record of actual men who actively decided to infiltrate women's dreams. This pointedly contrasts with frequent representations of men as passive or resisting recipients of dream invasions by flying erotic women or succubi, such as Lilith (see chapter 8). In the religious literature of the world, when men have erotic dreams they feel invaded by female demons,[40] but the

FIGURE 1.4 Winged woman arousing a sleeping man. Fragment of a marble relief, Roman, second century CE.
Photograph © 2018 Museum of Fine Arts, Boston.

evidence of the Greek spells shows that erotic psychic invasion was a conscious male pastime, not a female one. That such practices were widespread can be seen among the Mekeo of Melanesia, where a sorcerer uses the effluvia of the woman he or his client desires: feces, urine, sweat, blood, and sexual secretions. Through the manipulation of these substances the desired woman comes to the sorcerer or his client in a dream, with the final goal being that soon thereafter she will go to him in her physical body.[41]

A more positive view of flying dream women can be found in Tibetan Buddhism, where *ḍākinīs* often appear in dreams to tell adepts what teachings they need, and sometimes to predict the guru from whom they will receive them. Alternatively, just seeing a *ḍākinī* in a dream is evidence of spiritual accomplishment; they can grant spiritual powers that immediately manifest in waking life.[42]

Further associations of females with the dream realm include the Shekinah, the feminine presence of God in the world, which Jewish Kabbalists rely on to understand their prophetic dreams, while Ṣūfīs rely on Fatima, the daughter of the Prophet Muḥammad[43] (Muḥammad's Night Journey is included here because the horse he rode to paradise had the face of a woman, discussed in chapter 11).

But the most ancient source for this idea is in the myths and stories from around the world in which male heroes require a female guide in order to complete their quest, such as Odysseus and Circe. In the *Divine Comedy* Dante (1265–1321) draws on ancient understandings of women as guides to other worlds. Dante's poem prominently employs two women: St. Lucia (to whom Dante was devoted), who flies with his sleeping body to the gate of purgatory,[44] and his main guide, Beatrice, a young woman whom Dante loved and pined for his whole life.[45] She is like an angel to him, if not actually an angel, although he depicts her with wings (IX.50). The *Divine Comedy* is about the exaltation of Beatrice and her deification and enthronement in heaven[46] as well as Dante's own journey and transformation. Although he creates her as a character, it is she who leads him to paradise.

HUMANS, DIVINITIES, AND BIRDS

For ancient people the boundaries between human beings, divinities, and animals were porous. Gods could do whatever they wanted. Sometimes they appeared as animals and at other times as human beings; they could fly through the air, become invisible, or appear out of nowhere. This multiplicity of divine appearances was expressed by depicting the gods in human form with the addition of animal features, such as a pair of wings (see chapter 2), or attended by their special animal—for instance, Athena with her owl[47] or the Indian goddess Sarasvatī mounted on her swan.

Apotheosis

Human beings longed for the immortality of the gods. One way they hoped to achieve this was through heroic acts, after which they would be worshiped as a god, as was Hercules. The privilege of deification was also shared by Roman emperors and empresses. Several days after an emperor died and was cremated, a wax image of him was carved and placed on a heavily decorated, multistory funeral pyre with a wax cage at the top. As the pyre burned, the wax cage melted and released an eagle; its flight heavenward represented the ascent of the emperor's soul to the gods.[48] Empresses, too, could become gods, either with their husbands, as depicted in the column erected in honor of Emperor Antonius Pius (d. 161 CE) and his wife, Faustina,[49] or on their own, as in the beautiful second-century marble relief depicting the Empress Sabina's apotheosis (d. 136 CE, Figure 1.5), which shows her being

FIGURE 1.5 Apotheosis of Empress Sabina, c. 138 CE. Sabina is being carried by Victory (Nike). Capitoline Museums, Rome.

carried skyward by a winged Victory while her funeral pyre still burns below and her seated husband, Emperor Hadrian, bids her farewell. Chinese emperors were thought to be divinities—they were called the sons of heaven—and the death of one is glossed as his having mounted a dragon-chariot that returned him to heaven,[50] a reference to the legendary emperor Huang Ti, who, without dying, mounted a winged horse to return to heaven.[51] Similar beliefs in imperial divinity can be found in Pharaonic Egypt, pre-Columbian Peru, and Japan. The cult of Isis (see chapter 2) and the Hellenistic mystery cults promised initiates immortality, as well. The blending of the imperial cult with that of Christianity can be seen in a gold coin that shows the Christian emperor Constantine (272–337 CE) being carried into heaven in a chariot with the hand of God reaching down to him.[52] The persistence of this imagery is shown in François Rude's (1784–1885) monumental sculpture of Napoleon, which depicts him recumbent on top of an eagle.[53] This imagery was reinterpreted in President Ulysses S. Grant's tomb in New York City, which features an eagle with outstretched wings, as if about to take flight, in front of the tomb, which was dedicated in 1897.

Ancient Indian sages, through their mastery of ascetic techniques, were believed capable of becoming gods (see chapter 6) and, as mentioned, Tantric masters were believed to ascend into the sky at the time of their death. These beliefs express the possibility that humans could be godlike, yet humans also shared with animals characteristics such as mortality, sentience, fear, sexuality, and the ability to hunt and kill. Early human beings hovered uncertainly, halfway between the divine and the animal world, aspiring to one and capable of slipping into the other. The world around them was both familiar and mysterious; people who were alive to religious possibilities could never be quite sure what they were seeing. The animal slinking through the forest could be just that, or a god in disguise, or another human being whose spirit had entered it or who had the power to shape-shift.

Birds

Relationships of profound intimacy, identification, and complexity exist between humans and animals as well as between divinities and animals. Besides beliefs about humans and divinities shape-shifting into animals, animal totems were often used to define the members of a clan, while shamans and witches have their familiars (animal helpers). In Christianity, the Trinity expresses the intimate connection between God, humanity (Christ), and animals, in that the Holy Spirit is frequently represented as a bird, especially a dove, as when a dove descended from heaven after Jesus was baptized by John the Baptist, described in Mark 1:11, Matthew 3:16, and Luke 3:22.[54] Alternatively, the dove is replaced by a young woman.[55]

Birds have multiple rich associations with the divine, beginning with their ability to bridge the heavens and earth. The Bronze Age inhabitants of Crete believed that all gods appeared as birds.[56] In addition to being a form taken by goddesses and gods[57] or ridden as their vehicles (Figure 1.6), birds are used for epithets of divinities, such as "owl-eyed Athena," and many cultures believe birds to be divine messengers and thus connected to divination. In ancient India one word for bird, *śakuna*, came to mean omens.[58] The ancient Greeks carefully observed and interpreted the flight patterns, species, number, sounds, and other symbolic attributes of birds, while the Romans had a college of such diviners to learn the will of the gods,[59] and Tibetans had a manual on bird divination.[60] In ancient Egypt, the word for bird was connected to divinity,[61] and the Egyptians symbolized the human soul, the divine breath within the earthly body, as a human-headed bird,[62] while in Vedic India (c. second millennium BCE) the soul after death flies like a bird to the world of the ancestors or the gods.[63] The famous Muslim philosopher Avicenna (c. 980–1037) represents the ascension of the soul to God in the form of a bird, as do other

FIGURE 1.6 Aphrodite Riding a Goose, drinking cup found in a tomb on Rhodes, attributed to the Pistoxenos Painter, c. 470–460 BCE.

Muslim as well as Christian writers.[64] Appropriately for our topic, the soul (*psyche*) is understood to be female in many traditions.[65]

Birds are also associated with death, which was linked to many winged goddesses (see chapter 2), especially where bird wings are connected with reviving the dead,[66] as when Isis was said to have resurrected her husband Osiris by flapping her wings over his body.[67] (An ancient Egyptian name for the Land of the Dead was *ṭuat*, "bird-death."[68]) Similarly, when Odysseus descended into the Land of the Dead he met his mother, yet another woman knowledgeable about death, who explained to him that the souls of the dead fly about (*Odyssey* 11.221–222), which is the fate of Penelope's fallen suitors (*Odyssey* 24.5–9). Carrion birds, which strip the flesh from bones, are especially prevalent on battlefields, which connects them to the many flying goddesses of war who shape-shift into birds, such as the Valkyries and others. Most obviously, birds symbolize transcendence of and absolute freedom from earthly limitations.

People attempted to acquire avian attributes by sewing feathers on ritual clothing (see chapters 9 and 11) or dressing as birds,[69] making bird masks,[70] imitating birds' sounds and movements to stimulate shamanic flights (see chapter 9), or using bird shapes and motifs in ritual objects.[71] Eliade has suggested that "[i]t is probable that the mythico-ritual theme 'bird—soul—ecstatic flight' was already extant in the Paleolithic epoch; one can, indeed, interpret in this sense some of the designs at Altamira (man with the mask of a bird), and the famous relief of Lascaux (man with a bird's head),"[72] though there does not seem to be much reason to take these simple line drawings as representing men rather than women.[73]

In addition to totemic associations of birds and humans, such as the eagle clan, and the identification of shamans with their bird familiars, resemblances between birds and human beings are particularly striking: both are two-footed, and able to sing, hunt, gather, and build homes to rear offspring that they will defend to the death. These physical, linguistic, social, and psychological resemblances to human beings stirred ancient people's religious imagination.[74]

Bird Goddesses

Drawings and sculptures referred to as "bird goddesses" or "bird women"—human female figures with birdlike heads on long necks and sometimes winglike protuberances on their sides or wing-shaped arms—survive from the Neolithic period, most of which can be dated to 7000–3500 BCE.[75] One particularly striking figurine comes from a tomb in El Ma'mariya, Upper Egypt (c. 3500–3400 BCE, Figure 0.2)[76] that stands eleven and one-half inches high. Variations on this form from later periods have been discovered in many parts of the world (Figure 1.7),[77] and although their meanings and functions remain uncertain,[78] they may well be the forerunners of the various flying supernatural women who are the subject of this book.[79] A demonic winged female, called Lamashtu, from second-millennium BCE Mesopotamia, was a threat to infants and young children.[80] Lilith, discussed in chapter 8, was another winged, child-snatching demon with roots in the ancient Near East.

Ancient India is particularly rich in bird goddesses,[81] images of which go back at least to the Kushan era (first to third century BCE) and may be assumed to have existed in even earlier periods.[82] They are categorized both as mothers (mātṛkās)[83] and as seizers (grahīs), which suggests their ambivalent nature; both groups sometimes kill young children, but at other times they help with childbirth and protect children. The winged goddess Saṣṭhī has been worshiped since the Kushan period in connection with childbirth.[84] The association of fertility and children with aerial women is widely spread over time and space. Surviving images of Indian bird goddesses depict them with bird heads, feet, or wings. Their unpredictability is connected to their bird nature, for birds—especially carrion birds—are not always benevolent. Indeed, birds may have been understood as carriers of disease in

FIGURE 1.7 Terra-cotta statuette of woman with bird face, Cypriot culture, c. 1450–1200 BCE.
The Metropolitan Museum of Art.

ancient India,[85] and the Indian goddess of destruction and the mother of death,
Nirṛti, is associated with a black bird of omens (*Atharava Veda* VII.64). These characteristics are also attributed to Indian witches, who particularly threaten children
and women.[86] In China, Edward Schafer describes "The Roving Women Who Go
by Night," women believed to "fly by night and remain hidden by day, like ghosts
and spirits. They don plumage to become flying birds, and cast off the plumage to
become women. They have no children, and take pleasure in seizing the children of
men."[87] As will be shown in chapter 7, shape-shifting aerial women from India, such
as *ḍākinīs* and *yoginīs*, continue the ambiguous nature of the bird deities.[88]

Returning to the iconography of the second and first millennium BCE, suffice it to
say that it has frequent images of winged goddesses, for instance Isis, while iconography from Bronze Age Crete and Greece reveals two important facts: divinities appear in the shape of birds; and images of female divinities occur much more
frequently than male images.[89] Over time, the earlier animal form of a divinity
was incorporated into its anthropomorphic or human form.[90] An example of

FIGURE 1.8 Winged Artemis, a gold pendant, Eastern Greece, 650–600 BCE.
© The Cleveland Museum of Art.

this can be seen in a seventh-century BCE gold pendant depicting Artemis as the Mistress of the Beasts (*potnia theron*; Figure 1.8), in which her earlier form as a bird is recalled by her outspread wings.[91] The point is that religion is never static; it is always changing and evolving, as is its iconography.[92] As will be shown, other important Greek goddesses with clear origins as birds are Athena, Aphrodite, and Nike/Victory. It is to these historical goddesses that we now turn.

PART I

Supernatural Women

2

Winged Goddesses of Sexuality, Death, and Immortality

IN THE PREVIOUS CHAPTER, bird women and bird goddesses were introduced. In this chapter, we encounter the winged goddesses of the ancient Near East and ancient Greece—aerial goddesses who eventually lost their wings but nevertheless retained avian attributes. In both cultural contexts, the goddesses have rich mythologies, elaborate cults, and various literary texts that continually reinvent them. Through them we begin to observe history, narrowing the space of these originally untrammeled goddesses and introducing winged forms of the monstrous-feminine—female beings who could not or would not comply with the limitations that rising patriarchies attempted to impose on them—a theme that will arise again and again throughout this work.

ISIS

While the prominence of other gods waxed and waned, Isis—the winged goddess who resurrected her husband, Osiris, the first god-king of Egypt—was always widely worshiped among all classes from the earliest period (c. 2350 BCE) to the last dynasties.[1] While Isis was intimately connected with the earth and its concerns through her father, Geb, the god of earth, and especially with royal power (the pharaoh referred to himself as "the son of Isis"),[2] she was also a celestial goddess, given that she was the daughter of Nut, goddess of the sky. Her crown

held the sun, and she was identified with the star Sept (Sirius), the appearance
of which marked the start of the new year and the beginning of the Nile's annual
beneficent flooding, which restored the land and all who lived on it.[3] According to
ancient Egyptian texts, her beloved husband and brother, King Osiris, was killed
by their brother Seth, who scattered his dismembered body throughout the land.
The immediate consequence of this murder was that the kingdom did not have
a legitimate heir, because Isis and Osiris had been childless. Isis (in some redactions accompanied by her sister Nephthys[4]) made a sorrowful journey to gather
his body parts, a journey later duplicated by devotees who were initiated into her
cult. The sisters are sometimes depicted as birds watching over Osiris's corpse.[5] As
with many of the goddesses who traveled to the Land of the Dead, Isis journeyed
to revive the dead Osiris during the fallow period of the all-important agricul-
tural cycle; without her presence, the land is barren. After putting his body back
together, she restored Osiris to life by beating her wings over his body: "She [Isis]
sought thee [Osiris] without weariness, she went round about through this land in
sorrow, she did not set to the ground her foot until she had found thee. She made
light with her feathers, she made air to come into being with her wings."[6] She then
used Osiris's revived penis—the last body part she had found—to impregnate herself with their son, Horus, thereby securing the proper royal succession.[7] When
Seth learned about this, he attempted to kill Horus, but Isis hid with him in the
papyrus swamps. Still, Seth sent a scorpion, which stung the child, but Isis was able
to restore him to life.[8] This myth emphasizes that she was not only able to restore
life but was also essential to the sovereignty of the pharaohs. She was believed to
be their mother, who would protect and care for them as she did her own son—a
power later expanded to include all her devotees. In her we find the earliest articulation of the powers and features of winged goddesses: they can resurrect the
dead and grant immortality; they travel to and from the Land of the Dead; they
form relationships with particular men (kings or heroes); they confer sovereignty;
and they protect children and therefore fertility. Near Eastern winged goddesses
are sexually active, and their celestial nature, combined with their earthly appearances, enabled them to mediate between divinities and humans, transforming the
latter into the former through immortality. Variations of this belief appeared in
many places throughout history.

The early records of Egyptian religious life focus on the death rituals of the
god-king, during which the king's body was preserved and entombed in elaborate
structures along with possessions he might need in the afterlife. Though originally
this practice was the key feature of a royal cult that ensured the pharaohs' immortality and the special protection of the goddess, from early times Isis was depicted
as a more universal goddess of salvation, one who could grant immortality first

to nobles who had received the proper funerary rites and eventually to anyone who received these rites. Her mourning for and care of the dead Osiris came to dramatize her feelings for all her devotees, who hoped for immortality after their deaths. Stories about her magical abilities and restoration to life of various beings are found throughout ancient Egyptian literature; appropriately, they were frequently depicted on the walls of tombs.[9]

Ancient Egypt abounded with winged goddesses, and as noted, the sky itself was personified as the goddess Nut, one of the most ancient goddesses in the pantheon. Her body was depicted as arched above the earth, her torso representing the sky and her arms and legs the pillars on which the sky rested. The sun was believed to pass through her body at night, only to be reborn the next day. In her winged form she was depicted with long wings protectively wrapped around the dead, as can be seen, for example, on the coffin of Tutankhamun.[10] Maāt, the goddess of justice who heard the confession of the dead, is often depicted with wings or holding an ostrich feather in her hand or wearing one in her headdress.[11] Ritually, though, Isis was the most important goddess, given that so much of Egyptian ritual was devoted to the care of the dead. There are exquisite depictions of Isis and her sisters spreading their wings to protect the dead as they guide them to rebirth in the afterlife (Figure 2.1), and Isis is said to have restored Osiris to life

FIGURE 2.1 Isis and her sister Nephthys watching over a corpse. Temple of Hathor, Dendera, c. fourth century BCE.
Photograph by Francesco Gasparetti.

by beating her wings to create air for him to breathe. The Egyptian word for "bird" was connected to divinity;[12] consequently, birds were worshiped as the representatives of gods on earth, cared for in temples, paraded in ceremonies, and, when they died, mummified and buried in catacombs in individual pottery jars by the millions.[13] Birds also symbolized the human soul (*ba*), the divine breath within the earthly body, the hieroglyphic representation of which was a bird with a human head; small wooden statuettes in this shape were often placed in tombs.[14] These statuettes were of paramount importance because they represented the individual's postmortem power of mobility, especially of flight, so the deceased could fly with the sun god during the daily solar cycle and return to its corpse in the evening to be rejuvenated.[15] Birds were arguably the most significant creatures in Egyptian religion—they were used as amulets in life and after death were interred with their owner[16]—which may in no small part be related to the care and protection birds provide for their offspring.[17]

The prominence of goddesses in funeral rites was echoed in the participation of mortal women in those very rites. During the Old Kingdom (2686–2181 BCE), which saw the development of pyramids as royal tombs, and the Middle Kingdom (c. 2030–1786 BCE), a great number of women were priestesses, and women played various important roles in funerary rituals as priests, mourners, dancers, singers, and imitators of the sister goddesses Isis and Nephthys.[18] Wooden statuettes of female offering-bearers have been found in tombs throughout Egypt.[19]

Over time, Isis's cult spread far beyond Egypt. She had a sanctuary near Athens by the fourth century BCE, and she remained an important goddess into the Hellenistic period, when her cult spread to Rome, where it was eventually assimilated into that of the Virgin Mary.[20] Images of Isis holding her infant son Horus and Mary holding the infant Jesus made striking parallels possible.

This ancient tale contains all the primary topics and themes covered in this chapter: sexual, flying goddesses who have control over death, fertility, and immortality. To begin with, though, an exploration of the connections between human women and death accesses the deeper meanings of these goddesses and how their human devotees understood them.

WOMEN, DEATH, SEXUALITY, AND IMMORTALITY

The linking of women with death is ancient and pervasive. It began with early identifications of the earth as female, as the womb that brings forth life through the seasonal cycle and to which all living things return. This belief postulates that time is repetitive and cyclical, not linear; birth leads to death and death leads to birth, round and round.[21] It denies the permanence of death. Throughout the world, archaeologists have uncovered ancient graves that seem to be expressive of such an idea,[22] though the evidence needs to be viewed cautiously, especially where no corroborating evidence (such as funerary texts) survives. In some graves, bodies may have been ritually marked, as with red ochre;[23] others were positioned to face a particular direction that would presumably lead to the Land of the Dead or are curled in a fetal position to symbolize eventual rebirth from the earth's womb.[24] Ancient communal gravesites imply that the individual identities of the dead "dissolved into an anonymous collectivity of ancestors,"[25] which modern anthropological studies have revealed to be the source of continuing fertility for the living.[26] Some of the earliest human graves, both communal and individual, are in caves—natural, geologic forms that suggest womblike structures.[27]

Behind ancient associations of the earth with femaleness, and femaleness with death, lies the ambivalent nature of the feminine divine as simultaneously the giver and the taker of life. Like the earth's own cycle of generation and degeneration, women give birth, which inevitably leads to decay and death, signifying that women have a special knowledge of and relationship to death, and are a source of rebirth, either by giving birth to dead ancestors or, as divine women, by regenerating the dead in another realm.

In numerous ancient societies, burial rites were often in the hands of women, especially the laying out of the corpse, which was understood to be a prelude to rebirth.[28] And funeral rites were—and continue to be—linked with fertility, the denial of death, and the affirmation of new life.[29] Such rites can still be witnessed in the twenty-first century: a dramatic example of the identification of women with death and fertility can be seen in modern Cantonese funeral practices, in which women usually represent their families at funerals, as their female essence (*yin*) is associated with flesh, death, the dark, and the west (the direction of the dead), while men's *yang* essence is associated with bones, life, the light, and the east.[30] Consequently, young married women of the deceased's family (daughters and daughters-in-law) actively have contact with the corpse by rubbing the coffin with their unbound hair—hair being widely associated with sexuality and fertility—thereby soaking up the pollution of the decaying flesh. At this time the daughters-in-law wear a green cloth over their abdomens, an auspicious color representing spring and fertility, which therefore absorbs death pollution. At the end of the mourning ceremony the green cloths are purified by waving them through a fire, after which they prominently reappear, along with other accouterments from the funeral, in the back-strap harness women use to carry children,[31] thereby asserting that the women have renewed their powers of fertility through their contact with the dead.

Mourning women and their lamentations were and remain essential to death rituals;[32] the iconography of the Crucifixion is a case in point when it depicts women mourning beneath it (Figure 2.2), while widows who permanently wear black to express their ongoing mourning are still to be seen throughout the Mediterranean region.[33] It is notable that the Greek playwright Sophocles (c. 497–406 BCE) chose a woman, Antigone, to proclaim the right of the dead to a proper burial, and that this woman willingly lays down her own life in order to fulfill her obligations to bury the dead.[34] It is women who bring one to life and women who prepare one to leave it; rituals of death and mourning are an assertion of women's knowledge and control of these transitions.

A complement to these ideas is that part of the secret lore attributed to women is knowledge of the Land of the Dead. As one of their trials, male heroes often must go to the Land of the Dead, where they are usually guided by a woman—for example, Siduri in *Gilgamesh*, Circe in the *Odyssey*, the Cumae Sybil in the *Aeneid*, and Beatrice in the *Divine Comedy*. The *'das logs* of Tibet are usually woman shamans who journey to hell and bring back reports on how sins are punished there,[35]

FIGURE 2.2 Crucifixion with three Marys, sixteenth century. Gilded glass.
The Metropolitan Museum of Art, Gift of J. Pierpont Morgan, 1917.

as did the Nišan shaman (see chapter 9). Valkyries carry fallen warriors to Valhalla, and some Norse graves contained amulets in the shape of Valkyries (Figure 3.3, p. 62). Similarly, *apsarās* carry fallen heroes to heaven (Figure 6.2, p. 120), and the belief that a woman will beckon and greet one at the entrance to the other world is widespread.[36] Further, female witches and diviners were believed to get their information about the past and the future through the practice of necromancy, or the questioning of the dead, as when King Saul has the witch of Endor raise the dead prophet Samuel in order to learn the future.

Goddesses of the dead, or those associated with death, or personifying death,[37] abound in many cultures and time periods, from Kālī/Durgā, Isthar/Inanna, Isis, and Hel to the Furies and Morrigan. Some cultures even attributed the origin of death to a mistake or the breaking of a taboo by a woman, such as Eve or Pandora, or to the appearance of sexual desire, where sexuality is associated with women.[38] The identification of women with sexuality, and of sexuality with death, is dramatically played out among the Bara of southern Madagascar, who place a recently deceased body in a woman's hut from which men are rigorously excluded for three days and two nights. During the day everyone mourns, but at night the women abandon their usual modesty to perform erotic and provocative songs and dances that lead to promiscuous sexual pairings.[39] On the last day, the men force their way into the woman's hut and steal the corpse. The women run after them, physically struggling with the men as they carry the coffin to the mountain of the ancestors. Once at the tomb of the ancestors, "the deceased is reborn (head first like a foetus) into the world of the ancestors" by the ritual activity of the men.[40] This battle of the sexes is about the control of fertility. The temporary promiscuous sexuality of the women is not considered conducive to conception—it occurs at a time of death and leads to barrenness. It is only when the men restore order, and the women are subdued both sexually and as purveyors of death, that fertility returns, symbolized by the men rebirthing the corpse. Maurice Bloch elaborates on such beliefs:

Merging birth and death in the funerary ceremonies is what creates a picture of fertility which transcends the biology of mere dirty mortality and birth. Funeral rituals act out, therefore, not only the victory over death but the victory over the physical, biological nature of man as a whole. Birth and death and often sexuality are declared to be a low illusion, located in the world of women, and true life, fertility, is therefore elsewhere. This is why funerary rituals are an occasion for fertility.[41]

Women's connections with death frequently link them with immortality, suggesting that women control life and death to such a degree that they can free the individual from death. This brings us back to the many goddesses believed to control fertility, death, and rebirth—that is, the winged goddesses who guide or transport the dead to non-earthly realms. As discussed in chapter 1, among the earliest representations of female figures with wings are the so-called bird-women of prehistory, some of whom developed into winged goddesses. Fortunately, numerous textual references that more fully express the religious ideas underlying the winged female images of the ancient Near East, Greece, and Rome exist. The ancient Near East, as will be discussed, is a treasure trove of such texts and images.

THE ANCIENT NEAR EAST

As we saw in the story of Isis, winged goddesses of the ancient Near East are explicitly connected with sexuality, the realm of the dead, and rebirth. Yet the Egyptian and Mesopotamian worldviews differed. In Egypt, Isis held out the promise of immortality in a paradise,[42] but in Mesopotamia there was only a grim underworld.[43] These differing worldviews may have been influenced by ecological factors: both cultures relied on rivers, but the Nile was predictable and gentle, while the Tigris and Euphrates were unpredictable and sometimes treacherous. In Egypt the annual flooding of the Nile was peaceful and renewed the fertility of the land, due to the rich soil left behind by the receding waters. In Mesopotamia flooding was erratic and destructive as often as it was productive, bringing both drought or flooding without rhyme or reason.

The earliest Mesopotamian evidence of goddess worship shows a reverence especially for the winged goddess of love and war, Inanna, or Isthar (Figure 2.3). She is very much a sky goddess; her name means "the Queen of Heaven," and she is represented in tangible form as the moon and as the morning and evening star (the planet Venus).[44] Her connection with the moon makes plain her dual aspects as both the goddess of life and fertility (the full moon) and of death and rebirth (the new moon). One of her most important stories describes her journey to the Land of the Dead, ruled over by her sister Ereshkigal, who kills her and hangs her corpse on the wall. Inanna, suspecting foul play, left instructions for her faithful servant and fellow warrior Ninshubur to plead with the gods for her release if she does not return. To help Inanna, the god Enki fashions two creatures and gives them both the food and water of life. They retrieve Inanna's corpse and restore her to life.[45] Unlike Isis, Inanna cannot restore life to herself—she needs others to restore her, which is very suggestive of the active involvement of human beings in her cult, who help bring about rebirth and stimulate the arrival of spring with its renewal of the land.[46] Inanna knows the underworld of death, but she cannot save

FIGURE 2.3 The Burney Relief, Queen of the Night. Featuring winged Inanna/Isthar. Old Babylonian, c. 1800–1750 BCE.

anyone from it. She can, however, offer her devotees protection from it, through actions such as favoring certain warriors in battle. Her worship endured through four Mesopotamian empires: Sumer, Akkad, Babylonia, and Syria. Most of her story is contained in a collection of hymns composed by Princess Enheduanna, the daughter of the Akkadian king Sargon (rose to power c. 2350 BCE),[47] who conquered the Sumerian city-states. Sargon actively shaped the religious life of his conquered kingdoms by installing Enheduanna as a high priestess and by equating the conquered Sumerian Inanna with the Akkadian Ishtar, in which guise she spread to Babylonia and, as Astarte, to Assyria.[48] One of Enheduanna's hymns celebrates a winged image of Inanna:

In the vanguard of the battle,
    everything is beset by you.
My Lady, (flying about) on your own wings,
    you feed on (the carnage).[49]

The idea of winged or flying war goddesses, who can confer immortality as well, endured and morphed into less powerful females down through centuries and in many cultures, as shown by Valkyries, *apsarās*, *yoginīs*, *ḍākinīs*, and finally the female aviators of the twentieth century. Like the Valkyries, such goddesses are often depicted as carrion birds that feed on the dead left behind from battle, but they also have the ability to protect warriors and confer victory while demonstrating their powers of fertility through sexual relationship with kings and warriors. In brief, Inanna/Isthar "encompasses the two forms of potential disorder and violence—sex and war."[50]

Sacred prostitution was practiced in Inanna's temple, which was part of her royal cult as both the bestower and renewer of kingship, and the renewer of the land itself, through the ritual of sacred marriage (*hieros gamos*), during which the king had sexual intercourse with Inanna, presumably through her high priestess.[51] The king took the role of Inanna's husband, Dumuzi, whom she chose as the first king. Several rulers assumed the title "spouse of the goddess."[52] At Inanna's temple, women, often virgins, offered themselves to strangers. Other women, and men, fulfilled this role as staff members of temples, where they were considered living embodiments of Inanna. Such unions promised prosperity and fertility for the land and the livestock, and these practices were widespread throughout Mesopotamia for at least two thousand years. Importantly, these ritual practices were distinct from profane or commercial prostitution, which could exist at the same time in the same city.[53] Nonetheless, Inanna is specifically described as a prostitute in one inscription:

> Oh harlot, you set out for the alehouse
> O Inanna, you are bent on going into your (usual) window (namely to solicit)
>   for a lover . . .
> You, my lady, dress like one of no repute in a single garment
> The beads (the sign) of a harlot you put around your neck.[54]

Inanna's cult and mythology continued under her Babylonian name, Isthar, the Babylonian goddess of love and war.

Isthar could grant either victory or defeat, in romance or on the battlefield; as with so many aerial females, she could be benign or malefic. In the Babylonian texts, she makes a similar journey to the Land of the Dead as did Inanna, with whom she was assimilated and with whom she shared connections to death and fertility. Sisters in the underworld are an aspect of these this-worldly goddesses of fertility and sexuality. In the underworld Inanna/Isthar is held captive by her sister, named Ereshkigal, the Queen of the Underworld. While she is in captivity, all fertility on the earth ceases. Therefore the god Ea gains Ishtar's release by distracting Ereshkigal with a beautiful male eunuch (emphasizing the lack of fertility in Ereshkigal's realm), who wrangles the waters of life from Ereshkigal in order to free Ishtar.[55] The story reveals Isthar's knowledge of and success in both the realms of the living and the dead. The seven gates that she passes through upon entering and leaving the underworld, where she first leaves and then retrieves a possession, symbolize her loss of divine powers and their restoration, while the number seven is connected to the planetary symbolism much loved by the Babylonians.

A beautiful hymn extolling the charms and powers of Isthar dates from the reign of the Akkadian king Ammiditana (c. 1600 BCE). In it, the king lists the blessings he wishes to receive from her, such as long life and subjugation of the world and its people. It also presents her as the supreme god:

Praise the goddess, the most awesome of the goddesses.
Let one revere the mistress of the peoples, the greatest of the [gods] . . . .

She is clothed with pleasure and love.
She is laden with vitality, charm, and voluptuousness.

***

She is sought after among the gods; extraordinary is her station.
Respected is her word; it is *supreme* over them . . . .

She is their queen; they continually cause her commands to be executed.
All of them bow down before her . . . .[56]

Despite her many powers and such hymns of praise, in an ancient tale Isthar is mocked and defeated by the hero Gilgamesh. The earliest written stories about Gilgamesh are in Sumerian and date from around the turn of the second millennium BCE, although parts of his story are much older. The *Gilgamesh* available today is drawn mainly from a first-millennium BCE Babylonian text, though lacunae were filled in from fragments of earlier texts,[57] and it depicts events set in the third millennium BCE. Seams show in the text, underscoring changes in Isthar's status as a new, masculinized worldview emerges.

The hero of the epic, King Gilgamesh, is described as being two-thirds divine, because his mother was a minor goddess, and one-third human, because of his human father.[58] He may have been modeled on a historical king of Uruk named Gilgamesh who ruled in the middle of the third millennium BCE, about whom various tales were told, and around whom a cult developed in which he was called "king of the underworld."[59] The main conflict in the epic is that even though Gilgamesh has divine martial powers he remains mortal, doomed to die and go to the underworld.[60] Unlike the journeys of Isis and Inanna/Isthar, Gilgamesh's journey to the underworld will offer no escape. Even the greatest hero cannot achieve the immortality he seeks; yet he disparages an immortal goddess who can grant immortality and is closely aligned with kingship. Like Isis and Inanna, Isthar is essential for legitimizing kings. Gilgamesh starts off as an antihero: a bad king and a man who would deny his mortality. In the end, his acceptance of his mortality is also an acceptance of the superiority of the immortal gods; nonetheless, it remains a denial of Isthar's ability to grant immortality. Paradoxically, his story begins with a description of the magnificent temple he built for Isthar in his city of Uruk and concludes with a reference to it when he returns home.[61]

In the epic, after Gilgamesh has performed many heroic feats, the goddess Isthar begins to desire him, but Gilgamesh rejects her as a lover, taunting her with the miserable fates of her earlier lovers.[62] In truth they had not fared well. In one tale she chooses Tammuz, or Dumuzi in Sumerian versions, to be the first king. But when she is trapped in the underworld she offers him as her substitute, although he can return to earth and life for half the year. By sexually rejecting the goddess, Gilgamesh is breaking with the religious ritual of the *hieros gamos*,[63] that is, the sacred marriage in which mortal Mesopotamian kings participated in ritual sexuality with the goddess (through a priestess of the goddess called an *ishtaritu*) to ensure the fertility of the land and receive the goddess's endorsement of his right to rule. Thus Gilgamesh's rejection of Isthar has far-reaching implications for her status and that of other goddesses in the religious, social, and political life of Mesopotamia.

Temple prostitution was a celebration of the reproductive life force of nature that was most often conceived of as feminine.[64] In the Code of Hammurabi (no. 127), temple prostitutes were offered the same protections from molestation as married women, yet the story of Gilgamesh begins with his problematic kingship, given that he takes any woman he wants for his own pleasure. The gods hear his subjects' complaints and ask the goddess of creation, Aruru, to create his equal, Enkidu, the wild man who will become Gilgamesh's beloved companion.

Enkidu is raised by animals in the wilderness, where he destroys the traps of a hunter, who asks Gilgamesh for an *ishtaritu* to tame him. She seduces Enkidu, introducing him to the ways of civilization, after which the animals reject him and the *ishtaritu* takes him to Uruk. When Enkidu hears that Gilgamesh is about to exercise his *droit de seigneur* with yet another new bride, he challenges the king; they fight and then become friends. This is the taming of Gilgamesh, the way he is brought to righteous kingship. Another purpose of sacred prostitution is to ensure prosperity and peace (or, failing that, victory), a role admirably fulfilled by Enkidu's *ishtaritu* from Isthar's temple. Contradictorily, Gilgamesh and even Enkidu insult Isthar.[65] What stands out in the exchange between Isthar and Gilgamesh is that a mortal, even if partly divine, boldly insults and humiliates a divine female. This places the Gilgamesh and Isthar episode in the genre of stories about male heroes and gods who conquer divine females[66] and suggests the power of a new ideal: the (male) military hero. Unlike Egypt, whose wars were fought on foreign soil, Mesopotamia underwent a series of local conquests, leading to the idealization of the warrior-king personified by Gilgamesh. Isthar retaliates against their insults by sending a divine bull to kill Gilgamesh, but with the help of Enkidu the bull is killed. Isthar can only lament with the rest of the women; she is powerless against Gilgamesh.

The later parts of the *Gilgamesh* mark a transition from belief in a goddess who can grant immortality, to the exaltation of a heroic man who can gain immortality through the fame of his deeds. Gilgamesh, the man, accepts that he will die but ensures that he will live on in legend.[67]

ANCIENT GREECE

The ancient Greeks had equally complex winged females linked with the dead, such as the vengeful Furies, the terrifying Gorgon Medusa, the melodious Sirens, the life-snatching Harpies, and the riddling Sphinx. Included among these winged beings were well-known aerial divinities such as the war goddess Athena, the love goddess Aphrodite, and the fertility goddess Artemis, all of whom had ancient avian attributes.[68] Over time, the original animal forms of deities were changed into anthropomorphic images;[69] in the case of avian deities, wings were added to their humanized forms. Later iconography dropped the wings, though avian characterics were remembered through epithets, such as "owl-eyed Athena," depictions of the deity accompanied by birds or wearing bird motifs, and belief in their ability to shape-shift into birds; simultaneously, the belief lingered that birds were divine messengers.[70] Underneath the mythologies of classical Greece are archaic, often Minoan or Asiatic,[71] forms of female divinities that became problematic as the religious values of Greek culture evolved in favor of patriarchy.[72] Like Isthar, their powers would be contained.

Athena and the Monstrous-Feminine

With the exception of Nike, who primarily served patriarchal military ends and the athletic contests that were their training ground, the male defeat or rejection of ancient aerial females is a ubiquitous theme in Greek mythology. These are ugly, wrenching stories, several of which involve Athena, who was originally an ancient goddess from the Bronze Age of the Minoan-Mycenaean religion of Crete, where she was the goddess of war and protector of towns and the king.[73] Ongoing excavations of her sanctuary at Tegea near Sparta, which flourished from approximately the fourteenth through the fourth centuries BCE, reveal a complex fertility goddess who protected her devotees and granted immortality. Discovered among the votive offerings were pomegranate pendants and loom weights in the shape of pomegranates. The pomegranate's many seeds link this fruit with fertility, but also with death, because Persephone, while a captive in the underworld, was doomed to remain there after eating one. Further, the pomegranate's distinctive red color defined it as a "bloody" fruit, and it was considered an appropriate offering for the dead, who craved life, that is, blood.[74] From an early date Athena was the protector of weavers[75] as well as of life after death, which is understandable given the connections that were believed to exist between weaving and the length of life.[76] These characteristics are subdued in her later cult, when gestation and birth stories (Hesiod, *Theogony* 886ff.)[77] were created (eighth to seventh centuries BCE) to incorporate her into the male-dominated Olympian pantheon, as when it is said that her father, Zeus, impregnated her mother, Metis ("wisdom"), and then swallowed Athena out of fear that his child would one day overthrow him as he had his father, Kronos. Sometime later, Zeus developed a splitting headache and out popped Athena, full grown and fully armed, reconfigured as completely male-identified, the protector of male heroes such as Perseus, Bellerophon, Odysseus, and Jason, all known for thwarting or killing avian females.[78]

At Athens she was increasingly masculinized, as can be seen in the sculptural program of the Parthenon, her main temple in Athens, the pediment of which portrays scenes from her life. The main statue within the temple showed her wearing the *aegis*, an armored cloak, and was further adorned with the two leading examples of the monstrous-feminine: the winged Medusa's head across her chest and a winged Sphinx on the center of her helmet, both harbingers of death (Figure 2.4).[79] Her shield shows Greek men killing Amazons, while the statue's base features the birth of Pandora, the female source of evil in the world.[80] In this, her late and full iconographic representation, it is difficult to see her as anything but a destroyer of females and a perfect expression of the Greek patriarchal order,[81] a view supported by her later mythology. The defeated females carved into her armor defined her

FIGURE 2.4 Varvakeion Athena, a second-century CE copy of the original statue by Phidias, c. 423 BCE. The subjugation of Nike, shown as held in Athena's right hand, is part and parcel of Athena subduing other avian females, discussed further below.

National Archaeology Museum, Athens. Photograph by H.R. Goette. ©Hellenic Ministry of Culture and Sports/Archaelogical Receipts Fund.

appointed task—usurpation of ancient female powers that ironically included her earlier self.

Athena is ever helpful to men[82] attempting heroic, mostly murderous, deeds, such as Perseus, who killed perhaps the most monstrous winged female of them all, Medusa the Gorgon, a supernatural woman with avian and reptilian character- istics, who was an ancient goddess of life and death and a guardian of sacred pre- cincts.[83] Ovid (*Metamorphoses* 4.770ff.) writes that Medusa was a beautiful woman until Poseidon raped her in one of Athena's temples; in a rage against this pollu- tion of her sacred space, Athena punished the victim instead of the rapist by turn- ing Medusa's hair into snakes. From then on, Medusa's gaze turned men to stone. Later, Athena gave Perseus a polished shield to use as a mirror in order to deflect Medusa's gaze so that he could kill her. First Athena punished an innocent woman, creating a female monster, and then she transformed the monster through decapi- tation into the definitive monstrous-feminine, the *vagina dentata*, the quintessence of men's dread of women. A painted vase attributed to the Diosphos Painter (c. 500 BCE) shows Perseus fleeing from Medusa's fallen, winged body with the child of Poseidon's rape, the male flying-horse Pegasus, leaping from her throat.[84] By displaying Medusa's head on her *aegis*, Athena accentuates her own monstrous femininity, the male-born female and devourer of men (the enemies of her warriors). The *aegis* is trimmed with snakes, co-opting Medusa's chthonic powers or perhaps preserving a remnant of Athena's own earlier chthonic nature; the priestess of Athena would carry the *aegis* into the home of newly married couples to ensure their fertility, and snakes were associated with birth and death.[85] Initially, Perseus used her head as a weapon to paralyze his enemies before giving it to Athena, who impaled it on her *aegis* as a war trophy. Carvings of it were also used to protect sacred sites.[86] Medusa is silent—her story is told by others.

The Greek Sphinx, worn by Athena on her helmet, is an all-knowing, monstrous, winged female dealer-in-death who originated in Egypt. Sphinxes are depicted with a woman's head and a winged lion's body. In Greece the most famous Sphinx appeared outside Thebes, where she posed the riddle of the three ages of man: "What goes on four feet in the morning, two feet in the afternoon, and three feet in the evening?"[87] This riddle reveals the knowledge of all winged females, that of birth, decay, and death; her connection with death is further demonstrated by the many images of her as a protective ornament on tombs.[88] If someone could not solve the riddle, she killed him—that is, until Oedipus correctly answered "man," after which she is said to have died or committed suicide.[89]

The Furies

Athena's part in the defeat of powerful, somewhat murderous winged females, both divine and human, continues in the *Eumenides*, a play by Aeschylus (525–456 BCE) first performed in 458 BCE. The importance of theater for the dissemination of religious ideology in ancient Greece cannot be overstated. The play takes place shortly after the fall of Troy, when the victorious Greeks have returned to their homes. At the beginning of the war, the Greek leader, King Agamemnon, had raised a wind for the Greek ships to sail to Troy by sacrificing Iphigeneia, the daughter of his wife, Queen Clytemnestra. Agamemnon managed to get Iphigeneia away from her mother by claiming that he was planning to arrange for her marriage to the Greek hero Achilles; instead, he offered her as a sacrifice.[90] Clytemnestra is enraged when she learns of her daughter's death, and she waits ten long years, while the Greeks battle the Trojans, for her revenge. Upon Agamemnon's return home, she kills him. This places a blood obligation on their son, Orestes, to avenge his father's murder by killing the murderer, his mother—which he does.

The *Eumenides* opens after these events and focuses on Orestes, who is being tormented by the Furies (Greek: *Erīnyes*, "angry ones") for killing his mother. The Furies are ancient, winged-female earth deities associated with death and rebirth; they avenge wrongs (especially to relatives), send pestilence, and are said to fly swiftly among the clouds.[91] Hesiod claims that they were born from the blood of Ouranos, which flowed when his son Kronos cut off his genitals (*Theogony* 176–185), a primordial crime against a parent. They became known as the Furies (from the Latin *furia*) through the Roman poet Vergil (70–19 BCE, *Aeneid* 3.331). As avengers of familial crimes, they bring charges against Orestes, seeking a trial before the gods, and they speak as the chorus in the play. When questioned by Athena, who acts as his judge, Orestes freely admits to having killed his mother but argues that he is not really guilty because he was compelled to kill her to avenge the death of his father. Orestes's argument is that revenging his father was his primary duty, taking precedence over any injunctions against matricide. Apollo speaks in Orestes's defense by presenting the biological theory that women are mere incubators of male seed (a theory advocated by Aristotle[92]) and offers Athena, who was born from her father's head, as living evidence of his point. Apollo is eager to destroy the power of these ancient avian females who preceded his creation.

Athena declares that Orestes is innocent of his mother's murder, asserts the superiority of the male, and denies her own connection to the female by referencing her birth from the head of Zeus: "For there is no mother who bore me; and I approve the male in all things, short of accepting marriage, with all my heart, and I belong altogether to my father. Therefore I shall not give greater weight to the death of a woman."[93] In their protests over this judgment, the Furies reveal their understanding that their time has passed, and that a new order has replaced them, one that supports the rights of the father over the rights of the mother: "Ah, you younger gods, the ancient laws you have ridden down, and snatched them from my grasp!"[94] Underlying all this negative opinion about women and mothers is Clytemnestra's transgression in an increasingly male-dominated world. She is monstrous to the new order because she chose another sexual partner while her lawful husband was away at war, then murdered Agamemnon and thereby usurped his throne. Such a woman may have been accepted or tolerated in ancient times, as were the judgments of the Furies, but no longer.[95]

The *Eumenides* articulates the rejection of this early, monstrous group of female avian spirits in favor of more anthropomorphized aerial females, such as Athena, who support masculine domination. As she did with Medusa and the Sphinx, Athena once again took onto herself ancient female powers, saying that they shall be renamed the Eumenides (the "kindly ones") and shall be worshiped on the Acropolis next to her temple.[96] That Aeschylus used *Eumenides* as the play's title indicates and affirms their pacification and defeat.

The Furies may have been reduced, but they were not vanquished. Some continued to torment Orestes, as seen in Euripides's *Iphigeneia in Tauris*, first performed in 414 BCE, in which Orestes explains to his still living but long-lost sister Iphigeneia the details of his trial and acquittal by the gods. Yet "[t]hose Furies who were satisfied with judgment given established a sanctuary at the place of trial. But those who were not satisfied with the decree kept driving me in the chases that allowed no rest."[97]

Athena acts as the hand of patriarchy as she subdues ancient religious practices; her role is to help men hunt down and murder any such non-patriarchal females, human or divine.

Despite her co-optation into the service of patriarchy and its wars, Athena maintained connections to her early avian nature through her epithet "owl-eyed" and her frequent depictions with an owl, particularly on the silver *tetradrachm*, the most widely used Greek coin,[98] which depicted Athena's helmeted head on the obverse and an owl on the reverse. The association with birds continued in her temple on the Acropolis, which was filled with nesting owls.[99] In ancient Greece the owl symbolized death as well as wisdom,[100] continuing her linkage with death. Then there is her ability to shape-shift into other species of birds (*Odyssey* 1.319–320, 3.371–372 and 22.246), as when she changed into a vulture to watch the battle between Hector and Ajax (*Iliad* 7.58–59).[101] In order to fly in her anthropomorphic form, she is said to have possessed golden sandals that carried her over water and land (*Odyssey* 1.99–100), though Figure 2.5 shows her with wings, carrying the body of a slain warrior while flying over the sea,[102] somewhat like a Valkyrie. Also like a Valkyrie, she protected heroes, such as Hercules, Odysseus, and Jason—a relationship with the goddess that was passed on from father to son.[103] But, she had to leave the ancient feminine parts of herself behind in order to remain aerial.

Medea

A woman who is seen as the epitome of the monstrous-feminine is the semi-divine Medea—the destroyer of her own children. Hers is another story about the rejection of an ancient and powerful aerial woman. She is well known through Euripides's enduringly popular play, *Medea*. It was first performed in Athens in 431 BCE, though it depicts events thought to have taken place as much as a thousand years earlier. Her story will be discussed more fully in chapter 8, but briefly, Medea, the granddaughter of the sun god Helios, falls in love with the Greek hero Jason, for whom she betrays and abandons her family, fleeing with him to his home on Iolcus, where she renews the youth of Jason's father through

FIGURE 2.5 Athena flies, carrying a dead warrior, attributed to the Leagros Group, c. sixth century BCE.
Bibliothèque nationale de France.

magical herbs (Ovid, *Metamorphoses* 195). Medea has the power to restore life and, as we shall see, to take it as well. A significant part of Jason's reputation as a great hero, who stole the Golden Fleece from Medea's father, was built upon Medea's magical powers.[104] Euripides picks up her story in the city of Corinth, where she and Jason have lived happily for a time, and where Medea has had two sons. As the play opens, Jason plans to abandon Medea and marry the young daughter of the king of Corinth. Medea briefly ponders her fate and then calls upon Hekate, the goddess of witchcraft whom Medea serves as priestess, to help her take revenge, first by killing the bride and her father and then killing Jason's children—that is, her own children. She is withdrawing her fertility from him, and Jason will have no heirs. In the end, Medea flies off in a chariot drawn by two winged dragons provided by her grandfather, Helios.[105]

Harpies and Sirens

Two additional examples of the monstrous-feminine are the alarming Harpies and the alluring Sirens. The word "harpy" comes from *harpázdein*, "to seize" or "to snatch"—and the Harpies carried off various things and people, such as the young daughters of Pandareus, whom they gave to the Furies as servants (*Odyssey* 20.77). By snatching people's souls and carrying them to other worlds, especially young people like Pandareus's unmarried daughters, the Harpies are ministers of untimely death.[106] Hesiod, who said the Harpies carried off newborn babies, named two of them—names that survive today in Jewish amulets for protection against child stealing.[107] According to Jane Harrison, they were originally the enraged souls of people unjustly killed, but by Homer's time they were personified as avenging female spirits.[108]

A later story has the Harpies tormenting the blind King Phineus by carrying off his food and defiling what is left with their excrement. The story is depicted on an early fifth-century BCE terra-cotta bowl attributed to the Klephrades Painter[109] that shows three Harpies as clothed, winged women. This later representation, as winged women, became the standard one in Greece.[110] It is unclear exactly what Phineus did to deserve such punishment, but one version of the tale states that he had the gift of prophecy, which enabled him to learn, and then betray, divine secrets.[111] When Jason and his Argonauts asked Phineus for help in obtaining the Golden Fleece, he agreed to do so only if they could get rid of the Harpies. Jason called on the winged sons of Boreas, the north wind, who chased them until Iris, the winged goddess of the rainbow and messenger of Hera, intervened and promised they would never again disturb Phineus. Their story is of interest with regard to the discussion of Medea above, as it depicts Jason opposing aerial women even before he met Medea.

The Sirens, too, brought about untimely deaths. They were songstresses best known for luring sailors onto the sharp, dangerous rocks near their island; to hear their melodious song was to die.[112] Unlike the Harpies, they personify the dangers of sexuality and the role of song in seduction.[113] One hears their enticing song but does not see the heap of dead men's bones on their island: "Horror is kept in the background, seduction to the fore."[114] But like the Harpies, they are female birds of prey. They know the past and the future and also accompany the dead to the underworld. From very early times they were seen as protectors of the dead and singers of funeral dirges and were carved on the tops of tombs, depicted, like the Harpies, as birds with the heads of women[115]—a neat inversion of the ancient bird goddess, who had a woman's body and a bird's head, and perhaps signifying their exclusively sinister nature.

The Sirens are also defeated by two different heroes. The first, Odysseus, is told about them by Circe after he has journeyed to the Land of the Dead. He and his crew are already on the boundaries of the living world; they have survived the Land of the Dead and are now prepared to brave the Sirens. Circe warns

Odysseus that the only way he can hear their haunting song and survive is to be tied to the mast of his ship and to plug the ears of his crew so they will keep rowing (*Odyssey* 12.41–88). The second hero to subdue them is depicted in one of the earliest representations of Orpheus, on a vase dating from about 570 BCE: it shows him walking between two Sirens with bird bodies and the heads of women. Orpheus, the great master of song and another traveler to the underworld, trumps their death song, signaling his new religion, which grants immortality to its initiates.[116]

Both "siren" and "harpy" survive today as pejorative terms for women. "Harpy" is used for a rapacious woman or worse, while "siren" refers to an extremely alluring but deceptive woman, whom a man engages with at his peril.

Aphrodite

With Aphrodite, the goddess of love and fertility, and the moon and the stars,[117] we leave the monstrous-feminine behind. She, too, is a very ancient celestial goddess with roots in Cyprus and Asia Minor, among other places. The *Iliad* makes her eastern origins clear. She is the mother of the Trojan hero Aeneas and always sides with the Trojans, acting as protector of their warriors,[118] though she is no warrior goddess; her lover, Ares, serves the war god's role.[119] (Her Near Eastern counterpart Inanna/Isthar was both fertility and war goddess, but now the war function has been split off and given to a male deity.) Jane Harrison finds her prototype in Crete in the form of a goddess with a dove on her head that dates to around 1000 BCE, doves being sacred to her and associated with love and fertility,[120] though Walter Burkert sees clear connections to the Near Eastern Isthar/Inanna cults, possibly transmitted through her temples on Cyprus. Interestingly, Cyprian statuettes of her from the Bronze Age have bird faces.[121] Her chariot was thought to be drawn by doves or sparrows,[122] although she is also connected to the goose, as shown in Figure 1.6 (p. 23), which shows her being flown through the sky on a goose's back.[123] The Greek poet Sappho (c. 600 BCE) was devoted to her, especially for her ability to inspire love:

> You [Aphrodite] . . . yoked the birds to your gold
> Chariot, and came. Handsome swallows
> Brought you swiftly to the dark earth . . . .
> What does your mad heart desire?
> Whom shall I make love you, Sappho,
> Who is turning her back on you?[124]

Sappho's poetry greatly influenced people's understanding of Aphrodite's power to arouse erotic love, because Sappho was famous and traveled extensively throughout the Greek-speaking world to compete in poetry contests at festivals. Consequently, Sappho is a unique female voice shaping ancient Greek religion.[125] Regrettably, nearly all of her poems were lost or destroyed by early Christians, who did not celebrate carnal love.

As the goddess of love, both licit and illicit, Aphrodite is the driving force in the *Iliad* and the *Odyssey*, from the adulterous love of Helen that starts the war, to the marital love that propels Odysseus home to his faithful wife, Penelope. Like Athena and Artemis, she did not want to marry and soon made a cuckold of Hephaestus, the ugly and crippled blacksmith of the gods who made her his wife—but she had her share of lovers. She represented the erotic aspects of love so fully that she was the patron of prostitutes, and sacred prostitution was part of her cult at Corinth, Cyprus, Cythera, Eryn, and elsewhere. In this, she echoes her Near Eastern counterpart Inanna; in all these instances, sacred prostitution was believed to generate fertility and prosperity throughout the land. In ancient Greek her name could be used as a noun to mean sexual intercourse,[126] and there are frequent references in ancient Greek literature to "The Works of Aphrodite," which Paul Friedrich convincingly argues were love manuals.[127] Relevantly, she is the only Greek goddess portrayed in the nude (though sometimes, like Artemis, with only one breast exposed[128]). Aphrodite reveals her part in human love and fertility by raising her skirt to reveal her genitals in votive terra-cottas from seventh-century BCE Crete and Hellenistic Egypt.[129] Contrasting with these images is her most famous, most copied, and most innovative nude image: the larger-than-life statue by Praxiteles called the Knidian Aphrodite, produced around 340 BCE, in which she uses her hand to cover her genitals, a pose labeled *pudica* ("modest"). Her nudity and the *pudica* pose endured for centuries, perhaps most notably in Botticelli's *Birth of Venus*.[130]

Like Athena and Artemis, Aphrodite was incorporated into the Olympian pantheon through a birth story: Hesiod writes that she was born from the foam that arose when Ouranous's genitals landed in the sea—an expression of her powers of fertility—making her another non-womb-born goddess, created from the mixing of Ouranous's semen with the sea[131] ("sea," it should be noted, is a feminine noun in most, if not all, Indo-European languages).

Nike

This chapter ends with Nike, whose mythology encapsulates the many features of winged goddesses we have seen so far. The goddess of victory, she was also a symbol of victory over death, immortalizing heroes, and she was a favorite motif of Roman allegorical art. Hesiod is the first to mention her, describing her as the daughter of the Titan Pallas and the river Styx, which marked the boundary between earth and the underworld. This made her and her daughters goddesses of the boundaries between life and death. Styx brought her daughters Nike (Victory), Zelos (Rivalry), Kratos (Strength), and Bia (Force) to fight alongside Zeus against the old gods, the Titans (*Theogony* 383), for which they were rewarded with access to Olympus, home of the gods. Since she assisted in battle, Nike's popularity rose during the Persian Wars (499–449 BCE), and she began to appear more frequently on vases.[132] Like the Valkyries and *apsarās*, she transports heroes: Nike drives the chariot that carries the hero Heracles to Olympus.[133] Nike was also portrayed in vivid terms by fifth-century BCE poets as the bestower of victory in athletic and musical contests, and in this guise she frequently appeared on the coins of various Greek cities. Bacchylides (fifth century BCE) described her standing next to Zeus on Olympus, judging which gods and men should receive awards for excellence, and as flying over the victorious drivers of chariot races. In Pindar's (522–433 BCE) odes to the games at Nemea, he depicted an exhausted but victorious athlete sinking into her arms (*Nemean* 5.42).[134]

Marina Warner provides a thoughtful discussion of Nike's ancient and modern interpretations, although she is mistaken when she limits Nike to being an epithet for and/or emanation of Athena.[135] E. E. Sikes has shown that Nike had an independent existence both before and after she was appended to Athena in the Temple of Athena Nike on the Acropolis (completed c. 409 BCE) and on Athena's statue in the Parthenon (see again Figure 2.4), which had a diminutive Nike standing in Athena's outstretched hand. The Acropolis is, of course, in Athens, the city named after its protector, Athena. The city's victories were attributed to Athena's grace, so it was only to be expected that Nike (Victory) would be subsumed within Athena's already warlike iconographic program.[136] Notably, the most famous Nike, that of Samothrace, had nothing to do with Athena. Samothrace, a remote, mountainous island in the northern Aegean Sea, was the site of an important mystery cult devoted to the Great Gods, who were protectors from dangers such as war, drowning, and shipwreck; they may have been nameless or had names that were hidden from the public.[137] Many pilgrims were drawn to the island to participate in the cult's initiation ceremonies. The buildings and sculptures that they commissioned for the sanctuary were crucial to the development of art and architecture in the Hellenistic period, with the Victory of Samothrace being one of the era's finest pieces. Further, the Greek geographer Pausanias describes her cult in Olympia (5.14.8)—she had others at Ilion, Tralles, and elsewhere.[138] But by now we are familiar with Athena's destruction or co-optation of winged females.

In her Roman form, Nike was blended with the ancient Roman goddess Victoria and associated with the cults of Jupiter and Mars, while losing her connection to athletic and musical contests. In Rome she was strictly a military deity, worshiped by the army and given surnames associating her with particular legions and emperors. Her temple on the Palatine was dedicated in 294 BCE, but perhaps her most famous Roman monument was her altar in the Senate House, placed there by Augustus in 29 BCE[139] to commemorate the defeat of Antony and Cleopatra at the Battle of Actium. Here each senator offered libations of wine and burned incense to her as guardian of the empire.[140] She continued to evolve even among the early Christians, who did not discard her along with the other pagan gods. She remained a significant presence on Christian sarcophagi,[141] and later she influenced the iconography of Christian angels (see chapter 5), with whom she shared the function of being a messenger (*angelos*) of god(s).[142]

From the all-powerful Isis's diminishment into the Virgin Mary (who acts only as an intercessor, not an autonomous deity), to the betrayal of Medea, the defeat of the Furies, and the reduction of the other female gods and deities discussed throughout this chapter, we have seen a purposeful decline in the power of winged females. The ancient Greeks are a particularly good example of the constraints placed on winged females by their incorporation into and domestication within the patriarchal Greek pantheon. A staggering variety of constraints placed on winged females will be discussed in the chapters that follow.

3

The Fall of the Valkyries

VALKYRIES ARE BRAVE, wise,[1] and extraordinarily beautiful celestial women warriors. Mounted on horseback, they fly between this world and the heavens, choosing to protect some warriors by granting them victory or taking fallen heroes to Valhalla (Valhöll), the great hall of the Norse god Odin/Wotan, where they restore them to life. They confer immortality on and are the reward of heroic warriors in the afterlife.[2] The night sky reflects their glory: the Milky Way is said to be their road, and the Aurora Borealis the shine of their shields. The word *valkyrie* means "chooser of the slain," but they are much more than that. They are intermediaries between humans and gods, guides for the dead, and the means to rebirth. Like the winged goddesses of chapter 2, Valkyries act independently—though their independence is shown to be precarious. The earliest evidence for them are third-century altars dedicated to the Alaisiagae, the Germanic goddesses that preceded them.[3]

In legend and saga they were equally at home on the battlefield or in a royal court.[4] The greatest of all Valkyries is Brunhilde (variously spelled Brunhild, Brünnhilde, Byrnhild and Byrnhildr), though she is more often than not subsumed into the story of her lover, Sigurd/Sigmund.[5] Nonetheless, she caught and held the Nordic imagination for centuries. Her literary and iconographic development traces more than a thousand years of social and religious upheavals that changed ideologies about womanhood.

BRUNHILDE IN THE *VOLSUNGS SAGA*

The fullest surviving core of Brunhilde's story is told in the thirteenth-century Icelandic *Volsungs Saga*, a compilation of pre-Christian epic poetry, some of which dates back to the fifth century CE, the period depicted in the saga.[6] In it, Brunhilde is introduced as one of the Norse god Odin's (or Wotan's) "shield maidens," a term sometimes used to refer to Valkyries.[7] Her story begins when she disobeys Odin's order to give victory to one battling king over another. Odin's punishment is to stab her with a thorn that induces an enchanted sleep and to surround her in a ring of a magical fire. Just before she loses consciousness he declares that she will marry a mortal. Appalled by this fate, Brunhilde is quick to vow she will "marry no one who [knows] fear" (67).[8] Disobeying her father renders her unconscious, vulnerable, and subject to tragedy. What follows is a riveting tale of lovers deceived and love denied through deception and magic.

The hero of the *Volsungs Saga* is Sigurd (Siegfried in the German tradition), who becomes famous for killing the dragon Fafnir and capturing his vast treasure, which unfortunately includes a ring that is cursed and will bring about the death of any who possesses it (5–7). The popularity of Sigurd's story is attested by its frequent depiction on memorial stones in Scandinavia[9] and northern England, as well as on Christian artifacts such as stone crosses and the portals of Norwegian stave churches.[10] Sigurd may be the hero, but Brunhilde is the heart of the saga;[11] unlike other characters, she speaks often and at length.[12] She is a fallen celestial woman, no longer able to fly, held captive to the earth and its mortality, her divinity and powers gone, doomed to love any man who can brave the fire to awaken her. Yet, when one recalls the transformative power of fire to convert earthly offerings into sacred ones, or in this case to separate the sacred from the profane, the ring of fire marks Brunhilde as divine, as the divine gift of a celestial woman to a victorious warrior. It also prefigures her sacrificial death on Sigurd's funeral pyre. Brunhilde and Sigurd are both separated and joined by fire. She is trapped, unconscious, in hers, but he can breach it. When he is trapped, dead, on his funeral pyre, she reaches him. Being encircled by fire characterizes Brunhilde's ambiguous status throughout the saga as she shifts between being a supernatural Valkyrie and a human woman who traverses both the divine and mundane worlds.

After killing the dragon Sigurd drinks its blood, which enables him to understand the language of birds, who tell him about the sleeping Brunhilde. Sigurd can only reach his full heroic dimensions when he gains access to the sky through learning the language of birds and awakening Brunhilde, who will impart divine knowledge to him. Valkyries know the language of birds, an ability widely associated with divination,[13] and they often shape-shift into birds, including swans,[14] whose wings appear on nineteenth-century representations of their helmets (Figure 3.1).[15]

Sigurd walks through the ring of fire and awakens Brunhilde by cutting off her armor, a not very subtle indication of the power and protection she has lost. In spite of this, Brunhilde has retained certain divine qualities, mainly her great beauty and wisdom, which Sigurd says caused him to seek her (67). The awakening of Brunhilde has direct parallels to Norse stories about awakening the dead in order to obtain esoteric knowledge from them, such as when Odin travels to the underworld to awaken a dead female seer.[16] Brunhilde gives Sigurd esoteric knowledge about runes (a form of writing possessing magical power), but she also gives him exoteric knowledge via a code to live by, such as being patient, honoring oaths, and taking proper care of the dead—the last being the special province of Valkyries. The wisdom that Brunhilde imparts to Sigurd is key to his maturing into a full human being. He is still quite young and inexperienced, even mistaking her

FIGURE 3.1 Carl Emil Doepler (1824–1905), costume design for Brunhilde showing swan wings on helmet for the 1876 premiere of Richard Wagner's *Der Ring des Nibelungen*. Berliner Kundstdruckkund Verlags-Ansalt, 1889, Chromolithograph.
Gift of Hester Diamond, 2012. The Morgan Library & Museum.

for a man when he first sees her asleep in her armor. In a clear indication of its significance, Brunhilde's speech to him is the longest one in the saga (67).[17] Brunhilde
is not only teaching Sigurd; she is teaching all of Norse society. Because these rules
have been brought to earth by a divine woman, the consequences of breaking
them, particularly of breaking an oath, will lead to tragic events not only for the
humans involved, but for the gods as well. In Norse literature oaths imply a sacred
and solemn duty to oneself and one's honor—a matter of supreme importance—
and to the community.[18]

Though her divine powers are greatly reduced, Brunhilde becomes Sigurd's
guardian Valkyrie by giving him wisdom and by loving him. Before parting they
swear binding oaths to marry. Soon they meet again and renew their oaths to
marry, and Sigurd gives her Fafnir's cursed ring, thereby foreshadowing their
mutual doom. Since Brunhilde became pregnant during one of their encounters
(in an episode that has now been lost),[19] the ground is prepared for enacting the
Valkyries' theme of fertility, death, and rebirth.

Like many sagas, the *Volsungs Saga* was compiled from various prose and poetic
sources. Seams show, and story lines can be inconsistent. Magic and the supernatural are often used to move characters into situations they would not have
chosen, transitions can be abrupt, much is left unexplained, and in some cases
parts of the texts have been lost, such as Brunhilde's pregnancy. For the tragedy
to build, though, Brunhilde and Sigurd must be separated. Without explanation,
Sigurd goes off to seek adventure. He soon meets Queen Grimhild of Burgundy, a
sorceress who wants him to marry her daughter, Gudrun. Brunhilde and Gudrun
both anticipate future events when they dream of each other, meeting first in
the dream realm, before the fulfillment of their dreams tragically entangles
their waking lives. Brunhilde dreams that Gudrun is coming to see her, which
Gudrun eventually does because she has heard that Brunhilde is wise and can
interpret dreams. The ability to understand dreams, both one's own and those
of others, is a valued skill in the sagas and another indication of Brunhilde's prophetic powers—and part of her tragic fate because such foreknowledge will not
save her.

Gudrun told Brunhilde that she dreamed

"that many of us left my bower together and saw a huge stag. He far sur-
passed other deer. His hair was of gold. We all wanted to catch the stag, but
I alone was able to do so. The stag seemed finer to me than anything else.
But then you shot down the stag right in front of me. That was such a deep
sorrow to me that I could hardly stand it. Then you gave me a wolf's cub. It
spattered me with the blood of my brothers."

Brynhild replied; "I will tell you just what will happen. To you will come Sigurd, the man I have chosen for my husband. Grimhild will give him bewitched mead [of forgetfulness], which will bring us all to grief. You will marry him and quickly lose him. Then you will wed King Atli. You will lose your brothers, and then you will kill Atli."

Gudrun answered: "The grief of knowing such things overwhelms me." (77)

An important undercurrent in the saga is the tensions provoked by marriage—tensions that are exacerbated by the blood bonds between sisters and brothers.[20] Brunhilde and Sigurd are unattached figures in the *Volsungs Saga*. Both are without families, outsiders who are rootless in a tumultuous world defined and made safe by kinship ties. Additional sources of tension swirl around the changing forms of marriage that are enacted in Brunhilde's story: by one's own choice, by capture, by winning a contest, or by arrangement by one's family. And enormous efforts are brought to bear, including magic and deception, to get people married. Queen Grimhild is an excellent example of this—not once, but twice: she slips Sigurd a magic drink of forgetfulness and he marries Gudrun. They have a son. Grimhild then decides her son Gunnar should marry Brunhilde, which he can only accomplish through his mother's magic. For reasons that the saga does not explain, Brunhilde is residing in a castle surrounded by flames,[21] a reflection of her earlier position, when Sigurd first found her. Similarly, this ring of fire can only be breached by a great hero. Gunnar is not up to the task, so he asks Sigurd to shape-shift into his form. Sigurd, unfortunately, is still under the power of Grimhild's drink of forgetfulness and does not remember his sworn oaths to marry Brunhilde. Grimhild's magic is powerful enough for her to put a spell on Brunhilde so that she, too, does not recognize Sigurd in Gunnar's form. She takes him to be Gunnar, and when he asks her to marry him the text describes her appearance: "She answered gravely from her seat, like a swan on a wave, in her mail coat, with her sword in her hand and her helmet on her head" (81). This allusion to a swan evokes swan maiden tales (discussed in chapter 4) and foreshadows Brunhilde's captivity, like many a swan maiden, in a false marriage. Brunhilde's marriage will be false on several counts: it will be based on Gunnar's cowardice, Sigurd's deception, Grimhild's evil sorcery, and Odin's punishment. But she does not yet know this, so Brunhilde says she will marry Gunnar, but she sets a condition: he must kill anyone else who has asked to marry her. Again, the saga does not explain Brunhilde's motivation in marrying Gunnar, but in the oldest extant Brunhilde poem, any man who wishes to marry her must breach the flames around her castle.[22] In both tales, Brunhilde's acceptance of Gunnar sets into motion events that will lead to her own and Sigurd's deaths.

Brunhilde and Sigurd (in Gunnar's form) spend three nights together, sleeping in one bed with a sword between them, suggesting the marriage is not consummated, that Sigurd in Gunnar's body did not take advantage of his friend's future wife. Despite this, Sigurd's deception makes Brunhilde vulnerable to suspicion and betrayal. Before leaving her, he takes Fafnir's ring and replaces it with another ring.

Sigurd does not recover his memory until immediately after Brunhilde and Gunnar's wedding celebration, when he suddenly recognizes Brunhilde but chooses to remain silent, suffering silently in the knowledge that he is an oath breaker. Thus the tragedy begins to unfold, stimulated by tensions between the royal women, Brunhilde and Gudrun. This becomes an enduring theme in later versions of Brunhilde's story; arguments between women are enacted in order to depict women as divisive and ruled by jealousy. Matters come to a head because Gudrun cannot tolerate Brunhilde's pride, and in a fit of anger she tells Brunhilde that Sigurd "was your first man" (82), showing her Fafnir's ring as proof. This is a dreadful insult, and in that moment Brunhilde understands the full deception. She has a violent argument with Gunnar, saying she is "a breaker of oaths" because she does not have Sigurd and that her honor is lost. She tries to kill Gunnar but fails.

Before all this comes out, Brunhilde had been working on a tapestry—an earlier part of the saga notes that it depicts Sigurd's heroic deeds. Like one of the Norns, the goddesses who spin and then cut the length of a human life, she has been weaving his fate (73).[23] And, like a Norn, Brunhilde breaks the threads in her rage, tearing the tapestry to pieces, and with it both their lives (85).[24] The saga emphasizes the Norse belief that fate will play out; individuals act, swear oaths, have hopes and desires, but nevertheless are powerless against destiny. Some are noble, some are greedy, and some a mix of the two. All are masters of deceit, which was considered an honorable tactic during war and raiding. Women and men are equally active in moving the plot forward.

Brunhilde is constrained and therefore cannot act directly. She can no longer fly—surely a metaphor for loss of autonomy and independent action—and is trapped in a situation not entirely of her making. She has lost the divine powers available to a Valkyrie in battle, such as possessing great strength and the magical ability to bind men, rendering them powerless, for marriage has terminated her martial abilities. As she passively lies in bed, Brunhilde's laments echo throughout the house.

When Sigurd proposed to her on behalf of Gunnar, Brunhilde was dressed in armor, but later, when married to Gunnar, she no longer wears armor and fails in her attempt to kill him. Brunhilde's womanhood is regularized by marriage,[25] her warrior nature subdued. She lies in her room, passively holding the entire household in terror. No one goes near her for seven days—then Sigurd goes to her. He tells her he has always loved her and now wants to marry her, but Brunhilde will not have it. She is overcome with rage and shame due to Sigurd's deception when he came to her in Gunnar's form, and the honor she lost by not fulfilling her oath to marry Sigurd. She wants to die and she wants Sigurd dead, too. She sets out to accomplish this by telling her husband Gunnar to kill him or she will leave him. Of course, Sigurd has now asked her to marry him three times, thereby binding Gunnar to his oath to kill anyone who has proposed to Brunhilde. If Gunnar fails to keep his oath Brunhilde will be released from their marriage, but this is something he will not do.

Brunhilde has cornered Gunnar. He has to murder Sigurd to honor his oath to Brunhilde, yet he cannot do it himself because of the oaths of friendship he and Sigurd have sworn. He resorts to treachery; he convinces his younger brother Guttorm[26] to sneak into Sigurd's bedchamber and kill him while he sleeps. This is an ignoble end for Sigurd, but an appropriate one. While asleep he is as unconscious and unthinking—as when he deceived Brunhilde without any regard for her feelings or for the consequences, which have precipitated both their deaths. After he is dead, Brunhilde takes it upon herself to have his and Gudrun's son killed.[27] Once Sigurd's son and his assassin are dead, Brunhilde stabs herself, though not fatally, which may refer to the Norse custom of inflicting a wound when dying from an illness, wounds being a prerequisite for entry into Valhalla.[28] She then gives very specific instructions about the construction of Sigurd's funeral pyre: Sigurd, his son, Guttorm, and two hawks are laid on the same funeral pyre, which Brunhilde steps onto and dies upon (92–93). The two hawks are rich symbols, as guides for the dead, as the form sometimes taken by Valkyries, and as companions of Odin. Brunhilde may not have lived as a Valkyrie on earth, but she died as one, taking a warrior, Sigurd, to Odin's hall.[29]

IMAGES AND MEANINGS

The concept of supernatural female warriors may have originated from actual Germanic women warriors,[30] such as those described by the twelfth-century Danish historian Saxo Grammaticus,[31] as well as from the priestesses who officiated at sacrificial rites in which captives were put to death.[32] In Britain and Gaul and among the Germanic tribes, Roman soldiers encountered women warriors at a much earlier date.[33] Certain episodes in the thirteenth-century *Volsungs Saga* describe actual historical events from the fourth and fifth centuries, when pressure from the Huns pushed Germanic tribes into Roman territory and led to their eventual acceptance of Christianity.[34] It is possible that Brunhilde may have been based partly on Queen Brunhilda (d. 613), wife of King Sigibert (535–575 CE) of the Franks. When Sigibert was murdered by his brother's mistress, Brunhilda's efforts to revenge him seriously weakened the kingdom[35] and led to her own brutal death.

There is some evidence that the Valkyries may have been part of an early cult in which men worshiped a supernatural woman in order to gain her protection, a practice that was later displaced by the worship of the gods.[36] Valkyries were also worshiped through a special sacrifice (dísablót) offered only by women,[37] and it has been suggested they may have had an additional cult served by royal women seeking to become Valkyries.[38] Sigrun, whose story is told below, seems to have undergone the transformation from mortal woman to Valkyrie, since she first appears among beautifully attired women mounted on fine horses but is later referred to as a Valkyrie. Being shape-shifters, Valkyries easily slip between various kinds of being: divine, human, and animal.

The uncertainties surrounding the cultic practices associated with Valkyries and differences in their depictions reflect historical developments as well as contending conceptions of the afterlife far too complicated to detail here.[39] The Norse religious system was highly complex, and most of it is lost to us. It was practiced by a great variety of people over a wide and expanding geographical area for centuries, before the Norse were eventually converted to Christianity.[40] The Germanic people of continental Europe converted to Christianity beginning in the fifth century, while their Scandinavian cousins followed their traditional religion until around 1000 CE. This meant that Norse religion was practiced and continued to evolve, free from Christian influence, five hundred years longer in Scandinavia than in continental Europe. Consequently, Scandinavia provides the main sources of information about Norse religion, in which war and death played a major part. A generally held belief was that victory in battle could be gained by winning the favor of the gods (which was done through sacrifice), and gaining the protection of a Valkyrie.

Among the earliest iconographic representations of Valkyries is an eighth-century carved memorial stone from Tjängvide, Gotland, Sweden (Figure 3.2).[41] Such memorial stones tell a story in multiple timeframes defined by individual images. In Figure 3.2, the largest figure is an eight-legged horse, probably Odin's horse Sleipnir, with a rider. Slightly below and to the left is a large figure of a woman facing the rider and carrying a drinking horn and perhaps a key. Above her is a semicircular structure identified as Valhalla. It has been speculated that the rider is a fallen warrior and that the standing woman, a Valkyrie, is greeting him as he enters Valhalla.[42] This is a favored scene on memorial stones of the period, others of which show a female figure with a spear flying above a scene of conflict. Quite significantly, small silver and bronze amulets of women in long dresses

FIGURE 3.2 Tjängvide image stone, Viking era (800–1100 CE). 1.7 m h, 1.2 m w, and 0.3 m thick. Photograph: Ola Myrin/The Swedish History Museum, Stockholm.

holding drinking horns, similar to those in Figure 3.2, have been found in Viking Age graves (Figure 3.3),[43] suggesting that they were put there to guide the dead to the afterlife.

Valkyries divide into two types: the first, and possibly oldest, are frightening, often ugly, blood-thirsty goddesses of death who have the shape-shifting characteristics of werewolves,[44] or who ride wolves that feed on slain warriors. Grendel's mother in *Beowulf* is a good example of this type.[45] The second type are depicted as benevolent, radiantly beautiful court ladies with enviable martial skills. They dress in armor, often appear on horseback, and possess wisdom, eloquence, and the ability to prophesy, along with supernatural powers such as the ability to fly.[46] Sometimes the two types appear in one setting, battling for the future of the hero,[47] as in the *Gisli Saga* (thirteenth century). The hero Gisli describes them: "'There are two women I dream of. One is good to me. The other always tells me something that makes matters worse than ever, and she only prophesies ill for me.'"[48] The latter is appropriately called "the thread goddess," an allusion to her control over

FIGURE 3.3 Silver amulet of a Valkyrie.
Photograph: Christer Åhlin/The Swedish History Museum, Stockholm.

the thread of his life. As his death approaches, his dreams of her become more frequent and more gruesome.[49]

These conflicting dreams reflect the ambivalent nature of Valkyries as bringers of fertility, death, and rebirth. During battles they can act as protectors, or they can paralyze a warrior with their gaze, rendering him defenseless before his foes. In either case, though, the men ultimately emerge victorious, as they will survive the battle or the Valkyries will carry them to immortality.

The Valkyries' association with fertility, and thus sexuality, made them ideal for romantic tales. Over time this side of their nature persuaded some poets to recast Valkyries; no longer fierce, independent goddesses, they were reduced to mere components of male heroic tales.[50] In such tales they cannot fly and their other powers are also greatly diminished. This is especially clear in stories about Brunhilde. Later poets took the early tales about her, limited her powers, and then attached her tales to those about the hero Sigurd.[51] Long before Sigurd appeared, however, now-lost poems about Brunhilde were sung around Norse fires. Yet in the *Volsungs Saga*, even in reduced guise, Brunhilde maintained her individuality and foiled the plans of mortal men.

Like the ancient Near Eastern flying goddesses of war, love, and death, Valkyries are unpredictable beings, on the one hand bringing death and destruction, and on the other possessing powers of fertility and thus replenishment. Like Brunhilde, other Valkyries sometimes had sexual relations with heroes, and some of them acted as guardians of individual families and granted them children who would assure the continuation of the family line. Brunhilde not only taught Sigurd how to care for the dead, a subject she knew well, but one of the runes she taught him was used as an aid to women in childbirth.[52] Further, in many ancient cultures, female fertility was often represented by horse goddesses.[53] Jacob Grimm alluded to this and more by writing, "[W]hen the steeds of the valkyries shake themselves, dew drips from their manes into the valleys, and fertilizing hail falls on trees . . .,"[54] for the Valkyries are also ancient mare goddesses. This does not preclude them from being bird goddesses or swan maidens, as well; instead, it points to their plenitude of being because they can assume human, equine, or avian forms with ease. The Valkyries are divine women who ride, or are, horses, change into swans and other birds, and bestow blessings or death. Significantly, Valkyries are also connected to Freyja, the Norse goddess of love, fertility, and war. In her own realm, Folkvangr, she receives half of those who are slain, while the other half go to Odin. Both groups are delivered by Valkyries.[55] And, like the Valkyries, Freyja can fly by shape-shifting into a bird,[56] though she is also said to have a feather cloak that enables her and those who borrow it to fly.[57]

When a Valkyrie protected a particular warrior in battle, she also continued her protection in the afterlife, or upon his death she would transfer her protection to another man, often from the same family.[58] Richard Wagner made use of this belief when he had Brunhilde first attach herself to Siegmund, whom she tried to save from Odin/Wotan's decision that he should die, and then to his son Siegfried, whom she loved and with whom she chose to die, as discussed below. In this role of supernatural guardians Valkyries were occasionally looked on as the wives of their warriors.[59] Brunhilde's story suggests that the wives or lovers who followed their heroes through voluntary (sacrificial) deaths also went to Valhalla, where they were reunited.[60]

A syncretic poem included in the *Edda* is entitled "Brunhilde's Journey to the Underworld"; it brings together ideas about the Valkyries as swans or swan maidens. This poem presents an alternate immolation scene for Brunhilde and describes some of her afterlife. In this version, two funeral pyres are built, one for Sigurd and another for Brunhilde. Her body is placed in a wagon adorned with costly weavings. The poem describes her journey to Hel, where she meets a witch who challenges her right to enter Hel to be with another woman's husband, and calls Brunhilde the most ill-fated woman. This prompts Brunhilde to tell the witch about her early life, beginning when she was twelve years old and a king (or prince) carried off the *hamir*, a garment that allows her and her seven sisters to shape-shift. The poem is not completely clear in its connections, but Brunhilde then swore an oath to that king, perhaps in order to get the *hamir* back[61]—making it a classic swan-maiden tale (see chapter 4) and supporting the imagery of aerial women as part of a sisterhood or a flock. Similarly, in the Old Norse tale about Weyland, he and his three brothers capture three swan maidens, who are also called Valkyries, by stealing their swan costumes. They carry the women home and marry them, but seven years later the Valkyries, missing the heat of battle, find their swan cloaks while the brothers are out, and fly away.[62]

The independent spirit of the Valkyries was deeply connected to their ability to fly. Once this ability is taken away from them they lose any semblance of independence. Like swan maidens who have put aside their wings, they are inevitably captured and married off. The declining power of the Valkyries is further shown in the twelfth-century *Nibelungenlied*, to which we now turn.

BRUNHILDE IN THE *NIBELUNGENLIED*

The *Nibelungenlied* is based on the same pre-Christian, oral tradition of heroic poetry as the *Volsungs Saga*.[63] It follows a similar storyline, albeit one seen from a very different social and religious perspective. The *Nibelungenlied* was written down by an unknown author in southern Germany or Austria about 1200 CE—a few decades earlier than the *Volsungs Saga*. The continental Germanic tribes, however, had been converted to Christianity at least six hundred years prior to this, which heavily influenced their ideas about gender and marriage. Brunhilde retains barely an echo of her former divine power and wisdom, and she is rapidly shorn even of that. Further, all marriages in the *Nibelungenlied* are virilocal—that is, the bride leaves her natal home for her husband's. The *Volsungs Saga*, which was written down after only 130 years of Christianity in Iceland, presents more varied forms of marriage and preserves Norse religious ideas, reflecting a more pagan, and perhaps earlier, core of the story.

The *Nibelungenlied* begins with the beautiful Kriemhild (Gudrun in the *Volsungs Saga*), a princess of Burgundy who will become Brunhilde's enemy. In the Netherlands, Prince Siegfried (Sigurd of the *Volsungs Saga*), the hero of the tale, hears of Kriemhild's great beauty and decides to marry her. Prior to this, Siegfried had conquered the Nibelung people, taken all their treasure, and won a magic cloak that made him invisible and gave him the additional strength of twelve men. He had also killed a dragon and bathed in its blood, which has made him invincible, except for one place on his upper back, where a leaf fell between his shoulder blades. Unlike the *Volsungs Saga*, in which Brunhilde educates and empowers him, his character is fully developed from his first appearance in the *Nibelungenlied*.

Kriemhild's brother, Gunther, the king of Burgundy, has also heard about and desires a great beauty who lives far away: Brunhilde, the enormously strong warrior queen of Iceland. As in the *Volsungs Saga*, Gunther is the lesser man and requires help from Siegfried, the only hero equal to her. Siegfried agrees to help Gunther on the condition that Gunther will give Kriemhild to him, which Gunther swears to do so. They are trading women like baseball cards.

In the *Nibelungenlied*, Brunhilde has been demoted from a divine to a mortal woman, albeit a powerful royal woman. She has no desire to surrender her independence and refuses to marry unless a nobleman can defeat her in three contests: throwing the javelin, hurling a huge boulder a great distance, and making a long leap (*Nibelungenlied* 53 and 56). All three are aerial feats, with the last being a remnant of her original mythic power to fly.

Gunther and Siegfried sail to Iceland with a small group of companions. Gunther challenges Brunhilde and pretends to compete with her while Siegfried, invisible and possessing the strength of twelve men because of his magic cloak, actually performs the required feats. It is, after all, so much easier to dominate when one is invisible.[64] In this way, and with great effort despite his magic cloak, he barely defeats Brunhilde, who must now yield herself and her lands to Gunther (*Nibelungenlied* 64–69).

Brunhilde cannot accept her defeat, and she refuses to consummate the marriage on the voyage back to Burgundy, and continues to do so upon their arrival. Gunther is determined to have her and tries to force himself on her, but she easily ties him up and hangs him on a nail for the night (*Nibelungenlied* 87–88), an amusing allusion to the magical power of Valkyries to bind men. Once again, Gunther must ask Siegfried for help. Under cloak of darkness—another form of invisibility—Siegfried pretends to be Gunther, and with great effort, wears Brunhilde out with fighting. He then stands aside to let Gunther slip in and deflower her. Before Siegfried sneaks away, however, he takes a ring from Brunhilde's finger and her girdle, which he later gives to his wife, Kriemhild. This will have predictably disastrous consequences a few years later, as it does in the *Volsungs Saga*.

The regularization of womanhood through marriage is made more explicit in the *Nibelungenlied*, for when Brunhilde loses her virginity she also loses her great physical strength. Being sexual—actually, having been raped—domesticates her, yet neither Siegfried's nor Gunther's manhood is altered or reduced by personal sexuality. Rather, both retain their great sexual and masculine prowess. The text says,

> And now Gunther and the lovely girl lay together, and he took his pleasure with her as was his due, so that she had to resign her maiden shame and anger. But from his intimacy she grew somewhat pale, for at love's coming her

vast strength fled so that now she was no stronger than any other woman. Gunther had his delight of her lovely body, and had she renewed her resistance what good could it have done her? His loving had reduced her to this. (*Nibelungenlied* 93)

In the *Volsungs Saga*, too, Brunhilde is mostly passive after her marriage; both texts use marriage to regularize or pacify women. Interestingly, in the oldest surviving Brunhilde poem, nothing is said about her decreased physical strength after consummating her marriage to Gunther.[65] And in the *Nibelungenlied*, Brunhilde is reduced in other ways as well. She becomes petty and prickly, especially with regard to Kriemhild, even though she and Siegfried have moved back to his lands in the north. Brunhilde not only lacks the wisdom she possessed in the *Volsungs Saga*, but she actually appears to be stupid. Twice she has been tricked by Siegfried, first in Iceland and then in her own bed. And her resentment of Kriemhild is based on her rather vain idea that since she is the wife of a king, while Kriemhild is the wife of a vassal, Kriemhild should defer to her. Siegfried, a prince in his own lands, had assumed the disguise of a vassal in Iceland, and he maintains that disguise in Burgundy. Brunhilde resents Kriemhild, and wants to know why she does not defer to Brunhilde, her superior (*Nibelungenlied* 100). She arranges to find out by convincing Gunther to invite them to a feast.

Predictably, during this visit Kriemhild loses her temper and publicly accuses Brunhilde of being "a vassal's paramour" (*Nibelungenlied* 114), adding that it was Siegfried who deflowered her. Brunhilde bursts into tears. It is all she can do; she cannot even stand up to a pampered princess. The regularization of her womanhood, the loss of autonomy, has reduced her to teary helplessness and blinding pettiness.

Hagen, one of Gunther's vassal knights, now comes to the fore. He was one of the men who accompanied Gunther to Iceland, and because he formed an attachment to Brunhilde there, or because she is his lord's queen, or simply out of a jealous hatred for Siegfried, he vows to kill Siegfried when he sees Brunhilde in tears. Of course, he is no match for Siegfried, so he must resort to subterfuge. Hagan convinces Kriemhild that he wants to protect Siegfried in battle, and thus convinces her to tell him about Siegfried's one vulnerable spot. Kriemhild goes so far as to sew a mark on Siegfried's clothes that flags the exact spot on his back. A hunt is organized, and when Siegfried bends down to drink from a stream, Hagen kills him. In the *Volsungs Saga*, Siegfried, like all men, is vulnerable when asleep. Here, like all men, he is vulnerable to attack from behind. In addition to the treachery implied in being struck from behind or while asleep, these two attacks highlight Sigurd/Siegfried's blindness, because he cannot see them coming. He remains completely blind to the consequences of his deceptions and actions in relation to Brunhilde. Still, neither of these stories is Brunhilde's; she is reduced to being an aspect of Sigurd/Siegfried's story—she is just one of the accomplishments that define him as a great hero, a detail in his biography, like his killing of the dragon.

After Siegfried's death, Brunhilde all but disappears from the story, which resonates with her suicide in the *Volsungs Saga*. The *Nibelungenlied* not only denies her a heroic death; it also denies both her and the reader closure. Compared to other, earlier versions of her story, the Brunhilde of the *Nibelungenlied* is a lesser character, lacking almost any heroic or divine qualities, and she is never spoken of as wise. Its translator, A. T. Hatto, says her great physical strength did not conform to medieval ideas of the refined court lady and instead provided any minstrel reciting the epic with an opportunity for burlesque (*Nibelungenlied* 330).

In contrast to the Scandinavian *Volsungs Saga*, the Germanic *Nibelungenlied* is part of a continental European literature designed to educate courtiers in proper behavior and appearance; courtesy and hospitality are important virtues in these tales, while details about clothing determined fashion and emphasized stylish dressing for both women and men. They instruct rough warriors, female and male, in good manners. An important element in the medieval understanding of courtesy is the relations between women and men. Consequently, continental literature emphasizes different aspects of gender; it is shaping the gender roles of well-bred courtiers. There is no room here for the heroic women of earlier days, who lingered longer in Scandinavian literature. The realm of the *Nibelungenlied* is primarily that of the mostly helpless, overly refined court lady. Significantly, when he fights Brunhilde in her bedchamber, Siegfried steels his determination by reminding himself that if he loses his life "to a girl, the whole sex will grow uppish with their husbands for ever after, though they would otherwise never behave so" (*Nibelungenlied* 92). Fittingly, he does lose his life because of women: namely, through Brunhilde's revenge and his wife's naïveté. Beneath the veneer of this courtly romance, powerful, vengeful women seethe and eventually take their toll.

Kriemhild, though, also embodies characteristics of the Valkyrie. In the latter half of the *Volsungs Saga* and of the *Nibelungenlied*, the very ancient, destructive side of the Valkyrie surfaces in Kriemhild, who also longs to revenge Sigurd/Siegfried's murder. She can only obtain the power to accomplish this by marrying another powerful man, so she accepts the proposal of King Atli of Hungary, an event predicted long before by the dream she asked Brunhilde to interpret. Years later, Atli kills her brother Gunther and she takes her revenge by killing her two sons by Atli, having their hearts cooked for him and mixing their blood with his wine in cups made with their skulls. Later, when he is asleep, she kills him, and then burns the entire palace down. The modern reader may be repelled by Kriemhild's extreme, Medea-like revenge, but there is evidence Norse people took another view. It was generally assumed that a woman would maintain closer, deeper ties to her natal family than to her husband and children.[66]

In the *Nibelungenlied*, neither Brunhilde nor Kriemhild cares in the least about their actions' cost in human life, nor the political disorder that will inevitably follow the fall of two great royal houses. Being earthbound, unable to fly, is symbolic of their inability to transcend their situations; nor can they access the Valkyries' beneficial powers of fertility and rebirth. Kriemhild and Brunhilde can only destroy, and in that destruction, find comfort in their own deaths. The disempowerment of these two women leads to the destruction of two great kingdoms, Atli's and Gunther's, both of which are left without heirs. As women, neither Brunhilde nor Kriemhild are free to act independently or effectively in the world; therefore, their repressed desires drive them to destroy that world.

The passionate stories of Brunhilde and Kriemhild persist because they speak to two very deep and related issues in human experience: what it means to be gendered, and the power of fate and its possible antidote. Or, to put it another way: are our lives preordained? More specifically, if one does not adhere to traditional gender roles, how does that affect one's fate? We next turn to high culture's most successful appropriation of these themes.

WAGNER'S BRUNHILDE

Richard Wagner's magnificent and controversial opera cycle, *Der Ring des Nibelungen* (*The Ring of the Nibelung*), a feast for ear, eye, and soul that is performed over the course of four evenings, was composed between 1853 and 1874. It begins with the creation of the world and ends with its destruction, although there is the promise of renewal. Along the way, it debates the essence of human freedom mired in a world of greed and violence and the salvation that comes only from love. Heady stuff. Wagner takes liberties with earlier versions of the story—the *Volsungs Saga*, the *Nibelungenlied*, and Grimm's *Deutsche Mythologie*—in order to increase the dramatic tension, but as his title indicates, he centers the action on the cursed ring. In what follows, it is important to recall that Wagner wrote every word of the libretto as well as every note of music.[67] For Brunhilde's character he relied on the *Volsungs*;[68] she is still the fallen celestial woman, though he elaborates on her earlier history, before Siegfried is born. She now has eight sister Valkyries, whom Wagner calls the daughters of Wotan, and their mother is the goddess of the earth, Erda. Wagner uses this background to initially present Brunhilde as the devoted daughter.

She first appears in act 2 of the second opera in the cycle, which Wagner named for her, *Die Walküre* (The Valkyrie). The opera opens with an awesome storm of rain, wind, and lightning, establishing combat between earth and sky, the human realm and divine. At first Brunhilde seems energetic but unthinking, almost passive in relation to her father, Wotan. Indeed, they are more like lovers than father and daughter, incest being a prevalent theme in Wager's work.[69] Brunhilde is Wotan's favorite, and it is slowly revealed that he experiences her as the clearest expression of his will and of his most intimate thought.

Wotan tells Brunhilde to assist the hero Siegmund in an impending battle, which delights her. But after she leaves, Wotan's wife, Fricka, arrives. She wants Siegmund to lose the battle. In act 1 Siegmund met his long-lost sister, Sieglinde, and they fell in love. They are not just sister and brother, but twins who were separated at birth. When Sieglinde grew up she was forced into a loveless marriage. Siegmund grew up in the forest, and during a storm he unknowingly came upon her while she was alone in her hut. They soon recognized each other, became lovers, and ran away. Her husband, Hunding, pursued them, and it is Hunding whom Siegmund is about to fight. Fricka, as the defender of marriage, is offended by Siegmund and Sieglinde's adultery and also by their incest. This is truly odd, as she and Wotan are also both sister and brother, and wife and husband. But Fricka has an additional reason for hating Siegmund and Sieglinde: they are the offspring of Wotan's adulterous liaison with a mortal woman. There is an added poignancy to Brunhilde's eventual decision to help Siegmund and Sieglinde, because they are her half-brother and half-sister. The astute reader will notice that conflicting ideas about marriage and close blood-bonds between siblings remain potent elements in Wagner's telling of Brunhilde's story.

Wotan reluctantly agrees to Fricka's demand that he abandon Siegmund. When Brunhilde returns she finds Wotan slumped in grief and begs to know what is wrong. He asks, "Yet if I tell it, might I not lose the controlling power of my will?" To which Brunhilde immediately responds, "You are speaking to Wotan's will, tell me what you will. What am I, if I am not your will?" ("Zu Wotans Willen sprichst du, sagst du mir, was du willst; wer bin ich, war' ich dein Wille nicht?") Wotan agrees, saying that in speaking to her he is speaking to himself ("mit mir nur rat' ich, red' ich zu dir"), and thus does not reveal anything to anyone.[70] Wotan tells her that the gods are doomed to destruction unless a great hero comes to their aid, a hero who will also be the expression of Wotan's will. His deepest wish had been that Siegmund would be that hero, but this has been dashed by Fricka's demand. Brunhilde is uncertain which part of this information she should respond to: his command that she not save Siegmund, or his "unspoken" wish that she save him and thus save them all. This dilemma marks the beginning of her development into a psychologically complex character. (In a letter to Franz Liszt, Wagner wrote that this scene between Wotan and Brunhilde was "the most important scene in the whole of the great four-part drama."[71])

Brunhilde attempts to fulfill her father's command to abandon Siegmund when she appears before him, explaining that only those about to die see her, that she is death's herald.[72] But Siegmund refuses to go with her when she tells him that Sieglinde, who has collapsed from exhaustion, will not come with them. Siegmund's love and heroism impress Brunhilde and awaken within her the ability to choose her own destiny, while his arguments echo Wotan's wishes—wishes that now exist in Brunhilde not only as Wotan's, but as her own. She vows to aid Siegmund in the fight.

The production notes for this battle say that Brunhilde is seen "soaring over Siegmund and covering him with her shield,"[73] at least until Wotan shows up, tips the balance of power, and allows Siegmund to be killed. Brunhilde picks up the unconscious Sieglinde and flees on horseback to her sisters. The scene shifts to where the Valkyries are gathering, and the famous "*Ride of the Valkyries*" begins. The production notes say, "A flash of lightning breaks through a passing cloud: a Valkyrie on horseback is visible in it: over her saddle hangs a slain warrior"[74]—a clear reference to images from the Norse sagas and poems.

Brunhilde is now committed to protecting Sieglinde and the child she is bearing, who will become the hero the gods need, Siegfried. She gets Sieglinde to safety only moments before Wotan appears in a terrible rage. His punishment is severe. Since she has chosen personal freedom he gives it to her in spades: Brunhilde is banished from Valhalla and loses her divinity. She will be left defenseless and asleep by the wayside, available to the first man who wakes her. She shall spend her days at the spinning wheel in subjugation to a mortal man, scorned and mocked by all.

During their long dialogue, Brunhilde first pleads for mercy and then tries reasoning with Wotan, saying she fulfilled his wish because of her love for him. In the end, she asks him to temper his punishment by guaranteeing it will be a hero who awakens her. She begs him to put a ring of fire around her to drive away cowards.[75] Wotan agrees. She prophesies that Siegfried is to be born to Sieglinde, not mentioning the obvious—that she has saved Wotan's grandchild and her own nephew, and that this is whom she wants to awaken her. She plans to continue the actions that have brought her freedom and punishment. Moved by her love, Wotan, too, feels love for her. They embrace and he kisses her, removing her divinity as she slumps down into unconsciousness. He then strikes his spear against the rock on which she sleeps, causing a blazing fire to arise and protect her. The curtain closes on *Die Walküre*, leaving the story to be continued in the third opera, *Siegfried*.

Catherine Clément makes an important point about these multiple incestuous unions (Wotan and Fricka, Siegmund and Sieglinde, Brunhilde and Siegfried): given that the gods are not following the human custom of exchanging women through marriage in order to cement alliances and relationships with other families, the *Ring* can be read "as the progressive disappearance of a family that refuses exchange,"[76] a family that closes in on itself. In the *Volsungs Saga* and the *Nibelungenlied*, we have seen the conflicts that marriage generates when brothers and sisters marry out of their natal families. Wagner went back to the earlier, more deeply rooted ties of sister and brother as the most profound form of love.[77] In the last of the *Ring* operas, *Götterdämmerung* (The Twilight of the Gods), it is marriage that leads to the separation of Brunhilde and Siegfried, and ultimately to the destruction of the world and of Valhalla.

It is worth noting that Wagner's control of the *Ring* operas was not limited to the words, music, acting, and staging;[78] he influenced costume designs, as well.[79] Sketches from the 1876 premier of the full four operas at Bayreuth, the theater he had built for performances of the *Ring*, show the Valkyries wearing elaborate winged helmets (Figure 3.1).[80] The way these flow backward at ear level imitates flight and evokes swan maidens. Unwilling swan-maiden brides seem to be good company for Wagner's unmarried Valkyries.

It is only toward the end of the third opera, *Siegfried*, that the hero comes upon Brunhilde. Following the *Volsungs Saga*, he has killed the dragon, tasted its blood, and learned the language of birds, one of whom tells him about Brunhilde. In Wagner's hands the awakening scene is touching, glorious, and passionate, as Brunhilde sings her greeting to the sun, the light, and the day. She is ecstatic to realize it is Siegfried who has awoken her, and she tells him she has always loved him. As yet, Brunhilde is still wise, and she tells Siegfried she can teach him anything he wishes to learn, explaining that she is wise because she loves him. They embrace, and the curtain falls.

In the fourth and final opera, *Götterdämmerung*, Brunhilde is transformed by love and sex, as in the *Nibelungenlied*. Her great physical strength was tied to her virginity, and instead of divine wisdom she is now filled with human desire. She and Siegfried swear an oath that they will marry; he gives her the ring of the Nibelungs without knowing that it curses whoever wears it and goes looking for adventure, leaving her protected by the circle of flames.

Siegfried soon meets Gunther and his sister, called Gutrune, and their half-brother, the villainous Hagan. Encouraged by Hagan, Gunther has decided that Siegfried and his sister should marry; they seek non-incestuous unions that will enhance the family's honor and power. As an offering of hospitality, Gutrune offers Siegfried a magic drink of forgetfulness that also causes him to fall in love with her.

Siegfried and Gunther work out a traditional exchange of women: Siegfried will capture Brunhilde for Gunther, who will give his sister Gutrune to Siegfried. They swear blood brotherhood. For his part, Hagan wants the ring, which in addition to cursing its wearer endows him or her with world domination, and which only Siegfried can remove from Brunhilde's hand. Siegfried puts on a magical helmet that enables him to appear in Gunther's form, overcomes Brunhilde, and takes the ring from her. Later, when Gunther introduces her to his followers, she is a reluctant, miserable, and powerless bride. Wotan's original punishment has come to pass. Then she recognizes Siegfried, sees the ring, and believes he has betrayed her in order to marry Gutrune.

In a quiet moment, Brunhilde reveals that she fully understands her situation as a human woman—that she is a commodity of exchange between men. She complains to Hagan that she gave Siegfried everything she had, her love and wisdom, even her horse and shield, and now that she has nothing more to give, he is giving her away. Hagan promises to avenge her. Brunhilde tells him that Siegfried does not know that she has used magic to protect him, making him invulnerable in battle save for the spot on his back, because she knew he would never turn and run from any enemy.

In the last act the fateful hunt takes place, but with more cruelty than in earlier tales. Hagan encourages Siegfried to sing the story of his life and then gives him a drink that will help his memory. Siegfried remembers Brunhilde and is devastated. Then Hagan kills him, and Siegfried dies with Brunhilde's name on his lips. Gunther, Gutrune, and Hagan argue over who should have Siegfried's ring, but Brunhilde takes the cursed ring from his finger and throws it into the Rhine. Mounted on her horse, she leaps onto Siegfried's blazing funeral pyre.

Certain orchestral sections of Wagner's operas became the equivalent of pop hits. *The Ride of the Valkyries* was high on this list and the Paris Opera went so far as to erect an elaborate and expensive electric lantern presentation of it. A translucent blue screen showing drifting clouds faced the audience but did not reveal the immense scaffolding behind it (nine meters at its highest point and thirty meters long) that covered the entire background stage. This was the path of wooden horses drawn by a cable with their human riders revealed by flashes of electric lightning.[81] It was a huge hit and significantly contributed to the popularization of these mythological female figures. Ironically, when freed from the opera as a single piece, the Valkyries personify all the power, dynamism, and beauty of winged celestial women, but within the opera, although Brunhilde and her sisters are able to fly, they are far from being independent deities. They are ruled by the father-god Wotan.

4

Swan Maidens: Captivity and Sexuality

THE ELEGANT SWAN has captured the human imagination from time immemorial. It is most popularly known as a symbol of transformation through the widespread tale of the "Ugly Duckling," which suffers alienation and misery until it evolves into an adult swan, a creature of transcendent beauty and grace, equally at home in the elements of earth, water, and air.[1] The swan's ability to cross over these three elements with ease makes it expressive of longings for freedom, transformation, and transcendence. It is also the fastest aquatic bird both on water and in the air. Most extraordinarily, the swan can take flight from water by rising up and skimming the surface with its webbed feet while flapping its wings vigorously until it is airborne. When swans land on the ground their mobility is limited and they are vulnerable—a feature that easily fed into tales about captured swan maidens.

Swan maiden tales have been told all over the world from at least the first millennium BCE. The earliest extant tale of a swan maiden comes from India in the form of a hymn from the *Rig Veda*, an originally oral text composed between 1500 and 800 BCE.[2] It presents only the end of this multilayered myth,[3] which assumes its audience's familiarity with the entire tale. Urvaśī, a heavenly woman called an *apsarā*,[4] has left her mortal husband, King Purūravas, to whom she had been married against her will. The Sanskrit word *apsarā* means "one who goes in the waters" and "one who goes between the clouds."[5] *Apsarās* can shape-shift into swans, so some, like Urvaśī, are also swan maidens. They are divine women of enormous beauty and charm who are given as a reward to great heroes who have died in battle (and are discussed in more detail in chapter 6).

It is not clear how Purūravas won Urvaśī. Later versions of this tale explain that, because of a minor transgression (discussed below), she was thrown out of heaven and cursed by the gods to live with a mortal.[6] Even so, in the *Rig Veda* version she is able to impose a taboo on Purūravas to the effect that she will leave if she ever sees him naked. Other celestial beings conspire to help set her free by attempting to steal some of Purūravas's sheep late at night. Wakened by the sound of the sheep bleating, Purūravas jumps out of bed—stark naked—to stop the thieves. The heavenly beings then cause lightning to flash, revealing his nudity to Urvaśī,[7] whereupon she flies away, leaving him and their son behind (Figure 4.1).

After a sorrowful search, Purūravas finds Urvaśī swimming in a lake. A later text, the *Śatapatha Brāhmaṇa* (11.5.4), notes that when Purūravas finds her, she is swimming with other *apsarās*, who have all taken the form of water birds (*āti*);[8] Urvaśī has reverted to her swan body and to the companionship of her sister swan-*apsarās*.[9] Purūravas pleads with her to return to him, insisting that they had

FIGURE 4.1 Manuscript illustration of the story of Urvaśī and Purūravas, 1648. At the top center, a winged Urvaśī flies into Purūravas's home; their story unfolds, and Urvaśī is shown, once again with wings, flying away at the upper right.

Udaipur, Bhandarkar Oriental Research Institute, Pune, India. Courtesy of the Huntington Archive.

been happy together. She, however, contradicts his version of their happy married life: "Indeed, you pierced me with your rod three times a day, and filled me even when I had no desire. I followed your will, Purūravas; you were my man, king of my body."[10] Swan maidens, it seems, do not make happy wives.

Children are an important element in swan maiden tales, as symbols and examples of the maidens' powers of fertility. In Urvaśī's case, by having a son she also provides the country with an heir to the throne, which in Indian belief was a necessary prerequisite to ensure the ongoing fertility of the entire country.[11] Fittingly, the *Rig Veda* verses devoted to this story are a type of hymn associated with fertility, and may have been part of a ritual performance intended to bring about pregnancy.[12] The story ends with Purūravas intimating to Urvaśī that he might die without her, which moves her to promise that he will go to heaven when he dies, becoming immortal (v. 18).

IMAGES AND MEANINGS

Religious and mythical ideas about swans and swan maidens are also attributed, in varying degrees, to all flying females. They are believed to have the power to shapeshift; they can help men transcend death by leading them to rebirth or by granting them immortality; and they are a symbol of love, both faithful and adulterous, which connects them to sexuality and fertility.[13] More particularly, swan maiden stories are about men who are eager to grasp the divine and to obtain heirs, yet who are also unable to truly understand the women who flee these coerced marriages. Once free, like Urvaśī, swan maidens often say how unhappy they were as captured brides, although this appears to predominate primarily in the earliest tales. Gender issues, as well as sexuality and shape-shifting, are central to these tales. In many stories from around the world, female swans are trapped in human form and compelled into unwanted marriages and their attendant domestic chores until the women recover a stolen token (a feather, their wings, or animal skin) that will release them, or until their captor breaks a taboo. Though there are male variants of this tale, in their most ancient forms these stories are about immortal women who have the ability to bring prosperity and children, and to lift mortal men into higher states of being, even to transcend mortality.

In most cases the tale goes awry because the man breaks the condition set by the swan maiden, allowing her to regain her avian form and fly away. Thus they are often tales about unsuccessful male encounters with the feminine divine that reveal primordial and enduring tensions between women and men,[14] which is why we still tell them. All the tales emphasize a woman's sense of being trapped in a marriage and her quest to escape from premodern domestic drudgery and the mundane world into a larger, less encumbered life.[15] Swan maiden tales suggest that women need to be coerced into domesticity, either through captivity or the husband's performance of heroic deeds. The unhappiness of captured swan maidens is neatly summed up in a Bulgarian tale, in which they are called *samodivas*. In this story, the swan maiden manages to recover her stolen swan dress during a party in honor of the birth of her son. Before flying off, she then taunts her husband:

> Hear my words, O Stoian; seek not
> For thy wife a Samodiva—
> Samodivas are not thrifty,
> Know not how to tend the children.
> Said I not to thee, O Stoian,
> Samodivas are not housewives?[16]

These sentiments are echoed in a tale from the Buryat of Siberia in which a captured swan maiden, after giving birth to eleven sons and six daughters, is able to recover her feather robe and fly away. As she leaves, she says,

> "You are earthly beings and remain on earth, but I belong to Heaven and I am to fly back there!" Then, mounting ever higher, she continued: "Every spring, when the swans fly north, and every autumn when they return, you must perform special ceremonies in my honour!"[17]

Her astonishing fertility made her the ancestress of this particular clan, although other clans also claim swan maidens as ancestresses. Hatto explains that, "swans and their feathers are the subject of various taboos in this region, and the Buryat in fact provide a sacrifice of drink for the swans when they arrive in the spring, and their women bow to the first swan of that season."[18]

Being a monogamous bird, the swan is also an apt symbol of love. Swans were associated with love goddesses such as Aphrodite and Venus: swans drew Aphrodite's chariot and Venus's boat (see Figure 1.6, p. 23). Swans are also associated with eroticism, in part because they are among the few birds whose males have penises. This attribute is often emphasized in visual representations of Zeus's transformation into a swan in order to seduce the mortal woman Leda. The story of Zeus and Leda suggests the dangerous, seductive side of the swan, yet it also reinforces many of the swan's positive attributes because of the offspring of this union: the twin gods

Castor and Pollux, who become stars and are known as protectors of sailors from storms at sea. Another child of Zeus and Leda's union is Helen of Troy, who has the magnificent beauty of the swan and thus shares the guise in which Zeus covered his adulterous nature.

As Artemis's creature, the swan shares many of her characteristics, including her love of song and of marginal spaces, including those between life and death. In Plato's *Phaedo*, when friends gather in Socrates's prison cell as he awaits death, Socrates plays on the ancient belief that swans sing when they are about to die to argue that they know the soul is immortal:

> Will you not allow that I have as much of the spirit of prophecy in me as the swans? For they, when they perceive that they must die, having sung all their life long, do then sing more lustily than ever, rejoicing in the thought that they are about to go away to the God whose ministers they are. . . . And I too . . . would not go out of life less merrily than the swans.[19]

Swans' link to music is evident in another widespread belief: namely, that swans are drawn to beautiful music, especially that of harps and lutes.[20] We will see much more of this, especially in the Asian swan-maiden tales discussed below, in which swan maidens are often dancers and musicians.

Hatto has suggested that because swan maiden tales focus on women, they were most likely first told by women[21] and reflect women's symbolic role as outsiders in virilocal systems of marriage,[22] in which a bride moves into her husband's house, often in another village than the one she has grown up in. He has further argued that swan maiden tales are also connected to the migratory pattern of aquatic birds, which fly north in the spring to mate and rear their offspring, returning south in the autumn. While in the north, the parents cannot fly because they are molting, nor can their young. This natural cycle contains the main elements of the swan maiden tale: sudden appearance; molting of feathers (loss of the feather garment); temporary captivity; sex and fertility; and ultimately, escape. Such drama called out for human players. Parenthetically, Hatto asks, "What wife from a far land can fail to be affected when she sees a bird spread its wings to fly?" (333). Yet it must also be stated that these tales describe male fantasies about capturing and overpowering women, especially independent women, and they often continue with the husband undergoing heroic hardships while searching for his lost wife.[23]

The migration pattern of the swan also led to the belief that it carries souls to the Land of the Dead.[24] In this sense they overlap with the Valkyries of Norse mythology, who are able to transform themselves into swans. The swan's importance to the ancient Scandinavians is demonstrated by the fact that they depicted the vehicles of their sun god as bronze boats and chariots with swan motifs. This symbolism was incorporated into his epic *Parzival* by the poet Wolfram von Eschenbach (c. 1170–1220/30) and further developed by Richard Wagner as the vehicle of the swan knight Lohengrin, who, like the sun god, is life-saving, fruitful, and a source of joy. Christians, too, shared this solar imagery and easily connected Christ with swans: Christ descended from heaven, walked on water as well as earth, and ascended back to heaven, and belief in him leads to transformation, resurrection, and salvation. Swans' whiteness represents Christ's purity, and their wings resemble those of angels.[25]

To return to Urvaśī, the earliest known swan maiden: her basic story is retold and elaborated upon throughout Indian history.[26] While later versions retain the basic theme of the divine bird-woman who deserts her mortal lover, they also enlarge Purūravas's role and domesticate Urvaśī, making her a celestial woman who loved a mortal man so much that she longed to stay on earth with him.[27] Significantly, her ability to confer immortality is weakened. In some later versions, she asks the gods to teach Purūravas how to become immortal so that they can remain together, or the gods take it upon themselves to grant this gift, or they teach him a ritual that will help him to achieve immortality.[28] Once again, a winged woman loses much of her power and freedom as time goes on.

The most elegant of these later tales is the *Vikramorvaśī* ("Urvaśī Won by Valor"), attributed to the great Indian playwright Kālidāsa (c. fourth century CE).[29] In Kālidāsa's version, Urvaśī, described as an *apsarā*, is captured by demons while visiting earth.[30] King Purūravas, a renowned warrior, rescues her. Urvaśī is vulnerable, grateful, and deeply attracted to Purūravas, as he is to her. They fall instantly in love, but she must return to heaven when the gods call upon the *apsarās* to entertain them. (*Apsarās* are talented singers, dancers, and actresses, and are among the leading entertainers of heaven.) During one such performance, after having secretly met with Purūravas, Urvaśī flubs a line, saying she loves Purūravas instead of the required answer, which is that she loves the god Viṣṇu, the creator of drama. For this infraction she is cursed to lose her place in heaven. The god Indra intercedes, modifying the curse so that she needs remain with Purūravas only until she has a child.[31] The play also softens Urvaśī's abandonment of her child; in this version, she hides her pregnancy from Purūravas and then has their son raised secretly by others because Indra has doomed her to leave Purūravas when he sees his son. The dénouement comes when the boy, now a young man, is brought before the king (act 5, 93). But Indra lets the lovers stay together by making Purūravas immortal.

Although the play focuses on Purūravas, especially his suffering when he is separated from Urvaśī, it still offers telling details about divine aerial women. It frequently alludes to Urvaśī's shape-shifting powers: her ability to become invisible, her successfully disguising her pregnancy, and her fulfilling Purūravas's request that she change a cloud into a flying chariot to carry them back to his palace (*Vikramorvaśī*, 52 and 69, 93, 88). The play often refers to her power of flight, and it uses allusions to connect her with swans[32]—for example, utilizing the *Rig Veda*'s setting in which Purūravas looks for her near a lake[33] and describing swans longing for their mates in the opening verse to act 4, in which Purūravas searches for Urvaśī. This swan metaphor is repeated throughout act 4. In the play, Purūravas also questions other kinds of birds as to where Urvaśī might be. But by this time Urvaśī has been so completely transformed into an earthly creature that instead of swimming in the lake she is trapped in a creeper (66), one of the massive vines that grow up and around the trunks of trees and are poetic metaphors for sensuous women. In truth, she has not deserted her lover; rather, this is her punishment for having broken a taboo against women entering a forest dedicated to the god Śiva.

The Sanskrit word most often translated as swan is *haṃsa*, a term used for several web-footed birds, including geese as well as swans.[34] As with other birds associated with ascension and immortality, the *haṃsa* has decorated South Asian caskets and reliquaries—or reliquaries have been made in its shape[35]—at least since the first century CE. In the *Rig Veda*, swans are said to be able to separate *soma*, the drink of immortality, from water;[36] the *Rig Veda* also connects *soma* with the *apsarās* (IX.78.3), which is another indication of their ability to grant immortality. In India the *haṃsa* is noted for its discipline and beauty, and it also has solar associations (*Rig Veda* IV.40.5) similar to those of swans in ancient Greece and among the Scandinavians. The *haṃsa* symbolizes knowledge and cosmic breath and is thus the vehicle of the great creator god, Brahmā, and of his consort, the beautiful river goddess Sarasvatī, who is the patron of learning and the arts.[37] The bird's transcendent nature is further emphasized by the title *paramahaṃsa*, the "highest gander," an honorific given to Hindu ascetics who have achieved freedom from rebirth.

NORTHERN EUROPEAN TALES

The swan maiden received rich treatment in Norse and Scandinavian myth, beginning with the first swans to come into being, which are fed in the Well of the Norns,[38] linking them to prophecy.[39] In the tale of Weyland the Smith, an originally Saxon story preserved in the Icelandic *Völundarakvida* (c. thirteenth century), a Finnish king has three sons, Völund, Slagfith, and Egil. These three sons, all of them hunters, build a house on the shores of a lake. One morning they see three women on the shore, who put aside their swan dresses (*aptar-hamir*)[40] to spin flax. The three women, who are called Valkyries,[41] are daughters of kings, and each of the brothers takes one as his wife. Seven years later, while the brothers are away hunting, the women put on their swan dresses and fly away because they miss going to war. Their connection with Valkyries is plainly stated, in that two of their names, Hladgud and Hervor, are words connected with armies and war,[42] and their sexual relations with humans recall such relations between Valkyries and heroes.

In a fourteenth-century German telling of this story, a lone man, Weylan (or Weilan), comes upon three women who have put aside their dove-feathered dresses and are bathing in a fountain. He has a magic root that makes him invisible and is thus able to sneak up and steal their clothes. In order to get them back the women have to agree that one of them will marry him.[43] Notice once again the use of deception in capturing a supernatural woman in this story, which recalls Siegfried's defeat of Queen Brunhilde through invisibility.

In Western folklore, swans are sometimes human beings trapped in animal form who are redeemed and released by love—for example, in the Grimm Brothers' "The Six Swans" and, to a lesser degree, "The Crystal Ball." These tales exploit associations between sexuality and flying, the attraction to and fear of bestiality represented by animal lovers, and female shape-shifting abilities that transform domesticated, obedient wives into wild, uncontrollable, and free women. The gender disparity in these tales is of interest: while female swans are trapped when they become women, men are trapped when they become swans; women are trapped in domestic drudgery and men are trapped in a bestial state they can only transcend through a woman's love. Put differently, the tales about swan maidens have them running *from* men, while the tales about male swans have them running *to* women. In his ballet *Swan Lake*, Pyotr Ilyich Tchaikovsky turns this around, portraying a woman trapped in the body of a swan who can only be saved by a man's love. *Swan Lake* also highlights the sexual ambiguity of the swan by contrasting the good and chaste Odette with the evil and erotic Odile. In all their variants, though, swan maiden tales highlight the relationships between women and captivity, sexuality, and, frequently, immortality. As Hedwig von Beit noted about swans in his *Symbolik des Märchens*, "In archaic belief the swan is an escort on the journey to heaven . . . . [It] embodies as it were the yearning for immortality."[44]

Tchaikovsky's Swan Lake

In early nineteenth-century ballet, supernatural females such as sylphs, shades, water nymphs, and, later, swan maidens enjoyed great popularity, as they aligned with the interests of the Romantic movement, interested as it was in fantasy, the uncanny, and an idealized womanhood.[45] This art form, directed toward a male audience,[46] featured young women wearing less clothing than was usual for that period. Wealthy men were invited backstage, where they mingled freely with the young dancers who needed patrons; it was extremely fashionable for a prominent man to capture one of the ethereal females from the *corps de ballet* to be his mistress.[47]

Ballet movements, particularly *port de bras* (arm movements), are capable of imitating the flight of creatures of the air, as are certain leaps and jumps; dancers can appear weightless as they soar through the air. The great Italian-Swedish dancer Marie Taglioni (1804–1884) was the first to make defying gravity popular, especially in her title role in *La Sylphide* (1832; see Figure 4.2),[48] the story of a winged forest-spirit whose captivity by a young man kills her. Taglioni's ability to skim across the stage on her toes amazed audiences and led to the development of pointe shoes so other ballerinas could imitate her. Pointe shoes, the essential element in achieving this effect, are worn almost solely by female dancers. (They are sometimes, though very rarely, worn by men dancing female roles.) Within the shoes, the dancer's toes are encased in a "box" made of tightly packed layers of fabric and paper which are flattened to create a platform for the dancer's movements. As the dancer rises up and flutters across the stage, her tiptoeing footsteps seem to barely graze the earth.

The traditional costume for Odette, the swan queen of Tchaikovsky's masterpiece, was designed to extend the bird metaphor: the tightly fitted bodice with wings at the back and the fluffy, below-the-knee skirt in a light, white material evoking a swan's body. Her companions wore mid-thigh-length skirts[49] that revealed almost the whole leg, making the dancers appear spindly and birdlike. The way the swan queen and swan maidens move on their toes and their astonishing leaps into the air add to the impression of buoyancy. There is something supremely human about ballet movement and yet something totally inhuman, something transcendent,[50] which stimulated the melancholy longing of Romanticism for access to an alternative reality.

In Tchaikovsky's reversal of the swan maiden tale, she is a real woman trapped in a swan's body who longs for marriage with a man. She will make no attempt to transform him because she herself wants to be transformed. While hunting in the forest a young Prince Siegfried sees the leader of a flock of swans turn into a

TAGLIONI.
IN LA SYLPHIDE.

FIGURE 4.2 Marie Taglioni as *La Sylphide*. Eugène Lami designed this costume for Taglioni's debut; note the small wings on her back.
New York Public Library, Dance Collection.

woman, Princess Odette. She is under the spell of the evil sorcerer von Rothbart and only becomes a woman at night. This spell can be broken by someone who willingly vows eternal love to her, which Siegfried does, thus prefiguring the theme of betrayal. The next night there is a ball during which the prince must choose a wife. Among the guests are von Rothbart and his daughter, Odile, dressed in black and disguised as Odette. When the real Odette arrives at the ball, von Rothbart uses his sorcery to make her invisible and then gets Siegfried to declare his undying love to Odile, the false Odette, thus breaking his vow. Odette can see his betrayal but is helpless to do anything about it. She flees. Siegfried runs into the forest to find her and explains that he was bewitched. She forgives him, but the harm is already done. They vow to commit suicide so that they can be together. Von Rothbart tries to interfere, but, by leaping into the lake to their death, they also destroy him and his evil power.

ASIAN SWAN MAIDENS

Urvaśī is not the only swan maiden to receive elaborate and highly romantic treatment in Asian literature. In the Buddhist culture of South and Southeast Asia, the story of Manoharā is one of the most popular; it has been translated into many Asian languages, depicted on monuments, and continues to be performed today.[51] One of its earliest versions appears in a collection of Buddhist tales, the *Mahāvastu* (composed between the second century BCE and the fourth century CE).[52] This full-blown Indian romance runs the gamut of emotion: happiness, separation, longing, and reunion. Composed centuries after the *Rig Veda*'s tale of Urvaśī, it, too, emphasizes the role of the husband. Although Buddhist tales generally do not advocate romantic love,[53] the central character here is the Buddha, who narrates a story about one of his past lives to illustrate the great effort he made to win his wife Yaśodharā.[54] This complex tale, with multiple human, animal, and divine characters, begins when a king decides to sacrifice one of each kind of animal in existence (*Mahāvastu*, II.95), in the belief that this act will lead to his being reborn in heaven. The only missing being is a *kinnarī*, a divine, half-woman/half-bird creature who can fly between heaven and earth. The king sends the best hunter to find one. A *rishi*, a sage who acts as a bridge between the human and divine worlds, tells the hunter about Manoharā, the daughter of the king of the *kinnaras*, who plays with her many companions in the pond. The hunter easily captures her, because the *rishi* has told him her true name, a common way of capturing mythical beings across cultures and tales. The hunter brings her to the sacrifice, where a neighboring prince—the Buddha in his earlier incarnation as Prince Sudhana—falls in love with her. He preaches the Buddhist doctrine of non-injury (*ahiṃsā*) to the king, thus rescuing Manoharā from the sacrifice. He takes her home and marries her, and they are very happy. Their happiness is interrupted, however, because the prince is so enamored of her that he neglects his duties, and the king sends her away. The story now centers on Sudhana's longing and searching for her (II.104–111). Hoping that he would follow her, Manoharā gave instructions for finding her to two hunters she encountered on the way back to her own realm. These hunters eventually join Sudhana in his search, and they come across the *rishi* who had unknowingly brought about Manoharā's capture. The *rishi* gets the king of the monkeys to guide them to her home, where the king of the *kinnaras* accepts Sudhana as his daughter's husband. They live there happily for many years, but, being a dutiful son, Sudhana has to return to his parents. He takes Manoharā with him to the human realm, where—one hopes—they will live happily ever after.

Other versions conform more closely to the swan maiden tale type. In the *Divyāvadāna*, another collection of Buddhist tales composed in the second century CE, Manoharā is captured by different means and for different reasons. The story begins with a hunter saving a *naga*, a divine half-human/half-snake being, who rewards him with a magic chain that holds fast anything it captures.[55] The hunter then meets a *rishi* who lives near a large lake and who tells him about Manoharā. The hunter captures her with the magic chain. There is no feather suit in this tale, either; instead, Manoharā's power of flight comes from a jewel.[56] As the story continues in a fourteenth-century Tibetan redaction, Manoharā gives this jewel to the hunter when he promises that he will not touch her, but rather will give her to a king.[57] He brings her to Prince Sudhana, who immediately falls in love with her. For a while they are very happy, but then the prince must go to war. He entrusts his mother with Manoharā's jewel, instructing her to return it to Manoharā only if it is a matter of life or death.[58] Manoharā does not use trickery to obtain it; instead, evil courtiers plot her death, and Sudhana's mother readily gives the jewel back to her. Manoharā then flies toward her home, stopping only to visit the *rishi* en route. In true swan-maiden fashion, she first reminds the *rishi* of his interference in her life: "Great Rishi, in consequence of your directions, I have been captured and exposed to the touch of man, and have nearly lost my life."[59] But she tells him this in a respectful, not accusatory, way, in order to obligate him to tell Sudhana how to find her. The tale turns its attention to the heroic husband as she tells the *rishi* the complicated directions to her home and explains the many dangers along the way.

Meanwhile, Sudhana has subdued the kingdom's enemies and returned home, only to be devastated by Manoharā's flight. He is determined to find her, and the hunter helps by telling him about the *rishi*. The story unfolds as Sudhana overcomes all the obstacles that lie between him and Manoharā. Once safely in heaven, he obtains her father's permission to marry her, and she returns to earth with Sudhana. (As in later tales about Urvaśī, Manoharā does not confer immortality.)

Some swan maiden tales—Manoharā's in particular—hint at the tensions inherent in virilocal marriage practices, in which the bride must move into her husband's home, far away from those she knows and loves. When she recalls her natal home, and all the indulgences she enjoyed there, it must seem a lost paradise. Tales of fairy brides, too, touch on such issues.

Feather Robes and Dance

Asia is rich in tales about heavenly women who descend to earth.[60] One is a fourteenth-century Japanese Nō play, *Hagoromo* ("The Feather Robe"),[61] which was based on earlier material, and tells of a fisherman who, while admiring the beauty of the shore, finds a heavenly woman's feather robe hanging on a tree branch. (She is called a *tennin*, the Japanese translation of *apsarā*.) The fisherman steals the robe, and when the woman appears and asks him for it, he refuses to give it back. In this story, though, the man is eventually moved by the woman's sorrow and offers to return the robe to her if she will perform one of the dances of heaven for him. Donning her feather robe, she dances, and she and the chorus describe her heavenly home, the moon god's palace.[62]

The influence of the Indian *apsarās* on this story is clear, as they were known to be exquisite dancers (see chapter 6). And although this swan maiden does not lead the man to immortality, she reveals a higher and more refined way of being to mortals.

This heavenly swan maiden's dance also evokes images of female shamans who dance in bird suits in order to travel to other worlds (chapter 9), and of Daoist practitioners (chapter 11) who seek to transcend earthly limitations by flying to heaven and who have been known to wear feathers.

Her dance also recalls an extremely popular ancient Chinese dance, that of the Rainbow Skirt and Feathered Cape,[63] said to have been composed by the Tang emperor Xuanzong (r. 712–756) in honor of his favorite consort, the voluptuous Yang Guifei (700–755), whom he was later forced to put to death during a rebellion. She became legendary, as did her dance. It was a slow, courtly dance set to Chinese string and woodwind music with a humming chorus. The lead dancer wore "an oversized chignon and headdress, a cape evoking feathered clouds, and 'cloud-tip' slippers with a dramatic cloudlike upturned toe. The gentle swirling of the dancer's sleeves and skirt along with fluttering ornaments on the headdress mesmerized romantic rulers and poets. The appeal of the dance lay not in athletic skills but in an ephemeral grace paced by delicate footwork."[64] A popular song of the time described Yang Guifei's footwear as follows: she "soars on clogs with stilts ('teeth')." The aesthetics of this dance influenced the fashion trends of the day, as Tang ladies of the late eighth century combed their hair into high chignons and wore "cloudlike capes, [and] shawl-like ribbons draped on forearms."[65] This legend and this dance, in many variations, lived on long after Yang Guifei, and the dance traveled to Korea and Japan. Lady Nijō (b. 1258) witnessed its performance at the Itsukushima Shrine,[66] and the dance is still performed today.

From earliest times people have adorned themselves with feathers to gain spiritual powers, display wealth and prestige, or simply to beautify themselves.[67] During China's wealthy and cultured Tang dynasty (618–907), whole species of birds were brought almost to the point of extinction due to the high demand for clothes, jewelry, decorations, insignia, and fans made of exotic feathers;[68] the Tang-dynasty Chinese were not the last people to bring feathered creatures to the brink of extinction because they sought adornment.[69]

Two Chinese stories written down sometime before the tenth century[70] follow the pattern that divine women travel in groups, or flocks, with one member of the group being captured when her feather robe is stolen and then being forced to marry and eventually to have a child or children. In the first tale, the swan maiden instantly flies back to heaven when she recovers her robe. She then enlists the help of her two sisters, and all three return to earth and take her son to heaven, where he receives divine wisdom. He then returns to earth and becomes very wealthy.[71] In the second story, the swan maiden escapes, but then returns to earth with three feather robes for her three daughters. Like true swan maidens, the daughters fly away to heaven the moment they put on their robes.[72]

A Japanese story returns to the theme of the swan maiden who abandons her children. This swan maiden flies alone to earth, where she removes her feather robe and falls asleep. A farmer comes along and sees the robe (but not the woman), and he takes it. When the woman wakes up she is distraught, doomed to live on earth and forget about her life in heaven; memory, or divine consciousness, is, along with flight, an attribute of these robes. The story continues, "She felt the cold because her clothes were thin, and she also felt pangs of hunger. So she had to go down the mountain to the village and ask a farmer for some food."[73] The farmer is the same farmer who stole her robe, and, of course, she has no choice but to marry him. Eventually, she has two daughters, and, years later, the farmer—who has never connected the robe with his wife—brings it out for the oldest daughter to wear. The daughter puts it on and dances for the family, accompanied by her younger sister, who plays the flute. Their mother says, "The form of your arms is not good. I'll show you how." So she takes the feather robe and puts it on and begins to dance. As she does so, she loses her human heart. Her body becomes light and rises up in the air. Astonished, the girls shout, "What's the matter with you, Mother?" And the celestial lady answers, "Now I remember everything. I am the woman from the sky. I am going back to the heavens now. I should like to take you with me, but there is no room for human beings in heaven."[74]

TWO MIDDLE EASTERN TALES

This typology of swan maiden tales concludes with two Middle Eastern tales from the justly famous *Book of One Thousand and One Nights*. This text has a very complex history, drawing on Indian, Persian, and Arabic folklore compiled over a thousand years ago and more or less reaching the form we have today in the early 1500s.[75] Each story is told by a woman, Scheherazade (Shahrazâd), who has married a great king, or shah. Discovering his previous wife's infidelity, he had her killed; now, convinced of the perfidy of all women, he has decided to marry a new woman each day and have sex with her for one night only before having her killed, too.[76] This program is the antithesis of traditional marriage—and, as we have seen, swan maiden tales are very much about marriage. After a thousand women have been married, bedded, and killed, his young bride Scheherazade starts the process of normalizing the shah's marital life by beginning but not finishing a tale each night; the shah is amused and intrigued enough by each tale to let her live another day so he can hear the rest of it.[77] Scheherazade controls the narrative as she redirects the shah's desire and, it follows, his sexuality. "Her attempts to create a functioning heterosexual couple are played out against a greater civilizational pull for a male homosocial couple,"[78] to say nothing of Scheherazade's intent to curb his murderous nature. She is both buying time for herself and healing the shah. In the end, he falls in love with her after one thousand and one nights of storytelling and allows her to live. Intriguingly, Scheherazade had voluntarily gone to the king because she was convinced she could turn him away from murdering young women.[79]

Hasan of Basra

The swan maiden tales Scheherazade tells are quite long. The first starts on the 779th night but does not end until the 831st. It begins with a young man, Hasan of Basra, who, having squandered his inheritance on dalliances with lewd women and boys, is captured by an evil alchemist who takes him on a long sea voyage and abandons him in Japan.[80] He is saved by seven royal sisters who live in seclusion, if not captivity, because their father is too proud to let them marry. When their father sends for them, they give Hasan the keys to their palace but set a taboo on him not to open a certain door. Of course, he does so anyway. Behind the door a stairway leads upward to a magnificent bejeweled palace with a huge basin in the center. Soon a flock of glorious birds—ten in all—appears, and the birds take off their feather suits in order to bathe. Hasan falls madly in love with the flock's leader and pines away for her. When the seven sisters return the youngest asks why he is so sad and Hasan tells her. She agrees to help him capture his beloved.

She explains that the swan maidens' father is the great king of Japan, elsewhere called the King of the Jinns (supernatural beings, 793rd night, 52), who has confined them to an unreachable land guarded by an army of women. So the story has two fathers who are not fulfilling their obligation to find husbands for their daughters.[81] Though it will put her and her sisters in danger, she instructs Hasan to steal the feather suit of the one he loves so that her companions will flee for fear the same thing will happen to them. So much for sisterhood. After this takes place, it is the youngest sister who approaches the swan maiden, consoles her, and reconciles her to her fate, reminding her that women were made for men (790th night, 42)—a refrain echoed by her six sisters when they convince the maiden to marry Hasan because, or so they say, the feather suit has been burned (791st night, 46).

Forty days after their marriage, Hasan dreams of his mother and decides to go home, taking with him his wife, and unbeknown to her, the feather suit. Eventually he, his wife, and his mother move to Baghdad, where the wife gives birth to two sons. Hasan then decides to visit the seven princesses. He leaves his wife in the charge of his mother, telling her never to let his wife leave the house and to guard the feather suit that he has put away in a chest. The wife overhears them and makes her plans to escape. Three days later, she insists that she must go to the public baths. (Once again, bathing will lead to a swan maiden's transformation.) Once there her beauty causes a sensation, which is reported back to the caliph's queen, who demands to see her. The swan maiden, her children, and her mother-in-law are all brought to the palace. As they converse, the swan maiden tells the queen about a beautiful garment she owns, a feather suit. The mother-in-law tries to deny it, but the queen sends a guard to get it. The swan maiden puts the robe on, is transformed into a bird, and dances before the court, like the swan maiden in the Japanese tale discussed above. She then picks up her two children and flies to the ceiling, where she complains about being held captive, but she concludes by saying that should Hasan ever want to see her again, he must abandon house and home and travel to her faraway land (796th night, 59).

The story then becomes another husband's long quest-story, filled with suffering and sorrow as he seeks his lost wife. The story is, after all, named for him, while the swan maiden remains nameless,[82] as do most of the women in the story. He dreams that his wife repents of leaving him (798th night, 66), so he returns to the palace of the seven princesses, who once again agree to help him. Hasan eventually finds her, and she admits that a woman does not know a man's worth until she loses him (823rd night, 129). With some assistance, they return to Baghdad and supposedly live happily ever after.

Janshah

The second swan maiden tale that Scheherazade tells is quite strange. Prince Janshah of Kabul sets off to go hunting on a particular island with some companions, but they get lost at sea. As they are gradually pulled farther and farther from land, one by one, Janshah's companions are lost until he is completely alone. Bereft of everything, he accepts a richly paid job from a merchant, who requires him to kill a mule, empty its belly, crawl into the cavity, and be sewn in. A huge bird is attracted by the mule's belly and flies off with the mule—and Janshah—to the top of a mountain (507th night, 341).[83] This is the first of several transvections by birds that fly Janshah here and there. After he escapes from the bird he meets a man who is king of the birds and knows the language of birds.[84] This introduces an interesting parallel with Valkyries, since Sigurd/Siegfried learned the birds' language after killing a dragon, and the birds tell him about Brunhilde. This language is not only empowering; it grants access to aerial women such as Valkyries and, in the present story, *houris*, the divine women given to heroes who have fallen in battle.

Soon after Janshah's arrival, the king must leave for a few days. He gives Janshah all the keys to his palace, inviting him to explore it at his leisure—except, that is, for one room. Of course, Janshah chooses to unlock that room's door, revealing a huge room containing a very large basin and a pavilion where he falls asleep. When he awakes, he sees three dovelike birds the size of eagles, who take off their feathered clothes and became three young women. When Janshah asks who they are, the youngest tells him, "We are from the invisible world of Almighty Allah" (509th night, 346), which means they are heavenly women known as *houris*.[85] The next day they put their feathered clothes back on and fly away.

This variant on a swan maiden tale reveals the avian nature of *houris*. Figure 4.3 shows *houris* with birds perched on their heads and wearing feathers in their hair,[86] while winged *houris* were said to live on far-off Pacific islands that had many characteristics more marvelous than real.[87]

The Qur'ān discusses the future rewards faithful believers will enjoy in paradise (e.g., Sūra 53:32): each will be joined by family members who were faithful to God in life. Additionally, there are the *hur*, more familiarly known as the *houris*, the perpetually young and virginal women of paradise.[88] The Qur'ān makes reference to them as the reward of the faithful, presumably in statements addressed only to men, and refers to them as purified spouses (Qur'ān 2:23, 3:14, and 4:60). Because of their ever-renewing virginity, they will provide carnal joys a hundred times greater than those on earth. Each man will be given a different number of *houris*—for example, Jesus will receive one

FIGURE 4.3 Folio from a fifteenth-century manuscript of Muḥammad's Night Journey showing *hourīs* in paradise. A partial image of Muḥammad riding the flying horse Burāq that has a woman's face appears on the right.

From Mīr Haydar's *Mirāj Nāmeh*. Bibliothèque nationale, Paris (Supplément Turc 190).

hundred.[89] Here again is the motif of the celestial woman as a heavenly reward and sexual partner, like the Valkyries and *apsarās* (chapters 3 and 6). In Islam, this reward is broadened to all faithful male believers, not just warriors, in that *jihād* (striving or struggle) can refer to the inner spiritual struggle to reform oneself (the greater *jihād*) or to military struggle (the lesser *jihād*).[90] Nerina Rustomji makes the point, though, that *hourīs* are first mentioned in the context of warfare: in the eighth-century *Sira Rasul Allah* (Life of Muḥammad) by Ibn Ishaq, they are said to be present at battles, acting as comforters of slain warriors.[91] Utilizing an equally early source, the *Kitāb al-Jihād*, a collection of documents about the heavenly rewards of jihadists by 'Abd Allāh Ibn al-Mubārak, Maher Jarrar found several descriptions of *hourīs*, one of which was that they encouraged warriors during battles, although the warriors could not see them until their heroic deaths,[92] a theme also present in tales about Valkyries. Another common theme is a hero's dream or vision in which he goes to paradise and is invited by *hourīs* to return in the flesh *after* he experiences martyrdom at a time set by them,[93] once again recalling Valkyries who hold and then cut the thread of a man's life.

To return to Janshah's story: the king of the birds returns to find Janshah prostrate with grief, pining for the youngest bird-woman/*hourī*. The king explains that these women only come to that place one day a year. Janshah refuses to leave, and the king advises him to wait with him until the next year, when they will reappear. Then he can hide, and when they remove their feathered clothes he can steal those of the youngest one, named Princess Shamsah. The king will then get the birds to carry them both back to Janshah's homeland (510th night, 348–349). All this comes to pass. Before they leave, the king asks Shamsah to swear she will never betray Janshah, which she readily does, having fallen deeply in love with him. As with Brunhilde and Siegfried (with the sexes reversed), an oath is sworn that prefigures betrayal. Shamsah then asks for her feather clothes, puts them on, and tells Janshah to mount her back, and she flies him home to Kabul. A unique aspect of this tale is that the swan maiden immediately falls in love with her captor and uses her feather suit to fly him home.

In Kabul, Janshah's father builds a red silk pavilion for Shamsah, and she removes her feather clothes and puts on fine robes. The king then has a palace built, and Janshah buries her bird suit under its foundation. Nevertheless, Shamsah immediately smells it when she enters the palace, and she easily digs it up and puts it on. Before flying away, she calls out to Janshah, "If thou love me as I love thee," come to my homeland (516th night, 357). No explanation is given as to why she leaves Janshah—an act for which she is heavily criticized as the story unfolds—but it is easy to imagine her ire at his taking what was hers and also taking away her ability to fly, even though she had vowed to stay with him. He has not had faith in her vow and has attempted to undo her autonomy; therefore she doubts the intensity of his love. It is one thing to love an unattainable woman, and quite another to love an available one. When she was undomesticated he was consumed with love, but once she was domesticated his ardor seemed to fade. He treats her like a captive, not as a voluntary bride. So he must learn to value her through the ordeal of another arduous journey to reclaim her. Of course, no one has any idea where her homeland is.

For seven years, Janshah endures hardship, dangers, and hunger as he searches for Shamsah. He must repeat his original journey, this time not as a wanderer but as a man with a purpose: to regain his beloved. Janshah has many adventures, during which he is repeatedly helped by birds that fly him here and there. During this time, Princess Shamsah has returned home and told her parents all that has happened to her and of her love for Janshah. Her parents tell her that she did not deal righteously with him. They send birds out to look for him, and one finds him and carries him back to them (525th night, 374).

The king and queen joyously give their daughter to him. Shamsah is ashamed of her behavior toward him, which her parents call a sin (526th night, 375). This is, after all, his tale and thus told from his point of view, not hers. Here again, an otherworldly woman has been taken for granted, and, in traditional swan maiden style, she has set her lover a task to prove his love, yet she must act ashamed and be presented as an oath-breaker. She is docile and said to share the deceitfulness attributed to all women.

Meanwhile, war has broken out in Janshah's kingdom, and his father is under siege. Her parents give Janshah *marids*, who are powerful *jinns* and invincible warriors, to raise the siege of Kabul. The terms of Janshah and Shamsah's marriage are that they will alternately live one year with her family and one with his. Here again, uxorilocal and virilocal issues are in conflict. Part of Princess Shamsah's final domestication is to be given to Janshah by her father, not to give herself to him as an independent woman. Though it is not stated, Shamsah's wings are clipped. They are flown to Kabul not by Shamsah, as in the first journey, but by the *marids*, who scatter the enemy army and save Janshah's kingdom (528th and 529th nights, 378–379).

Unfortunately, Janshah and Shamsah do not live happily ever after, although they have several joyous years together until, on the way to Princess Shamsah's home, they decide to rest by a riverbank, where she and her female attendants take off their clothes to bathe. Alas, a huge shark grabs and kills the princess. Her family buries her by the river, and Janshah asks that they dig a grave for him beside hers, where he will wait for death (530th night, 381).

Given the complex historical transmission of these tales, it is understandable that a variety of cultural values have been infused into them. Except for the nineteenth-century *Swan Lake*, this seems to be the only tale in which the swan maiden dies. Her death is more than domestication; it is the complete removal of Princess Shamsah's divine, and therefore immortal, nature as a *hourī*. Her marriage takes away her immortality, and at her death she is exactly as he had first seen her, bathing in water. Then, she was a shape-shifter at home in the air, in the water, and on the earth. But now she is not, and her immersion in water is her death—the shark singles her out, ignoring her female attendants. Note that both Hasan's and Janshah's stories take their titles from the hero's name, not the swan maiden's, making them definitively male-centered tales. Shamsah dies halfway en route to her natal home, so there will not even be a part-time uxorilocal marriage. Janshah, however, shows his love for her not only by waiting for death, but by doing so in that middle space that is neither patrilocal nor uxorilocal, human nor divine.

It is worth looking more closely at the role and status of mothers in many of these stories. When their sons return to them, the sons' marriages are jeopardized. Leaving Freud aside, the swan maidens are made helpless by captivity but prove themselves otherwise through their cleverness, while the mothers' powerful influence on their sons inevitably leads to the swan maidens' escape and the loss of their sons. Yet the men who perform heroic searches for their escaped avian brides do return to their patriarchal houses, placing the brides once again under the watchful eye of their parents. Hatto suggests that these stories should be understood as tales of conflict between wives and mothers-in-law[94]—a theme of assorted ancient tales. Needless to say, swan maiden tales spoke to the realities of many women's lives. At the same time, though, the husbands' journeys through mysterious and magical lands, encounters with strange beings, and accomplishment of heroic tasks puts these journeys in the category of transformative experiences. The man who recovers his otherworldly wife is not the same man who initially captured her. The swan maiden has set the man a seemingly impossible task: a journey requiring bravery and the ability to endure hardships. The swan maiden knows her worth—something the husband has forgotten but recalls as he struggles to find her. He will not take her for granted again and has learned the hard way to respect her ability to disentangle herself from patriarchal marriage. If he wants an extraordinary woman, he must adjust, must be willing to change to suit her. When the bride willingly returns to her marriage, she has asserted her independence and is no longer a captive. She has won her freedom. Nevertheless, one can also read these stories as tales about the male desire for an extraordinary woman only in order to make her ordinary, to render pointless the power of avian females to make men more than they are, even to make them immortal. As aerial females move through time from an ancient, undifferentiated period into a distinctly patriarchal one, their power is denied. They become just another ornament for male pride.

Swan maiden tales represent such powerful ideas about gender and social relations, immanence and transcendence, that they connect with tales about other categories of beings, such as *apsarās*, Valkyries, *hourīs*, and even fairies. In Siberia, swan maidens continue to play a role in both tales and rituals to welcome the spring migration of swans, and there are also traces of the swan maiden in the rituals of shamans from all around the world (chapter 9), who dance in bird costumes to cross over the divide between the lands of the living and the dead in order to heal the sick or to make the barren fertile.[95] Similarly, the levitations of Christian and Asian mystics (chapters 10 and 11) are also escapes from the mundane world and its attendant domesticity.

Even in modern times, the story of the captured bride continues to be lived out. Princess Diana captured the world's attention and imagination to a degree almost unprecedented by any other royal figure in history. The media was excessive in describing—and thus defining—her "fairy tale" romance, wedding, and happily-ever-after life. They just never got which fairy tale it was. On the one hand, she was the modern "wonder woman," having and doing it all: a handsome and charming husband, beautiful male children, and a full-time job as a royal princess. The fairy tale she really lived out, though, was that of the captured bride. Prince Charles obviously broke the taboos she pressed on him, but this did not lead to the recovery of her stolen wings. Ugly, public divorce with all its attendant humiliations is the cost of freedom for today's swan maidens and fairy brides. That, and the apotheosis of death.

5

Angels and Fairies: Male Flight and Contrary Females

RELIGIONS BASED ON REVELATION, as well as folktales from around the world, group together an intriguing assortment of aerial and elemental beings who bring the otherworld to the natural world, offering otherwise unattainable gifts and knowledge to human beings. Angels act as messengers between God and human beings singled out to hear God's word, while fairies remind humans that there is a realm beyond the world they think they know. The latter are mostly beautiful, capricious, and somewhat eerie occasional visitors to the world who can bring wealth and happiness to men—who, inevitably, do not take the fairy's independent nature seriously and thus lose her and the wealth she brought. In contrast, God's word, delivered by mostly terrifying angels, is usually followed to the letter. Both have been conflated with goddesses: angels share the imagery of Nike, while fairies, especially Morgan le Fay, have absorbed aspects of earlier goddesses. Fairies are slippery beings who impose taboos and inevitably escape back to their own world, while angels evolved into females encased in male fantasies of obedient and domestic women.

As we will see, neither fairies nor angels are truly domestic. Once again the male attempt to grasp aerial females is a failure. However, they both lose power as they are gradually feminized: the venerated angel is reduced to "the angel of the house" while the sometimes violent, always mercurial, fairies are diminished to little winged people in Victorian children's books. We have to ask ourselves, how was such a powerful and threatening fairy as Morgan le Fay reduced to Tinkerbell? So much of women's history has been trivialized that recovering defiant and powerful females requires a great deal of unpacking of the familiar.

From the perspective of gender, the most important thing about angels is that they are all male. This is obvious from their descriptions in scripture and from artistic depictions up until the late medieval and early Renaissance periods, when angels first began to be portrayed as female (Figure 5.1).[1] The angel who drives Adam and Eve out of paradise, the one with whom Jacob wrestles, and those that appear to Hagar, Daniel, Abraham, the Virgin Mary, the women at Jesus's tomb, and Muḥammad are all male.[2] Even the angels that appear in the biblical dreams of Jacob and Joseph are male, as are the angels that became visible to the medieval Christian women mystics, discussed in chapter 10. Angels' maleness even plays a part in Paul's admonishment that praying women should veil their heads: "A woman ought to have a veil on her head because of the angels."[3] Seemingly, the angels would either be aroused by women's hair or offended by it. A possible exception occurs in Zechariah 5:9 when the speaker says of two women: "The wind was in their wings; they had wings like the wings of a stork."

The word "angel" comes from the Greek *angelos*, which is a translation of the Hebrew *mal'akh*, meaning "messenger." They are God's winged messengers, mostly benevolent spirits who mediate between humans and the divine, and thus they are prominent in religious movements based on revelation, such as Zoroastrianism, Judaism, Christianity, Gnosticism, and Islam.[4] In all of these traditions, angels are incorporeal beings without gender; nonetheless, they are understood to be male because human beings tend to gender the world and the male body is widely considered the normative body, making the female body deviant.[5] For example, Matthew describes the angel appearing at Christ's tomb as male (Matthew 28:3). On the scale of existence, they are as different from God as they are from human beings; they are formless, bodiless, immaterial, and often considered as "elementals" made up of air, water, fire, and earth.[6] This makes them mostly invisible, except when becoming visible is necessary. The Jewish Bible (*Tanakh*) is replete with their appearances as messengers of God: They are necessary intermediaries between God and human beings, because humans cannot look upon God directly and live (Exodus 3:6). Despite Solomon's having had carvings made of them in the Temple (1 Kings 6:23–35), Judaism did not allow any figurative representations of its religious concepts, following the second of the Ten Commandments: "You shall

FIGURE 5.1 Adriaen and Jan Collaert, after Hendrik Goltzius, *The Angel Calming Joseph's Suspicion*, engraving, c. 1586.

Anonymous woodcut, c. 1481, from *The Illustrated Bartsch*, vol. 3. ©Abaris Books.

not make for yourself a graven image . . . of anything in heaven . . . or that is in the earth beneath" (Exodus 20:4).[7] Consequently, angels presented an iconographic challenge to early Christian artists, a problem largely solved by presenting them as winged men, examples of which already existed in pre-Christian art,[8] such as the naked Erotes (members of Aphrodite's/Venus's retinue). Christian sculptures, paintings, illuminations, and texts presented angels as male in both popular and high art, while liturgies ritually recalled angelic appearances at pivotal moments in Christian history. Interestingly, in Byzantium after the tenth century, angels were thought of as male eunuchs—a notion brought about by the church's assumed parallelism between the imperial court, with its eunuchs, and God's heavenly court.[9] According to this model, angels serve God in heaven, and as his messengers to humanity they are agents of God's plan for human redemption.[10]

In Islam angels have an unprecedented role, especially the angel Gabriel (Jibra'il).[11] It is Gabriel who brought Muḥammad (c. 570–632) the word of God during the twenty-two years of revelations that became the Qur'ān. He also accompanied Muḥammad on his Night Journey to Paradise, though he could not enter into the presence of God,[12] an important indication not only of Muḥammad's superiority over Gabriel but of all of humanity's as well. Sunni Muslims believe angels have neither self-knowledge nor free will. Therefore, only human beings— not angels—can know God. A further indication of human superiority over the angels is revealed in the fall from heaven of those who refused God's command to bow to Adam—that is, to God's creation of human beings. Led by Iblīs, the Devil (Shaitan), some say they became *jinns*, a low spiritual form that usually does evil,[13] although other sources define them as a class of beings different from both humans and angels, and they are sometimes conflated with fairies (*perīs*) and *hourīs*.[14] *Jinns* are actually pre-Islamic spirits that can be female or male. Like fairies, they are unpredictable: sometimes benevolent, sometimes malevolent. They love music and are irresistibly drawn to it. Beautiful and sexually alluring, *jinns* are also possessors of great wealth.[15]

Despite their lesser status, angels accompany the human soul at death to the gate of heaven,[16] a belief shared by Christians. Shi'a Muslims have more diverse beliefs about angels, considering them superior to ordinary humans,[17] which is closer to the Christian understanding of angels.[18] Shi'a images of male angels and cherubs can be found in the Mughal art of India.

Of further historical interest, it is the traditional belief in the three biggest monotheistic religions that the northern Arab people, from whom Muḥammad descended, were preserved through the intervention of God and one of his angels. Abraham abandoned his concubine Hagar and their son Ishmael in the desert because Abraham's wife, Sara, was jealous. Desperate to find water, Hagar ran back and forth between two hills searching, an act that pilgrims duplicate during the Hajj, the pilgrimage to Mecca expected of all Muslims with the means to do so. Although Hagar is not mentioned by name in the Qur'ān, her story is preserved in Genesis, which tells us that an angel spoke to her from heaven, saying Ishmael would be the head of a great nation, the Arabs, and that God then opened her eyes and she saw a well (Genesis 21:17–21).

Angels are distinguished from demons or devils, which are malevolent mediating spirits, but both benevolent and malevolent spirits have wings and can fly.[19] Satan is said to have been one of God's favorite angels (in Islam he is a *jinn* called

Iblīs, as mentioned above), until he rose up in rebellion and was thrown out of heaven, along with his followers, into the infernal regions (Qur'ān, Sūra 7:10–12). This story points to even earlier concepts of angels as ambivalent beings, equally capable of good or evil; thus angels could be associated with malefic magic in Judaism and Islam.[20] Jewish ideas about angels were elaborated upon during the Babylonian exile (sixth century BCE) under the influence of the many winged figures of the ancient Near East,[21] as well as the Zoroastrian notion of a good god, Ahura Mazda, battling it out with a bad god, Angra Mainyu. Both these gods are accompanied by an army of spirits,[22] and this military aspect added to the belief that angels were male. After the Babylonian exile, Judaism was increasingly concerned with angelic hierarchies, ranks, numbers, and names—the last being particularly important in magic.[23] There was also a growing devotion to individual guardian angels assigned to each person,[24] which was absorbed into Christianity and Islam. Christians and Muslims inherited the Jewish conception of angels, and Shi'a Muslims followed the Christians' visual images of them (as in the image of Jonah and the whale from Iran, shown in Figure 5.2), as well as drawing on some Asian examples.[25]

FIGURE 5.2 *Jonah and Whale*, folio from a Jami al-Tavarikh (Compendium of Chronicles), c. 1400, Iran.
The Metropolitan Museum of Art, New York.

The Greek goddess Nike and her Roman counterpart, Victory, though female, provided a model with their impressive wingspans as well as their positive associations as divine messengers of success (Figure 0.1, see p. 2).[26] Speaking more broadly, Gunnar Berefelt explains, "The classical idea of wings as a symbol of speed, as the attribute of a being occupying an intermediate position between mortals and gods and as a symbol of spirituality lies at the root of the investment of Christian angels with wings." The Jewish Bible, the New Testament, and the Qur'ān imply that angels have wings and can fly[27] and that, like Nike, they are "bearers of good tidings."[28] On the Day of Judgment, angels will sound their trumpets and the dead will be resurrected.[29] Singly and in groups, however, Nikes or Victories continued to appear in Christian art as late as the sixth century.[30] As shown in chapter 2, winged goddesses commonly appeared on sarcophagi, and it was not long before Christians adopted this motif by placing Victories and winged Erotes on their sarcophagi as escorts of the soul,[31] indicating the central Christian tenet of victory over death, or the achievement of eternal life. Eventually they were replaced by angels, with the Erotes providing a convenient male model.[32] Male angels acted as escorts in depictions of the Ascension of Christ, the Assumption of Mary, and the Crucifixion. Early Christian angels were even depicted holding wreaths similar to those carried by Victories; in the case of angels, the wreaths indicated the triumph of Christianity over pagan Rome. The Romans had proclaimed their invincibility through images of Victory, and the church utilized her imagery to proclaim its dominance. Angels and Victories often appeared in pairs, but they were clearly distinguished by their costumes and gender: both wore tunics, but male angels had mantles draped over their flat chests, while mantle-less Victories displayed prominent breasts.[33] Occasionally, halos were added to define the figures as angels.

The feminization of angels and the introduction of child angels (*putti*, later conflated with cherubs) began in early Italian Renaissance art (thirteenth to fourteenth centuries). Neither female angels nor child angels have any basis in Christian literature or thought; they are an innovation introduced by artists of the period, based on the classical female forms of the goddess Victory and the childlike forms of the Erotes.[34] While masculine angels remained dominant, female angels began to perform some of their functions, appearing on tombs and flanking the Cross, while *putti* appeared in nativity scenes and scenes from Christ's childhood, as well as in scenes showing them crowning Mary as Queen of Heaven.[35] Berefelt makes the point that not only was this "a departure from traditional conceptions but also a change of attitude towards the important position formerly held by the angel in Christian mythology."[36] Belief in angels was waning, and the appearance of child and female angels was an indication of angels' declining status: if women

FIGURE 5.3 Daniel Chester French, *The Angel of Death and the Sculptor*, 1889–1893. Marble copy (1921-1926) of original bronze sculpture from the Milmore Memorial.
The Metropolitan Museum of Art, New York.

and children could be angels, then angels were less significant.[37] Be that as it may, when one recalls that the Renaissance was inspired by the discovery of ancient Greek and Roman texts and iconography, the appearance of female angels can be seen as a return to the female Victories on which angels were originally based, as well as a recurrence of ancient and enduring beliefs about female, not male, guides for the dead and restorers of life (Figure 5.3). Female angels also invoked other aerial women of the battlefield, such as goddesses of war, the Valkyries, and so on (Figure 5.4).[38]

Female angels began to appear in large numbers during the nineteenth-century Romantic movement, and as the Victorian era arose, the word angel began to be used most often in connection with women, as in "the angel of the house,"[39] a widely popular conception in England and the United States at the time. The Victorian social myth of woman as the presiding angel of the hearth is one indication of how quickly female angels were domesticated in both winged and wingless forms. By requiring a daily prayer session involving the entire household (family and staff), the wife/mother fulfilled the traditional angelic role of mediating

FIGURE 5.4 Francis Luis Mora, *Flanders Field with Angel of Victory*, c. 1918.
Collection of Jason and Rena Pilalas.

between the members of her household and God. She further participated in Christian philanthropy in visiting the poor.[40] M. Jeanne Peterson adds:

> [She] was the one near to God, the pious one who kept the family on the Christian path. In secular terms the angel provided the home environment that promoted her husband's and children's well-being in the world; she also provided a haven from its worst pressures through her sound household management and sweetness of temperament. The latter meaning suggests the angel's domesticity, unworldliness, asexuality, innocence, even helplessness in matters outside the domestic sphere.[41]

The idea was popularized by the essays of John Ruskin (1819–1900), who, in his essay "Of Queens Gardens," set forth the "argument that women (read middle-class women) are peculiarly suited to moral 'gardening,' to cultivating human plants not only at home but also abroad to remedy social ills,"[42] and by the nineteenth-century memoirists and biographers who wrote "about their own mothers, sisters, and wives."[43] A book-length poem of a minor poet, Coventry Patmore (1823–1896), entitled *The Angel in the House* (published serially, 1854–1863) took the lead in formulating this ideology, which played out in subsequent nineteenth-century novels that presented the angel in the house as the ideal woman, one who was often pitted against a less pliant woman. Virginia Woolf's (1882–1941) *To the Lighthouse* (published 1927) is a late example of a work presenting examples of these two types of women.[44] But Woolf put the final nail in this coffin of male fantasy in her autobiographical comments in "Professions for Women," in which she explicitly railed against the detrimental effects of the stifling "angel in the house" ideal:

> I discovered if I were going to review books I should need to do battle with a certain phantom. And the phantom was a woman, and when I came to know her better I called her after the heroine of a famous poem, "The Angel in the House." It was she who used to come between me and my paper when I was writing reviews. It was she who bothered me and wasted my time and so tormented me that at last I killed her. . . . I will describe her as shortly as I can. She was immensely charming. She was utterly unselfish. She excelled in the difficult arts of family life. She sacrificed herself daily. . . . [I]n short she was so constituted that she never had a mind or wish of her own, but preferred to sympathize always with the minds and wishes of others. Above all . . . she was pure. . . . and when I came to write I encountered her with the very first words. The shadow of her wings fell on my page. . . . Had I not killed her she would have killed me.[45]

I quote Woolf at length because of her articulate rendering of the enormous effort required to resist and reject such idealizations placed on women. How can a woman create anything of her own if she must devote all of her time and energy to the needs of others?

The thing about angels (and devils) is that they are spirits and therefore do not actually have bodies, let alone sexual characteristics;[46] rather, they can assume the appearance of a human being. Yet in the medieval period it was not just the maleness of angels that was asserted; Nancy Caciola has traced the parallel feminization of demons in art and theology: "Among spirits, a female appearance is an exclusive signifier of demonic status. Male appearance, conversely, is angelic."[47] Angels' masculinity echoes the masculinity of Christ, which Leo Steinberg has shown increased in importance in the later Middle Ages,[48] and even though demons were fallen angels and would therefore presumably be male, their depictions are feminized. For example, the serpent that tempts Eve is sometimes depicted with the face of a woman.[49] More commonly, Satan is depicted in hell giving birth to sinners, as in Giotto di Bondone's 1306 "Last Judgment."[50] In fact, it is precisely their fall that feminizes them; just as Eve is the first human sinner so, too, are the fallen angels the first heavenly sinners. Woman and demon have a shared status as primordial sinners, who continue to drag others (specifically, men) into sin.[51]

What we see in this history is the male appropriation of a primal female power and the suggestion that when males fly it is good but when women fly it is bad—so much so that female angels are linked to the decline of the cult of angels. Even the saint of aviation, Joseph of Campolino, is male, despite the more numerous flying female mystics discussed in chapter 10.

FAIRIES

The term "fairies" encompasses a wide variety of unpredictable and contrary creatures believed to exist throughout the British Isles, continental Europe, and Scandinavia, and who are related to similar ethereal beings in the Middle East and Asia. Like angels they are thought of as "elementals"—that is, creatures of the air, fire, water, and earth. In contrast to angels, who can visit earth but are essentially of the heavens, fairies are of the earth, though their elusiveness suggests they occupy an earth parallel to, rather than part of, the earth known to humans. Often it is said they can become invisible. Fairies encompass helpful brownies, banshees who announce impending deaths, sly elves, and pixies who mislead travelers.[52] Like Valkyries, some fairies were said to attach themselves to particular households or families.[53] Their closeness to the earth is connected to the belief that they were the ancestors of an aboriginal people who lived before the Europeans, or that they were the old gods from before Christianity,[54] and they are closely identified with the dead.[55] Another view links them to the air and with angels—specifically, the fallen angels who followed Lucifer. They are therefore often conflated with devils and, once again, with the dead, as in the belief that they go forth in troops at night, riding the wind or on horseback.[56]

There are many references to flying fairies.[57] In the fourteenth-century romance *Richard Coeur de Lion*, Richard's father, Henry II, married a princess of great beauty who turned out not to be what she seemed. Over fifteen years she bore him a daughter and a son, though she refused to take Holy Communion—that is, until one of the king's knights grew suspicious and held her captive during Mass. Just before Communion began the queen grabbed both her children "and flew out of the roof," but she lost her grip on the boy and dropped him. He became King John,[58] a not very subtle jab at Eleanor of Aquitaine (d. 1204) who, in real life, supported her sons in their war against her husband Henry. Additionally, banshees are prolific shape-shifters who are said to fly;[59] in Romania fairies have wings and fly.[60] Sicilian fairies traditionally flew on goats and were conflated with witches,[61] as were Scottish fairies, because both loved dancing, whether at a witches' sabbath or in a fairies' circle, and because both rode through the night on the air or on horses.[62] The conflation of fairies and witches seems to be widespread, as in the well-documented case of Bridget Cleary (c. 1869–1895) who was mostly described as fairy-possessed, but was also said to have been bewitched or even to be a witch herself.[63] Fairies are also great lovers of music, and gifted musicians were thought to have been taught by them.[64] One of the most famous fairies, Titania, Queen of the Fairies, was introduced by William Shakespeare in *A Midsummer Night's Dream*. Sir Joseph Noel Paton's 1849 painting, "The Quarrel of Oberon and Titania," depicts her as winged and the fairies surrounding her have butterfly-like wings, a common European belief.

Morgan le Fay

Another well-known fairy is Morgan le Fay (Morgan the Fairy), said to be the half-sister of Arthur, the semi-legendary sixth-century king of the Britons.[65] She is a complex figure woven from many ancient threads and is variously represented as a dangerous sorceress who enchants men with her magic and her beauty; a woman famous for her wisdom, esoteric knowledge, and abilities as a healer; a fairy; or a goddess, who can bless or curse, or confer sovereignty, as she pleases. She opposes Arthur and constantly seeks ways to harm him, yet in the end it is she who takes him to Avalon, the Land of the Dead and of immortality. This is consistent with the belief that fairies can be helpful to humans—for instance, by doing their work—or can steal and make trouble.[66] It is never fully explained how Morgan's human status as Arthur's sister coexists with her supernatural fairy and goddess nature, though there are many stories of Celtic goddesses and fairies who become women in order to be with the heroes they choose. The medieval tale *Lancelot* (II:lxix) offers the explanation that Morgan's interest in magic caused her to leave human society and to live in the forests. Eventually people began to think of her more as a fairy than a mortal and gave her that title.[67]

Even the earliest sources for Morgan[68] were composed several centuries after the events they describe (although the historical basis of Arthur's existence remains highly questionable). By that time, Christianity had been established in Britain (an event that is often anticipated in the Arthurian legends), and the British Isles had suffered several invasions of foreign people.[69] The Christianization of the Celtic people of the British Isles began in the third century CE, and they maintained their new faith even after the invasion of pagan Anglo-Saxons, who established permanent settlements. The Anglo-Saxons, in turn, began to be Christianized during the last decade of the sixth century. This process took several centuries to complete and entailed a change in, among other things, the status of women, a change that is generally understood to have been a reduction of status.[70] Bits and pieces of Morgan's story are contained in the oral Arthurian legends that developed into medieval story cycles, such as those of Sir Thomas Malory (d. 1471), whose writings are the source of most modern interpretations of Morgan and Arthur.[71]

As I discussed in the introduction to this book, Maureen Fries defined the female counter-hero,[72] so well personified by Morgan, who is indifferent to patriarchal values and who harkens back to an earlier, generally pre-Christian time and earlier sources of knowledge. In an age not known for its love of learning, she is a woman of knowledge. Her story was written down just as the courtly poetry of unconsummated love began to be popularized by the troubadours, yet she exhibits a sexual freedom unknown to other female characters. Morgan le Fay goes her own way.

In *Le Morte d'Arthur*, Malory presents Morgan as a decadent, adulterous, and murderous woman who uses magic to achieve her ends. Her ability to cast spells defines her, in the terms of Arthurian romance, as a female counter-hero, but she also acts in the male heroic mode, choosing her lovers and fighting her enemies.[73] The easy sexual relations she pursues echo the earlier, self-motivated behavior of pre-Christian Celtic women and goddesses who also frequently chose their own mates. One of Morgan's functions in this text is to be a counterpoint to the new, idealized Christian woman of the period.

Morgan's hatred for Arthur can be surmised from her early history in Malory's tale, when King Uther kills her father in battle, claims her mother for his wife, begets Arthur, and then marries off Morgan's two sisters. Morgan is one of the conquered royal women who make up Uther's spoils of war, to use as he wishes. Perhaps Morgan was too young to marry; instead she is sent away from her mother to school,[74] and replaced by Arthur, the son and heir.

Later in Malory's telling, Morgan is married and also has a lover. While Arthur is out hunting with her husband, King Uryens, and her lover, Sir Accolon, Morgan uses magic to cause the three men to fall into an enchanted sleep from which each one awakens in a different place. King Uryens wakes up in Camelot with Morgan.

Sir Accolon wakes up in the company of a dwarf, who gives him a message from Morgan together with Excalibur, Arthur's magical sword, which makes its wielder invincible. She wants Accolon to use it in combat against Arthur. King Arthur awakens in a dungeon, where he is coerced into fighting the disguised Accolon. Ultimately, Morgan is thwarted in her efforts by the counter-magic of the Lady of the Lake, who protects Arthur and helps him defeat and kill Accolon. Meanwhile Morgan attempts to kill her husband, but is prevented from doing so by a female servant who warns him. These are two examples of Malory's use of other women to contain Morgan and to contrast their benevolent behavior with Morgan's malevolency. Malory particularly uses the Lady of the Lake to usurp Morgan's positive qualities. Undeterred, Morgan then rides off to once again steal Arthur's sword, but she succeeds only in capturing its magic scabbard (which prevents its owner from bleeding to death). Pursued by Arthur, she flings it into a lake, saying, "'Whatsoever com of me, my brothir shall nat have this scawberde!'" She and her followers then ride into a valley "where many grete stonys were," and she shape-shifts herself, her followers, and their horses into similar great stones.[75]

Morgan's persistent efforts to capture Arthur's sword as a means to destroy him can be read as a struggle against the various forces that were undermining the power of royal women, and pre-Christian goddesses, to grant the kingship to a male hero of their own choosing. Indeed, legend says Excalibur had been forged on Avalon, the island of the fairies, Morgan's true home. While there are no explicit connections in Malory between the sword and kingship, Excalibur empowers Arthur, while the source of its power lies with the fairies. Significantly, as Arthur lies mortally wounded, Morgan displays her divine connections. In the company of two other queens (thus forming a divine trinity, similar to that of the Celtic goddesses Macha, Martrona, and Morrigan, and echoing the trio she formed with her two sisters), Morgan takes him to the mystical island of Avalon, where time stands still, to be healed.[76] It is from Avalon, a land where no one ages, that Arthur will someday return to rule again, this time as a wiser king, one worthy of sovereignty. Even in Malory, Arthur returns to the pre-Christian roots that drive his legend: divine kings who receive their sovereignty from exacting goddesses. The clearest surviving Celtic component in Arthur's, and thus Morgan's, story is that of the king who will renew himself on the magical island of Avalon, from which he will someday return to rule again.

For Malory, Morgan represents a subversive force within Arthurian society. She opposes and sabotages the political and social structure of her brother's realm through her beauty, sexuality, magical powers, and occult knowledge. Malory's text transforms Arthur, the legendary pagan king, into a righteous Christian king, while demonizing his semi-divine half-sister. In this regard it is of interest that

Merlin, too, has magic, which he uses to place Arthur on the throne and keep him there. As discussed in chapter 8, in the medieval period it was acceptable for literate men to dabble in ritual magic, but not women.[77]

Morgan's supernatural nature is shown, in part, by her title "le Fay." *Fay* is an early word for fairy, which Venetia Newall opines may come from the Latin *Fata*, the Fates—"supernatural women who appear beside the cradle of a newborn infant to decide its future."[78] A good example comes from Sleeping Beauty's christening, which was attended by both benevolent and malevolent fairies. The fairies' connection with fate links them to other aerial women, such as the Valkyries (chapter 3) and winged goddesses of war throughout the ancient Near East (chapter 2), who decide the fate of warriors. Additionally, like the Celtic goddesses, fairies were believed to be magical.[79] Morgan, too, displays supernatural powers, for example when she casts spells on Arthur, Accolon, and her husband, magically transporting them to distant places, and when she shape-shifts. Of particular interest is her ability to turn herself into a stone, as when she entered a valley of great stones, possibly monoliths similar to those at the ancient site of Stonehenge. It is thought that Stonehenge was used as an astronomical site to measure the solstices and other important astronomical phenomena, a science Morgan is said to have mastered, but more recent evidence suggests it was a burial site.[80] Thus her shape-shifting is suggestive of the renewal of life through burial rites. Finally, Morgan's choosing and disposing of lovers, even going so far as to attempt to kill her husband, identifies her both with the fairies and with the more autonomous Celtic women, especially royal women, of the past.[81]

Roger Loomis argues that the fays in medieval romance and modern folklore were derived from the goddesses of pre-Christian Europe and that this explains Morgan le Fay's multiple personalities: "She has acquired not only the attributes and activities of Macha, the Morrigan, and Matrona, but also the mythic heritage of other Celtic deities. She is a female pantheon in miniature."[82] Morgan's name is derived from Morrigan, the Irish warrior goddess, with whom she shares many characteristics.[83] The second part of her name, *rigan*, means queen, while *mor* is "cognate to Old High German and Old Norse *mara*, Anglo-Saxon *maere*, German *Nicht-mahr*, French *cauche-mar*, and English *night-mare*. She is thus the nightmare queen, a fitting title for a goddess of war and death."[84]

Morgan was also allied with prosperity, as in Geoffrey of Monmouth's *Vita Merlini* (twelfth century), where she first appears as a lovely, learned, and potent woman—a shape-shifter knowledgeable in healing and astrology. And in *Vita Merlini* she is not Arthur's sister; rather, she is one of nine divine sisters from the island of Avalon, where Arthur's sword Excalibur was forged, where he is taken to be healed after his final battle, and from which he will return to the world in the future. These sisters also have custody of a magic cauldron that provides an inexhaustible supply of food.[85] Overall, though, in these early stories Morgan's positive aspects and her divine nature are in conflict with changing social and religious ideologies about the proper behavior of women and new ideologies about royalty, which are reducing the power of queens. In slightly later literature, such as "Lancelot" and "Sir Gawain and the Green Knight," she becomes more malevolent, predatory, ugly, and lecherous.

The sources for Morgan are contained in the literatures of two peoples: the Celts, among whom the Arthurian legend began, and the Normans, who first wrote the legends down. The significant and active roles played by women in Arthurian literature suggest pre-Christian models for women, both Celtic and Norse, though one should not overlook the influence of later, aristocratic women on this literature—for example, Eleanor of Aquitaine—as both audience members and patrons. Such women may not have been satisfied with a literature characterized by passive women. Among both Celts and Normans, there is evidence for the high status of at least some upper-class women: they could own property, initiate divorce and choose whom they would next marry, rule countries, and command men. Some were powerful warriors or achieved status in the priesthood—among the Celts they were often *faiths*, or soothsayers. This is consistent with the role of many of the women in Celtic literature, who act as intermediaries between the natural and supernatural worlds or are from the supernatural world.

The frequent association of women with magic and the supernatural among both the Norse and Celtic people suggests suspicions about women and a fear of their power, which contributed to negative assessments of womankind in general and the imposition of limitations on their rights and privileges. Some of the conflicts surrounding the proper position of women are brought out in the Arthurian stories, which often depicted attempts to undercut women's power, or to put limits on it.

As already noted in the discussion of the *Nibelungenlied* (chapter 3), much of the literature composed during the medieval period was designed to educate courtiers in proper behavior; courtesy and hospitality were important virtues. An equally important facet in the medieval understanding of courtesy has to do with the relations between women and men—consequently, this literature was reshaping gender roles.[86]

The contradictory roles that fairies had in relation to an increasingly patriarchal society moved from literature to actuality in several medieval incidents that connected fairies with political and social discontent, such as protests against new laws in England forbidding peasants access to the wood and game of forests, in 1450–1451. Men with blackened faces, who called themselves servants of the

Queen of the Fairies, broke into the Duke of Buckingham's park and helped themselves to the restricted wood and game.[87] A similar group roamed Ireland from
1760 to 1790; called the Whiteboys, they also blackened their faces and wore long
white frocks suggestive of women's clothes, tore down enclosures, and otherwise
punished greedy landowners, claiming that they acted under "sanction of being
fairies." Their legacy surfaced once again in the nineteenth-century social-protest
movements known as the Molly Maguires and Ribbon Societies.[88]

Fairy Brides

There are many stories about fairies who marry mortal men, but such marriages
usually end badly because, like swan maidens and Valkyries, the fairy imposes a
taboo on her husband. Inevitably he breaks it and she returns to fairyland, desert-
ing her husband and children.[89] One cannot help but observe in this some face-
saving device for deserted husbands, who could claim that their departed wives
were fairies and not actual women. As we continually see, many of the stories
about flying women involve escaping from domesticity back into the wild. And let
us recall that many of these stories were told by women, even though they were
later collected and written down by men in the early nineteenth century,[90] or, in
the case of the Arthurian romances, beginning in the twelfth century.

In Arthurian romances a great hero often wins the love of a fairy, a woman of
exceptional, indeed supernatural, beauty. She may be his greatest prize, the seal
of his heroism, or she helps him to display his courage and strength by assigning
him an almost impossible task. Thus fairies are prized, beautiful, and challenging.
They also show a marked streak of independence, coming and going as they please,
and are highly sexual and seductive.[91] In folklore they are sometimes perceived as
succubi, dream-women who cause sleeping men to ejaculate and eventually to lose
their souls.[92]

Marie de France was a twelfth-century writer of romances, possibly at the court
of Eleanor of Aquitaine and Henry II. Her stories insist upon the right of women
to choose their own lovers, despite the prevalence of arranged marriage during her
lifetime. Like most of the courtly romances of this period, her stories harken back
to earlier, pre-Christian tales, in which powerful women decided their own fates.
Marie claimed that she was retelling stories she had read or heard recited from
long ago so that they would not be forgotten. These stories challenged prevail-
ing Christian sentiments that represented sex as only acceptable within marriage
for procreation by describing adulterous affairs conducted for personal pleasure.
Courtly love, by definition, takes place outside the strictures of patriarchal marriage. One of Marie's fairy tales, "The Lay of Sir Launfal," describes the romance

of an impoverished Arthurian knight and a beautiful fairy woman endowed with magical powers. While resting in a meadow one day, Sir Launfal is approached by two beautiful women who invite him to meet their mistress in a nearby pavilion. She offers him her love and a magic purse that can never be emptied no matter how much he spends. (Fairies were thought to possess great wealth.) She does, of course, impose a taboo: if he ever speaks of her, he will lose her forever. He is besotted, and not long after he returns to Arthur's court he rejects the overtures of Queen Guenevere—Marie de France goes so far as to villainize Guenevere—and brags that his lover is more beautiful than the queen. He is rapidly brought to trial for this insult, and his fairy lover must appear at court to save him by displaying her greater beauty. Launfal is proved not guilty, and his fairy takes him away to the island of Avalon, from which he never returns.[93]

Two of the earliest European stories about fairies underscore the quality of immortality, or timelessness, associated with fairies, a component that is essential to the ongoing popularity of Arthur's legendary status as the king who will return. Both come from Irish literature. The first is from the *Imram Brain maic Febail* ("The Voyage of Bran, Son of Febal"), a tale told perhaps as early as the seventh century.[94] In it, a fairy queen appears to the hero and takes him back with her to a "Land of Women." Eventually the hero grows homesick and decides to return home, only to find out that centuries have passed during what he experienced as years. He crumbles to dust as he steps off the ship onto land. In another early Irish story, the *Echtra Condla* ("The Adventures of Connla"), a hero is called to this Land of Women, lured by a fairy and the apple she has brought with her. He is never heard of again.[95] These stories suggest the immortal nature of the fairies, and their ability to predict a human's future because time is relative for them.

Unlike humans, fairies do not age, remaining eternally young and beautiful even though they freely pass between the land of humans and fairyland. They are as unaffected by time as they are by other human limitations; hence they are perceived to have magical powers allowing them to achieve their ends. It is love that draws them to the human world—these are romances, after all—yet their love for mortal men has a misogynist edge, suggesting that great heroes can never find their equals among mortal women. It is a view that does not embrace the idea of heroic roles for women, unless they are supernatural; human women must be obedient, patient, kind, and faithful. Fairy women can be the opposite of all this: they can be commanding, impatient, or cruel, and fidelity is not one of their virtues. In fact, they act just like the heroes, only they are even more powerful because of their supernatural abilities. In their behavior they display an inability to fit into the real world as it is structured by patriarchal society. Further, they represent the disturbing otherness of women, their tendency toward willfulness, while their bestiality is shown by their shape-shifting powers, and consequently, their greater sexuality. Morgan le Fay is their greatest literary representation.

Fairies also had an early militant aspect. Although early folklorists deemphasized this aspect, they did retain the associated behaviors of hunting, riding, and roaming where they chose, and the folklorists retained references to them as "troops of fairies."[96] For example, the warrior queen Medb of the seventh-century Irish epic the *Tain* lingers as Mab, queen of the fairies. Nonetheless, a militant strain runs through fairies, swan maidens, Valkyries, and *apsāras*, all of whom are similar in multiple ways.

Fairies are also known for stealing human babies, a clear parallel to Lilith (chapter 8). It was believed that they took children, and sometimes young women, in order to replenish their own dwindling numbers.[97] On occasion, they were said to leave a changeling, or a fairy child, in the stolen infant's place. This story may have helped parents deal with a deformed child, since they could deny that it was really their child.[98] There are recorded cases of such children being burned or almost drowned in an attempt to drive the fairy out and recover the "real" child, thereby exacerbating the child's weak physical condition.[99] Despite this view, in one of the Grimm Brothers' tales, fairies are shown to be fond of human children.[100]

Asian Fairies

East Asians have always believed in a variety of spirits, both as natural forces and as supernatural beings in either human or animal form. The ancient Chinese understood that the natural world sometimes could draw close and temporarily assume a faint human shape, most often a female shape, although as upper-class Chinese society became increasingly male-oriented, these female spirits became less benevolent.[101] As Indian Buddhism spread eastward it brought along stories of *apsāras*, who became more fairy-like and were believed to inhabit mountains and bodies of water.[102] Chinese Daoism also contributed to these beliefs, and from China the Buddhist and Daoist stories spread throughout Asia, mixing with indigenous beliefs about divine women who could be ghosts or immortals and who, like Western fairies, might either benefit humans or bring them harm.[103] Another similarity between Western and Eastern versions of such tales is that time can be much slower in fairyland, with one human day equaling many fairy years.[104] In a Chinese folktale, two young boys happen upon a cave where two fairies[105] are playing chess. Unobserved, the boys sit for a few hours watching the game while a rabbit jumps up and down. When it rises, flowers bloom, and when it descends, they fade. Eventually the fairies notice the boys and tell them to stay with them instead of going home, because no one will recognize them. Of course, the boys do not listen and return home to find that seven generations have passed. When, in despair, they try to return to the cave of the fairies, it is shut tight. They had been given magical reeds to open the cave but have carelessly lost them.[106]

This tale reveals the common belief that fairyland is parallel to earthly life; it is "just over there"—easily fallen into when there is an opening, inaccessible when closed off. The rabbit is an amusing image of transcendence; when it's aerial there is fertility, when earthbound there is decay. In Chinese culture rabbits symbolize fertility, and they are also associated with the moon and immortality through a well-known ancient tale and the extremely important Mid-Autumn Festival, which commemorates the Chinese overthrow of the Mongols in the fourteenth century. Supposedly, rebels hid notes to fellow conspirators in moon-shaped cakes like those made for this holiday. More relevantly for our purposes here, it is also a celebration of the legend of Chang'e, the Lady of the Moon, who is believed to have lived around 2170 BCE and to have been married to a great archer.[107] At that time there were ten suns in the sky, which was too many, so the emperor ordered the archer to shoot down nine of them. For his success, the archer was rewarded with a pill of immortality. He did not want to take it, though, because he wanted his beloved wife to be immortal as well. One day when he was hunting, his villainous apprentice broke into the house and tried to force Chang'e to give the elixir to him. In desperation, Chang'e drank it as the only way to escape him, and she flew up to the moon (Figure 5.5) to be close to her husband, who became the constellation of the Archer. She became the moon goddess and was given a rabbit to keep her company, hence its connection with longevity and immortality.

The supernatural wife is a common motif in Daoist fairy tales.[108] Most often she is a celestial woman of great beauty who for some reason marries a mortal man, thereby transforming his life into one of graciousness, luxury, and tranquility. Sometimes the husbands make mistakes and lose their divine wives, but in other tales the wife takes her earthly husband up to heaven with her—conferring immortality on him.[109] While idealized and romantic, these tales also suggest the transformative power of aerial women over men's lives.

Asian fairies, like their European counterparts, can also confer wealth. One Daoist tale plays with the idea of wealth and desire, and the interconnectedness of the heavenly and earthly realms. In it, a poor widow supports her three sons through her extraordinary talent as a weaver of brocades in which the scenes are completely lifelike. While in town one day to sell her brocades, she sees a picture of a rich estate. She cannot resist buying it, but her desire to live in such a place is so intense that she becomes ill. Her youngest son suggests she weave a copy of it. It takes her three years, but when it is done it is perfect. Unfortunately, a great breeze picks it up into the sky and sends it sailing toward the east. The mother asks

FIGURE 5.5 Tsukioka Yoshitoshi, *Jōga hongetsu* (Taoist deity Chang'e, flying away on a cloud after having stolen the elixir of immortality), Woodcut, c. 1880.
Library of Congress Prints and Photographs Division, Washington, D.C.

each son in turn to find it. Each comes upon an old woman who explains that the fairies have taken it to copy, gives him directions, and offers him aid during the dangerous journey. Only the youngest is devoted enough to do so. A magic horse carries him to heaven, where he comes upon the fairies, who are weaving a copy of his mother's brocade. They say they are almost finished and ask him to wait. One fairy finishes her section first, and she is so entranced by the widow's brocade that she wants to live in it—so she embroiders a picture of herself into it. The youngest son reaches home to find his mother on her deathbed, but the return of her brocade revives her. They take it outside their hut to admire it in the daylight, where it grows as large, and as real, as the estate it depicts. The fairy is there, too, and the youngest son marries her and they live happily ever after.[110]

In a seventeenth-century Korean story ("The Home of the Fairies"), a young scholar loses his way on a strange road during a rainstorm. An old, sage-like man appears, gives him directions, and then disappears. Soon the young man has crossed into fairyland, a place of wealth, beauty, and tranquility. There he is accepted as the bridegroom of the fairy king's beautiful daughter. Time passes pleasantly and they have two sons, but the young man is a dutiful son and longs to see his mother. His wife sends him on his way, and he spends a few years in his home village, until a messenger comes from fairyland warning him to return because everyone in the village is going to be killed. So he leaves before the village is destroyed by foreign troops. In this tale, time in fairyland is not different from earthly time, and—equally unusual—the man is able to regain entry to fairyland.[111] Clearly, tales such as this one are an attempt to reconcile male fantasies about sexually available supernatural woman and their filial duty toward their mothers, something we have already seen in the Middle Eastern swan maiden tales discussed in chapter 4.

Sometimes the fairies come to human beings. A seventh-century Japanese tale describes an episode in the life of Emperor Temmu, who one day is playing the *koto* (a stringed instrument) among the cherry blossoms. Five fairies appear in the sky, adding their instruments to his and performing a dance. From then on, their music and dance became part of the imperial coronation festivities. This story also became the basis of a Nō play, *Hagoromo* ("The Feather Robe"),[112] and is a variant on the story told in chapter 4. The tale shows the influence of Indian beliefs on Japan, in that such divine women are often called *tennyo* or *tennin* in Japan, a translation of the Indian term *apsarās*, the heavenly women known for their talent as dancers and musicians. Like them, *tennin* roam the sky, often on clouds, without wings but with flowing scarves and playing musical instruments.[113]

Fairies also visit three young Chinese men who have been sent to the country to study, which the eldest does but the two younger ones do not—a sure indication that things will not end well. A fairy, here also a heavenly woman, appears to them, and when she finds out they are single she brings her three beautiful daughters to be their wives. Miraculously, their humble shack is transformed into three separate palatial homes, one for each couple. She also promises them immortal fame through the high promotions she will obtain for them. She calls on Confucius himself to teach them what they need to know for their government examinations. In a twinkling, their understanding is complete and their comportment noble. Their father intrudes on this scene by sending a messenger to check on them. The messenger is astonished by their circumstances and rushes home. The father then sends for the three young men. The fairy warns them not to reveal anything. Once home, the father beats them until they tell the secrets of heaven that they have learned, after which he locks them up. When he asks a famous scholar what it all means, the scholar explains that everything will be lost. The father attempts to alter matters by sending the three young men back to the country, but their wives ignore them. The fairy explains that because they broke her taboo, they will lose everything. She makes the men drink something that turns them back into the uncouth youths they were at the beginning. All their wives, attendants, houses, and riches are gone.[114] Once again, aerial women raise men to a higher state of being only to be betrayed, after which the men lose everything they had gained from their benevolence.

6

Apsarās: Enabling Male Immortality, Part 1

THE SANSKRIT WORD *apsarā* means one who "goes in the waters," including "between the water of the clouds."[1] These celestial women of Hindu and Buddhist mythology are equally at home on the earth, in streams and rivers, in the sky, or in heaven. Being shape-shifters, *apsarās* often appear in legend as aquatic birds[2]— that is, creatures equally at home in water, on the earth, and in the air. *Apsarās* bring together three lines of ancient Indian religious thought: the ambivalent powers of ancient bird goddesses; the belief that the boundaries between humans, divinities, and animals are porous; and the spiritual importance of the power of flight. Like the *ḍākinīs* and *yoginīs* discussed in the next chapter, they are related to the bird goddesses of ancient India. They retain the aerial abilities of their Vedic cousins as well as their powers to bestow new life or snatch it away, but they are wingless and without other specifically birdlike features. All three are understood to be divine, although in courtly settings and rituals, human women sometimes impersonated them. In their earliest forms *apsarās*, *ḍākinīs*, and *yoginīs* are more powerful than humans but not quite as powerful as gods. Being closer to human-kind than the distant gods, they were thought to be more accessible to appeals from human beings and, over time, people began to believe that they themselves could accede to the same semi-divine state.

Iconographically, their ability to fly is signaled by images of them hovering in the sky, sitting on clouds, being surrounded by rainbows, or wearing flowing, winglike scarves. They are transcendent beings, in that they reside in heavenly abodes, but they are also immanent, appearing on earth. All have the ample, curvaceous, and beautiful bodies of young, fertile women idealized in Indian art and literature, which signal their ability to confer fertility as well as to renew life through the blessing of immortality. Historically, all three first appeared as unpredictable, independent deities, but over the centuries they lost their autonomous status as they were incorporated into increasingly male-identified religious traditions within Buddhism and Hinduism,[3] while *apsarās* were placed firmly under the control of the Hindu gods Indra, Brahma, and Viṣṇu, who often employed them as seductresses.

In different ways that all involve their common ability to fly, *apsarās*, *ḍākinīs*, and *yoginīs* either challenge or assist men who desire immortality, spiritual liberation, or more immanent supernatural powers. In exceptional cases, *ḍākinīs* and *yoginīs* also help women, but these are women who are locked into a male-defined religious system. Overall, the powers of fertility and renewal of *apsarās*, *ḍākinīs*, and to a lesser degree, *yoginīs*, are not available to women; these powers are exclusively used to serve men.

Apsarās are an important iconographic presence in both Hinduism and Buddhism, including in the texts of both traditions. To offer just two examples, they are abundantly present at the tenth-century Hindu temple complex of Khajuraho, and in the Buddhist cave paintings of Ajanta (c. sixth century CE). Through both Hinduism and Buddhism their beautiful images spread throughout Asia to such diverse sites as Dun Huang in Central Asia and Borobudur in Indonesia (Figure 6.1).[4] They add their beauty to these sites, act as potent symbols of heavenly delight, and, contradictorily, signify the threat of unbridled female sexuality for celibate men. As a heavenly reward promised to valiant warriors and to men of great spiritual accomplishment, they symbolize both immortality and sexuality. Indeed, they are sometimes referred to as heavenly courtesans. On earth they often act as temptresses who can and do undermine men's spiritual power.

IN HINDUISM

For centuries, Hindu stories about individual *apsarās* captured the South Asian imagination. These *apsarās* are divine, yet earthly, both immanent in art and transcendent in theology, simultaneously erotic and pure. Their voluptuousness promises new life but they are connected to death and immortality. Western observers often mistakenly thought of *apsarās* as angels, but they can hardly be compared to those sexless beings.

FIGURE 6.1 *Apsarā* from Borobudur, Java, Indonesia, ninth century. Sitting on a cloud with flowing scarves and birds.

Photograph by Gunawan Kartapranata.

Relations with Heroes

Apsarās provide one of the most ancient examples of the role of celestial women as a heavenly reward for fallen warriors. Urvaśī, the first named *apsarā* in Indian literature,[5] who was discussed in chapter 4, was won by the warrior-king Purūravas. *Apsarās* share some characteristics with Valkyries: most notably, several battle hymns from the *Atharva Veda* (c. 1000 BCE) call upon the *apsarās* to help slay the opposing army (VIII.8 and XI.9), while the *Mahābhārata* (dated to the beginning of the Common Era) depicts them as leading fallen Hindu warriors to heaven, saying to them, "be my husband" (XII.99.45).[6] Elsewhere in the *Mahābhārata* they carry fallen warriors off in brilliantly colored chariots (*Mahābhārata* VIII.4.9).[7] Iconographic depictions of this can be seen in hero stones (Figure 6.2),[8] which are memorials for fallen heroes in which three ascending scenes are carved in relief: the hero's death in battle; his being carried to heaven by two beautiful women; and the hero in heaven.[9] A sixth-century inscription describes the heroic death of King Damodaragupta (d. c. 550–560 CE), who died on the battlefield and was greeted

FIGURE 6.2 Memorial stone, c. 950 CE, Ron, Dharwar, Karnataka, India. The bottom tier depicting a battle is broken; the middle tier shows two *apsarās* flying on either side of a fallen warrior; and the top tier shows the warrior in heaven, flanked by his two *apsarās*.
Photograph: American Institute of Indian Studies.

by heavenly women called *suradhu*, meaning "bountiful" and "victorious."[10] This idea continued into the medieval period, as is shown by an inscription that contrasts the earthly female ghouls (*vetālīs*), who drink the blood of fallen enemies, with the *apsarās*, who deliver flirtatious glances while flying over a battlefield,[11] and then into the modern period as well among the Rajputs, who envisioned the *apsarās* hovering above the battlefield.[12] The idea of the *apsarās* becoming the wives of fallen warriors recalls the amorous relations between Valkyries and heroes who have died in battle. In this context, the *apsarās* serve under the rule of the thunderbolt-wielding sky god Indra, a not very distant cousin of the hammer-wielding sky god Thor/Wotan. Also like the Valkyries, who could spread confusion and bind men to their will, *apsarās* were believed to be able to possess men and to drive them mad.

The divine beauty, voluptuous bodies, and gracefully erotic movements of the *apsarās* could drive men, overcome by arousing passion, to insanity. They even mesmerize the gods: Indra and Śiva are said to have sprouted extra eyes in order to better see them;[13] while Brahmā was so delighted by one *apsarā* that he sprouted three additional heads in order to watch her without moving.[14] As accomplished singers, musicians, actors, and dancers, *apsarās* fill the heavens with their beauty and art, and they are depicted wearing the elaborate costumes, ornaments, and headdresses of their human counterparts, namely, court and temple dancers.[15] Appropriately, given their powers of seduction, a troop of *apsarās* is said to accompany Kāma, the god of love and desire.[16]

Seducing Ascetics

In other traditional tales, *apsarās* act as seductresses at the behest of the gods, especially Indra. For example, the *apsarā* Menakā brings about the fall of the mighty sage Viśvāmitra, who, through his austere lifestyle, especially his celibacy, has built up so much supernatural power (*tapas*) that even the gods tremble before him. To subvert his growing power, they send Menakā to seduce him. According to the *Rāmāyaṇa* (c. second century BCE), she flies down to earth to bathe in a lake on whose shores Viśvāmitra has practiced his ascetic ways for more than a thousand years. Upon seeing her beautiful nude body, which we are told resembles "lightning athwart a cloud,"[17] he is overcome with desire and asks her to live with him, which she does for ten years. It was and remains a strong belief in Hinduism that men can gain spiritual power by withholding their semen, something *apsarās* excel at undoing, and when all of Viśvāmitra's spiritual power is gone, he reflects that "ten years have seemed to me to be but a day and night."[18] Like a European fairy, Menakā has so intoxicated him that it is as if he entered a fairyland, where time as humans know it does not exist.

In the *Mahābhārata* version of the story, Menakā is afraid Viśvāmitra will burn her to ashes with his spiritual power if she tries to seduce him. She asks Indra to create fragrant, intoxicating breezes that blow off her clothes, and to enlist the assistance of the god of love, all making her less culpable. Then,

Menakā, callipygous [with well-shaped buttocks] nymph, set timid eyes on Viśvāmitra, who, all his evil burned off by his austerities, was yet engaged in more in his hermitage. She greeted him and began to play in front of him. Off with the wind went her moonlight skirt, the fair-skinned nymph dropped to the ground embracing it, bashfully smiling at the wind. And so that strictest of seers saw Menakā nude, nervously clutching at her skirt, indescribably young and beautiful. And remarking the virtue of her beauty the bull among Brahmins fell victim to love and lusted to lie with her. He asked her, and she was blamelessly willing.

The pair of them whiled away a very long time in the woods, making love when the spirit seized them, and it seemed only a day.[19]

Again we see that *apsarās* are so entrancing that they make time stand still.

Continuing with the *Mahābhārata* version: Menakā gives birth to a daughter, after which she deserts both child and father to fly back to Indra's heaven. Half-human/half-divine children are special beings in Indian legend, and the child of this union, Śakuntalā, is one of the most famous Indian heroines, who becomes the mother of a great king. Her father, Viśvāmitra, also abandons her as an infant in order to devote himself to asceticism, but birds (*śakunta*) protect her from dangerous animals until the sage Kaṇva finds and raises her. Thus, she is half-*apsarā* and half-human with a touch of bird goddess, as is reflected in her name, which evokes both her adoptive bird-mothers and her flying *apsarā* mother, who has her own bird goddess antecedents.

Śakuntalā lives independently, pursuing her own spiritual path, until one day she meets a powerful king who is hunting near her home. She is the discovered divine woman in a wild place—a place like Brunhilde's mountain crag—where lovers can make their own rules. Unlike an *apsarā*, she chooses to enter into a secret marriage with a human, and in place of the usual taboo an aerial female would impose on such a marriage, Śakuntalā imposes the condition that if she bears the king a son, he will become the heir to the throne. After the king leaves, she remains at her forest hermitage and does give birth to a son. When she brings the child before the king, however, he denies paternity. Śakuntalā puts up a spirited public defense of her honor, during which—again like Brunhilde—she has a civilizing influence on the king, explaining all the important duties (*dharma*) of a wife, a father, and so on. Finally, she points out that her lineage is higher than the king's since she is half-divine; while he walks on the earth, she flies in the sky. This calls the king to task: he makes her son the heir to the kingdom, and she becomes queen.[20] Śakuntalā's story demonstrates a movement into a new era in which these independent women on the margins of civilization and humanity are domesticated. No doubt, it is her human half that causes her to keep her child and leave the wilds for the palace.

A shorter but nonetheless wonderful seduction story comes from the *Brahma Purāṇa*, 1.69.7–101 (c. 200–1000 CE), which describes the fall of another powerful sage, Kaṇḍu, before whom the great god Indra trembles. This time, Indra sends the *apsarā* Pramloca to seduce the sage. Pramloca is described as "fine-waisted, with beautiful teeth, full hips and ample breasts, and endowed with all the fine marks of beauty."[21] Like Menakā, Pramloca is irresistibly beautiful, and she, too, is afraid of the sage's power to curse her, so Indra promises to send the powers of Love, Spring, and Wind to help her.

Pramloca flies down to earth and begins to sing near Kaṇḍu's hut. Spring causes the birds to sing, while Wind blows fragrant air, and Love sends his arrows to disturb the sage. Kaṇḍu succumbs in a moment, totally smitten. He gives up all his religious practices and instead makes love to Pramloca, day and night, for one hundred years. When Pramloca repeatedly tries to return to heaven he asks her to stay, again and again. She remains, still fearful of his power to curse her. But, finally, after 1,600 years, all his spiritual power is depleted and he comes to his senses. As in the story of Menakā and Viśvāmitra, Kaṇḍu has been so deluded that he thinks only a day has passed. He berates Pramloca but recognizes his own weakness and does not curse her. Instead, he tells her to go, and she flies back to heaven.[22] The yearning love of the *apsarā* is believed only to affect her victims, not the *apsarā* herself; she possess the maddening power of love but does not participate in it.

In the *apsarā* we once again encounter the ambivalent nature of aerial women; *apsarās* are fertile, but not nurturing mothers. As we have seen with Menakā and the swan maiden/*apsarā* Urvaśī, if children are conceived from such unions they are usually abandoned at birth by their *apsarā* mother, an event presented as a sign of her wantonness and indifference.[23] Indeed, the mythic mother of the *apsarās* is listed among the "seizers"—that is, semi-divine and often malevolent beings who cause miscarriages.[24] The *apsarās* are meant to be childless women, unencumbered and available to generate love madness, although, contradictorily, their ability to have children is proof of their powers of fertility.[25] Menakā's grandson and Urvaśī's son were both heirs to thrones, thus renewing the fertility of an entire kingdom, as well. Even so, as an *apsarā*, Menakā has no interest in motherhood, while the half-*apsarā*/half-human Śakuntalā does. I will return shortly to the complicated subject of the *apsarā*'s fertility and infertility.

Other signs of the indifferent nature of *apsarās* are shown in an *Atharva Veda* spell that empowers a woman to arouse the love of a man. It tells us that "yearning love" comes from the *apsarās*, and it asks the gods to send it to the man, adding that while the man should long for the woman, the woman will never again long for him:

This yearning love comes from the Apsaras, the victorious, imbued with victory. Ye gods, send for the yearning love: may yonder man burn after me! . . . .

That yonder man shall long for me, (but) I for him nevermore, ye gods, send for the yearning love: may yonder man burn after me! (VI.130)

Further, *apsarās* were believed to possess men, and even to cause insanity. The *Atharva Veda* (II.2) and *Rig Veda* (X.11) contain hymns to protect people from the madness *apsarās* can bring, and *Atharva Veda* VI.3 beseeches them to restore sanity.[26] The belief is that since *apsarās* have the power to induce harm, they must also have the power to remove harm. Thus they are listed among the divine beings who can protect from misfortune (*Atharva Veda* XI.6). Two other hymns simply attempt to drive them away, rather than appeal to their benevolent side (*Atharva Veda* II.1 and IV.37)—a clear indication of their unpredictable nature to bless or harm. This is further shown in *Atharva Veda* IV.38, where an *apsarā* is called on for help in gambling because *apsarās* are believed to be skillful with dice and to dance with them. The arbitrariness of a roll of the dice is the perfect expression of their double-sided nature.

Although *apsarās* can inspire men to feats of spiritual as well as martial heroism that will ensure them a place in heaven, *apsarās* also are a reminder of human limitations. They are not of this world, but they personify its attractions: beauty, sexuality, and wealth. *Apsarās* are the essential counterpoint to the requirement that males remain celibate for spiritual advancement or to gain spiritual power;[27] they show that spiritual power is equally at odds with earthly power as well as divine power.

The contradictory nature of *apsarās* is further shown when they are depicted as the reward of spiritual heroes, that is, men whose spiritual advancement allows them entry to heaven. In the *Kauṣītaka Upaniṣad* (composed c. sixth century–fifth century BCE), the god Brahmā instructs the *apsarās* to greet those men who have died after achieving the highest spiritual knowledge:

"Run to him with my glory! . . . He will never grow old!" Five hundred celestial nymphs [*apsarās* then] go out to meet him—one hundred carrying garlands, one hundred carrying lotions, one hundred carrying cosmetic powders, one hundred carrying clothes, and one hundred carrying fruits.[28]

Further, when the great hero Arjuna visits Indra's heaven, he sees "these . . . beautiful lotus-eyed nymphs danc[ing] everywhere, bent upon enticing the hearts of the Siddhas [holy men], with wide-flanked buttocks and bouncing breasts, stealing hearts and minds with their quick glances, allurements, and sweetness."[29] After a lifetime of celibacy, the spiritual hero is rewarded with the favors of the *apsarās*. Like *hourīs*, they are beautiful, sexually enticing women gifted by the gods to heroic men, whether that heroism is spiritual or martial.

Spiritual power is a dicey business in Indic religion, as it brings about both rewards and pitfalls. Devotion to asceticism can ensure one a place in heaven, but since great sages can acquire divine capabilities that threaten even the gods, the gods seek to reduce their power. A large part of the ascetic power of men comes from the practice of celibacy, from the strength they are believed to gain by withholding their semen. Thus if Indra wishes to undermine their power, he sends *apsarās* to seduce them.[30] By ejaculating, these sages once again become mere mortals, bereft of supernatural power. This does not require sexual intercourse, because some sages, such as Mankaṇaka and Gautama, are so aroused by just seeing and smelling the fragrant beauty of an *apsarā* that they ejaculate without touching her.[31]

The lesson seems to be that only the practice of asceticism due to devotion to the gods, rather than for the personal achievement of supernatural power, will ensure entry to heaven and access to the *apsarās*. In the medieval tradition of Tantra, however, the search for such powers became an end in itself for some—an end that also brought the reward of sexual union with a divine woman, the *yoginīs* discussed in chapter 7.

Kings, Devadāsīs, and Fertility

The dangerous supernatural powers of celibate ascetics are also depicted in stories about ancient and medieval Indian kings, who were perceived as semi-divine beings possessed of superhuman powers that enabled them to ensure the prosperity of their realms. Kings were believed to maintain the fertility of the fields and herds. Like the god Indra, whom they imitated, kings kept beautiful women in their courts. These women, in turn, imitated the *apsarās* in their charm, beauty, and artistic talent,[32] but when ordered by the king, they would seduce and betray those who threatened royal power. Such women are connected to the many tales in which a king can only end a drought by sending a courtesan, an imitator par excellence of *apsarās*,[33] to seduce a local celibate sage. Into the twentieth century, this theme continued to be enacted in an annual ritual to hasten the monsoon rains that was performed by *devadāsīs*, the sacred courtesans and dancers at the temple of Jagannātha in Puri.[34] The connections between semen and rain have a long history in the ancient world; both are connected to fecundity and thus to power. By withholding his semen, a sage not only challenges Indra's power, but he can actually blight the land, unless the king has a greater command over the powers of fertility or can command the auspicious powers of a beautiful and fertile woman.[35]

Devadāsī means "servant of god," a title given to women who, as children, were dedicated to temples, where they became the wives of the temple's presiding god and were trained to sing and dance for him. They were human embodiments of the *apsarās*, known for their beauty and musical talents.[36] Though sexually active, they, too, remained childless; they were never mothers. The *devadāsīs* belonged to the god, but through them, and through the ubiquitous images of *apsarās* in temples,[37] human men could glimpse the heavenly reward that awaited them if they were heroic in battle or strict in their spiritual practice.

Given that the gods are immortal, *devadāsīs* could never become widows; they were *nityasumaṃgalī*, forever auspicious. As such they were able to bestow their excess of auspiciousness on others, and they participated in rituals focused on renewal, fertility, regeneration, and rebirth.[38]

Apsarās linger at the margins of womanhood—a select, divine, and immortal group who are beautiful, talented, sexually assertive, and appear to be independent. They meet sages by traveling alone through the wild forests to the sages' retreats. Because they belong to no man—they have neither fathers nor husbands—they can say and do things not allowed to mortal women. In some texts, though, they are said to be married to or to be the mistresses of the *gandharvas*, equally ambivalent male deities who are the heavenly musicians who play while the *apsarās* dance and sing.[39] A hymn from the *Atharva Veda* that emphasizes their ambivalence and their sexuality is actually a spell to drive away *apsarās* and *gandharvas*, whom it accuses of sexually preying on innocent men and women. The last stanza states, "The Apsaras, you know, are your wives; ye, the Gandharvas, are their husbands. Speed away, ye immortals, do not go after mortals!" (IV.37). In this hymn, Maurice Winternitz sees the *apsarās* and *gandharvas* as succubi and incubi.[40]

Apsarās also personify the wives of Kāma, the god of love, who are called the *ādhis*, or "the yearnings."[41] However, when *apsarās* appear alone, they are represented as sexually available women. This idea is connected to the story of their creation. Long ago, the gods were threatened by a powerful group of demons, and they appealed to the great god Viṣṇu to save them. Viṣṇu helped them to create *amṛta*, the drink of immortality, which would make them stronger than the demons. He did this by having them churn the ocean, from whose depths arose not only *amṛta* but many beneficial things and beings, including the *apsarās*.[42] The *Rāmāyaṇa* adds that no one would take them as wives, so they were called *sādāraṇā*,[43] or "common to all." It emphasizes this point when the demon king Rāvaṇa rapes the *apsarā* Rambhā. When Rāvaṇa comes across her walking alone in the forest, she pleads with him, saying she is married to his nephew. Rāvaṇa rapes her anyway, saying,

"For those who have but one husband, this argument is valid but in Devaloka [the realm of the gods], the Gods have established a law that is said to be eternal, that Apsaras have no appointed consorts."[44]

Apsarās confer the blessings of fertility in epic literature when they appear dancing and singing in the sky above weddings, such as that of Rāma and Sītā,[45] and at the birth festivals of famous heroes.[46] Urvaśī's child is proof of the blessings of fertility that *apsarās* can confer, and her story was told in a conversation hymn (*ākhyāna*), a type of hymn associated with fertility. Wendy Doniger O'Flaherty suggests such hymns may have been part of a ritual performance involving actors and dancers which was intended to promote fertility,[47] just as plays featuring courtesans were performed during spring fertility festivals to help promote the fruitfulness of humans, animals, and crops.[48]

IN BUDDHISM

Apsarās were one of the many aspects of South Asian culture and religious thought that were incorporated into the earliest Buddhist beliefs,[49] and they are present in all forms of Buddhism. Unlike Hinduism, Buddhism rarely emphasizes individual *apsarās*; for the most part they are nameless, often appearing in groups, which keeps them firmly in the background of male Buddhist experience, where they remain on call either to serve as expressions of female turpitude, or to sing and dance for the spiritual victory of mostly male saints, as when the Buddha achieved enlightenment,[50] and when he preached his first sermon. Such roles do tell us something about the overall development of the *apsarā*.

Buddhist saints are thought of as heroic; they have won a great victory by conquering their passions and piercing the veil of illusion that traps all beings in this earthly realm. The Sanskrit word *vīra*, "hero," is used to describe brave warriors and Buddhist men who achieve enlightenment; hence they share the hero's reward of *apsarās*, though for different ends. As on the memorial stones of martial heroes, *apsarās* are depicted in Buddhist art and literature hovering over great saints when they preach, expressing the heavenly joy of their conquest of this illusory world. In this context, the sexuality of *apsarās* is played down in favor of their general auspiciousness.

Because of their beauty and powers, *apsarās* were widely used in the decoration of Buddhist and Hindu temples and sanctuaries in Southeast Asia.[51] In Buddhist Tibet they appear in cloth paintings (*thangkas*), where they are often depicted floating on clouds either above the four gates of *maṇḍalas*,[52] or as participants in assemblies of human and divine beings connected to a particular teaching lineage, where they frame the central group.[53] They were painted and carved throughout Buddhist East Asia as well, sometimes in surprising venues, as in a bas-relief on the bronze bell of King Seong-deog of Korea, cast in 711,[54] or as a Japanese ivory netsuke (Figure 6.3).[55] An overabundance of *apsarās* decorates the painted caves of Dun Huang, on the Silk Road in northwestern China.[56] Some of most charming images of *apsarās* come from the royal fifth-century CE mountain site of Sigiriya, in Sri Lanka, which contains the remains of innumerable paintings of *apsarās*.[57] For centuries, pilgrims visited this site and wrote poems to the *apsarās* on the walls beneath their images, such as the following:

Ladies like you
Make men pour out their hearts
And you also have thrilled the body
Making its hair
Stiffen with desire.[58]

Seductresses

Seduction stories were as popular among Buddhists as among Hindus,[59] and the Buddhists used similar scenarios, most famously when the demonic god Māra

FIGURE 6.3 A netsuke carved as an *apsarā* (*tennin*) carrying a musical instrument.
Courtesy of the Division of Anthropology, American Museum of Natural History.

attempts to prevent the Buddha's enlightenment by sending his *apsarā*-like daughters to seduce the Buddha. In these scenarios, *apsarās* are embodiments of pure sexuality, and human "seductresses" are unfavorably compared to them. Like Indra, Māra has a bevy of seductive beauties at his command to undermine the spiritual power of a male ascetic. Māra rules over the realm of desire—this earthly realm—and Buddhists assert that it is desire that keeps us chained to the wheel of becoming, which draws us endlessly to death and rebirth, again and again. By successfully rejecting desire and by entering the meditative state that will lead to his enlightenment, the Buddha is about to break free of Māra's realm, never again to be reborn. Māra must oppose this challenge to his sovereignty, so, like Indra, he sends beautiful women to seduce the celibate sage. Of course, they fail to seduce the Buddha, but stories in which seduction fails served several purposes; the encounter between ascetic and seductress is often a literary device to highlight the ascetic's control of his sexuality. They also serve as warnings of the dangers of sexuality to male spiritual power and define women as sexual temptresses. For the most part, early Buddhist texts were under the control of monks committed to celibacy among whom seduction stories proliferated. They tended to focus on women as temptresses and on failed seductions, emphasizing the oppositions of *dharma* and *kāma*, religious obligation and pleasure, where dharma is clearly associated with men and pleasure with women.[60]

Another well-known story about women trying to seduce the Buddha once again has women acting at the behest of a powerful male figure who wants to prevent the Buddha from obtaining enlightenment. In Aśvaghoṣa's *Buddhacarita*, one of the earliest full-length biographies of the Buddha (c. beginning of the Common Era), the Buddha asks his father's permission to leave home in order to pursue the life of an ascetic. Instead, his father, King Śuddhodana, commands his guards to prevent this, and he also orders the women of the harem, whom the text repeatedly compares to *apsarās*, to use their beauty and sexuality to distract the Buddha.[61] Udāyin, the Buddha's friend, is part of this conspiracy, and he takes the Buddha to a pleasure grove filled with harem women, whom he has instructed in the art of seduction. Udāyin encourages them by saying, "You could make even lust-free seers waver, and captivate even gods who are accustomed to the Apsarases" (iv.11). Later in the same scene, the text says, "In that lovely grove he [the Buddha] shone with the women in attendance on him, like Vivasvat surrounded by Apsarases" (iv.28).[62] The women act out page after page of sexual ensnarement, such as stumbling against the Buddha, whispering in his ear, letting their garments slip, and so on[63]—all ploys used by *apsarās* in their seduction episodes.

The harem women are a nameless collective, partly because they are meant to represent all women; but in reality they represent only one aspect of woman—the sexual seductress. The harem women, like the *apsarās* they imitate, are not individuals; they are the ocean in which men's spiritual hopes may founder.[64]

The later Mahāyāna school of Buddhism also plays with seduction tales. In a widely known Mahāyāna text, the *Vimalakīrti Sutra*, composed between the first century BCE and second century CE,[65] Māra attempts to seduce a Buddhist saint, the bodhisattva Jagatīṃdhara, by disguising himself as the god Indra and offering him the gift of 12,000 *apsarās*. Appropriately, at least from the Buddhist point of view, the demon god of the realm of desire is said to have *apsarās* at his command. A more spiritually advanced Buddhist (called a bodhisattva), Vimalakīrti, sees through the subterfuge and tells Māra to give the *apsarās* to him. He then proceeds to teach them about enlightenment. Māra decides he wants them back, but the *apsarās* protest, saying they prefer the teachings of the Buddha to the pleasures of desire. Māra, however, challenges Vimalakīrti's right to them by saying that a bodhisattva must give away all his possessions, so the women are returned to him. Before leaving, they ask Vimalakīrti how they should live in Māra's desire realm. Vimalakīrti tells them to teach others about enlightenment.[66] Once again, Māra's use of women fails.

Around the same time, another story was told about the *apsarā* Alambusā in the *Alambusā Jātaka*,[67] a past-life story. This story is said to have been told after one of the Buddha's monks was seduced by his former wife.[68] The Buddha explains that in a past life the monk was a great ascetic who threatened the power of Indra, who, of course, orders the beautiful *apsarā* Alambusā to seduce him. But she is reluctant to do so, calling it a "hateful task,"[69] and pointing out that there are many other *apsarās* who could do it. Indra insists that she must be the one to carry out the seduction because she possesses the greatest of women's wiles (*itthikuttavilāsehi*): she is a master of deceit.[70] For example, when the ascetic is so astonished by her beauty that he cannot move, she runs away from him ever so slowly, which prompts him to action: he catches and passionately embraces her. He spends three years with her, thinking it is only a day. Finally, he recalls his father's warning against women and recovers himself.

Alambusā is now afraid of him and asks for forgiveness, which he grants, and she mounts a golden chariot to fly back to heaven, where Indra is so pleased with her that he offers her whatever she wants. She asks to be released from having to seduce an ascetic ever again. Even though she repents her unwilling actions, thereby revealing some spiritual feeling, the second part of the *jātaka* tale still emphasizes the evil, seductive nature of women by having her reborn as a human being. According to the law of karma, even the gods' good karma—and apparently that of *apsarās*, too—will eventually wear out, causing them to fall into lower rebirths as human beings. Thus Alambusā is reborn as a wife whose husband became a monk, and despite all her previous good intentions, she seduces him.

Apsarās thus play two roles in Buddhism: as celebrants in the victories of male Buddhist celibates; and as threats to that celibacy. In the *Saundarānanda,* the Buddha uses their seductive appeal to turn his half-brother to celibacy.

The Saundarānanda

According to early Buddhist tradition, the Buddha was never one to shirk from using women as a teaching device,[71] as in the sophisticated and beautifully written epic about the Buddha's half-brother Nanda, the *Saundarānanda.*[72] It was composed around the beginning of the Common Era by Aśvaghoṣa, the learned Buddhist monk who also wrote the *Buddhacarita.* The *Saundarānanda* was an extremely popular story, translated into many languages and widely depicted throughout Asia.[73] The story revolves around the relationship of Nanda, who is so handsome that he is called Nanda the Fair (*Saundarānanda*), and his equally beautiful wife, Sundarī. They are madly in love. Indeed, they are so involved with each other that they do not hear the Buddha when he arrives on his daily round of begging for alms. When Nanda learns of this lack of hospitality and respect for his older brother, he is terribly upset and runs after the Buddha, though all the while looking longingly back toward his wife. The Buddha leads Nanda to his community of celibate monks and nuns and has him initiated into that group. In this way Nanda ends up among the monks, as a monk, but a reluctant one,[74] given that he never ceases longing for his beautiful wife.

In an attempt to free Nanda from Sundarī's charms, the Buddha flies with him to Indra's heaven. On the way they see an ugly, one-eyed female monkey, and the Buddha asks Nanda whether Sundarī, who is said to be as beautiful as an *apsarā* (VI.3), is more beautiful than the monkey, to which Nanda emphatically answers yes (X.15–17). Once in Indra's heaven Nanda is overwhelmed by its beauty, lack of disease, and luxurious living. Then the *apsarās* begin to surround him:

> They were ever young, ever busied in love alone and enjoyed jointly by those who have earned merit; [as] celestial beings, union with them was no sin. In them centered the reward of the divine world for past austerities.
>
> Some of them sang softly and proudly, some pulled lotuses to pieces for sport; others again danced because of their pleasure in each other with varied gesticulations, their pearl necklaces thrown into disorder by their breasts.

The faces of some with dangling earrings peeped from out of the forest glades, as lotus flowers, shaken by *kāraṇḍava* birds, peep out from the scattered leaves of the plants.

As Nanda saw them come out from the forest like lightning banners from a cloud, his body trembled with passion like moonlight trembling on rippling water.[75]

The Buddha then asks Nanda to compare them to Sundarī, and Nanda answers that the difference between them and his wife is just as great as that between her and the ugly monkey. His wife is completely forgotten as his ardent desire for the *apsarās* grows, and he begs the Buddha to help him obtain them. The Buddha explains that they can only be won by strenuous austerities. This is, after all, Indra's heaven, to which spiritual heroes go upon death, and where they are rewarded with *apsarās*.

Buddha and Nanda return to earth, and Nanda devotes himself to ascetic practices in order to ultimately reach this heaven and those divine women. This being a Buddhist story, however, he slowly comes to understand that even heavenly pleasures are transitory—that having obtained entry to heaven through his austere practices, his time there will run out and he will be reborn on earth. After further instruction by the Buddha, he is a changed man. He retires into the forest, devotes himself to meditation, and achieves enlightenment (XVII). His wife, Sundarī, does not appear again in the story. Her role was to hold a man back, and the Buddha's was to break that role by using other women—namely, the *apsarās*.

The *Saundarānanda* maintains the ancient South Asia idea of aerial females as especially dangerous to ascetic men, who are frequently referred to as *vīras* (heroes), a term formerly used for warriors in Sanskrit, but the danger of war has now been converted into a stimulus toward salvation. *Apsarās* goad Buddhist ascetics' desire to obtain them, but once they achieve enlightenment the ascetics are carried beyond desire. Their ancient role of transforming heroic men into immortals is redefined through the Buddhist goal of going beyond the gods and immortality into *nirvana*, nonexistence.

These incredibly beautiful, irresistible, and sexualized women, while distinctly South Asian, are clearly related to Valkyries and *hourīs* in their capacity to reward fallen warriors with immortality and sexual pleasure—a linking of aerial females with war that we have seen in ancient winged goddesses of love and war. In the next chapter we will see some intriguing physical evidence for the belief in divine aerial women.

7

Yoginīs and *Ḍākinīs*: Enabling Male Immortality, Part 2

LIKE FLOCKS OF BIRDS, *yoginīs* and *ḍākinīs* often appear in groups as they fly through the air. For the most part they are nameless and lack individuality, though there are lists of *yoginī* names, and individual named *ḍākinīs* can appear to adepts. Contradictions abound among them: elusive beings who are often conflated with one another, they escape neat definition, even as to the question of whether they are divine, demonic, or human.[1] Despite their differences, *yoginīs* and *ḍākinīs* are both examined in this chapter, within the Hindu Tantric context and the Buddhist Tantric context, respectively, where they receive their fullest expositions.

TANTRA

Tantra developed as a religious movement in India beginning about the fourth century CE; though its earliest history is unclear,[2] we know it drew extensively on preexisting traditions such as yoga, Vedic sacrifice, rituals of sexual union, sorcery, and tribal practices.[3] Both Hindu and Buddhist Tantra began as marginal religious practices among wandering *yogīs* who often frequented cremation grounds[4] and experienced metaphysical ritual journeys in which they met and subdued deities and demons in order to gain their powers (*siddhas*), including the ability to fly. Tantra is described as a fast path to enlightenment (in a single lifetime), and one of its essential features is an abundance of female symbolism

and deities,[5] and the incorporation of divine, demonic, and human females called
yoginīs and *ḍākinīs*.

Hindu and Buddhist Tantric rituals were often performed at night in cemeteries, presumed to be the favorite haunts of bloodthirsty, nonhuman *yoginīs*
and *ḍākinīs* who could either terrify or confer supernatural powers on intrepid
devotees.[6] Their rituals are described in *tantras*—sacred, often revealed texts,
composed by both Hindu and Buddhist Tantric groups, that emphasize sexual
practices (whether actual or visualized), the use of human skulls, alcohol and
meat, song and dance,[7] descriptions of sacred sites for their practice,[8] and the
overpowering of deities and spirits in order to bend them to one's will. In Tantra,
the lines between religious traditions are often blurred,[9] as are the boundaries between human and divine, since Tantra affirms—indeed emphasizes—the
divine potential of human beings. (Tantric practices will be discussed more below
and in chapter 11).

YOGINĪS

Yoginī is a term used for a variety of female beings. It is the feminine form of
the masculine noun *yogī* and thus can refer to human women who practice nonTantric yoga, or to those who practice Tantra or sorcery, as well as divine and
demonic beings.[10] The last three categories are believed to be capable of flight.
They appear in groups connected to Śiva, among other deities both Hindu and
Buddhist. Varieties of their cult flourished from the ninth to the twelfth centuries
throughout central India[11] and continued in some places into the early sixteenth
century, after which the cult and its temples were for the most part abandoned,[12]
though in the twenty-first century practicing *tantrikas* still exist and local people
remain in awe of divine *yoginīs*.[13] Additionally, Indo-Muslim rulers sought their
favor for successful military actions,[14] although their depictions of *yoginīs* were
markedly more subdued.[15]

More usually, *yoginīs* appeared as wild, half-naked, devouring aerial females who
consumed the sexual fluids or flesh of their human victims, while at other times
they are described as bestowing blessings and supernatural powers (*siddhas*). As
noted in chapter 1, from the most ancient times in India certain divine females
have been regarded as beings whose curses were feared and blessings were sought.
These include the ancient bird goddesses and the village goddesses (*grāma devatās*)
that abound throughout India.[16] The fear they inspired undoubtedly helped the
yoginī cult remain a well-guarded secret—so much so that the *yoginī* temple in
Hirapur, Orissa, was not known to the general public until 1953.[17]

Yoginī *Temples*

The most dramatic element of the *yoginī* cult is its circular and roofless temple style (Figure 7.1).[18] These structures are unique in South Asian religious architecture, which is predominantly roofed.[19] The openness of *yoginī* temples to the sky not only evokes magical flight; it is material evidence that the ritual interactions between human and divine *yoginīs* and male adepts involved belief in the ability of human adepts to ascend to heaven and of divine *yoginīs* to descend to earth. In summarizing his findings from the textual descriptions of how these temples should be built and drawing on the archaeological evidence, Michael Rabe writes, "[H]omologies are presupposed between the physical space and forms of temple architecture, the divine order of the universe, and a mapping of the individual worshipper's subtle body[20]—or more simply, between the macro- and microcosmos: as it is in heaven, so may it be on earth."[21] In their architectural distinction, *yoginī* temples exemplify this view. At the same time, they reflect the *maṇḍalas*, sacred circles created for worship and initiation, described in the *yoginī tantras*.[22]

FIGURE 7.1 Inner wall of Chausaṭh Yoginī Temple, built between 975 and 1025, Bheraghat, India. The wall is eight feet high, with eighty-one niches for life-size *yoginīs*. Dehejia comments that the eighty-one niches have "not particularly disturbed scholars who continue to refer to Bheraghat as a Caunsaṭh or Sixty-four Yoginī temple," *Yoginī* 125.

Photograph by the author.

The Hirapur temple, dating from perhaps as early as the ninth century,[23] is a telling example of the relationship between astral phenomena and the uniqueness of the round, hypaethral (unroofed) *yoginī* temples. Heinrich von Stietencron argues, quite convincingly and supported by detailed diagrams, that its structure represents the ability to coordinate solar and lunar (ritual) time,[24] with the *yoginīs* representing the *nakṣatras* (the lunar mansions). A circle of *yoginīs* is enshrined into the round temple walls in relation to the *Kālacakra,* thereby allowing rituals enacted by human participants (*yoginīs* and their consorts) at astronomically appropriate times to celebrate the harmony of the cosmos within themselves.

A recently discovered twelfth-century CE text glorifying the ancient city of Vārāṇasī as a pilgrimage site describes a roofless *yoginī* temple found there. The text describes rituals performed within it that reveal the roofless temple's function. The rituals are linked to astral phenomena such as the waxing and waning of the moon, when Śiva was believed to descend in the form of the moon during *Mārgaśīrṣa* (November–December), and the requirement in the month of *Vaiśākha* (April–May) that practitioners worship Śiva all night so that at daybreak they will achieve union with him. Further, the text describes the relationship between the *Khecarīcakra* (Circle of Sky-Travelers), presumably the one installed at the site in a circle of stone figures (*yoginīs*), and the heavenly *Khecarīcakra,* that adepts can see in the sky, which is the subject of so many Indian narratives about encounters with *yoginīs.* For those who can see the *Khecarīcakra* in the sky, "the bond of *saṃsāra* has been cut"[25]—that is, liberation has been achieved. There are also descriptions of night festivals of song and dance that culminate in dawn worship of the circle of *yoginīs* to obtain their esoteric knowledge.[26]

Yoginī temples are usually found on the tops of hills, further adding to their emphasis on the sky, and in remote areas that are difficult to reach, which helped the *yoginī* cult to remain hidden. In striking contrast to the majority of elaborately carved exteriors of Indian temples, the outer walls of *yoginī* temples, which might only be eight feet high, were usually completely devoid of decoration. The inner circular walls usually had niches adorned with life-sized sculptures that depicted the *yoginīs* as seminude yet bejeweled women, carrying various auspicious and inauspicious implements, and some having bird and animal heads (like prehistoric goddesses) or seated on animals that act as their vehicles, such as the statues from the Chausaṭh Yoginī Temple, which was built between 975 and 1025 (Figures 7.1 and 7.2). Vandals or iconoclasts have damaged many of its statues. Its outer wall is about ten feet high and the inner wall about eight feet high with a diameter of 125 feet.[27]

Where the statues are missing, it is generally assumed that they have been carried off, but Michael Rabe has suggested that, instead of holding statues, the empty

FIGURE 7.2 The *yoginī* Śrī Ṭhākinī with flower offering, Chausaṭh Yoginī Temple, Bheraghat, India.
Photograph by the author.

niches may have been the places for living women to stand and participate in rituals, particularly those designed to secure military victories.[28] The *yoginī* cult received generous support from Hindu royal families who were besieged by Muslim factions during the medieval period[29] because, like *apsarā*s, Valkyries, and Nikes, they could confer military prowess. The *Silpa Parkāśa*, an eleventh-century Tantric text on Hindu architecture, describes the drawing and empowering of the *yoginī yantra* (a magical drawing) in which the king participated. At the conclusion of this stage of construction the text says: "Thus the king's aspirations for victory are fulfilled."[30] As already mentioned, Indo-Islamic rulers were quick to follow suit in appealing to these deities.

Practices and Stories

Yoginī cult practices are not so esoteric as Tantric rites were and are performed to gain advantages that can be used for worldly as well as spiritual ends. Aristocrats, warriors, and the politically ambitious were and remain participants in Tantric rituals.[31] A connection is made between *yoginīs* and the conferring of sovereignty in a set of oral tales going back to perhaps the fourth century CE and anonymously compiled in the thirteenth century as the *Simhāsana Dvātrimsīkā* ("The Thirty-Two Tales of the Royal Throne").[32] These tales are about a fabled king, Vikramaditya, and his magic throne, which is supported by thirty-two statuettes of divine women (*surāṅganā*). The throne is said to have been buried after Vikramaditya died and later dug up by King Bhoja (r. c. 1018–1055 CE), who repeatedly tries to ascend it but is thwarted by the thirty-two statuettes, which come alive one by one to tell a story about King Vikramaditya's virtues. Though they are not specifically called *yoginīs*, the number thirty-two (half of sixty-four, their more usual numerical grouping) evokes them, and some of their names appear in the *yoginī* names lists collected by Vidya Dehejia.[33] In iconography and literature, *yoginīs* were gathered into potent numerical groupings that were believed to enhance their individual powers. Additionally, in the twenty-first story, King Bhoja goes to the city of *yoginīs* (*yoginīpura*),[34] where he is given magical powers by eight *yoginīs* (a base number of thirty-two and sixty-four).

A further example of the *yoginīs'* connection to sovereignty comes from the twelfth-century *Rājataraṅginī*, which tells the story of a Kashmiri royal minister, Sandhimati, who was wrongfully accused of treason and put to death on a stake. Wild wolves fed on his body, reducing it to a skeleton, until one night a group of divine *yoginīs* arrived, put him back together, and recalled his spirit back to his body. Each *yoginī* then had sex with him; in yogic parlance they consumed his sexual fluids. Subsequently, he was made king, which meant the *yoginīs* repaid his sexual offering with kingship. David White succinctly sums up the intricate parts of this story:

Like Osiris by Isis in Egyptian mythology, he is given new life by these Yoginīs through their mending of him. Yet who was it who had torn apart and devoured his lifeless body in the first place? The wolves that haunt cremation grounds are but animal forms of the same shape-changing Yoginīs, who are very frequently portrayed as the wolf's female cousins—she-jackals (*śivās*). Having enjoyed him as food and thereby devoured his mortal body, they put him back together again in order to enjoy him a second time, as a source of sexual pleasure.[35]

The story describes magical-religious activities involving sexuality, shape-shifting, cannibalism, and death, followed by regeneration and the gift of sovereignty, a not insignificant earthly empowerment (*siddhi*).

Sexual Yoga

Yoginīs (and, as we will see, *ḍākinīs*) represent a well-known theme in world religion and mythology, that of a male's dependence on a female guide in order to complete his quest, win his goal, or achieve enlightenment.[36] Wisdom (*prajñā*) is a feminine term in South Asian languages as well as in the languages of other religious traditions, and it is frequently personified by divine women whose aid must be won in order to succeed in gaining spiritual knowledge or power.[37] In all these cases they serve male aims, which is made explicit through the practice of sexual yoga.[38] Through them (and through *ḍākinīs*, for Buddhists) is illustrated to the fullest articulation thus far of the purpose of sexuality between aerial women and human men. In Hinduism, sexual yoga is represented by images of the goddess Kālī astride the prone and dead figure of Śiva, the *liṅgam* (penis) placed in the *yoni* (vagina) (Figure 7.3), the Śrī Yantra, and other portrayals of divine beings in sexual union.[39] These images express the oneness of the two necessary elements for the generation of liberation: energy/power (*Śakti*, an active female principle), and consciousness (Śiva, a passive male principle),[40] sexually joined together on the plane of ultimate reality. Thus Tantra needs sexually active females—real or envisioned, human or divine—to enact its rituals and appear in its iconography.

Sexual yoga reverses orthodox sexuality, in which the female partner absorbs the sexual fluids of the male. This reversal underscores the point that Tantric sexual activity is not about normal, biological procreation, but rather about procreating the energy that will lead to liberation. It does not produce life; rather, it produces the cessation of life through liberation. In this it participates fully in the Tantric emphasis on practicing in places connected to death, such as cremation grounds. Like many of the aerial women examined thus far, *yoginīs* (and *ḍākinīs*), while sexual, are not meant to be mothers. They only give birth to male empowerment.

Tantric Hindu initiates sought worldly or spiritual powers as well as bodily immortality (*jīvanmukti*) through direct sexual encounters with divine *yoginīs*. Rituals were established to draw them down from the sky into human *yoginīs*, who were the Tantric consorts of male adepts. In other words, human *yoginīs* became possessed by the divine *yoginīs*, and roofless, circular temples were constructed to enable their easy descent.[41] Just as female practitioners were believed to be possessed by the divine *yoginīs*, the male adepts (*siddhas*) were similarly believed to be possessed by divine *siddhas*.[42] Unlike Buddhist rituals of

FIGURE 7.3 *Yoni* and *liṅgam*, c. ninth century CE, Pancesvara Temple, Gujarat, India.
Photograph: American Institute of Indian Studies.

sexual yoga, in which the male does not ejaculate,[43] these male adepts would offer the *yoginī*s their semen, for which the *yoginī*s exchanged their own sexual discharge. The sexual discharge of the *yoginī* was understood to be the divine fluid of the universe, and receiving it was the point of the ritual.[44] For her part, the female consort "gained raw materials necessary for her refinement of the high energy fuel that powered her flight,"[45] flight being one of the goals of female and male devotees alike.

The basic idea is that men fed *yoginī*s the bodily constituents they craved, sometimes including their own blood,[46] while the *yoginī*s shared their sexual fluids and conferred *siddhi*.[47] Much of the *yoginī* cult is about obtaining magical power here and now,[48] though this did not preclude spiritual powers.[49]

There are several stories dating from the medieval period that describe human *yoginī*s who gathered together in groups numbering multiples of eight to perform rituals involving the consumption of liquor and the sacrifice of human beings, usually men, in order to gain the power of flight. An eighth-century play by Bhavabhūti, the *Mālatīmādhava*, depicts the *yoginī* Kapālakuṇḍalā, who is the consort of a Tantric practitioner.[50] It is of some interest that her part would probably have been played by a woman, thereby concretizing the existence of such women, as Indian classical theater utilized both women and men as actors. In the play, Kapālakuṇḍalā is flying to a cremation ground to meet her consort. As she flies onto the stage she describes herself:

The swiftness of my flight along the surface of the sky gives to me in the amplest measure a charming frightfulness, with the harsh bells [of my neck-lace] ringing in consequence of the garland of skulls striking against them, as it slips down in the winging movement.

The mass of my matted locks [of an ascetic], though firmly secured by knots, yet streams loosely on every side; the bell attached to my staff moving circui-tously produces a piercing sound prolonged by incessant tinkling; and the vio-lent wind howling through the hollows of the line of the bare skulls of corpses, and causing the continuous pealing of bells, flutters my banners upwards.[51]

She is about to perform a ritual with her consort during which they will consume human flesh.

There is a clear connection between the power of flight and the consumption of human flesh in the medieval period.[52] Somadeva (eleventh century) relates several stories on this topic. In one, a heavenly woman, called a *vidyādharī*, is captured by an ascetic when he takes her clothes while she is swimming. In this typical swan maiden/*apsarā* story, she is forced to live with him until she gives birth to a child. There is a twist, though, to this tale. Before leaving him she says that if he wants to see her again, he must cook and eat the child. He does this and is immediately able to fly up to heaven after her.[53] In another tale from this collection a witch (*śākinī*) says that supernatural powers such as flying arise from eating human flesh (II:103–105 and 112–113).

Other stories circulated during this period said that *yoginīs*, conflated with witches, could transform men into animals by tying magical strings around their necks.[54] Somadeva tells of a man changed into a monkey by such a spell (III.191–193).[55] In this way, the *yoginīs* held men captive and would only turn them back into men when they wanted to have sex with them. Overall, in medieval literature human *yoginīs* are presented as drunken, dangerous, sexually voracious eaters of human flesh who have magical powers and who can shape-shift into birds or fly on their own.[56] In some cases Indian folklore describes them as virtuous women by day and wild furies by night.[57]

Dehejia argues that human sacrifice was not part of the *yoginī* cult, even though corpses were used in cult rituals. This, of course, fits with the Tantric propensity to perform rituals in cemeteries. Part of the *yoginīs*' cult involved sitting on a corpse while practicing ritual breathing, performing sexual yoga on a corpse, ritually cut-ting off its head, or eating its flesh.[58] Human and divine *yoginīs* are often portrayed flying on enlivened corpses or skulls, a possible reference to the many images of Kālī straddling Śiva's corpse to enliven him. Whatever the case may be, we once again see connections between aerial women and death.

In other literature, however, the *yoginīs* are described as "self-propelled, flying through the air under their own power."[59] David White tells us that "there was a notion in the medieval period that women had, in some way, a natural propensity for flight that was absent in men, as a statement from the twelfth-century alchemical text *Kākacaṇḍeśvarīmata* clearly implies: 'I will now speak of other female aviators who move through the heavens. Difficult of attainment for all women, how much more must it (i.e., the power of flight) be for a man!'"[60] This may be connected to ideas about the subtle body, as several yogic and Tantric works state that, unlike men's, women's flow through the channels of the subtle body is constant and strong.[61]

Divine *yoginīs* are generally understood to belong to the retinue of Śiva in his fierce form Bhairava, where they are wild, blood-drinking female spirits who, like Kapālakuṇḍalā, wear human skulls as ornaments and fly through the air.[62] Some legends trace their origins to goddesses, such as Kālī just after she conquered the demon Mahākālā,[63] or Durgā after killing the demon Mahiṣa, or Pārvatī (Śiva's wife) while she was practicing asceticism. They have also been variously traced back to the *mātṛkās* ("the mothers"—seven, later eight, unpredictable goddesses who sometimes kill but at other times protect children),[64] to Śakti,[65] and to village cults, each of which had its own goddess (*grāma devatā*) who, though generally hot-tempered and unpredictable, protected the village.[66] The archaeological evidence reflects this varied background, as some *yoginī* temples have Durgā or Kālī as the central deity,[67] while others have Śiva.[68] *Yoginīs* elude categorization, yet they were consistently perceived by their devotees as all-powerful goddesses.

Taming

Yoginīs are clearly associated with death, sexuality, and the granting of both spiritual and earthly powers; they are unpredictable beings whose good will may be obtained through proper offerings and rituals. As they are absorbed into Tantric practices, male adepts seek to control these divine women for different purposes and through various means. This begins with the *yoginī tantras*, in which Hindus and Buddhists alike first domesticated them and then incorporated them into mainstream practice.[69] The literature also reflects this gendered shift of power. Paul Dundas has translated part of a seventeenth-century Jain hagiographic collection that describes a Jain adept neutralizing the power of the sixty-four *yoginīs* and bringing them under his will by instructing a disciple to place sixty-four mats on the ground as offerings to sixty-four *yoginīs* disguised as laywomen as they stood in the southern direction (the inauspicious region of death) and wore the white clothes of widows (reiterating their association with death).

Once they sat on the mats he recited powerful mantras, and through his superior powers they remained pinned to the ground and had to grant him several concessions.[70]

Very little is known about the human *yoginīs* who were involved in sexual practices, but Alexis Sanderson's research into the early Śaiva (or Śiva tradition) Tantric texts and practices from around 400 to 800 CE sheds some light on them. To begin with, pregnancies could result from these practices, and the daughters born from such unions were considered divine from birth. *Yogīs* recruited girls who lived in the vicinity where such ceremonies took place. They were probably poor or low-caste girls, either sold or offered by their parents to the *yogīs*. Another group were older, untouchable women—women below or outside the caste system.[71] These women were powerless in the mundane world, while in a ritual context they were all-powerful. The idea was for men to manifest the fiercest forms of feminine power, propitiate and co-opt it, and then to disempower and de-divinize the human women who embodied it by ending the ritual context.[72]

ḌĀKINĪS

In their most ancient form, Indian *ḍākinīs* were known as malevolent and dangerous flying demonesses or witches who could inflict all kinds of suffering on humanity.[73] They haunted cemeteries, where they fed on the human flesh that gave them the power to fly.[74] To a large extent, they remain in this guise in Hinduism, where they are cannibalistic members of the retinues of the goddesses Śakti and Kālī, as well as that of Śiva in his fierce form, known as Bhairava. South Asian witches, who can be alive or dead, are also believed to congregate secretly at night in cemeteries, where they are said to consume the blood and flesh of the dead, and where they dance naked with loose hair.[75] *Ḍākinīs* and *yoginīs* are also depicted as practically nude, except for some ornaments.[76] Since witches are female they were easily confused with female Tantric practitioners, some of whom were called *ḍākinīs*, so much so that in Nepali *dakini* can mean witch,[77] while in Orissa, which is famous for its numerous witches, the word for witch is *dahani*, a corruption of *dakini*.[78] Complicating matters further, some female *tantrika*s were and are active sorceresses.[79] In India, the earliest archaeological evidence for the worship of *ḍākinīs* is a stone-tablet inscription, dated to 423 CE, from Gangdhar, which records the building of a temple to the *mātṛkās* and the *ḍākinīs* who are said to accompany them. It describes *ḍākinīs* traveling in groups, being joyous, and banging gongs and says they "are pumped up to the rain clouds (in) the powerful winds raised by the Tantras (in this context, 'ritual practices')."[80]

Given their powers to bless or curse, Tibetan magicians also try to gain power over *ḍākinīs* for their own ends, such as controlling a group of five *ḍākinīs* with vulture heads in order to use them to harm an enemy's flock of sheep. On other occasions they are magically called upon to consume a corpse that has been put out for sky burial,[81] thereby maintaining their ancient connection to, and consumption of, the dead. In a gentler vein, *ḍākinīs* are also said to disguise themselves as pigeons,[82] and one is said to have transformed into a bat.[83] Such shape-shifting into flying creatures brings us to the etymology for *ḍākinī*, one of which is obtained from the Sanskrit root √*di*, or √*dai*, "to fly,"[84] meaning "she who flies," which is similar to the Tibetan translation of *ḍākinī* as *khadoma* (*mKha' 'gro ma*), meaning "she who moves in the air," which is also a colloquial term for bird.[85] We will see that *ḍākinīs* can cross between realms, those of the living and the dead, as well as between species and boundaries of time and space, appearing in visions, in dreams, or in earthly forms.

Subduing

Beliefs about *ḍākinīs* are presented in the vast biographical literature of Tantric Buddhism, such as those of the eighty-four *mahāsiddhas*, who were eighty male and four female[86] wandering Tantric *yogīs* who flourished in northern India between the eighth and twelfth centuries. They were believed to be capable of flying and deeply influenced Tibetan Buddhism. Tantra's origins were outside the great monastic institutions of the period; it began and flourished among wandering *yogīs* from a wide range of social backgrounds, though eventually, in modified form, Tantra became part of the monastic curriculum. *Mahāsiddha* biographies reveal the magical powers these *siddhas* possessed. They constantly interacted with the divine *ḍākinīs* while they were alive, and almost all the biographies end with them going to the Land of the *Ḍākas*,[87] a heaven, in their mortal bodies. Examples include Virūpa, who became so frustrated with his lack of progress in meditation that he threw away his prayer beads, only to have them returned by a *ḍākinī* who then instructed him on his practice; Lūyipa, who received instructions from them, as did Kukkuripa, from a *ḍākinī* disguised as a dog; and Dharmapa, who also received instructions, but through a dream, among other examples.[88] The divine *ḍākinī* Vajrayoginī[89] (Figure 7.4) frequently appears to *siddhas*, especially in Tāranātha's version of their lives.[90] *Ḍākinīs* are frequently shown dancing naked except for their ornaments (often human skulls), and sometimes a scarf floating over their shoulders and under their arms (signifying their ability to fly), with supernatural skin colors. Like most aerial women, they easily shape-shift between human and animal forms, or have human bodies with animal heads,[91] some of which are distinctly fierce in appearance, and they are also believed to reside in the practitioner's body, where they can be awakened by meditational practices.[92] Being initiatory goddesses, they have important salvational roles and also represent wisdom (*prajñā*), which they can bestow along with *siddhis*. The point is that, whether frightening or in disguise, they were all at the service of male adepts to whom they granted teachings and empowerments.

When Tantric Buddhism arrived in Tibet, local goddesses were subdued by powerful *mahāsiddhas* and converted into initiation-granting *ḍākinīs* and guardians of Buddhism. Into the twenty-first century, they continue to have an important

FIGURE 7.4 Vajrayoginī in the form of Khecarī ("the airborne one").
Courtesy of the Division of Anthropology, American Museum of Natural History.

place in Indo-Tibetan texts, iconography, and rituals, as well as in the spiritual lives of individuals. The great *mahāsiddha* Padmasambhava (traditionally, eighth century CE), believed to have brought Buddhism to Tibet, is a well-known subduer of *ḍākinīs*. His biography is full of his encounters with their multiple forms. Like a true *tantrika*, he practiced in many cemeteries, in one of which he saw innumerable *ḍākinīs* riding various animals, brandishing weapons, wearing corpses, and eating corpses or their own intestines. He subdued them all,[93] yet maintained a healthy respect for some of them. One of the most dramatic stories capturing their ability to take adepts beyond death has Padmasambhava visiting a cemetery to gain initiations and teachings from them. Here he meets the highest *ḍākinī*, Sūryacandrasiddhi, and requests teachings. In a refined enactment of the cannibalism associated with *ḍākinīs*, she transforms him into the sacred syllable *hūm*, which she then swallows. While he is inside her body, she confers blessings upon him, and she then gives birth to him.[94] It would be difficult indeed to find a more vivid example of the *ḍākinīs'* power to transform death into eternal life.

Padmasambhava's connection to subdued *ḍākinīs* continues in the Tibetan tradition of *termas* (*gterma*), texts and other treasures he is believed to have hidden that have been discovered over the centuries, up to recent times.[95] Many of these texts are written in what is called *ḍākinī* script, making them inaccessible to the non-initiate. *Ḍākinīs* lead the discoverer to such texts and also help him decode the writing. Frequently they are also the sexual consorts of the discoverers,[96] as they are of other human and divine practitioners; by sexual means they lead their male companions to ultimate understanding.

Like *yoginīs*, *ḍākinīs* also represent the theme, prevalent across world religions and mythology, of males' dependence on female guides to achieve a goal, in this case that of achieving enlightenment.[97] They sometimes serve male aims through the practice of sexual yoga.[98] In Buddhism, sexual yoga is represented iconographically by the *yab yum* couple,[99] mainly divine beings in sexual union. These images express the oneness of the two necessary elements for the generation of enlightenment—wisdom (*prajñā*), a passive female principle,[100] and skillful means (*upāya*), an active male principle[101]—sexually joined together on the plane of ultimate reality. Buddhist Tantra, like Hindu Tantra, needs sexually active females—real or envisioned, human or divine—to enact its rituals and appear in its iconography.

Tantric Buddhist sexual yoga also reverses orthodox sexuality through the prohibition against ejaculation, and thus emphasizes that its goal is not procreation. Sexual union, whether enacted or visualized, involves the belief that women inherently possess something men do not: *prajñā*, that is, "wisdom" or "insight." Male adepts seek to access and appropriate that wisdom through sexual yoga. For female practitioners, men are the source of *upāya* ("skillful means") which they want to appropriate. During sexual union, the adept will lose any spiritual benefit if he ejaculates,[102] so he attempts to absorb his consort's red drops (uterine fluids),[103] mixing them with his white drops (semen), which he then absorbs through his penis (*vajrolī mudrā*) into the subtle body channels leading to the top of the head. Thus, it is a sexual contest, to see who will obtain whose fluids and their benefits.[104]

Tibetan Practitioners

In many Tibetan biographies of Buddhist saints, *ḍākinīs* appear in the sky at the birth of the saint, thereby predicting his or her illustrious future,[105] or they appear in the dreams of future mothers and fathers as portents of a saintly child.[106] As crossing-over deities, symbolized by the rainbow, they not only appear at births— bringing life, as it were—but they also make dramatic appearances at the deaths of great saints, helping them to cross over to the next realm.[107] The pervasiveness of this idea in Tibetan Buddhism is shown in the biography of the beloved poet-saint Milarepa (1040–1123), whose life was filled with encounters with *ḍākinīs*.[108] In it, his disciple Rechungpa has parallel dreams that begin and end the biography. As the biography begins, he dreams he is in the abode of the *ḍākinīs*, a paradise, where five *ḍākinīs* encourage him to ask Milarepa for his life story. At the end of the biography, Rechungpa again dreams of these five *ḍākinīs*, who carry away the relics from Milarepa's cremation.[109] The function of the *ḍākinīs* is to instigate the telling of the biography, to bring it to life, and to end it by carrying away Milarepa's remains. Adelheid Herrmann-Pfandt has shown that, "*ḍākinīs* accompany the adept's life and guide it, so to speak, as forces from within,"[110] even acting as guides during the inter-mediate state (*bar do*) between life and death.[111]

Seringma

Despite the foregoing, some *ḍākinīs* remained unpredictable, and therefore dan-gerous. The five aforementioned *ḍākinīs* originally tried, unsuccessfully, to over-power Milarepa. These five *ḍākinīs* align with the ancient pre-Buddhist mountain deities, the goddess Seringma and her four sisters (*Tshe ring mched lnga*), who usu-ally accompany her.[112] René de Nebesky-Wojkowitz describes each one's skin as a different color: white, yellow, blue, green, and red,[113] representing the rainbow. They are also known as the Five Sisters of Long Life, and they reside on the Himalayan summit of Gaurishankar, known to Tibetans as Jomo Seringma. (*Sering* means "long life" and *ma* is the feminine ending.) It is believed that at the foot of this mountain, there are five glacial lakes consecrated to these goddesses, each with a different color water. Therefore, the Five Sisters are connected to both the greatest heights and lakes, recalling again the swan maidens.

In one of Milarepa's songs, they are described as "five extremely dreadful, wild-looking, flesh-eating female demons who displayed themselves in a number of ugly and ferocious forms." Milarepa refers to them as "the five cannibal demonesses/Who, with abusive language, curse me,/And shout, 'Die you shall, you must!'" Somewhat like Padmasambhava, he offers his body to them as a sacrifice:

This human body, composed of Skandhas [aggregates]
Is transient, mortal, and illusory.
Since in time I must discard it,
He who would, may take it now.[114]

In responding to this offer they shift their position, saying, "The fact that you have no attachment or concern for your body is truly marvelous! We did not come here with so much hatred and determination really to harm you. We came only to test your Realization and understanding" (*Songs* I:302–304). *Ḍākinīs* represent both the accomplishment of enlightenment and the dangers that must be overcome to achieve it, by which they test a spiritual candidate's courage and determination.

The oral tradition relates that Seringma and her sisters were subdued by Padmasambhava, though this event does not appear in his biography.[115] Seringma talks about being subdued by Padmasambhava both in Milarepa's collected poems (*Songs* I:343), and in a Tibetan pilgrim's guide that claims to be a *terma* composed by Padmasambhava, who gave it to her and her sisters to conceal for future genera-tions.[116] This guide focuses primarily on the acts of Padmasambhava and Milarepa in the area of Lapchi and on their interactions with these five *ḍākinīs*.

By this point in the oral tradition, although Seringma and her sisters maintain their shape-shifting abilities and occasional wrathful appearance, they are now in the service of Buddhism, so much so that at one point during their exchange Milarepa addresses Seringma:

Queen of Heaven.
Oh cruel Lady Tserinma of the Snow Lakes,
Your hair is decked with the mountain snow;
Embroidered on your skirt in all their beauty,
Are the verdant fields of Medicine Valley.[117]

Seringma can also be translated as "she [who can grant] long life," a fact empha-sized by the display on her skirt of Medicine Valley, a place where therapeutic medicinal herbs grow and are gathered. This contrast with her initially malevolent character is strengthened further when they all make offerings to Milarepa, each one giving him a particular supernatural power. Seringma gives him the ability of "protecting and increasing one's progeny," revealing her connection with fertility. The remaining four *ḍākinīs* give him similar powers regarding fertility and prosperity: "refilling a storehouse with jewels . . . winning food and prosperity . . . [and] increasing livestock." The fifth one gives him the power to divine with a mirror—that is, the ability to see the future[118]—calling to mind the Norns, who spin the thread of life and see into the future.

Another telling incident is contained in a pilgrimage guide to Lapchi, the place in Tibet where Milarepa is said to have met with Seringma and her sisters. It contains an additional story in which Seringma, despite her healing powers, becomes deathly ill and sends for Milarepa to heal her, which he does. Without irony, he prolongs the life of this *ḍākinī* of long life through a ritual. He then instructs her in Buddhist teachings and takes her as his "ritual sex consort. Thus, as she was the chief [of all the deities] and was now under his power, all the celestial heroes and . . . [*ḍākinīs*] of the region of Lapchi perforce came under his power and were bound by oath."[119] Seringma's story depicts the thoroughgoing and heavy-handed demonizing and eventual subduing of indigenous deities.[120]

The multiple forms of *ḍākinīs* led to a plethora of terms for them, including goddess, *yoginī*, consort, and *ākāśagāminī* ("sky-goer"), among others.[121] *Ḍākinīs* can be either divine females, or actual women who have achieved tremendous spiritual power,[122] and some are transformed from women into divinities.[123] In some cases, divine *ḍākinīs* are said to possess (Tib.: *babs*) female practitioners in order to confirm or protect an adept's progress.[124] (These women and their practices [sexual and otherwise] will be discussed in chapter 11.) Such a rich assortment of terms, disguises, and human and divine forms only begins to convey the scope of the many characteristics and roles applied to these beings.[125] Despite attempts to box them into a single category, *ḍākinīs* blur all boundaries, for that is their purpose: to cross boundaries between human and divine, human and animal, sacred and profane, life and death.

In Buddhism and Hinduism both women and men are believed to be capable of flight. But even so, a gendered distinction exists. Most important, these are male-oriented traditions: their texts, art, and teachings are framed in a male-dominated discourse that presumes men to be the main actors and the main audience. As we have seen, divine women who are central to this tradition are represented as wild, unpredictable, and dangerous beings who can bestow supernatural powers, blessings, and even enlightenment, but who at other times may withhold these gifts and even be malevolent. This goes back, in part, to ancient Indian beliefs about the ambivalence of divinity in general, but most particularly to the ancient Indian bird godesses discussed in chapter 1. Coercion was required to direct their powers toward the desired male goal. Regardless of whether they are human or divine, the females are subordinate to males and their needs; the contrary behavior of females is but an echo of their former independence—and perhaps signals a lingering male fear that too heavy-handed a domination of the feminine will lead to a terrifying revenge.

PART II

Human Women

8

Witches and Succubi: Male Sexual Fantasies

BELIEFS ABOUT WHO witches are and what they do have varied from one historical period and geographical area to another.[1] Magical flight, however, has been a fairly consistent element in witches' repertoire, from Medea escaping in her flying chariot, to medieval European witches riding their brooms. As we shall see, though, their history is one generally marked by increasing restraint. Christina Larner most succinctly sums up the characteristics of European witches, who first and foremost were women:

> The stereotype witch is an independent adult woman who does not conform to the male idea of proper female behaviour. She is assertive; she does not require or give love (though she may enchant); she does not nurture men or children, nor care for the weak. She has the power of words—to defend herself or to curse. In addition, she may have other, more mysterious powers which do not derive from the established order. All women threaten male hegemony with their exclusive power to give life; and social order depends on women conforming to male ideals of female behaviour. The identification of any woman as a witch will, therefore, set against her not only males, but also conforming females and their children.[2]

Much of this is true of all aerial women, but beliefs about witches are especially key to a society's concept of womanhood because witches, especially, contradict the characteristics of the ideal woman. The witch is an inversion of the good woman, who embodies the categories of wife, mother, and upholder of morality,[3] an inversion so ably personified by Euripides's depiction of Medea.

MEDEA

Medea (who was also discussed in chapter 2) is best known to us through the Greek playwright Euripides (c. 485–c. 406 BCE),[4] whose *Medea* was first performed in Athens in 431 BCE, though it depicts events thought to have taken place as much as a thousand years earlier. The play opens with Medea's nurse briefly recounting the events that have led up Medea's desperate situation. She fell in love with the Greek hero Jason when he came to her father's kingdom to steal the Golden Fleece of a ram that had been a gift from the god Hermes. Driven by her passion for Jason, and based on his sworn oath to marry her,[5] Medea betrayed her father, used her magical powers to help Jason steal the Golden Fleece, and killed her brother when he pursued them. Jason and Medea fled to the city of Corinth, where they lived happily for a time and had two sons. As the play opens, it is now Jason who has betrayed Medea, by planning to marry the young daughter of the king of Corinth. Through this union Jason will secure a place of prominence for himself, though Medea and her sons will have to be banished. Medea is enraged. She calls on Hekate, the goddess of witches,[6] saying:

> For, by Queen Hecate, whom above all divinities
> I venerate, my chosen accomplice, to whose presence
> My central hearth is dedicated, no one of them
> Shall hurt me and not suffer for it! Let me work:
> In bitterness and pain they shall repent this marriage,
> Repent their houses joined, repent my banishment.[7]

Medea is partly divine, being the granddaughter of the Titan Helios, who drives the chariot of the sun across the sky. While pretending to acquiesce to Jason's remarriage, Medea makes her plans. First, she secures the protection of the king of Athens by promising to cure his impotence. (She has the power to rejuvenate people, to bestow youth and fertility, which she had also done for Jason's father, but she also has the power to cause great bodily harm.) Medea's revenge is to send Jason's new bride a crown and a robe that catch fire when she puts them on, consuming both her and her father, who desperately tries to tear them off her. Medea then kills her children—Jason's children—and takes their bodies with her into a flying chariot drawn by two dragons.[8] Jason arrives, screaming curses at her, and accuses her of causing all this destruction simply because he will no longer have sex with her. Medea acknowledges this before she flies off. Interestingly, Euripides's play is the first account in which Medea kills her children; in other versions, the Corinthians kill them.[9]

Medea is a beautiful and sexually dangerous woman who can fly, has knowledge of potions, herbs,[10] spells, and charms, and is both a threat to and a bestower of children. Her tragic and gruesome tale represents witches as independent women and objects of fear. Often, witches were women who lived apart from society and made their own decisions, in social environments that left little room for non-conformist or independent women. Traditional forms of patriarchy cannot make room for a lone woman not identified by her relationship to a man—any man, whether father, brother, husband, or son.

ANCIENT WITCHES AND SEXUALITY

Medea introduces us to the concept of witches as highly sexed beings, a point that will be emphasized again in the European Middle Ages. She is ruled by her sexual passion for Jason and acknowledges his claim that she created havoc because he would not have sex with her. Another sexy witch is Circe, the daughter of Helios, one of the Titans who existed before the Olympian gods, and who is also the grandfather of Medea, making Circe Medea's aunt. Whether or not any of these women actually lived is far less important than the larger issue of the effect these stories have had on shaping our understanding of witches. These are the stories that were passed down through the generations.

Witches were also conflated with succubi (discussed below), who predate them back to ancient times. Succubi are night-flying female spirits who lay on top of men while they sleep in order to have sex with them. It is quite likely that the male imagination created the succubi in response to the common male experience of nightly emissions. This belief in the overpowering sexuality of witches was especially strong in the European Middle Ages, emphasizing as it did their deviant sexuality; it was also believed that witches' sabbaths were hotbeds of sexual activity.

Circe

Circe has already been discussed in the context of her role as a guide to the Land of the Dead (chapter 2). Here, the focus is on the Circe episode contained in book

10 of Homer's *Odyssey*—a richly detailed story that describes many of the characteristics of later witches, while also presenting Circe as a witch very different than those examined thus far. Homer's dates are uncertain (perhaps eighth century BCE), but the events of his two great works, the *Iliad* and the *Odyssey*, took place much earlier, during the thirteenth century BCE. In book 10, Odysseus and his men have been wandering for some time following the fall of Troy, unable to reach their homeland of Ithaca. One of the many places they visit is the island of Aeaea, where Circe lives with four maids and assorted animals that are actually men she has transformed into beasts. Odysseus and his men variously describe her as a beautiful woman, a witch, and a goddess (her father is Helios). Circe is an enchantress who knows how to shape-shift into other beings. Under the guise of offering Odysseus's men hospitality, Circe transforms some of them into swine. She does this by means of a magic potion and her magic wand. As Homer describes it, she offered the men food:

> Adding her own vile pinch, to make them lose desire or thought of our dear fatherland. Scarce had they drunk when she flew after them with her long stick and shut them in a pigsty—bodies, voices, head, and bristles, all swinish now, though minds were still unchanged.[11]

On his way to rescue his men, Odysseus meets Hermes, the messenger of the gods, who offers to help. Hermes assists Odysseus in three ways: he gives Odysseus an herb called *moly* that will act as an antidote to Circe's magic potion; he advises him to have sexual relations with Circe; and he tells him to make her swear an oath not to harm him when he is naked. With Hermes's help Odysseus is successful in avoiding Circe's magic and convinces her to transform his men back into their human forms, which she does by rubbing them with a magic salve. Odysseus then quite happily lived with her for about a year.

When Odysseus wants to return home, he asks Circe to fulfill her promise to help him. She tells him that before he can go home he must journey to the Land of the Dead to consult with a dead prophet. A witch acts as medium between the living and the dead (a trope which shall be discussed in more detail with the example of the Witch of Endor). Circe gives Odysseus detailed instructions on how to find the Land of the Dead, how to protect himself once he is there, and the particular rituals he should perform while waiting for the dead prophet to appear. Circe commands esoteric knowledge about both the Land of the Living and the Land of the Dead.

The chapter ends with Odysseus and his men going down to the sea to get ready to sail to the Land of the Dead. When they arrive, they find that Circe has been there before them—that she has passed by them unseen through the power of transvection, the ability to instantaneously transport oneself from one place to another, which is yet another attribute of witches.

Circe is a beautiful and dangerous woman, one who enchants men, turning them into beasts with her potions and her wand. Her sexuality also makes her dangerous, as is shown by Odysseus's need to bind her with an oath before they go to her bed, which reveals men's vulnerability to women when they are naked and asleep. In a large number of European folktales, the lovers of a sorceress are transformed into animals when she is through with them. There are two connected issues here. The first has to do with women whose sexuality is not controlled by a man—always problematic in patriarchal societies. The second has to do with the fear of being trapped in the body of an animal while retaining human consciousness. In the ancient imagination, populated by gods who could transform themselves into animals, this seemed a real possibility. A wonderfully amusing presentation of this situation appears in Apuleius's *The Golden Ass*, in which the hero is transformed into a donkey but restored by his devotion to the goddess Isis. These beliefs linger in folktales (e.g., "The Frog Prince," "Beauty and the Beast"), where such a spell can be reversed by the love of a maiden, meaning a sexually inactive female. Ideas about the dangerous sexuality of witches continued into the Middle Ages, which connected their sexuality to their ability to transform men into animals, perhaps to "bring out the beast in men." They are the definitive evil flying women.

The Witch of Endor

In the Bible, chapter 28 of I Samuel recounts the meeting of King Saul (r. c. 1020–1000 BCE) with the Witch of Endor on the eve of his final battle. Prior to this, Saul had exiled anyone who summoned the dead for purposes of divination. Subsequently, he lost favor with God, who would no longer answer his inquiries "either by dreams . . . or by prophets" (I Sam. 28:7). Dreams and prophecy were common ways of divining the future in ancient Israel, while necromancy was not (see, e.g., Isaiah 8:19 and 65:3–4). Anxious about the outcome of the battle, Saul found someone who had not heeded his decree, a woman living at Endor. He commanded her to bring up the spirit of Samuel, the great judge and prophet who had anointed him king. When questioned, Samuel told Saul that he and his sons would be killed in battle the next day. And, indeed, that is what occurred.

The book of I Samuel highlights another of the main attributes of witches: they can commune with the spirits of the dead and thereby foretell the future. Such necromancy is presented as a possible form of divination, but not a righteous one, so the power of these diviners or witches was acknowledged even as they were relegated to the margins of society, where they lived under the threat of exile. This incident and the famous injunction of Exodus 22:18—"Thou shalt not suffer a witch to live"—helped shape later European ideas about witches.

Witches recall or are a resurgence of ancient malevolent bird goddesses, such as the Harpies.[12] They are monstrous women. Additional descriptions from the ancient world that connect witches with flight and birds include Ovid's description of the witch Dipsas, who, he noted, could fly when clad in feathers,[13] while the second-century Roman grammarian Festus defined *strigae* as "the name given to women who practice sorcery, and who are also called flying women."[14] Apuleius (c. 125–c. 180) dramatized such beliefs in *The Golden Ass* when the witch Pamphile transformed herself into an owl by rubbing her body with a magic ointment and chanting a charm. Then she shook herself and "her limbs became gradually fledged with feathers, her arms changed into sturdy wings, her nose grew crooked and horny, her nails turned into talons, and soon there was no longer any doubt about it: Pamphile had become an owl. She gave a querulous hoot and made a few little hopping flights until she was sure enough of her wings to glide off, away over the roof-tops."[15] Certain features of Pamphile's story continued to endure in European beliefs about witches: namely, that ointments they brew and rub on their bodies enable them to fly or be transformed into birds, specifically owls, because they are night-flying birds.

SUCCUBI AND INCUBI

Like Medea, another example who emphasizes that witches are dangerous to children is Lilith, yet another sexy witch, who has roots in the ancient Near East, where she was a goddess of the underworld known as Lilitu (meaning "demon") and connected with the goddess Isthar.[16] She was believed to be a creature of the night, often appearing in the guise of an owl as she roused the dead. She holds a rod and ring of justice in her hands, which may symbolize the span of life as well as judgment of the dead.[17] According to Jewish legend, Lilith was the first wife of Adam, who was created simultaneously with Adam (Gen. 1) and was therefore equal to him. Lilith is not only the first woman; she is the first monster, the origin of the monstrous-feminine (chapter 2), as she soon deserts Adam because he does not treat her as an equal and refuses to lie beneath her during sexual intercourse.[18] She flies off, and even though God sends angels after her, she refuses to return to Adam, choosing instead to take demons as her lovers. God then creates a second, more obedient wife, named Eve, from Adam's rib (Gen. 2) and punishes Lilith by having one hundred of her children die each day,[19] which led to her identification as a killer of children, especially infants, and as a threat to pregnant women.[20] This belief (and a high infant mortality rate up until relatively recent times) led to a proliferation of amulets to protect infants from her.[21] The later Talmudic tradition elaborates upon Lilith's sexuality, as she becomes a witchlike figure, a night demon with long, loose hair. Referred to as a succubus, she causes men to emit their semen while they are sleeping, no doubt by lying on top of them.[22] Such emissions were believed to be particularly dangerous because they allowed demons to be born into the human world. In Europe, stories about Lilith mixed with those of European folk tales,[23] such as stories of the night-flying women who hunted with the goddess Diana or with the Germanic witch figure Holda.[24] Even more pertinently, Lilith, with her owl-like nature, was easily assimilated with the Roman *striga* (from the word *strix*, meaning a screech-owl), ill-omened night birds that Ovid described as killers of infants, adding that certain old women can change themselves into *strix*.[25] It is interesting to note, however, that while the practice of killing children is attributed to night-flying women and to witches in general, this contradicts the role of Hekate, goddess of the witches, who, according to Hesiod (eighth century BCE) was the protector of children.[26]

The belief in succubi is connected to Greek and Roman stories about divinities who had sex with human beings, as well as the ancient Near Eastern goddesses who had sex with human men. Other divine and semi-divine women had succubi characteristics, such as Circe and Medea, Valkyries, swan maidens, fairies, *apsarās*, *ḍākinīs*, and *yoginīs*, who took or were taken by human lovers with greater and lesser success and always with a residue of terror or dread on the part of their human companions.

Stories about flying succubi who visited men and incubi who visited women in the night to have sex with them, which circulated in the early church,[27] drew on Genesis 6:1–2, in which the sons of God have sex with human women. Like all demons, succubi and incubi were believed to be more powerful at night, when human beings are made vulnerable by sleep.[28] Demons were simply a part of the Judeo-Christian worldview. Medieval Christian theologians, however, gave new life to succubi/incubi by reviving the belief that they were actual beings.[29] In contrast to the parallel Jewish tradition, which was more concerned with sleeping men being visited by female demons,[30] the vast majority of female Europeans accused of being witches were believed to have had sex with demons, and were seen as willing, active participants in this unnatural intercourse. In the anecdotes conveyed by the medieval church, victims often turn to a priest or monk to protect them from their demon lovers. Contrastingly, accused witches were believed to ignore ecclesiastical help and to deny they had demon lovers. This shift in emphasis from succubi to incubi is important to the ideology that set the groundwork for the imprisonment and killing of thousands of women in large part because of their supposed deviant and demonic sexuality—a form of female sexuality that will be shown to have existed only in the male imagination.

An important, if not the most important, basis for the belief in succubi and incubi is the prevalence of sex and sexuality in dreams. Sexually satisfying and sometimes sexually terrifying dreams have been reported in all societies. Quite often such dreams involve intercourse with attractive and seductive spirits, although elements of dread and terror may also accompany the experience.[31] See, for example, Figure 1.4 (p. 19) of a winged succubus with a sleeping man. The belief that women could conceive children through such dream experiences is equally widespread. Examples include the mothers of Alexander the Great and the Buddha as well as the wizard Merlin, who is said to have been fathered by an incubus who had sex with a nun.[32] Needless to say, religious attitudes toward sexuality were active in shaping how such dream experiences were interpreted.[33]

WITCHES IN CHRISTIAN EUROPE

The history leading up to the witchcraft craze in Europe is a long sweep of both subtle and overt transformations in law and theology, the increasing power of individual kingdoms and of the church (whose monasteries preserved literacy and education), cultural shifts regarding sexuality and concepts of womanhood, and redefinitions of witchcraft—all arising against a background of fear, superstition, war, plague, climate change, and famine. The fifteenth century was the most critical time in terms of documented changes, but the roots of the witch hunts stretch deep into the past.

As with Lilith, during the early Middle Ages stories from the classical world and biblical notions about witches began to mix with European folk beliefs about night-flying witches.[34] This mythopoeic canon contributed to what would become entrenched and heavily documented evidence for the existence of witchcraft. Before turning to this evidence, much of which was extracted by torture,[35] it will be helpful to understand the tenor of the times.

The enormously powerful Catholic Church believed it was the guardian of religious truth, and as such was under a divine obligation to destroy contrary religious beliefs. In the eleventh century the church began to flex its muscles and actively persecute any individuals or groups advocating other religious faiths. These included the frequent Christian heterodoxies that sprang up throughout the Middle Ages, and extended to Jews and Muslims both in and outside of Europe. This was the period of the Crusades, the so-called holy war to wrest the Holy Land from the hands of the heathen, and of the Inquisition,[36] the goal of which was to preserve the unity of the one true church by rooting out all heresy. It was a time of tremendous religious intolerance on the part of orthodox Christians as well as some of the so-called heretics they opposed, such as the Waldensians and the Cathars. Simultaneously, beginning around 1315, Europe experienced a radical drop in temperature known as the Little Ice Age, which lasted until around 1850 and caused the so-called Great Famine of 1315–1317, followed by the Black Death (1346–1353) and the Hundred Years' War (1337–1453), all adding to the fanaticism and fear already in the air.[37] There is some irony in all this, in that Christianity was not the uniform religion theologians thought it was or wanted it to be. Then, as today, popular Christianity was inclusive of practices and beliefs that would not be completely approved by the highest church authorities. As Christianity had spread throughout pagan Europe it incorporated some pagan elements, modifying them where possible toward Christian ends.[38] The descriptions of witchcraft brought out by the trials of so-called witches horrified conservative theologians, who reacted with all the unrestrained force a hegemonic institution could muster, casting a harsh light on many of these practices.[39]

As was briefly discussed in chapter 5, most Christians believed that the world was in the midst of a cosmic battle between the forces of good and the forces of evil. The side of good was led by God, supported by the angels and the Christian saints. The other side was led by the devil, his demons (fallen angels), and his human helpers, soon to be named witches.[40] In the Christian mind, the devil and his demons had grown in power over time. The numerous biographies of saints in which they were tormented by demons were taken as evidence that such a battle was continually being waged. Witches became members of this battle in the fifteenth century, when they began to be thought of as worshipers of the devil—that is, women who had renounced Christ and aligned themselves with the forces of evil.[41] The demonization of witches was part of a theodicy; witches empowered by demons helped explain the existence of evil in the world. Henceforth, a refusal to believe in witches was heresy.[42]

Iconography played an important part in spreading this ideology, which is demonstrated by the almost complete absence of visual representations of witches before 1450 and the abundance of images thereafter.[43] Additional factors contributed to the redefinition and persecution of witches as well. First, changes in medieval law beginning in the thirteenth century made it easier to bring accusations of *maleficium*, or harmful witchcraft,[44] which underscores that it was the secular authority, in the form of courts and judges, who acted upon the changing theology of the church.[45] Nonetheless, the witchcraft trials created a space where elite and popular ideas about religious life met, clashed, and ultimately merged.

Prior to this period, *maleficium* was in large part understood to be an imaginary rather than an actual crime.[46] The shared belief of literate people was based on a passage in the *Canon Episcopi*[47] that states that some wicked women dreamed, or were deluded, that with the help of the devil they could fly at night by riding animals in order to revel with the pagan goddess Diana (Artemis), who was associated with Hekate and the moon, spirits of the dead, witches, and sexuality[48] It flatly denied actual bodily interaction between the women and devils.[49] Later "witchcraft theorists," to use a term coined by Walter Stephens,[50] contradicted the *Canon Episcopi* by asserting that women were awake, not asleep, and by insisting on the reality of devils and witches, and of corporeal interactions between them.[51] Stories of nocturnal revels drawn from pre-Christian tradition now took on a more sinister shape, as the notion of a malevolent witches' sabbath developed.[52] This process was enhanced by the practice of gathering evidence by means of torture during the early witchcraft trials of the 1420s.[53] Through interrogation and torture, the accused were led to fulfill their examiners' ideas about witchcraft. They were forced to confess that they attended witches' sabbaths, to which they generally flew, where they worshiped the devil; killed, cooked, and ate children; and had promiscuous sex with humans and demons. This meant that witchcraft began to be defined as the rejection of Christianity and the simultaneous embrace of devil worship, which was understood to involve deviant forms of sexuality.

The Witches' Sabbath

The witches' sabbath was a distinctly new addition to the repertoire of witchcraft. Before the fifteenth century, malefic witches were solitary figures,[54] but now they were perceived to be members of large and therefore frightening groups that threatened all of society. Most scholars agree that the witches' sabbath was fabricated by witchcraft theorists who drew on a composite tradition: there is no hard evidence that such ceremonies ever took place.[55] Stated differently, malefic witchcraft became an accepted part of reality through the efforts of so-called "learned" witchcraft theorists who elaborated on folk beliefs about witches, either from confessions or from stories they were told, which they then linked expressly to Satanic worship, by claiming that witches worshiped the devil at witches' sabbaths (Figure 8.1).[56]

Women and the Demonic

An additional factor that helped define witchcraft was the reconfiguration of the functions and processes of exorcism in the fifteenth century. Barbara Newman has documented the active role of thirteenth-century women saints in curing the

FIGURE 8.1 Hans Baldung Grien, *Witches' Sabbath*, woodblock print, 1510. Female nudity, loose hair, and riding backward suggest the disorderly and contrary nature of the witch.
The Metropolitan Museum of Art, New York.

possessed,[57] but gradually this role came to be dominated by a male clergy bent on exorcising female bodies. Exorcism dramatically asserted the spiritual power of the exorcist, who expelled demons that were thought to cause the physical or mental illness of the possessed.[58] Public exorcisms showed the male clergy to be part of God's army against the demonic, and a formal liturgy for exorcism developed, which, in Nancy Caciola's words, "enact[ed] a performative convergence between the divine, the masculine, and the clerical, on the one hand, and the demonic, the feminine, and the lay, on the other."[59] The language of exorcism texts reveals that only women were thought to be possessed by demons.[60]

Recognizing the importance of women in transmitting and preserving popular culture, some of which contained pre-Christian elements, helps us to understand how this placed women in opposition to church theologians and their monolithic view of Christianity.[61] At the same time there was an increasing scrutiny of female mystics, with some women saints accused of witchcraft.[62] Caroline Walker Bynum summarizes the similarities between the female Christian mystic and the witch:

By 1500, indeed, the model of the female saint, expressed both in popular veneration and in official canonizations, was in many ways the mirror image of society's notion of the witch. Each was thought to be possessed, whether by God or by Satan; each seemed able to read the minds and hearts of others with uncanny shrewdness; each was suspected of flying through the air, whether in saintly levitations or bilocation, or in a witches' Sabbath. Moreover, each bore mysterious wounds, whether stigmata or the marks of incubi, on her body. The similarity of witch and saint—at least in the eyes of the theologians, canon lawyers, inquisitors, and male hagiographers who are, by the fifteenth century, almost our only sources for their lives—suggests how threatening both were to clerical authorities. Woman's religious role as inspired vessel had come to seem utterly different from man's role as priest, preacher, and leader by virtue of clerical office. And because it seemed so different, it titillated—and was both encouraged and feared.[63]

It is commonly accepted that the vast majority of those accused of witchcraft were women.[64] One must look to more nuanced social causes, beyond the basic fact that celibate male hierarchies tend to diminish the spiritual potential of women, to explain why secular and religious institutions, both Catholic and, later, Protestant, acted upon such beliefs to the point where they imprisoned, tortured, and executed innumerable women. Larner has shown that the accused women appeared as disorderly and threatening to patriarchal order.[65] Bengt Ankarloo found similar instances of disorderly females during the witch hunts in Sweden. Here the social fabric was torn by the deaths of so many men during the continental wars that left many women unmarried, perhaps self-sufficient, and involved with pre-Christian practices. He says: "The world of God and men was thus set in opposition to a realm where Satan and women ruled."[66]

The social reality of the women accused of witchcraft was that they were mostly single (either unmarried or widowed), rural (and thus less influenced by elite religious and social views), poor (and thus powerless), and often older.[67] In short, they were women free of male supervision in an age that had no way of conceptualizing such women; they had to be disorderly because they were "out of order," that is, outside the hierarchy of God over man and man over woman. If they were not under the rule of a man, they must be under the rule of the devil. It was inconceivable that they could be autonomous.[68]

The stake on which witches would burn was finally raised in 1484, when, at the behest of and based on a report given to him by the Dominican inquisitors Heinrich Kramer and Jakob Sprenger, Pope Innocent VIII issued the papal bull *Summis desiderantes* to strengthen the inquisitors' abilities to seek out and punish witches and other heretics.[69]

Two years later, in 1486, Kramer and Sprenger published the *Malleus Maleficarum* (*The Hammer of Witches*),[70] with the papal bull included as a preface. Aided by the new technology of the printing press, it went through multiple printings throughout Europe and became the authoritative handbook describing the heretical activities of witches and serving as a guide to their conviction. It increased the number of people who could be persecuted, as well as the geographical scope of the investigation to include most of Europe, and from there to the Americas, and it focused attention especially on women. The appearance and activities of witches became familiar to the general population through discussion of this and other texts and the trials and executions they generated. Concurrently, easily disseminated iconography such as printed woodblocks and engravings helped spread Kramer and Sprenger's ideas.[71]

The *Malleus Maleficarum,* an extremely misogynist text, almost always uses *malefica*, the feminine form of the Latin word for witch. Underlying the text, though, is the belief that when witches confess to having had sex with devils, usually referred to as incubi, they provide proof that bodily contact with demons is possible. The theological point is that evil spirits actually can take on bodily forms and have physical contact with human beings. As already stated, this idea can be traced back to stories of the Greek and Roman gods who had sex with humans. In the *City of God* (8.14–10.332), Augustine (354–430 CE) had classified all the pagan gods as demons, thus laying the groundwork for Christian beliefs about demon lovers.[72] The *Malleus Maleficarum* blends this theology with its negative view of women when it states, "All witchcraft comes from carnal lust, which is in women insatiable. See *Proverbs* XXX: There are three things that are never satisfied, yea, a fourth thing which says not, It is enough; that is, the mouth of the womb. Wherefore for the sake of fulfilling their lust they consort even with devils."[73] There is no evidence dating to before 1400 of the connection of *maleficium* (witchcraft) with demon lovers. This develops out of the trial testimonies of women accused of witchcraft, which, it must be recalled, were extracted under torture.[74] Indeed, Kramer went so far as to argue that the number of witches rapidly increased after 1400 because of widespread voluntary copulation with demons, which led to the birth of more witches.[75] Yet before 1400 it was literate men—necromancers or ritual magicians—who deliberately invoked demons. Unlike female witches, they were understood to be skilled specialists who commanded demons and were not commanded by them, nor were they their sexual partners.

Kramer combined beliefs about women's greater sexual appetite with their greater susceptibility to demonic possession to posit them as likely candidates to have demon lovers;[76] ultimately these were women accused of unlicensed sexual activity.[77] The discussion here comes full circle when Kramer and Sprenger cite Medea as an example of the ungovernable nature of women, especially in their desire to follow their own impulses.[78]

The idea that witches, like Medea, kill children reappears in tales about witches' sabbaths. It was said that the participants would sacrifice an infant in a perverse variation on the Christian mass, or drink a broth made from murdered infants as part of their initiation ceremony.[79] As the notion of witches cooking infants in cauldrons took hold, it was believed that the witches derived an unguent from the residue left at the cauldron's bottom—and that this unguent enabled witches to fly and could also be used to harm others by sprinkling some of it on them.[80] The infant mortality rate was high during the medieval period, and what we refer to today as "crib death" or "sudden infant death syndrome" left parents without an obvious explanation for their child's death. In a suspicious age with a growing acceptance of malefic witchcraft, blame was frequently assigned to witches, who were believed to shape-shift into animal form, especially that of cats, and who could then easily and silently gain access to houses where they smothered babies or sucked away their breath.[81]

Flying

From the 1420s on, the notion that witches flew at night to attend witches' sabbaths[82] became part of the general understanding of what witches did. At least some of the inquisitors and other elite men believed that witches could fly.[83] Details of such flights were elicited from accused witches through a combination of torture and continuous interrogation by men who presupposed the possibility of flight. Flying was an essential component in defining witches' sabbaths as a threat to Christendom, because flying meant witches could travel quickly from distant places, thereby increasing the number of attendees and making it easier to meet frequently.[84] As Robert Rowland puts it, "Symbolically, flying established the dangerous ambiguity of the witch: she was an apparent member of the community while belonging in reality to an anti-world which threatens and negates it . . . . The witch's flight is an expression of the fact that she combines in her person two contradictory and mutually incompatible modes of existence: only by unnatural and extraordinary means can the two worlds be placed in a spatio-temporal relation to one another."[85]

Under the influence of witch theorists, the image of the flying witch caught the imagination of many artists. As mentioned, visual representations of witches are extremely rare prior to 1450, but after this period they are abundant.[86] Albrecht Dürer (1471–1528) was one of the first artists to visually represent the ideology of the demonologists. One of his famous engravings, *Four Witches*, defines the witch as female, sinister, and naked—and therefore sexually voracious.[87] In 1510, Hans Baldung Grien elaborated on these beliefs in his famous woodcut *Witches' Sabbath* (Figure 8.1), which depicts a naked female witch flying through the air by riding backward on a goat and with long, loose and unkempt hair. The goat has ancient and longstanding associations with sexual excess, while riding backward connotes the endless reversals believed to occur at a witches' sabbath: a black mass rather than a Christian mass, sexual promiscuity rather than tempered Christian sexual relations, and, perhaps worst of all, uncontrollable women with supernatural powers. To her right another witch flies through a cloud of vapor, while beneath them equally naked witches concoct an evil brew that they are releasing into the air. A proliferation of phallic pitchforks—some lying on the ground, one carried by the goat-riding witch, and one, partially obscured on the left edge, draped in sausages, widely associated with penises in medieval times[88]—all point to the sexual power, voraciousness, and danger of witches.[89] A later, anonymous image (Figure 8.2) shows the full development of this motif, as clothed witches fly on pitchforks placed between their legs—just as they fly on broomsticks (Figure 8.3) in images (for example, Halloween decorations) that endure to our own day.

It was also an accepted belief that witches rubbed their bodies with a magic ointment in order to fly through the air to attend their unholy sabbath meetings.[90] This belief, too, began to be depicted in the fifteenth century, in images of witches rubbing such ointment on their bodies or preparing it in "witches' kitchens."[91] Like the witch Pamphile in Apuleius's *The Golden Ass*, some European women, such as Agnes Gerhardts in 1596 and Ursula Kollarin in 1661, testified at their trials that by spreading an ointment on their bodies they were able to grow wings and fly.[92] In other cases, witches were believed to apply the ointment to household items such as brooms or the paddles used to load bread into the oven, thereby demonstrating their perversion of women's domestic role. Sometimes they were believed to apply the ointment to an animal that would then carry them through the air.[93] *Malleus Maleficarum* describes the latter process:

FIGURE 8.2 Anonymous, *The Infernal Sorceress Circe*, illustration from D. Faber, *Die Höllische Zauberin Circe*, 1699.
Columbia University Library.

Now the following is their method of being transported. They take the
unguent which, as we have said, they make at the devil's instruction from the
limbs of children, particularly of those whom they have killed before a baptism, and anoint with it a chair or a broomstick; whereupon they are immediately carried up into the air, either by day or by night, and either visibly, or
if they wish, invisibly.[94]

The text also offers a documented example of a witch flying by a third means: that
of being carried by a devil.[95]

FIGURE 8.3. Illumination from Martin Le Franc, *Le Champion des Dames*, 1440. This is probably the earliest illustration of a witch on a broomstick.
Bibliothéque nationale de France.

The *Malleus Maleficarum* also affirms that in some instances these flights are imaginary and that witches could attend sabbaths in spirit only by lying down "on their left side, and then a sort of bluish vapour came from their mouth, through which they can clearly see what was happening"[96] at the sabbath. Of course, there is also the earliest statement of the *Canon Episcopi* that these women only dreamed of flying, and a great deal of ink has been spilled over the possibility that they used an ointment with psychotropic properties—in other words, dreams of flying were stimulated by the ointment or, indeed, the women just hallucinated such flights.[97]

For all the detailed testimony elicited by the inquisitors, Hans Peter Duerr is struck by their apparent lack of interest in the actual contents of the ointment, beyond the fat of unbaptized babies and other repellent ingredients. He concludes that the influence of mind-altering plants was actually suppressed because it would have led to a natural explanation for reports of flying, and therefore would not have provided evidence for the existence of devils and their ability to physically

interact with human beings.[98] It is clear that finding the truth was not the domi-
nating motive of the witch theorists, given that where the belief in flying witches
was widespread so, too, was the persecution of witches, and given that, as the
number of witchcraft trials increased, so did the proportion of women accused.[99]
First and foremost, the inquisitors projected a terrible evil out into the world that
needed to be destroyed. Second, they located that evil in what they saw as its natural recipients: namely, women, and especially in transgressive women who pur-
portedly transcended human limitations in their flight, an ability granted only to
the most saintly beings (see chapter 10), and maintained control of their sexuality
in *choosing* to participate in the sexual promiscuity of the witches' sabbath.

Once begun, witch hunts continued into the late seventeenth century. No certain figures exist for the exact number of people killed; some scholars put the figure at the suspiciously high number of four million, while others put it as low as
30,000.[100] Much depends on the length of time and the extent of the geographical
area examined. Recent scholarship has shown that different countries and regions
viewed witchcraft through different lenses and with different social agendas.
For example, the continental obsession with demon lovers was totally absent in
England, although it was a concern in Scotland. This seems to be connected to the
fact that English law did not allow torture in such cases.[101] Relevantly, the witches'
sabbath was not an issue in England, and English witches were not believed to
fly, though that did not prevent Anne Boleyn (1501–1536) from being executed
by Henry VIII for witchcraft, along with other crimes. About 80 percent of those
killed all over Europe were female, varying in age from young girls to old women.
Even if some of these women truly believed themselves to be witches, or truly did
practice what they considered witchcraft, by far the larger number were victims of
false accusations, usually by malicious neighbors.

Ideas about witches became entangled with Christian notions of evil, the devil,
sexuality, and womanhood to such a remarkable degree that Christianity faced
the problem of distinguishing itself from witchcraft. The contrasts between good
Christians and witches, miracles and magic, could be very thin, in part because
the early policy of the church had been to incorporate pagan practices and to dress
them in a Christian guise where possible.[102] It becomes hard to draw a line between
good Christians who prayed[103] to dead saints to ask for miracles and witches
who worked spells on the dead to ask about the future. Such overlaps compelled
Christianity to define witchcraft as the perversion of Christian activities, as the
evil opposite of Christianity's good. Consequently, all evil was placed outside the
church; anything that was not inside the church—for example, other religious
ideas—was also evil. In this way the church, with a few notable exceptions, did not
have to examine its own practices, such as sanctioning the use of torture.[104]

From ancient times through the medieval period[105] witches were seen as preservers of earlier religious traditions: Circe and Medea were descendants of the Titan Helios, divine beings who preceded the Olympian gods,[106] and both are outliers in Greek cultures, women living on the fringes of the Greek world. As we have seen, European witches were often practitioners of folk religions, mostly patched-together remnants of pagan religions. Christianity's influence on medieval Europe was widely spread, but not necessarily deep. Lingering stories about Circe, Medea, the Witch of Endor, and others contributed to both the elite and popular understanding of witches as outliers of the patriarchal orders; they are defined by being disorderly and disrespectful of male authority. They are perverters of domesticity, using its tools such as broomsticks to fly and cauldrons to cook babies, and they controlled their own sexuality—thus undermining the patriarchal goal of controlling women's reproduction, but not men's. The control of women's sexuality is essential to patriarchy. Sexually autonomous and powerful women are a threat to men and their institutions. Circe turned men into swine (a domestic animal) and European witches were believed capable of causing male impotence and in control of love spells that could make men a woman's slave.

Interestingly enough, the next chapter examines a so-called pagan religion, shamanism, that presents parallels to the repression and persecution of women by patriarchal religious authorities.

9

Women Shamans: Fluctuations in Female Spiritual Power

WOMEN SHAMANS HAVE a long and varied history, stretching back from our own modern era to the dawn of human culture, and spanning the globe. Shamanism has traditionally been strongly linked with birds; shamans frequently have been described with birdlike features, and as using magical flight as they have sought to cure the sick, heal communities fractured by dissent or change, commune with spirits, see the future, and understand the past. They have also struggled to maintain their autonomy as outsiders have encroached on their environments, bringing deprivations, sickness, and new religions with no leading roles for women.

The term "shamanism" encompasses a great variety of religious practices performed in many parts of the world from the earliest times to the present day. These practices center on a religious expert called a "shaman," a word that comes from the Tungusic languages of northeastern Siberia (šaman, from the root sa, meaning "to know, think, understand"),[1] and thus most specifically refers to a religious role in Siberian cultures. Early scholars of religion and anthropology found it a useful term to apply to a geographically and temporally wide variety of religious practitioners whom they perceived as similar.[2] There is some justification for this, but ultimately this tendency downplays the complexity of some richly detailed practices.[3] The goal of this chapter is to attempt to respect cultural contexts while elaborating on and privileging descriptions of shamanic flight by women from different historical periods and various, mostly Asian, cultures.[4]

THE NIŠAN SHAMAN

The Manchu folk epic known as the *Tale of the Nišan Shaman* is told in various forms across Siberia and northeast Asia. The heroine is simply called "the Nišan shaman," after the place where she lives.[5] She is a woman of an uncertain age, widowed but still young, and is said to be more powerful than any other shaman because she can revive the dead. When she first appears in the epic, she is hanging laundry out to dry—a typically female task, but one that also foreshadows the spiritual purification that will soon occur.[6] Her atypical female behavior is soon revealed when she breaks the social rules constraining female behavior in relation to men, especially men of higher social status, by teasing the powerful, Sinicized, and wealthy official who comes to seek her help. She tells him that the shaman he wants to see lives across the river, but, once he gets there, someone else has to tell him to go back to the Nišan shaman's side. This short scene both suggests her trickster nature and hints at the tensions within Manchu society between traditional culture and Chinese, especially Confucian, influences. The Manchus were a tribal people originally living on the edges of the Chinese empire, which they eventually conquered in the seventeenth century, creating the Qing dynasty (1644–1911). This divided Manchus into Sinicized followers of the imperial court, and those who remained faithful to older, more traditional Manchu ways; the former group gained power, while the latter became marginal.[7] Confucianism, the dominant Chinese ideology, tended to suppress shamanism[8] and favored a male-dominated hierarchy, with the husband ruling over the wife, the father over the son, and the emperor—regarded as the son of heaven—over all. But the brief conflict between a Confucianized male Manchu (the official) and a traditional female Manchu (the shaman) in this tale also reveals the internal tensions within traditional Manchu society, where women had low social status yet could be powerful shamans.[9] At the end of the epic, in what is probably an interpolation, she once again comes up against the all-male Confucian hierarchy, though with less success.

Despite being tricked by her, the official humbly begs for her help and offers her half his wealth if she will bring his fifteen-year-old son back to life. After protesting that she has little skill, she finally agrees. Then and there, she readies herself for a brief divination by washing her face, thus cleansing herself of this world in preparation for entering another realm—a physical acknowledgement that a break with everyday reality is a necessary prelude to the trance state—and then by burning incense to attract the spirits. Encouraged by the outcome of the divination, she begins to beat on her tambourine and to chant, calling her familiar spirit into her body. Speaking through her, the spirit reveals the circumstances of the boy's death: while he was out hunting, an evil spirit took his soul.[10] To bring back his soul, a powerful shaman will have to journey to the Land of the Dead. This requires a more formal ceremony, which is held at the official's home. The Nišan shaman calls for her male ritual assistant, whose expert drumming will support her shamanic journey. As the ceremony begins there is some playful sexual innuendo in her instructions to him, to which he responds with laughter. She says to him:

> According to that which was established of old, I confidently entrust the tambourine and drum to you, brother and assistant. If you are unable, I will beat your thighs with a dampened, leather-covered drumstick. If you do not harmonize with the chanting and murmuring, I will beat your buttocks with a wet drumstick made of cherry wood![11]

The erotic undertone in the exchange between the female shaman and her male assistant at the beginning of her journey is brought to the forefront in the later revelation that he is her lover. As will be discussed in the pages to follow, sexual energy is often an important component of shamanic rituals,[12] which is consistent with the connections between aerial females and sexuality that have been discussed in previous chapters.

The Nišan shaman then puts on ritual clothing trimmed with bells and a cap decorated with nine birds. She calls on the spirit that will speak through her to descend, which announces it will go to the Land of the Dead (or, the underworld).[13] Then she falls down. Her assistant attends to her, preparing the sacrificial animals (a rooster and a dog).[14] He then takes up the drum and chants to the animal spirits of the sky, earth, and water, notifying them of the shaman's journey to the Land of the Dead and requesting that they accompany her.

Her journey begins with the crossing of two rivers, symbolizing her transition from the earthly realm to that of the spirits and ghosts. At the first river, she bribes a boatman to take her across. Significantly, she tells him that she is going to visit her natal family, specifically mentioning various maternal relatives.[15] Manchu shamanism is based on or empowered by clan affiliations; thus the Nišan shaman's spirits are those of her natal clan.[16] When she comes to the second river there is no one to help her across, so she calls on her spirit helpers and throws her drum into the river so that she can ride it across. Still, she pays a fee to the god of this river, and farther on she pays fees to two gatekeepers. The element of exchange is pivotal in the shamanic journey; sacrificial offerings are usually given in exchange for a human life or for knowledge of the future. (The shaman is also paid by the sponsor of the ritual.[17]) The third and final gatekeeper is argumentative, but she angrily dismisses him and proceeds to a fourth and final gate that leads to the city of the Lord of the Underworld, who has adopted the official's dead son. Since she cannot enter, she once again calls on her spirit helpers, one of whom—a great bird—flies in and plucks up the boy. The Lord of the Underworld is not pleased by this, and he sends the third gatekeeper after them to demand a fee. A tough negotiation ensues, with the shaman slowly increasing her payment. The gatekeeper also wants the rooster and dog, which she withholds until he agrees to give the boy one hundred more years of life and good health, as well as nine children, eight of them boys.[18] Her trickster side surfaces again as she walks away: the sacrificial animals follow her instead of the gatekeeper because she has not told him the correct way to call them. Laughing, she finally tells him the sounds for commanding them. This is a display of her confidence and power in the underworld; only a mighty shaman would dare tease a gatekeeper of the underworld.

Still in the underworld, she walks along a road, holding the hand of the boy, when she suddenly meets her dead husband. He berates and threatens to kill her for not restoring him to life, as well. She explains that he has been dead too long and that his body is too decayed, but to appease his angry ghost she promises to make offerings at his grave and to continue taking care of his mother. He refuses this offer, accusing her of not treating him well when he was alive and of having acted according to her own whims.[19] Then she gets angry and accuses him of leaving her destitute and with his mother to support, which she has done and for which he should be grateful. In discussing this scene, Stephen Durrant points out "the tensions between her immanent status and her recognized capacity for transcendence."[20] In other words, her spiritual powers as a shaman are in conflict with her low status as a woman, which she challenges by arguing with her husband. In the end, she easily gets rid of him by calling on her great bird-spirit and telling it to snatch him up and drop him in the city of Lord of the Underworld. She then sings:

Without a husband
I shall live happily.
Without a man
I shall live proudly.
Among mother's relatives
I shall live enjoyably.
Facing the years
I shall live happily.
Without children
I shall live on.
Without a family
I shall live lovingly.
Pursuing my own youth
I shall live as [well as] a guest.[21]

Her song is provocatively female-centered, focusing on independence from men and life with her maternal relatives. After all, she has just shown that she can bring back the dead, but she would not bother to do so for her husband.[22] She connects the avoidance of patriarchal expectations with not growing old before her time. Her rejection of children and the patriarchal family is brazen, though it must be mentioned that not all women shamans reject motherhood.[23]

Continuing her journey back to the land of the living, the Nišan shaman comes to the tower of the female spirit who distributes souls. She pays another fee to a guard, enters the tower, and finds a woman who shows her where children are taken in order to be reborn. Another woman takes her to the place where souls are judged and sent to their reward or punishment, depending on the good or bad deeds they committed while alive.[24] This female-centered activity reflects the beliefs of an ancient cult, widespread in Inner Asia, that was practiced almost entirely by women and that featured female shamans. Caroline Humphrey discusses it in the context of the Daur cult of Niang-Niang, the Womb Goddess in the sky, who granted fertility, prosperity, health, and longevity. This cult was prevalent among the Manchu as well.[25] Chinese influences intrude in this part of the Nišan shaman's story, however, in the descriptions of Daoist and Buddhist hells, which conflict with traditional Manchu depictions of the Land of the Dead. The depiction of these hells also foreshadows the public punishment awaiting the Nišan shaman at the end of the epic.

After leaving the tower, the shaman continues on the road back to the land of the living. At the first river she gives another fee to its god, throws her tambourine on the water, picks up the boy, and rides across. She also pays an additional fee to the boatman at the second river and soon arrives back at the official's house.

At this point, her assistant pours water around her face, burns incense,[26] chants the story of her journey, and names her spirit helpers. Still in trance, the Nišan shaman chants the details of her journey, after which she wakes up and becomes herself again. She then fans "the soul into the empty body"[27] of the official's son, who wakes up. (Presumably, he went on to have a long and happy life.) After recounting how the shaman became rich and famous, the epic would seem to have reached its end, but there is a Confucian coda attached.[28] It relates that the shaman, who, we are now told, had been having an affair with her assistant, ended the relationship because of what she had learned about the punishment of sins during her journey to the Land of the Dead.[29] Her misfortune is that her mother-in-law has heard from others what happened when she met her husband in the Land of the Dead. The mother-in-law brings charges against her, claiming she killed her husband a second time. The Nišan shaman is found guilty, and the emperor of China decides to punish her by having all her shamanic clothing and implements destroyed.[30] In the end, the Confucian state takes away her power.

This richly detailed tale is useful for unpacking the complexities of a shaman's life, placing seemingly timeless shamanic practices within a specific historical context. The elements of shamanic practice include the shaman's costume, especially the bird cap, whose ascension imagery enables flight or a swift journey, and the bells, which are connected to important aural elements of shamanic trance: namely, the drumming and chanting (Figure 9.1). She is helped to fly not only by the birds on her cap; she is also carried by the sounds of the ritual—a point echoed in the Nišan shaman's tale when she crosses rivers on her drum and tambourine—and by one of her spirit helpers, a giant bird. As discussed in chapter 1, birds help shamans ascend to the heavens, and water birds, which dive below the surface, assist shamans in descending to the underworld. Such aerial and avian imagery maps the overall flight path of women who fly.

The epic's historical elements reveal the pressures of clashing cultures.[31] Through conquest, the Manchus had absorbed the Chinese state, but they, in turn, were absorbed by Chinese culture. The *Nišan Shaman* is a Manchu work, composed by traditional Manchus living on the margins of the Manchu empire, which was centered in Beijing. Appropriately, the Sinicization of the older Manchu culture appears at the edges of the epic, that is, the beginning and the end: the tale opens with a Chinese-style official seeking the shaman's help, and closes with her being

FIGURE 9.1 Koryak female shaman with drum. Photographer unknown, 1897–1902.
Courtesy of the Division of Anthropology, American Museum of Natural History.

judged by the emperor of China. It is more than likely that in the root story, the official was a Manchu chieftain. Changing him into a Manchu working as a Chinese official signals a foreign influence that is more completely revealed by the epic's discordant moral coda, which calls upon the awesome temporal and spiritual powers of the emperor of China. The clash of these two cultures is revealed through the inherent contradiction in the text between its positive presentation of a powerful female heroine, and her destruction. This is first and foremost a text about shamanic power and the shamanic journey, yet the coda undermines such power, even though the shaman has served patriarchal interests by saving the official's only male heir and by negotiating with spirits to ensure that he will have eight sons. The epic clearly associates shamanic power with women, but the coda pointedly takes this power away from them. Read through a patriarchal lens, the epic shows what women do when they have power: they are completely untraditional; do not respect their husbands or have children; take lovers; and generally live as they like. This was not acceptable in a Confucian state, which actually did suppress what it called Manchu "wild shamanism" during the nineteenth century.[32]

BECOMING A SHAMAN

Historically, shamans are found in tribal societies, but in the twenty-first century they survive and even flourish in modern, urban societies.[33] As with the Nišan shaman, the central ability of the shaman is to enter into alternate states of consciousness[34] in which she or he travels to other realms, such as the heavens, the underworld, the Land of the Ancestors, or the Land of the Dead,[35] where he or she becomes a conduit for the voices of the spirits. Shamans do this to cure the sick, guide the dead to the next world, divine the future, aid hunters and warriors, and repair conflict in the community.[36] In sum, they perform life-giving rituals that ensure the continuing flourishing of their society and its natural resources.[37] These and other shamanic characteristics appear in almost all parts of the world— for example, among Native Americans, Africans, Pacific Islanders, Asians, and Australian Aborigines. Quite often, shamans were and are women. Interestingly, the earliest known remains of a shaman, who was female, date from the Upper Paleolithic in central Europe. Barbara Tedlock discusses Neolithic and Bronze Age gravesites of female shamans that have been discovered,[38] while Siberians believe that the first shaman was a woman, an idea shared by the Manchu, who claim that the Nišan shaman was the first shaman.[39]

Shamanism is not a textual religion: it has few sacred books, and most of these were written down fairly recently or recorded by outsiders. Instead, it is an incredibly rich oral tradition of storytelling, mythmaking, and ritual, all of a highly complex and somewhat flexible nature. Significantly, by the time reports and studies about traditional people were available, they were no longer living in isolation; they had been colonized, missionized, and ravaged by European diseases, and quite often their ecological systems had been irreparably damaged. All of this affected the way shamanism was practiced, because shamanism is so responsive to its social, political, and ecological environments.[40] The practice of shamanism before these historical incursions is relatively uncertain.

Generally, shamans either inherit their office, or they are called to it.[41] In the latter case they usually undergo a process that begins with a crisis, often an illness that may be mental or physical. The illness is understood to be the call of the spirits, who then cure the future shaman when she or he accepts initiation from an experienced shaman and submits to a period of training. Frequently it is not a vocation the shaman willingly chooses,[42] because in one way or another it sets him or her apart from the rest of the group and can entail physical and mental suffering. It is generally believed that if people refuse the call they will die, and they or their families will suffer misfortune.

Shamans enter altered states of consciousness in a variety of ways. As with the Nišan shaman, they do so through drumming, dancing, or singing, as well as through ascetic practices such as fasting, going without sleep, and meditation. Some take a variety of mind-altering substances, such as the *soma* of the ancient Indians and the peyote and tobacco of Native Americans.[43] Hallucinogens are especially common in South American shamanism. Most tribal people have a formidable knowledge of pharmacology, and shamans, through their work as healers, can be quite knowledgeable about such substances.

MAGICAL FLIGHT, RITUAL DRESS, AND SPIRIT ANIMALS

Shamanic journeys are frequently referred to as "magical flight," indicating the shaman's use of magical or religious means of flight, during which her soul or spirit flies while her body mostly remains on the ground. This is particularly common among Siberian shamans,[44] as well as throughout Himalayan cultures,[45] though examples can be found among many other peoples as well.[46] Becoming a bird or being accompanied by a bird while in trance empowers the shaman to journey to the sky.[47] For example, a Daur (Mongolian) shaman song states: "Putting on my bird skin I have flown away/Putting on my feather gown I have leapt out."[48]

This song calls our attention to the shaman's ritual dress, which is rich with bird and flying imagery; such images have been found dating back to the Bronze Age rock art in Siberia.[49] For Mircea Eliade, shamanic clothing "constitutes a religious hierophany and cosmography; it discloses not only a sacred presence but also cosmic symbols and metaphysic itineraries. Properly studied, it reveals the system of shamanism as clearly as do the shamanic myths and techniques."[50] Pendants sewn onto the ritual shamanic clothing can be made of metal, bone, feathers, or cloth; they frequently depict bird spirits as well as celestial phenomena, such as the sun and the moon that will light the shaman's aerial journey. The costume's fringe represents a bird's feathers[51] and marks the shaman's ornithomorphic nature, which empowers her or him to transform into a bird or to fly. These avian aspects are thought to be the most ancient characteristic of the shaman costume.[52] Feathers, whether real or simulated, also lend buoyancy to the costume and simulate flight, an effect enhanced by the shaman's ritualized movements. Among Siberian shamans, ritual dress is commonly a bird suit believed to facilitate journeys of ascent and descent. A nineteenth-century Yukaghir shaman's coat had "[t]wo iron circles on the back [that] represent the shamanistic sun . . . and the shamanistic moon . . . . The tassels on the back represent the feathers . . . of a bird; the fringe at the bottom represents the tail . . ., while the sleeves stand for the wings . . . . The entire coat thus represents a bird's skin by means of which the shaman is able to fly"[53] (Figure 9.2). Additionally, fringe decorates the headdress and the footwear,[54] so that from head to toe the total costume is designed to represent flight. Such costumes are believed to transform shamans into birds,[55] because they are thought to possess supernatural powers and to be the dwelling place of spirits.[56] Thus they also become vehicles for passing shamanic power on to another person.[57]

Correspondingly, shamanic rituals often simulate birdlike movements and cries,[58] while ascension, whether actual or symbolic, is enacted. The Zen master Myōe (1173–1232) reported that while in trance a female shaman (a *miko*) rose into the air "like a moth fluttering its wings" and descended "as silently as a swan's feather falling."[59] Modern *miko*, while more ornamental and less shamanistic, still wear white robes decorated with images of birds. Among the Altai people of Siberia, shamans both straddle a scarecrow in the shape of a goose and climb a tree with nine notches in its trunk representing the nine heavens,[60] while Dolgan shamans erect nine wooden pillars with birds carved on their tops to represent the nine stories of heaven. These constructed birds are believed to help the shamans fly through the heavens.[61] The acts of jumping and leaping into the air are central to Korean shamanism, as well as to Siberian, Southeast Asian, and Japanese practices,[62] while ladders, ropes, and swings are used to simulate flying.[63] Equally important are the drum, well known from northeastern Asia, on which the shaman rides or flies, as we have seen when the Nišan shaman used her drum to fly or float across a river in the underworld, while the rattle serves this purpose in South

FIGURE 9.2 Yukaghir shaman suit, cap, and drum. The fringe on the cap goes around to cover the shaman's face, 1902.

Photograph: Waldemar Jochelson. Courtesy of the Division of Anthropology, American Museum National History.

America.[64] Images of these drums, and the paintings that decorated them, are preserved in Siberian rock art from various times and locations; they are noticeably similar to the shapes and decorations of more recent shamanic drums, signaling a remarkable historical continuity.[65] The frame of the drum usually comes from a special tree, one that may represent a cosmic tree that grows through all three levels of the cosmos: underworld, earth, and sky.[66] While drumming and singing to call her spirit-animal helper, the shaman imitates the sounds it makes, and through dancing mimics its movements. In many cases the spirit animal is thought to enter the shaman's body and speak through her; therefore, while in trance, the shaman moves and sounds like her spirit-animal helper.

In their everyday lives, shamans continued to be associated with their spirit animals. Sometimes they were called by their spirit-animal names, such as Swan Shaman, and in tales of their exploits, they shape-shift into the forms of their spirit animals.[67] Their bodies were not buried like those of ordinary people, but rather were placed on platforms or structures raised above the ground, or in tree branches or on mountain tops in order to release their "soul-birds."[68] The think-ing behind these practices is expressed in an analogous custom: "If a Yakut finds a dead eagle or the skeleton of one, he regards it as his duty to bury the bird on a special erection of wood, or in a tree .... While doing this, he utters the following words: 'Lift up thyself, fly to thy birthplace, come not down on the earth.'"[69] At the conclusion of a Gurung shaman's funeral this is literally enacted by releasing a bird from its cage atop the effigy of the deceased,[70] a practice that recalls the eagle released from the Roman emperor's funeral pyre (as noted in chapter 1).

Among indigenous Siberian people, certain birds are considered sacred and may not be killed, in part because a bird of that type was the clan ancestress, but also because myths describe the first shaman as a bird, often an eagle, or recall that a woman gained powers from a bird and became the first shaman. These stories have an element of sexuality and fertility: the woman sometimes becomes pregnant by the bird or, in other versions, a being called Bird-of-Prey-Mother makes nests on the gigantic first tree and lays eggs from which shamans hatch.[71] Among the Sakha, female shamans cured other women of barrenness or protected their child-ren against early death by placing bird nests on a sacred tree to attract the soul of a potential newborn.[72]

GENDER

The earliest forms of shamanism seem to be lost in the mists of time, though Lewis-Williams persuasively argues that it was the earliest form of religion, an idea shared by other scholars[73] and popularized by various neo-shamanic move-ments.[74] Waldemar Bogoras and Waldemar Jochelson, who studied the traditional people of northeastern Siberia in the late nineteenth and early twentieth centu-ries, thought the earliest forms of shamanism were embedded into family life: periodically, individual family members would beat a drum and sing to the spirits or ancestors.[75] Whatever shamanism's origins, certain individuals appear to have shown greater skill in this area, and the role was left to them. In many cultures, women assumed this role.[76] The *Chu Ci*, an anthology of Chinese poems said to date back to the fourth century BCE, tells of female and male shamans who drew the goddesses and gods down from heaven through their erotic longing,[77] while the ancient Japanese empress Himiko is said to have had shamanic powers.[78]

As I have argued in earlier chapters, women often were perceived to have access to other worlds and were therefore appropriate intermediaries between the mun-dane and spiritual realms. Additionally, in the past and in the present, women seem to have been more active in, and were believed to have greater access to, the trance practices associated with shamanism.[79] Moreover, shamanic powers are frequently inherited through the female line.[80] Some scholars have suggested that male shamans who dress as women (to be discussed further shortly) are evidence for an earlier female dominance of shamanism,[81] and Weston La Barre has a provocative psychoanalytic argument for the feminine quality of shamanism, regardless of whether it is practiced by men or women.[82]

I. M. Lewis has presented the very influential argument that in some regions there was a gradual and widespread displacement of female spiritual power from women to men by which politically powerful central cults came under the control of men, although usually some women were retained in decorative capacities,[83] which left women in charge of the local folk practices that emphasize shamanic experiences.[84] In other areas, the incursion of great missionary religions, such as Buddhism,[85] Confucianism,[86] Islam,[87] and Christianity,[88] with their organized male priesthoods, sought to control and diminish shamanism. Their criticism of shamanism reduced its prestige, making it less attractive as a religious specialization for men, and in many places clearing the way for women to once again assume and preserve these roles. Several scholars have challenged this as a universal thesis,[89] although some cases of this scenario have been acknowledged.[90] Most tellingly, Barbara Tedlock has written at length about the multiple ways through which the roles of women in shamanism have been ignored or gone unrecognized by scholars.[91]

Given the scarcity of accurate information, all that can be said with any certainty is that traditionally some form of shamanism has been widely practiced among tribal people for whom gender distinctions are central to religious life, as can be seen in the initiation ceremonies that mark the passages of the human life cycle.[92] These distinctions are most often complementary, but sometimes they are oppositional. In either case they ritualize, or make sacred, the separate spheres of male and female activities.

At the same time there can be an emphasis on female pollution, specifically through menstruation and childbirth. As with shamanism, most of the available material on female pollution has been gathered by men from other men, so there is limited knowledge about how tribal women themselves perceived these gender distinctions.[93] A case in point is Caroline Humphrey's reflection on her years of studying Siberian people. She has shown that among the Daur of Mongolia, single-sex rituals and the restrictions placed on women, when carefully analyzed and explored from the point of view of women, reveal that women have much more social and religious power than was suggested by earlier studies. Interestingly, Humphrey considers the *Nišan Shaman*, despite its negative ending, to be a critical marker of this power.[94]

TRANSVESTISM AND SEX CHANGE

Any hard-and-fast rules about gender are further compromised by changes of sex that occur or are sought during shamanic rituals. This belief in gender fluidity, and its reflection in social reality, has ancient and widespread roots extending back into the Upper Paleolithic and Mesolithic periods in Eurasia, and spread by migration across the Bering land bridge into the New World.[95] Among these and other peoples, shamans are conceived of as a third sex, beyond the polarity of male and female.[96] Among the Chukchi of Siberia, sex change could become permanent; outside ritual contexts, male shamans wore their hair like women, dressed in women's clothes (Figure 9.3), and took on traditionally feminine activities, such as sewing. Such shamans even marry; men thus transformed into women marry other men, and women transformed into men marry other women.[97] Some Native American peoples of North America recognize Two-Spirit people (often referred to as *berdaches* in the anthropological literature). Biologically male Two-Spirits dress, act, and live as women, often marrying men; biologically female Two-Spirits adopt male roles and have sometimes risen to prominence as warriors. Two-Spirit people who become shamans are considered more powerful than other shamans.[98] Additional examples can be found among the tribal peoples of Borneo and the Celebes.[99]

More ambiguous transformations arise when sex change is only experienced within a ritual context, after which the shaman returns to his or her original sex. Female and male shamans among the Mapuche of Chile ritually enter a primordial state in which they are simultaneously female and male.[100] During ceremonies, the men wear some women's clothing, but return to their male status upon completion of the ceremony. In the 1970s, Laurel Kendall noted: "The rare male shaman in Korea . . . performs *kut* [shamanic ritual] wearing women's clothing, down to the pantaloons that hide beneath his billowing skirt and slip,"[101] but, again, these shamans revert back to male status in non-ritual contexts. At some goddess festivals in South India, men dress as the goddess, complete with artificial breasts, then dance and sing their way into trance,[102] while in New Guinea men wearing costumes and with painted bodies dance as the red bird of paradise, even though this bird is the preeminent natural form of spirit women. Women accompany the dancing with their singing, thereby becoming complicit in the belief that only the men can represent the divine, whether it is gendered female or male.[103] Jochelson discusses the incorporation of female dress by male Yukaghir shamans, speculating that it may indicate that the first shamans were women, or that women's clothing was thought to possess spiritual and healing power.[104] He also notes instances of male shamans who, during rituals, wore women's clothes to which some of them attached two

The Chukchee.

FIGURE 9.3 Transvestite Chukchi shaman, drawing, c. 1902.
Courtesy of the Division of Anthropology, American Museum of Natural History.

iron circles to represent breasts.[105] Similarly, Marjorie Mandelstam Balzer found that, "numerous male shamans . . . wore cloaks fashioned in patterns of women's dressing during their séances."[106] And Tedlock describes how, during their training as shamans, she and her husband were encouraged to perceive themselves as co-gendered and to each take on the social role of the opposite sex.[107] In China these ideas go back to at least the fourth century BCE, when the shaman's gender could switch during rituals, as could that of the spirit possessing her or him.[108]

Gender transformations were a source of sacred power, and people who utilized the energies of both sexes were often sacralized.[109] At the same time, such acts shatter the category of gender, as well as the distinction between the sacred and the profane. In some cases, when male shamans put on female attire, it suggests a return to a time when only women were shamans, when only women had access to the sacred. In other cases, it signals the breakdown of the cultural categories of female/male and sacred/profane in order to enter a primordial state, or at least a state of undistinguished potentiality from which all existence, and consequently all fecundity, arise.

Before leaving this topic, it is important to acknowledge that male transformations into females or their assumptions of female dress do not necessarily indicate
a valuing of the "feminine" or of actual women. Rather, such transformations are
a usurpation and control of feminine powers. There is no equal exchange of power
in gender transformation, as the majority of transformations are of men into
women, even as they for the most part retain their cultural advantages as men.[110]

SEXUALITY

A final aspect of shamanic rituals that is consistent with the characteristics of
other aerial women is sexuality, which returns us to the *Nišan Shaman* and the
sexual play between the shaman and her male assistant at the beginning of her
shamanic ritual. Shamans seek access to spiritual realms in which sexuality, procreation, and death are merged. Such realms of potentiality are believed to be the
source of new life, generated by both sexes, and the realms to which both return in
death. Consequently, ritualized sexual innuendo places shamans in a procreative
mode that is believed to endow them with the ability to restore the dead and to
heal the sick. This is made explicit in various versions of "Princess Pari," an undated
folktale that plays an important role in Korean shamanism.[111] In this tale, the heroine makes a journey to the Land of the Dead in order to obtain divine medicines.
Since she does not have enough money to pay the guardian of this realm she has to
marry him, and eventually she bears seven sons, the ultimate sign of fecundity in
a patriarchal context.[112] Similarly, a Tibetan legend describes the shamanic journey
of Yid Thogma, which is fraught with sexuality. When we first meet Yid Thogma,
she is a barmaid, a profession that is traditionally often associated with sexually
loose women, and one that is a gloss for a sexual consort, that is, someone with
whom a Tantric adept practices ritual sexuality. Yid Thogma's sexuality, however,
gets her in trouble when she is caught having sex with a monk. Her punishment
is to be put in a covered box and set adrift on the ocean. She lands on the island
of a great spiritual practitioner, for whom she promptly brews beer; he becomes
inebriated and she seduces him. She stays with him for seven days, during which
he gives her teachings and magic charms that will help her on the rest of her journey. As she continues to travel she meets a variety of beings, both human and
semi-divine, with whom she has sex and who give her additional magic charms
and medicines.[113]

Textual evidence for the antiquity of such ideas comes from the fourth-century
BCE anthology of Chinese poems called the *Chu Ci*. Some of the poems in this collection are shaman songs. They begin with an invocation that usually has erotic

overtones and continue by describing the sexual longing of the female shaman for the divinity who has just left.[114]

Echoing these ideas are the many examples of the purposeful inclusion of women in male-dominated shamanic practices as ritual assistants and in order to attract male spirits.[115] In medieval Japan, shamans, who worked in male and female pairs, were often married.[116] Among the Yukaghir the sexual purpose behind the inclusion of women is underscored by the occasional requirement that female participants must be virgins, because male spirits were thought to like girls who had not yet had intercourse with men,[117] while the Inuit practice of wife exchange was sometimes connected to shamanic rituals.[118]

Some female shamans have spirit husbands to assist them, just as male shamans may have spirit wives.[119] This is particularly the case among Burmese shamans, the vast majority of whom are women.[120] A woman becomes a shaman when a *nat* (a spirit) falls in love with her and wishes to marry her.[121] The woman usually resists this marriage because Burmese shamans (*nat kadaw*s) have a low social status.[122] The low status of shamans is deeply connected to sexuality in several ways. First, it is thought to be shameful to have sexual relations with spirits, which often represent forbidden sexual relations such as premarital sex or adultery, while shamans are generally thought to be sexually immoral and promiscuous. In part, this opinion arises from the shaman's public performances while possessed by her *nat*, during which she dances with wild abandon.[123] Given the cultural emphasis on female modesty and decorum, this in itself is shameful, but their public performance also equates shamans with female actors and dancers who are regarded as sexually loose. Needless to say, this moral gloss defines shamans as highly sexualized and thus powerful beings.

Beyond this, though, shamans transgress gender roles not only when they are possessed but in daily life, as well. A female shaman personifies her *nat* husband by wearing his costume, reenacting his life, and completely identifying with him. "[S]he may guzzle alcoholic drinks, brandish a sword, cavort like a buffalo,"[124] and so on. When female shamans take on a male persona during their rituals, that persona often carries over into their daily life, causing Melford Spiro to comment that, "many are highly masculine in manner."[125] Of course, the same is true of the small number of male shamans who personify their *nat* wives and are quite effeminate in daily life.[126]

Spirit wives and husbands, who make love to shamans in their dreams, were common among the Goldi tribe of Siberia.[127] In 1910 a male shaman reported to Leo Sternberg that his spirit wife, who came to him in his dreams, could shapeshift, sometimes appearing as an old woman, sometimes as a wolf, and at other times as a winged tiger.[128] The theme of the supernatural animal-spouse is found throughout the folklore of the world, some of which has been discussed in the context of swan maidens, and is suggestive of shamanic spirit marriages.[129] After making love, the spirit spouse gives the shaman additional spirit assistants, usually in the form of animal spirits. Another shaman told Sternberg that he inherited his three spirit wives from his father, who had also been a shaman.[130] This is similar to the shape-shifting Valkyries, some of whom also remain connected to one family. The spirit spouse possesses the shaman and empowers her or his ritual activities, during which the shaman makes movements that imitate sexual intercourse.[131] Occasionally spirit spouses are jealous of the shaman's earthly spouse, and are thought to cause sterility, or even to kill the earthly spouses. Some shamans become so completely enraptured by their spirit spouses that they ignore their earthly spouses, or refuse to marry at all.

This summary of flying female shamans reflects several factors that appear among aerial females: shape-shifting; otherworldliness; profound connections to birds; a struggle for power between the sexes; and sexuality. The aerial women presented in the next chapter also wage battles with male religious authority, though much of their power is gained through celibacy, among other ascetic practices, and they visit other worlds: namely, the realms of heaven, hell, and purgatory.

10

Flying Mystics, or the Exceptional Woman, Part I

THIS CHAPTER AND the next one detail the aerial experiences of women from a broad spectrum of religions, unified by their single-minded devotion to the divine and their yearning for union with it. Presented here are a number of well-known, and some lesser-known, women who symbolically—and often physically—temporarily left the world behind and the men who tried to restrain them, if only by taking control of their narratives.

The Christian women discussed in this chapter are but a small representation of a rich tradition. All had visionary experiences, which gave them enough religious authority to have their views accepted and their works preserved, yet they were unique individuals. They lived in various countries, came from different classes, and had widely diverging educations. Most were cloistered but found ways to move about in the secular world. Each, in her own way, led a heroic life by being a woman of formidable will who overcame obstacles and stayed true to her own visions. Several affirm the connections between women and death, in that they visited the lands of the dead—specifically, hell and purgatory. These aerial female saints form an intriguing contrast with the maleness of the winged angels that often appeared to them.

ST. CHRISTINA THE ASTONISHING

Christina Saint-Trond (1150–1224) of France, a laywoman from a poor family, became known as Christina Mirabilis (Christina the Astonishing), a title she fully earned. Christina was no merely visionary flier; according to her hagiographer, the Dominican friar Thomas de Cantimpré, the witnesses he assembled testified that they actually saw her fly with their own eyes.

The Life of Christina the Astonishing was written in 1232.[1] Its popularity is attested to by the survival of twelve manuscripts in Latin, one in Middle English, and three in Dutch.[2] Given the extraordinary events of Christina's life, Thomas de Cantimpré is quick to cite the testimony of Cardinal Jacques de Vitry (d. 1240) that he had been an eyewitness to her life and exploits[3] and adds that he relied on many other "straightforward witnesses."[4]

The Life of Christina begins with her death—that is, her death and resurrection.[5] When she was about thirty-two years old, she grew ill and died. During the Requiem Mass said for her, "the body stirred in the coffin and rose up and, like a bird, immediately ascended to the rafters of the church" (*Life* 18), the first of many references to her birdlike activities. She is soon forced to descend by the officiating priest and is questioned by her friends about what she saw while she lay dead. Christina answers that she had been taken by angels to see the suffering souls in purgatory and in hell (Figure 10.1) and that then she had been led before God, who gave her a choice:

> "either to remain with me now or to return to the body and suffer there the sufferings of an immortal soul in a mortal body without damage to it, and by these your sufferings to deliver all those souls on whom you had compassion in that place of purgatory, and by the example of your suffering and your way of life to convert living men to me and to turn aside from their sins, and after you have done all these things to return to me having accumulated for yourself a reward of such great profit." I answered without hesitation that I wished to return under the terms which had been offered to me. (*Life* 19)

Christina continued to display her aerial abilities, and her talent for more terrestrial forms of flight, as she time and again escaped the chains with which her family and friends bound her in the belief that she was mad or possessed by demons. The chaining and restraining of visionary women appears not to have been unusual.[6]

Christina never joined an order of nuns. Instead she struggled to maintain an independent and solitary life. She "lived in trees after the manner of birds" (*Life* 20) or at the top of any lofty structure she could find. In this practice, Christina

FIGURE 10.1 Prayer card depicting an aerial St. Christina (top center) receiving a soul from hell carried by an angel. From the *Fasti Mariani* calendar of saints, 1630.

used her body to demonstrate her interstitial state: by her choice she was nei-ther fully with God, nor willing to be fully in this world. Dendrites (hermits who lived in trees) and stylites (hermits who lived on high pillars) had existed since the early centuries of Christianity, especially in Syro-Mesopotamian Christianity.[7] Christina is, of course, imitating them—whether consciously or unconsciously—while combining shamanic behavior and sympathetic magic, whereby enact-ing one's desire—in this case, literally climbing toward heaven—can lead to its accomplishment—that is, arriving in heaven. She is said to have survived in such places by drinking the sweet milk that dripped from her own virginal breasts; later, her breasts dripped a pure oil that sustained her and healed the wounds caused by her chains.[8] During the medieval period, other female saints were said to have fed people from their bodies.[9]

To fulfill her promise to God to take onto her own body the torments of those in hell and purgatory, Christina threw herself into fires, from which she emerged without any marks, or stood in freezing water in the winter. She also hung on the gallows between thieves and entered into graves (*Life* 10–13, 21–22).[10] It is possible that Christina may have been an epileptic, perhaps falling into rivers and fires rather than choosing to enter them. She also continually fasted, creating the lightest body possible; being so poor, she had nothing else but food to give up for Christ.

When she was imprisoned and chained to prevent her perceived self-destructive behavior, she broke free and again flew "through the empty air like a bird" (*Life* 18, 25). Thomas de Cantimpré's *Life of Christina* frequently describes her flying and compares her to birds:

> Her body was so sensitive and light that she walked on dizzy heights and, like a sparrow, hung suspended from the topmost branches of the loftiest trees.
>
> When she wanted to pray, she had to flee to tree-tops or towers or any lofty spot so that, remote from every one, she might find rest for her spirit. . . . Many times she would stand erect on fence palings and in that position would chant all the Psalms for it was very painful indeed for her to touch the ground while she was praying.[11]

This quote reveals the power of a male hand in devising a new interpretation of Christina's somatic experiences as those of a holy woman and not a madwoman, an interpretation begun by Jacques de Vitry. Time and again male hagiographers interpret the mystical experiences of medieval women.[12] De Vitry protected Christina, and under his guidance she became more pious, modeling her behavior as best she could on other holy people.[13] Being a laywoman from a very poor family, Christina especially needed protectors.

Elsewhere the *Life* explains that Christina flew because she could not tolerate the smell of human beings (*Life* 18, 20, 27), but her flight and birdlike nature were surely expressions of spiritual longing. As we have seen in many times and places, birds and flight are associated with the soul. Christina had already died and ascended to heaven; in her mind she was only her soul, not her resurrected mortal body. Despite this, the *Life* is all about her extraordinary body: so light from fasting that it can fly; undamaged by her self-imposed austerities such as sitting in ovens or blazing fires; and self-sustaining in its production of first breast milk (even though she is a virgin) and later a healing oil. Two final examples go beyond even what a contortionist can do with her or his body:

[W]hen she prayed and the divine grace of contemplation descended upon her, all her limbs were gathered together into a ball as if they were hot wax and all that could be perceived of her was a round mass. After her spiritual inebriation was finished and her active physical senses had restored her limbs to their proper place, like a hedgehog her rolled up body returned to its proper shape and the limbs which had been bent formlessly once again were spread out. (*Life* 16)

Though her body suffered from her penances on the behalf of souls in purgatory and hell—she often screamed in agony—it showed no marks from such ordeals.[14] Christina Stern summarizes Christina and her *Life* as follows:

Christina is a living marvel, the text suggests, because she moves, flies, walks across water, metamorphosizes [*sic*], spins in mystic ecstasy, escapes chains, and performs a whole repertoire of bodily movements that entrance, stupefy, and otherwise attract the eyes of those around her. Her unique body dramatizes important religious messages not only about purgatory—which is fundamentally her primary mission—but other theological matters as well. By the inclinations of her body she exhibits the mercy of God, the nature of the soul, the power of divine will, and the joys of prayer, mysticism, and spiritual life.[15]

Indeed, it is reasonable to suggest that Christina's journeys to the Land of the Dead (hell and purgatory) and expressions of fertility through her body (a virgin whose breasts provide milk and healing oil), including her propensity to cry out "as if in childbirth" (*clamabatque quasi parturiens*) over the suffering of sinners,[16] connect her to ancient and not-so-ancient beliefs in the power of females to bring the dead to eternal life—in Christina's case, rebirthing them from hell and purgatory to heaven.

Despite her physical suffering, she lived to the ripe old age (for the medieval era) of seventy-four.

FLIGHT AND SANCTITY

Devout people of many faiths have experienced miraculous flights and moments of transvection (being carried through the air) and levitation (rising into the air). The Old and New Testaments mention several incidents of transvection: Enoch is carried up in a whirlwind (Gen. 5:24); Habakkuk is carried by an angel to bring food to

Daniel in the lion's den (Dan. 14:32–38); Philip is carried to Gaza (Acts 8:39); and, not least, Christ is transported by Satan to the top of the Temple of Jerusalem and then to a high mountain (Matt. 4:2–8; Luke 4:5–8). A later transvection was that of St. Catherine of Alexandria (traditionally, fourth century), whose martyred body was carried by angels to Mt. Sinai for burial.[17] Mention should also be made of St. Mary of Bethany, the sister of Lazarus, who was said to have risen above the ground seven times a day during her contemplations.[18] Then there is St. Mary the Egyptian, whose *Life* reports that, in 430, St. Zosimus came across her living in the desert. While they prayed together he looked up and saw her floating in the air.[19] Several other female saints levitated, including Lutgard of Aywières, Vanna of Orvieto,[20] St. Bona of Pisa, St. Umiltà of Faenza,[21] and Teresa of Ávila.[22] To this list can be added Beatrice of Ornacieux, who moved miraculously through or over walls; Douceline of Marseilles; Christina of Stommeln;[23] and St Rita de Cascia.[24] Bilocation is also a familiar motif. The Virgin Mary is the earliest Christian example. She is said to have bilocated to what is now Spain, appearing on top of a pillar, in order to encourage the apostle James the Elder to continue his efforts to convert the pagans.[25] Maria of Ágreda (1602–1665) was said to have flown to isolated villages in the American Southwest, "where she inspired the Indians to seek out priests for baptism,"[26] at the same time that she was residing in Spain.

As noted earlier in the discussion of witches, Christians eventually demonized human flight. Churchmen were made anxious by any supernatural acts, because the source for such powers could be the devil (as in the transvection of Christ) as well as God. In general, they perceived flying as a sign of demonic power, as in the case of witches, but the occasional levitations by a saint while engrossed in prayer were merely frowned upon. Demoniacs (those thought to be possessed by demons) were, however, commonly believed to levitate as well.

St. Irene of Chrysobalanton

The Eastern Orthodox Church has also given us flying female mystics, as in the example of St. Irene. The author of the late tenth-century *Life of St. Irene, Abbess of Chrysobalanton* is unknown, although there are reasons for believing the author was a woman;[27] Irene's precise dates are also uncertain, although she lived in the ninth century, during the period of the Triumph of Orthodoxy, which had seen the defeat of several heresies.[28]

Irene came from a noble Byzantine family and rejected several offers of marriage in order to pursue her vocation as a nun. In the convent she performed ascetic practices such as fasting, standing in prayer all night. Her *Life* tells us that her success in these practices attracted the devil's envy, but Irene defeated him through prayer, after which God made her immune to the devil's attacks and gave her power against demons. Additional incidents of black magic and sorcery were defeated by Irene's marshaling her sister nuns to intense prayer for hours on end, and again by fasting. In chapter 13 of the *Life*, a young nun becomes possessed because her former suitor hires a sorcerer. She is overcome by an intense sexual desire to get out of the convent so that she can see the suitor. Irene organizes the nuns to fight back with prayer and fasting, which culminated in Irene's having a dream in which the Virgin Mary promises that the possessed nun will be healed. As the nuns continue to pray over the young nun, St. Anastasia and St. Basil the Great are "seen flying through the air" (*Life* 61). A voice tells Irene to hold out her robe, and as she does so the saints drop a package into it containing the magic devices used to possess the nun, such as images of her and the man bound together. Irene sends the package, the possessed nun, and two other nuns to the Church of St. Anastasia, which also served as a kind of mental asylum.[29] Here a priest burns its contents, which causes the nun to slowly regain her wits.

This aerial vision prefigures Irene's own experience of flight. Chapter 16 of the *Life* describes her practice of standing prayer, during which Irene strikes a posture of flight by extending her arms toward heaven. She remains in this position for days, even a week, so that

> when she was to lower her hands, she was unable to draw her arms together by herself, since the elbows and the shoulders, in consequence of the severe stretching and the prolonged extension, resisted their natural flexibility. Calling for those among the sisters that were closest to her she received help, and one could hear the joints emit a terrible cracking. (*Life* 75)

These long vigils required her to go without sleep for days at a time, even as she maintained such an intense fast that the skin was said to hang off her bones. This rejection of bodily needs obviously led to an extreme loss of weight and a continual state of lightheadedness that would be conducive to Irene's own sense of flight or, more accurately, her levitation. This seems to have been a frequent event for Irene, though there is only one witnessed account by an unnamed nun, who

> happened to peep out of her cell just [in time] to behold Irene hanging in the air about two cubits above the ground and praying with her hands extended towards heaven. Two lofty cypresses were standing on either side of the forecourt, reaching far up into the air. As Irene bent forward and prostrated herself before God, they trembled gently together and bowed their crowns to the ground along with her, waiting for her to rise. But even when the holy

woman stood upright, the trees did not raise their crowns until approaching she made the sign of the cross on each of them, then, as if blessed, they returned to their erect position.[30]

The observing nun later claimed that Irene had lingered in the air for three hours or more (*Life* 77). This event reminds us of Christina the Astonishing's special relationship with trees, as well as of the visions of Hadewijch of Brabant, to be discussed shortly.

Irene was also able to penetrate the dreams of others, as when the Byzantine emperor Basil I saw her in a dream. The next day he sent high-ranking officials and a painter to her convent. The officials kept her engaged in conversation long enough for the painter to finish her portrait. Of course, the emperor was startled and somewhat afraid when he saw the similarities between his dream image and the painting of the actual woman.[31]

St. Elisabeth of Schönau

Christianity's early acceptance of aerial females included the Assumption of the Virgin Mary,[32] which remains an enduringly popular image in Christian iconography. Several of the Christian mystics who follow, including Elisabeth of Schönau, Hadewijch, and Teresa of Ávila, focused on Mary's Assumption. Angels, assumptions, and ascensions are all expressions of a core Christian belief in an ongoing downward spiritual movement of God's grace to human beings and an upward movement of human beings to a heavenly salvation. This belief is expressed in texts and displayed in iconography, not infrequently through the depiction of God's creating the birds in Genesis 1.[33] Christ's Resurrection and Ascension and Mary's Assumption into heaven are not just their individual experiences; they are a promise that all faithful Christians will be bodily called to heaven on the Day of Judgment.[34] Elisabeth of Schönau (1128/9–1164/5)[35] embodies this dual movement in that she claims to have been transported to other realms, and also to have been visited in this world by heavenly beings.[36] In her *Poem of the Assumption*, she described her vision of Mary's Assumption, which popularized this belief, defined its imagery, and influenced its iconography.[37]

Elisabeth frequently described being "carried aloft" by a male angel, as when he carried her to purgatory, where three young girls asked for her prayers so that they could ascend to heaven.[38] This is a reversal of the usual saintly intercession, in which living human beings pray to dead saints to help them; here, the dead seek the help of a saintly and living human being to secure a better afterlife. In this, one of Elisabeth's many visions, we see the familiar association of aerial women with the realm of the dead, as we did with Christina the Astonishing. Elisabeth was more than that, though; based on her visions she claimed an independent authority to address matters of religious truth, including the moral corruption in the church, and in keeping with her aerial nature she found her own path and peopled it with authoritative women represented by the supportive community of her sister nuns and by her visions of the Virgin Mary and of powerful, often royal, women. Book II of her *Visions* opens with an explanation of why she should be blessed with visions:

> Because in these times the Lord deigns to show His mercy most gloriously in the weak sex, such men [who sneer at her visions] are offended and led into sin. But why do they not remember that something similar happened in the days of our fathers? While the men were given over to sluggishness, holy women were filled with the spirit of God, that they might prophesy, govern God's people forcefully, and indeed triumph gloriously over the foes of Israel: so it happened with Olda, Deborah, Judith, Jahel, and other women of this sort.[39]

One of the most gifted women of the Middle Ages, Hildegard of Bingen, believed that Christianity was in an effeminate age (*muliebre tempus*),[40] in which the failure of male leadership required women to define their own spiritual paths. Fittingly, Elisabeth maintained a correspondence with and was influenced by Hildegard: Elisabeth's visions began one year after the publication of Hildegard's visions, the *Scivias*, in 1151 (Figure 10.2).[41]

Anne Clark classifies Elisabeth's aerial experiences as "raptures," during which she "perceived herself to be taken away from her room or her place in the chapel and brought somewhere else . . . . In each case of rapture, Elisabeth perceives her soul lifted up into heaven or, at least, lifted up into 'the height,' which is ostensibly closer to heaven and thus affords a better view of what is going on among the celestial citizens."[42] For example, Elisabeth tells us:

> On the vigil of All Saints Day, at Vespers, I struggled in agony for a long time, and while I was doubled over with violent pain, I tightly bound the sign of the crucified Lord to my breast, and at last coming into ecstasy I became quiet. Then, in an unusual way, it seemed to me as if my spirit had been snatched up into the height, and I saw an open door in the heavens and such a multitude of saints, more than I had ever seen before[43]

FIGURE 10.2 St. Elisabeth reading St. Hildegard's *Scivias*, engraving, Germany, c. eighteenth century.
Austrian National Library.

Clark opines that "the distinctiveness of this experience seems to refer to Elisabeth's perception that her soul was forcibly taken up into heaven, and there, in heaven, she saw visions. She continues this narration with the report that the next day, also at Vespers, she was again raised up."[44]

Between these two raptures Elisabeth first describes her angel, whom she identifies as Jacob's angel (Gen. 48:16). Clark says, "[A]t this point she ceases to qualify her descriptions of rapture. Her variations on the formula, 'It seemed to me that my spirit was seized,' give way to a new model: 'The angel of the Lord seized my spirit.'"[45]

Elisabeth's family, probably members of the minor nobility, dedicated her to a Benedictine monastery when she was twelve years old; she remained there for the rest of her short life. Her ecstatic visions, which usually occurred after she had been ill for a period of time, began when she was about twenty-three and continued until her death thirteen years later. Her poor health and frequent illnesses were probably exacerbated by her lack of interest in food or drink and her practices of physical mortification, such as wearing coarse garments and a harsh belt that tore at her flesh, as well as the many tribulations in her life, which she attributed to the "hand of the Lord upon her."[46] One prolonged difficult period occurred when a vision that told her that the Apocalypse would occur in the year 1155 was widely reported. When it did not come to pass,[47] she suffered mockery and no doubt developed anxieties about her visions. These anxieties were somewhat eased by Hildegard of Bingen, who wrote a letter in which she reassured Elisabeth that this was God's way of testing her. This vision was later removed from her text.[48]

Her brother Ekbert (d. 1184), who was a monk and later the abbot of Schönau, wrote down, edited, and disseminated her experiences but neglected to write her biography, save for his description of the last two weeks of Elisabeth's life, *De Obitu Elisabeth*.[49] From him we learn that her visions occurred on Sundays or other holy days and that they began with physical pain, after which she lay as if lifeless, seemingly not breathing, although she would eventually speak from her trance-like state in Latin, German, or a combination of the two. Not surprisingly, the visions occurred after she had taken the Eucharist,[50] as they did for many female mystics. She had several visionary experiences of the Eucharist—the miracle of communion, when bread and wine are transformed into the body and blood of Christ—including vision 26, in which she saw a dove depositing tongues of fire above the heads of her sister nuns as they received Communion,[51] and again when she saw a dove plunge its beak into the chalice, turning the wine to blood.[52] Ekbert said he set down her words as she related them, but he did suppress some of her experiences; he also discussed her visions with her, and sought revelations from her on topics of interest to himself, making the record of her visions a complex collaboration.

Returning to Elisabeth's vision of being flown to purgatory, where three girls asked her to pray for them: this vision not only trespasses on the powers of dead saints, but it creates a startling parallelism between Elisabeth's earthly intercession for the three dead girls, and the Virgin Mary's primary role as the heavenly intercessor on behalf of the living. The living Elisabeth is to the dead what the dead Mary is to the living. Elisabeth both reflects Mary's power and turns that reflection back on Mary through a series of visions she had of the Virgin Mary over more than three years, during which Elisabeth questioned her about the nature and time of her Assumption into heaven.[53] Given that the New Testament is silent about Mary's death, there was uncertainty about the exact date of her Assumption, which was celebrated on the same day as her Dormition, her "falling asleep"—that is, dying but ready to be awakened.[54] It was revealed to Elisabeth, however, that the Virgin Mary was resurrected forty days after her burial and then flown to heaven by a host of angels.[55] There was also uncertainty as to whether Mary's Assumption was only in the spirit or in the flesh as well, in answer to which Elisabeth is granted the following vision:

> And I saw in a very distant place a sepulcher bathed in a strong light, and in it what seemed the form of a woman, and all about stood a large throng of angels. And after a little while, she rose up out of the sepulcher and together with that throng of angels was lifted up into the heavens.[56]

Elisabeth's angel is by her side during this vision to explain that it reveals the Virgin Mary "was assumed into the heavens in the flesh as well as in the spirit."[57] Like the Virgin Mary, Elisabeth is transvected skyward by an angel, but in spirit only. Elisabeth identifies with and enacts not only Mary's compassionate role as intercessor but also her Assumption. Fittingly, the wide circulation of Elisabeth's visions in manuscript form popularized Mary's Assumption and influenced its iconography.[58]

Her most popular work, *Revelations of the Sacred Band of Virgins of Cologne*,[59] is about the martyred British princess St. Ursula (variously said to have died in the third, fourth, fifth, or seventh century) and her 11,000 companion virgins, all of whom ascended to heaven,[60] though this was a visionary ascension as their bodies were left behind. Their martyrdom is said to have been at the hands of the Huns in Cologne, Ursula being the last one killed:

> And so Ursula, the queen of the most radiant army [the 11,000 virgins] pierced through by the shot of an arrow sank upon the noble heap of her followers like a heavenly pearl. She was purified by the royal purple of her own blood as if she had been baptized again. With all her victorious troops she ascended, crowned with laurels, to the celestial palace.[61]

In *Revelations of the Sacred Band*, and through her ecstatic trance visions, Elisabeth elaborated upon Ursula's basic legend, which led to its validation and its wide circulation.[62] These visions were stimulated by the discovery of corpses thought to be those of St. Ursula and her companions and the delivery of the relics of two bodies to her convent; Elisabeth had a vision of their impending arrival accompanied by an angel.[63] Her influence on ideas about female sanctity, the development of Ursula's cult, and the nature of Mary's Assumption indicates the remarkable acceptance of women's visionary experiences and a growing acceptance of saintly female imagery.

But Elisabeth goes further. In perhaps her most astonishing vision, received during Mass on Christmas Eve, Christ appears to her in the body of a young female virgin, crowned and sitting on a throne.[64] When questioned, her angel explains to her that the virgin "is the sacred humanity of the Lord Jesus."[65] In this vision, Elisabeth then questions St. John the Evangelist, asking why Christ has appeared in a woman's, rather than a man's, form. He answers that Christ has chosen the female form "to signify his blessed mother as well," because it is she who intercedes with her son to forgive the sins of humanity.[66] Hildegard got it right; Christianity had entered an effeminate age.

FEMALE AND MALE MYSTICS

There were consistent differences between medieval women's and men's spirituality. Female mystics primarily experienced union with God within their bodies: levitations, immobile and insensible trances, uncontrollable fits, and reception of the stigmata were all bodily manifestations of and authentications of access to the divine.[67] Flying and levitation were considered supernatural, but not always problematic, signs of grace.[68] In part, female mystics had internalized the association of women with flesh (and men with soul) articulated by philosophers and theologians, and thus they manifested their mystical experiences through their bodies, while male mystics did so through their intellects.[69] They also profoundly enacted belief in the resurrection of the body as well as the soul on Judgment Day.[70] As we have seen in Christina's life, their religious authority arose in large part from their somatic experiences.

Women's religious lives were not always institutionalized. Beguines, such as Hadewijch of Brabant (1202?–1268), were independent religious women living and working all over northern Europe.[71] (Likewise, Christina the Astonishing was always moving about when not actually escaping confinement, and she was not a member of a religious order.) Many of these women found a religious significance in ordinary life and its chores that "seemed odd and dangerous to male sensibilities."[72]

The experience of union with God through his spirit or that of the Holy Spirit penetrating an individual's body was new to Christianity and, unfortunately for many, appeared to resemble the longstanding conception of demonic possession.[73]

That is, the external behaviors of the possessed, whether divine or demonic, were perceived to be similar. The only distinction between them was internal and therefore dependent on the claims of the possessed person.[74] Miraculous abilities, such as levitation, could just as well be conferred by an evil spirit as by God,[75] and women were considered more susceptible to demonic possession than men.[76] Some people thought Hildegard of Bingen had been seduced by evil spirits,[77] while she herself expressed fears of the devil's influence, which may explain why she waited so many years to record her visions.[78] Concurrently, women's low status in medieval society fostered suspicion that their claims to religious authority were attempts to gain prestige. Underlying the notion of women's vulnerability to possession may have been their sexual role as the ones penetrated during the sexual act, as well as their ability to become pregnant—that is, to carry another being within their body.[79] Even cloistered women mystics were figures of public renown and thus both more challenging to, and vulnerable to, male ecclesiastical authorities, many of whom thought their claims to sanctity usurped male authority; these men tended to couch their questioning of such women in their beliefs about women's greater vulnerability to the demonic. This was the time of the Inquisition, and women such as Hadewijch of Brabant and Teresa of Ávila (1515–1582) came under its scrutiny. In contrast, male mystics were more often questioned in terms of doctrinal error or heresy.[80] Carole Slade explains a female mystic's conundrum:

> The *Directorium Inquisitorum*, the most authoritative manual for Inquisitors during the fifteenth and sixteenth centuries, traces heresy etymologically to the verb *to elect* (*eligo*); the heretic, then, is one who "refuses the true doctrine and chooses as true a false and perverse doctrine." This definition, implying deliberate choice of an erroneous doctrine, applied to male heretics only, however: women were not considered to possess the faculty of reason. While the heretical man was considered to have chosen his belief, the heretical woman was thought to be deluded by the devil. Defining possession by the devil in terms of sexual intercourse, medieval theologians held that the inordinate sexual appetite attributed to women made them particularly susceptible to heresy.[81]

Given the similarities between divine and demonic possession, a widespread campaign was initiated to educate clerics and laity in the discernment of evil spirits. In the case of women, it was usually presumed that possession was caused by an evil spirit, which required women to defend themselves, sometimes again and again for years.[82] Beginning in the late twelfth century, one consequence of this campaign was a concurrent increase in reports of demonic possession just as reports of women claiming divine possession first appeared.[83] Similarly, Bynum discusses the conflation of the female mystic and the witch, noting that "[a] number of women saints were suspected of witchcraft or demonic possession: e.g., Catherine of Siena, Lidwina of Schiedam, and Columba Rieti."[84] Indeed,

> [b]y 1500 . . . the model of the female saint, expressed both in popular venera-
> tion and in official canonizations, was in many ways the mirror image of soci-
> ety's notion of the witch. Each was thought to be possessed, whether by God
> or by Satan; each seemed able to read the minds and hearts of others with
> uncanny shrewdness; each was suspected of flying through the air, whether
> in saintly levitation or bilocation, or in a witches' sabbath. Moreover, each
> bore mysterious wounds, whether stigmata or the marks of incubi, on her
> body. The similarity of witch and saint—at least in the eye of the theologians,
> canon lawyers, inquisitors, and male hagiographers who are, by the fifteenth
> century, almost our only sources for their lives—suggests how threatening
> both were to clerical authorities.[85]

Two prominent elements defined the sanctity of medieval women saints. First, they were celibate, despite the sometimes erotic language with which they described their connections to Christ,[86] which altered their status and gave them potential authority. Celibacy, for the most part, placed them beyond common assumptions about female weakness and corruption; it also freed them from the constraints of gender roles.[87] It could also be the first step in denying the needs of the body in order to reconstruct that body into a different vehicle.

The second element was excessive fasting, for which women saints were famous.[88] This denial of and attempt to transform the body actually does make the body lighter, perhaps light enough to fly,[89] as was suggested in *The Life of Christina* and the *Life of St. Irene*. Unfortunately, witches were also great fasters, so not eating could be attributed to either a demonic or divine source.[90] In the case of witches, it was assumed they were "fed by the devil in a symbolic rapport with a familiar or an incubus."[91] An important aspect of fasting among holy women included devotion to the Eucharist—that is, eating the sacred host, a thin wafer representing the body of Christ.[92] Taking the Eucharist released a significant number of medieval women—including Elisabeth of Schönau and Hadewijch of Brabant—into ecstatic union with Christ.[93] Extreme female fasters were said to live on the communion host alone, thereby taking Christ's transcendent and elevated nature into their extremely light and thin bodies. In the medieval period levitation was frequently "attributed to a divine spiritualizing of the physical body that rendered it lighter than air."[94] Fasting is deeply connected to female miracles involving manipulation of their bodies, including flying, levitation, transvection, and bilocation. Their consciousness was undoubtedly altered by the act of fasting, making them light-headed as well as light in weight and stimulating visions involving aerial events. Their bodies were further transformed by physical suffering, illness, and harsh forms of asceticism.[95]

Of some importance, female mystics, unlike various male mystics, mostly employed the vernacular, which gave them "access to a whole system of imme-diate meanings and images in the erotic category."[96] Jacques de Vitry says of the Beguines: "They melted altogether in wondrous love for God until it seemed that they bowed under the burden of desire and for many years they did not leave their beds except on rare occasions. . . . Resting in tranquility and with the Lord, they became deformed in body but comforted and made strong in spirit."[97]

Often, female mystics write about or describe images that are aerial and involve birds and ascents. For example, Mechthild of Magdeburg (c. 1210–c. 1285) described God receiving the soul as follows: "Be welcome, darling dove; you have flown so fervently over earth's kingdom that your feathers rise strong to the kingdom of heaven."[98] Beatrijs of Nazareth (1200–1268) also used the image of an ascending bird for the soul: "[L]ike a bird that boldly soars in the space and immen-sity of the air—so the soul feels her spirit move freely in the space and depth and extent and height of Minne [Love]."[99] Hildegard of Bingen understood the soul to have wings,[100] which was a very ancient idea (chapter 2), and Hadewijch of Brabant (1202?–1268) also used this imagery when she described the soul as an eagle.[101] Similarly, Teresa of Ávila (1515–1582) asserted that the soul grows wings after expe-riencing rapture and can fly,[102] and she also described seeing a heavenly dove above her head during an ecstatic experience.[103] And, as has been mentioned, Elisabeth of Schönau had visions of a dove, seemingly representing the Holy Spirit, including one in which the dove deposited tongues of fire above the heads of her sister nuns as they received communion.[104]

The ready acceptance of medieval women's visions is quite notable. There is a long tradition of visions and prophecy, by both women and men, in the Jewish tradition and in the Christian tradition that grew out of it.[105] Consequently, the visions of medieval women were perceived as being within the category of prophe-cies, but they had to be proved. When Hildegard of Bingen's visions were sent up the chain of church hierarchy to the archbishop, the verdict was "that these things were from God and from the prophecy which in the past the prophets had proph-esied."[106] Even Pope Eugene III (d. 1153) promulgated her *Scivias* at the urging of Bernard of Clairvaux (1090–1153). Bernard did this at the same time that he was condemning the works of male visionaries such as Abelard (1079–1142), William of Conchés (c. 1090–after 1154), and others, while the pope also rejected the claims of the male visionary Eudo de Stella.[107] The importance of this papal recognition of a woman receiving divine revelations cannot be overestimated in an age that declared women inferior to men. There was even room for failed or erroneous prophecy, in that a prophet was not considered infallible. (Elisabeth of Schönau provides a painful experience of failed prophecy in her vision the Apocalypse recounted earlier.) But in many cases women mystics were also concerned with more immanent matters, such as church reformation and redemption of sinners—concerns often shared by the male hierarchy of the church. Nonetheless, they struggled with a church that circumscribed their roles and constrained their abilities. Women such as Christina, Irene, Hildegard, Hadewijch, and Teresa breached the boundaries of decorum, gender expectations, hierarchy, perception, and reality.

Hadewijch of Brabant

Hadewijch of Brabant (1202?–1268) was a Flemish Beguine,[108] one of the laywomen who lived in small groups and could be single, married, or widowed (but who took an informal vow to remain celibate while living as a Beguine), retained private property, and earned their living mostly as weavers. They were part of a movement that sought to live as Christ's apostles had: simply, in poverty, and doing manual labor. They also nursed the sick and worked as teachers. Though its origins remain obscure, the Beguine movement began in northern Europe in the late twelfth century and received papal recognition in 1216. It was successful in that it spread rapidly in northern Europe, but it was frequently criticized and viewed with suspicion, so much so that Pope Clement V condemned it in 1312. Through a gradual process, the women who had joined Beguine communities were regularized and eventually enclosed in convents.[109] A large part of the problem they faced was that they were under no ecclesiastical authority—no men had a final say over their lives and practices, for which each community created its own guidelines. Joining a group of Beguines only required a sincere desire to live as they did, and one was free to leave at any time. Today there are only a handful of Beguines left in Belgium.[110]

Very little biographical information about Hadewijch is available to us. She was not well known in her lifetime; her writings were not discovered until 1838 in the Royal Library of Brussels.[111] There are no images available of her, nor has any written "life" of her been discovered.[112] Among her published works is a book of her visions, which she wrote in the vernacular Middle Dutch used in Brabant,[113] and which demonstrates that she was well read in theology and scripture. This indicates that she had received a good education, making it likely that she had an aristocratic upbringing and education—she knew French and Latin as well as her native dialect, and her poems were written in the sophisticated troubadour style.[114] Due to the eventual obscurity of her life, and since she was not enclosed in a convent, there was little male influence on her writing, although the Inquisition was an ominous presence and she was required to use priests for confession and in order to receive the Eucharist.

At some point Hadewijch became the head of a Beguine group, but eventually she was forced to leave amid criticism from some of her sister Beguines and from outsiders, although she continued to write to those Beguines who had been under her care. Some of her sister Beguines may have found her high standards too exacting, and her visionary experiences of union with God could have provoked their jealousy. Outsiders threatened her with the charge "of teaching quietism," which if brought before the Inquisition could have led to her imprisonment, and she was the subject of gossip for teaching that one must live Love (*Minne*)—that is, subsume oneself in and act out of love, which is where one finds union with God (Letter 6).[115] *Minne* is an ambiguous word, connoting the nature of love itself, in contrast to *Liebe*, the more common term for love.[116] The term was used by many Beguines to suggest the complexity of their mystical union with God.

Hadewijch's first recorded vision occurred just after she had received the Eucharist, which caused her to enter a trance. As with other female mystics, the Eucharist was her chosen form of sustenance, and she transformed the hunger caused by fasting into hunger for Christ.[117] This was not necessarily the first vision she experienced as she did not leave a complete record of all her visions; she chose only fourteen for publication.[118] In this vision an angel leads her to a meadow with seven trees, and he explains the meaning of each one to her. One is the tree of wisdom, with Love in its highest branches. Another is the tree of knowledge, which stands

> with its roots upward and its summit downward. This tree had many branches. Of the lowest branches, which formed the summit, the first is faith, and the second hope, by which persons begin. The Angel said to me again: "O mistress, you climb this tree from the beginning to the end, all the way to the profound roots of the incomprehensible God! Understand that this is the way of beginners and of those who persevere to perfection!"[119]

With the angelic command to climb this tree, a visionary life is born, one that is rich in aerial imagery. Hadewijch's relationship with trees is reminiscent of that of Christina the Astonishing: climbing trees brings one closer to God, and they are the habitat of birds, which can fly even higher and are expressive of the soul's longing to reach God.

Hadewijch frequently described her mystical flights as being "taken up in the spirit" and transported to a heavenly place. In the fifth vision in her writings, she says, "I was taken up for a short while in the spirit: and I was shown the three highest heavens."[120] Angels (visions 1 and 4) and seraphim (vision 13), who along with cherubim occupy the three highest heavens, appear in this and other visions, and they talk to her.

Even God is depicted with avian imagery in vision 13, in which Hadewijch explains that the countenance of God has six wings: "[T]hey were all closed outwardly, but within they were ceaselessly in flying motion."[121] Wings, representing the power of flight, are intimately connected to Hadewijch's understanding of union with God. Her ability, through her visionary experiences, to be transported through the air affirmed her belief that her soul was close to God.

Birds, especially eagles, are also prominent in her visions.[122] In one of her letters, Hadewijch writes that, "the interior soul, which is to be an eagle, must fly above itself in God . . . . [and] it does not turn its eyes from God . . . . There we shall think no longer of the saints or of men, but only fly in the heights of God." Even more vividly in vision 11, which occurs on a Christmas night, she is "taken up in the spirit," where she sees a phoenix devour a young gray eagle and an old yellow eagle. Christ's voice explains that Hadewijch is the young eagle and St. Augustine the old. "The phoenix that swallowed the eagle was the Unity in which the Trinity dwells, wherein both of us are lost [i.e., where she and St. Augustine achieved union]."[123] In this vision, Hadewijch sees herself as a bird, as a soul set free and able to fly, which complements her experiences of mystical flight.

Despite the preponderance of airborne female saints, the patron saint of aviation is often said to be St. Joseph of Copertino (1603–1663),[124] one of the very few male levitating saints.[125] Clive Hart opines that Joseph's childlike nature—many referred to him as mentally retarded[126]—made him "a convenient vehicle for the expression of a powerful and suppressed longing: endowed with spiritual authority by the participant's sanctified state, the idea of free flight is purged both of its physical terrors and of its taint of the ridiculous."[127] That, or it's miraculous when a man flies, but threatening, even demonic, when a woman does.

11

Flying Mystics, or the Exceptional Woman, Part II

WHILE THE SPECTRUM of Asian mystical experience presents many unique voices, a constant theme among them is the urge to transcend the limits of ordinary human experience in order to reach a higher reality. Women's voices express longing for a more profound spiritual experience, often within the framework of the need to escape the confinement of patriarchal society to achieve full spiritual transformation. Working within and around male-defined traditions of spirituality, women nevertheless found ways to soar.

ISLAM

Ṣūfīs are the mystics of Islam, who first and foremost seek union with God. They lead simple, self-disciplined lives devoted to God, and welcome others to do so as well. They take their name from the Arabic word ṣūf, "wool," which refers to their modest attire of coarse woolen cloth.[1] This form of dress traditionally served to distinguish the Ṣūfīs from their more worldly minded, richly dressed brethren and to evoke the memory of the austere life in the desert lived by Muḥammad and his companions. This emphasis on a simple, self-disciplined life devoted to God reveals Sufism's origins in the early ascetic movements of Islam. Ṣūfī movements began to arise in various parts of the Muslim empire during the eighth century, eventually developing into particular schools, many of which still exist, claiming descent from individual Ṣūfī masters. Some Ṣūfī masters were married, but large numbers of Ṣūfīs chose celibacy in the belief that this enabled them to be closer to God. Monasteries and convents were established to support their pursuit of the spiritual life.[2] In this environment, freed from domestic and social obligations, many women rose to prominence as spiritual guides and were renowned for their devotion. As with their male counterparts, some of these women were venerated as saints both before and after their deaths.

Rābiʿah al-ʿAdawiyya

One of the most famous Ṣūfī mystics was Rābiʿah al-ʿAdawiyya of Baṣra (717–801),[3] who lived her entire life as a celibate in semi-seclusion and great poverty. Even after she became well known and many people offered to help her, she refused the goods of the world as distractions; she wanted to remain in a state of total focus and dependence on God, not the material world.[4] An acquaintance, Muḥammad b. ʿAmr, described visiting her one day:

> I went in to Rābiʿa [her name receives various spellings (added by author)],
> and she was a very old woman of eighty years, as if she were a worn-out skin
> almost falling down, and I saw in her house a reed-mat and clothes-stand of
> Persian reed of the height of two cubits from the ground and upon it were
> her shrouds and the curtain of the house was made of palm-leaves, and per-
> haps there was a mat and an earthen jug and a bed of felt, which was also her
> prayer-carpet.[5]

She was given the name Rābiʿah, which means "four," by her father because she was his fourth daughter. After the death of her parents, she was sold into slavery but later released because of her piety; she is said to have fasted all day and prayed all night, a common Ṣūfī trope. Much of her life is shrouded in legend, but the basic outline is that after her release from bondage she spent time in retreat and in the desert, where God spoke to her,[6] and on pilgrimage to Mecca, where the Kaʿbah is said to have moved halfway to meet her.[7] She rejected several offers of marriage, choosing to remain celibate, and became a respected teacher of Sufism, which helped preserve many of her sayings and verses. Several sources report her constantly weeping over her sins because they might deny her God's presence after her death[8]—a great source of sorrow among Ṣūfīs of this period.

Rābiʿah had an important and continuing influence on Sufism[9] in that it was she who emphasized the importance of loving God, often quoting the Qurʾanic verse "He loves them and they love him" (Sūra 5.59). This pure love for God is a constant theme in the prayers and poems attributed to her, as well as in stories about her. One of the most vivid stories describes Rābi'ah racing through the streets with a bucket of water in one hand and a burning torch in the other. When asked where she is going Rābi'ah replies, "To burn down paradise and to put out the fires of hell."[10] Her point is that good Muslims are so concerned about avoiding the sufferings of hell and trying to get into paradise that they forget about God.

One of the earliest and fullest biographical sources for Rābi'ah, and therefore the one that has had the strongest influence on Ṣūfī understandings of her life and mystical experience, is *Tadhkirat al-awliyā* (Biographies of the Saints), by Farid al-Din 'Aṭṭār (1145/6–1221).[11] The inclusion of a woman in this collection is something that 'Aṭṭār felt he needed to explain,[12] which contrasts with Ibn 'Arabī's (1164–1240) collection of saints' lives, which includes four women as a matter of course (see below). 'Aṭṭār's awkwardness with this subject grows patently obvious as he twists all logic in making three points about Rābi'ah's gender: first, he claims it is irrelevant; then, if it is relevant, he invokes the precedent of one other important woman with religious authority, Ā'isha, the wife of Muḥammad and the source of many *hadīths* (documented stories about Muḥammad); last, he denies her gender entirely, claiming that she became a man.[13] Nonetheless, he preserves the following marvelous story about her and another famous Ṣūfī, Ḥasan of Baṣra, who is often linked to Rābi'ah (although this is highly unlikely, if not impossible, since he died in 728, when Rābi'ah was just eleven years old[14]). One day, Ḥasan saw Rābi'ah when she was near a lake,

> Throwing his prayer rug on the surface of the water he called,
> "Rabe'a, come! Let us pray two *rak'as* [units of ritual prayer] here!"
> "Hasan," Rabe'a replied, "when you are showing off your spiritual goods in this worldly market, it should be things that your fellow-men are incapable of displaying."
> And she flung her prayer rug into the air, and flew up on it.
> "Come up here, Hasan, where people can see us!" she cried.
> Hasan, who had not attained that station, said nothing. Rabe'a sought to console him.
> "Hasan," she said, "what you did fishes also do, and what I did flies also do. The real business is outside both these tricks. One must apply one's self to the real business [of loving God]."[15]

Aṭṭār explains that Ḥasan's spiritual attainment was not as advanced as Rābi'ah's, so he could not do as she did, even though she discredits such feats as irrelevant to loving God.

As in the above story, Ṣūfīs often were said to walk on water,[16] and flying is believed to be another of the spiritual powers developed during advanced stages of spiritual growth.[17] Such miraculous acts reflect the Ṣūfī's special relationship with God.

The belief in magical flight dates to Muḥammad's famous ascension to paradise on a winged horse (named Burāq and often depicted with a woman's face), referred to as Muḥammad's Night Journey (*Mi'rāj*).[18] This is sometimes said to have been a dream, though many faithful Muslims believe his actual, physical body was indeed carried to paradise.[19] For instance, when a disciple of the Ṣūfī master Nizam ad-din Awliya (1242–1325) asked whether this ascension was bodily or spiritual, the master replied, "'Imagine the best, ask not for details! In matters of religion,' he added, 'one must have faith; one should not show excessive zeal in either asserting or exploring them.'"[20]

Muḥammad was accompanied on this journey by the angel Gabriel, who brought him the word of God during the twenty-two years of revelations that became the Qur'ān, and who also acted as his guide when they reached paradise.[21] Gabriel has a long history in the Judeo-Christian-Islamic traditions as a bridge between the divine and earthly worlds, as when he announced the conception of Jesus to the Virgin Mary, leading to the incarnation of the divine into the terrestrial world, an act replicated in his bringing the word of God to Muḥammad, another insertion of the divine into the terrestrial.

Muḥammad's Night Journey is a beautiful model for the spiritual ascent of the soul.[22] Annemarie Schimmel describes it as "the first link in the spiritual chain of Sufism . . . the prototype of the mystic's ascension into the intimate presence of God," and a model for other mystical aerial experiences.[23] The leading example of another such experience is the dancing of the Mawlawīyah (or Mevlevis), founded by Jalāl al-Dīn Rūmī (1207–1273), more generally known as the whirling dervishes,[24] who spin[25] their way into an ecstatic trance[26] that feels like flying as they invoke the descent of creation (a movement away from God) and then of ascent (a movement back to God).[27] Their dance was sometimes referred to as the "ascension of the saints," and some dervishes were said to have "disappeared in the air in a flight produced by their spinning movement."[28]

Other Aerial Ṣūfī Women

Sayyida Fatima (fl. thirteenth century) of Fez, Morocco, provides an interesting contrast to the independent Rābi'ah. Fatima was said to fly or teleport from her home in Fez to the middle of the Sahara in order to bring food and medicine to a male Ṣūfī saint. She attributed her ability to fly to her selfless devotion to her husband, which she understood to be a duty from Allah.[29] Devotion to a male saint and conformity to patriarchal family expectations were the more common path to religious freedom for female Ṣūfī saints.[30]

Among the numerous works of the great Ṣūfī mystic and philosopher Ibn ʿArabī (1164–1240) are two collections of biographies of Ṣūfī masters who lived primarily in Spain from the twelfth to the thirteenth centuries. These two texts are the *Rūḥal-quds fī munāsaḥat al-nafs* (The Spirit of Holiness in the Counseling of the Soul) and *al-Durrat al-fākhirah fī dhikr man intafaʾtu bihi fī ṭarīq al-ākhirah* (The Precious Pearl Concerned with the Mention of Those from Whom I Have Derived Benefit in the Way of the Hereafter). Ibn ʿArabī is an important and influential figure in Sufism for two reasons. First, he united the thinking of Eastern and Western Sufism. He was born and raised in Spain, where he first studied Sufism, but later he traveled throughout the Muslim world to the Middle East, where he spent the latter half of his life. Second, he was a bridge between the rich oral tradition of Spanish Sufism, which he preserved and explained in his writings, and the Sufism that developed after him.[31] His two collections of biographies reveal the deep respect Ibn ʿArabī had for Ṣūfī women and their paranormal powers. Two aerial women stand out in his writings. The first is nameless, known only as a slave girl of Qasim al-Dawlah, who lived in Mecca. Ibn ʿArabī tells us:

> She was unique in her time and had attained the power to cover great distances quickly [i.e., to fly (added by author)]. When she was away on her wanderings she would commune with the mountains, rocks and trees, saying to them, "Welcome, welcome!" Her spiritual state was strong and she served the Folk [Ṣūfīs] and followed the Way with unswerving sincerity. She had the virtues of chivalry and was most strenuous in self-discipline, frequently practicing day-and-night fasting. Despite this she was strong and her exertions seemed to suit her well. I have never seen one more chivalrous than her in our time. Dedicated to the exaltation of God's majesty, she attached no worth to herself.[32]

The second woman was Zainab al-Qalʾiyyah, who was

> the foremost ascetic of her day. Although she possessed both great beauty and considerable wealth she freely abandoned the world and went to live in the region of Mecca, a woman ennobled by God. I had contact with her both in Seville and at Mecca. She was the companion of many eminent men of the Folk ....

When she sat down to practice Invocation [of God's name] she would rise into the air from the ground to a height of thirty cubits; when she had finished she would descend again. I accompanied her from Mecca to Jerusalem and I have never seen anyone more strict in observing the times of prayer than her. She was one of the most intelligent people of her time.[33]

As with other aerial women, birds are associated with Ṣūfī women such as Lala Imma Tifellut, who, when abducted by a suitor, turned into a bird. This story seems to be commemorated at her shrine, which is surrounded by cedar trees[34] considered too sacred to be cut down or damaged—a protection extended to the birds that make their nests in them.[35]

DAOISM

Perhaps as early as the sixth century BCE, Daoism drew together philosophical ideas about the harmony of the universe, expressed through the Dao or the Way, and indigenous religious practices associated with shamanism, such as trance and dream experiences, breathing techniques, healing, and herbology. Daoist practitioners later added magical techniques, exorcism, and dietary restrictions to their practices, while their main goal became the search for immortality. The first chapter of the *Chuang Tzu*[36] (fourth century BCE) describes such practices:

> Inhale the wind, drink the dew,
> Do not eat the Five Cereals:
> Mount cloudy vapors
> Rein flying dragons—
> Then wander (*yu*) beyond the Four Seas![37]

Daoists considered a number of practices as key to achieving immortality, including alchemy, ingestion of substances such as cinnabar and mercury, and carefully regulated sexual intercourse.[38] For Daoists, immortality essentially consisted of the ability to prolong life in the physical body (longevity) and the acquisition of magical powers such as flight,[39] although becoming an Immortal and reaching the Land of Immortals were also goals.[40] Based on his reading of the first collection of Daoist biographies, the *Lieh Hsien Chuan*[41] (first century BCE), Max Kaltemark explains, "The Daoist ideal is not to die but to prolong life through physical and spiritual purification that makes the body light enough to take flight and escape the world. . . . After one thousand years of life a Daoist sage mounts a white cloud and rises to heaven."[42] An early esoteric text, the *Scripture and Chart for the Mysterious Contemplation of Man-Bird Mountain* (c. 619–907), describes a mountain range inhabited by beings with human faces and bird bodies. The adept who can visualize these beings will be able to fly like a bird, become immortal, and ascend to heaven.[43]

Sun Bu'er

The twelfth-century female sage Sun Bu'er (1119–1182) wrote a poem called "Flying" that beautifully captures the Daoist life and its goals in complex imagery:

> At the right time, just out of the valley,
> You rise lightly into the spiritual firmament.
> The jade girl rides a blue phoenix,
> The gold boy offers a scarlet peach.
> One strums a brocade lute amidst the flowers,
> One plays jewel pipes under the moon.
> One day immortal and mortal are separated,
> And you coolly cross the ocean.[44]

This poem connects music with elevation—usually of spirit, though here of the body—and a mix of female imagery (the girl, the valley, the moon, the lute) and male imagery (the boy and the pipes). Blending the female and the male, the yin and the yang, can lead to attaining the Dao, when one leaves mortality behind to become immortal, freed from the earth and death. Poetry, paradox, dance,[45] metaphor, nature, and music best express the ineffable Dao (sometimes Tao)[46] of Daoism, a philosophy, a religion, and a way of life said to have originated with the semi-legendary figure Laozi (traditionally between the sixth and fourth centuries BCE).

Sun Bu'er is one of the best-known female sages (someone who has attained the Dao, also known as an Immortal); she passed into folklore as one of the famous Seven Immortals—all the rest were men. She has had an enduring impact on Daoism. Her life is depicted in the popular anonymous sixteenth-century novel, *Seven Taoist Masters*, which blends legend, history, and Daoist training instructions.[47] It describes her as a beautiful woman, happily married to a fellow Daoist practitioner. She received instruction from the master teacher Wang Changyan, became a local Daoist leader, and quickly advanced along the path to immortality. The master then told her that she had to leave home and make an arduous thousand-mile journey to the city of Loyang to complete her training, but, since her beauty would attract rapists, he did not think she could do it. Sun Bu'er immediately went into the kitchen and disfigured her face with hot oil and pretended to be insane. When her wounds were healed, she ran away, setting off on her journey.[48]

The novel says she lived in Luoyang for twelve years as an insane beggar woman, all the while secretly practicing, until she attained immortality. She then decided to display her powers to the people through a ruse, one that suggests the sexual elements of Daoist practice. She created a man and a woman who looked like her and who behaved sexually in public,[49] offending the people to the point where they decided to burn the man and woman alive in their house. Above the flames Sun Bu'er appeared, seated on clouds, with the man and the woman on either side of her. She told the people she would give the man and woman to them as guardians of the village and that they would also ensure ample harvests,[50] suggesting the ancient and widespread belief that sexual activity in freshly plowed and seeded fields would positively influence the fertility of the crops. According to the historical record, she received the highest level of ordination, with the right to both teach and ordain others, and was one of several Daoist women who had an enduring cult.[51]

Other hagiographies describe divine aspects connected with Sun Bu'er's conception, such as her mother's dream of seeing seven cranes, one of which entered her breast. The crane is the bird of long life and a vehicle of Immortals (Figure 11.1).[52] She grew up in a family of educated bureaucrats; she received a good education and showed exceptional intelligence along with a saintly nature. In traditional China, Confucian, Buddhist, and Daoist ideas found their way into each other's texts, examples of which are found in the conflicting ideas expressed in descriptions of Sun Bu'er's life. Some sources assert that when her husband became a follower of Wang Changyan, Sun Bu'er saw this as a threat to her family life—a typical Confucian reaction to the challenging Daoist lifestyle and values. More reliable sources assert it was Wang who advised her and her husband to separate in order to become Daoist monastics. Her husband promptly did so, while Sun Bu'er is said to have resisted this threat to family stability, social status, and worldly comfort. She was finally convinced by an argument based on the Confucian ideal of wifely duty. Rather than fulfilling her traditional duty as a wife to her husband and his family, she should fulfill her duty to her husband by becoming a renunciate herself, thereby freeing him of family ties and enabling him to pursue immortality. In this version of her life, she became a Daoist nun and spent several years in various parts of China before moving to Luoyang, where she chose to live in the grotto of the Immortal Lady Feng, an eccentric practitioner who had died a few years earlier. In this way she entered a female lineage and empowered herself to follow Lady Feng's path of eccentricity, eventually acquiring magical powers. At the time of her

FIGURE 11.1 Zhang Lu, *He Xiangu* [a female Immortal] *on a Flying Crane*, ink and color drawing, early sixteenth century.
Shanghai Museum.

departure for the Land of Immortals, her former husband, though far away, is said to have seen her rise up to heaven on a five-colored cloud.[53]

Daoist Beliefs and Practices

Little of the foregoing is contained in the so-called founding text attributed to Laozi, the *Dao De Jing*.[54] Rich in paradox and mystical insight, the text accepts Chinese cosmological beliefs such as the harmonious nature of the cosmos and the relationship of yin/yang (female/male). In general, the *Dao De Jing* recommends that individuals model themselves after nature, which demonstrates the ideal of cosmic harmony, by pursuing a passive quietism and seeking mystical union with the Dao (understood to be the foundation of all that exists). The *Dao De Jing* lends itself to the ideal of the sage as recluse, someone who has left society and its values to pursue self-cultivation in harmony with nature, where communion with the Dao is more accessible.

Many of the images Laozi used to describe the Dao are associated with the female, such as "the valley," "water," and muddy water (yin, the feminine principle, is dark as well as moist),[55] and Daoism affirms the social and philosophical position of women, asserting that the weakness and passivity that are part of women's nature represent yin and should, in fact, be emulated by men. Significantly, the female body was thought to be ideal for the inner alchemical transformation that leads to immortality.[56] It also describes the Dao as like the "babe," that is, unformed, and not yet socialized, because socialization blinds one to the Dao. A fourth-century alchemical text, the *Nei P'ien*, written by Ko Hung (c. 280–340), tells the story about such a babe, a four-year-old girl who was abandoned in a pit during a time of great unrest. Three years later, her father returned to the pit to claim her bones but found her alive and well. She explained that when she became hungry she imitated the actions of a tortoise (the symbol of long life), which was also in the pit, "that stretched its neck and swallowed its breath."[57] She imitated its actions and became less hungry. The unsocialized girl was an ideal Dao practitioner because she did not know such a thing was possible before nature taught her.

Attaining the Dao through nature and losing it when returning to civilization is described in another tale from the *Nei P'ien*: "Under Emperor Ch'eng of the Han, hunters in the Chung-nan Mountains saw a naked [female] person whose body was covered with black hair. They wanted to capture this individual, but it passed over pits and valleys [suggesting aerial abilities] like a thoroughbred and could not be overtaken." After she was captured, she explained that she had been a concubine who had run away to the mountains during the fall of the Qin dynasty (207 BCE), which made her over two hundred years old. In the mountains, an old man taught her to eat the leaves and fruits of the pines, after which she did not experience hunger, thirst, heat, or cold. Once captured, she was nauseated by normal food, but she seemed to adjust to it—and then two years later she became old and died.[58] This story seems to have enjoyed some popularity, as a variant of it has been preserved in the *Lieh Hsien Chuan* (or *Liexian Zhuan*), the earliest collection of Daoist biographies, some of which are of a legendary nature.[59] A similar story passed into Japanese literature in the *Nihon Ryōiki* (eighth to ninth century), the first Buddhist collection of tales, compiled by the monk Kyōkai, although the story is clearly Daoist. In it another concubine, abandoned by her lover along with her seven children, raises them in great poverty, weaving vines for their clothes and feeding them only the herbs she gathers. She does all this with great reverence and dignity until one day she flies up to heaven.[60] Additional examples of Daoist flight come from stories and poems composed as early as the third century BCE.[61]

When Daoism began to develop community organizations in the second century CE, it reflected the cosmic balancing of yin and yang by having women fill active religious roles. Beginning in the sixth century there were convents in which women pursued the goals of Daoism in a communal setting,[62] and several women, like Sun Bu'er, became figures of widespread and enduring cults.[63] Despite the positive value it ascribes to yin, Daoism, like so many other religions, is a tradition predominantly shaped by and for men. Tellingly, its rich biographical tradition is dominated by men; very few biographies of women Daoists exist, and we have seen Sun Bu'er's autonomy diminished by Confucian views of proper female roles.

Also, women's roles in the biographies of Daoist men are generally quite passive. Consequently, the majority of Daoist stories describing flight are about males, with some notable exceptions.

"Feather clothed" is a well-known metaphor for a Daoist who has attained immortality, and some Daoists actually wore feather garments[64] (such as the short feathered cape seen in Figure 11.2) to express their symbolic association with birds through the lightness of their bodies and their ability to fly.[65] Evidence from the Han dynasty (206 BCE–220 CE) is particularly rich. Edward H. Schafer mentions the alchemist Luan Ta (second century BCE) who wore a dress of feathers. Commenting on this, the Tang-dynasty (618–906) scholar Yen Shih-ku wrote: "In using the plumage of birds to make his dress, he was seizing on the conception of the flying and soaring of a divinity or sylph-being."[66] Winged spirits depicted on the stone sculpture of Han-period tombs have bodies covered with long filaments that we know represent feathers because bird sculptures are treated in a similar way.[67] Other Daoists wore feathers in imitation of deities such as the Cinnabar Mother of the Highest Prime, who is described as wearing "an embroidered feathery, flying skirt of flowery pattern, and has her top knot in the design 'whirlwind cloud.'"[68] She is one of the nine yin forces of the Northern Dipper constellation, who, when cultivated through worship and visualization, can grant the higher powers of immortality, such as invisibility, multilocation, and free travel through the cosmos[69]—that is, flying. Interestingly, the ideogram for "immortal," *xian*, is written with components meaning "flying person."[70] This last meaning explicitly connects flying and ascending into the sky with immortality, which the stories that follow also demonstrate, and recalls the feather robes of Chinese swan maidens (see chapter 4) and fairies (see chapter 5). This aerial theme is continued in the shoes, worn by Daoists, inscribed with cloud motifs, symbolizing their ability to walk on clouds.[71] The famous Tang-period poet Li Po (b. 701) wrote a poem about his friend, the Daoist priestess Chu'u, on the occasion of her departure for the south. Here, such shoes are called "far-wandering shoes":

Lady of the Tao from the Kiang in Wu,
With lotus flower kerchief borne on her head,
And a rainbow dress unwetted by the rain—
Unique and rare—a cloud from Yang'-t'ai [home of the ancient fertility
goddess, the rainbow woman of Wu Shan].

Under her feet far-wandering shoes
To skim the waves, raising pure-white dust,

FIGURE 11.2 Female Immortal, tapestry, c. 1575–1725. Note the short feathered cape around her shoulders. A similar feather cape is worn by another female sage in a painting on silk at the Freer Gallery of Art, accession number F1916.46.

Freer Gallery of Art, Washington, D.C., Gift of Charles Lang Freer.

To find the transcendents, head for South Marchmount—
Where surely she will see the dame of Wei [divine protector of the
   mountain].[72]

The Land of Immortals is an otherworldly place, but immortals can and do appear on earth. They are shape-shifters who can fly and are not ruled by the laws of time and space. As elsewhere, this fluidity between worlds opens up the idea that such flights can take place in both directions, and such flights duplicate shamanic flights[73]—one

cannot ignore the many shamanic elements in Daoism. Both immortals and shamans are described as birdlike creatures, which implies their ability to fly.[74]

One important Daoist school, Shangqing, or Highest Clarity, began in 364 CE,
based on revelations received by the medium and shaman Yang Zi (fl. 364–370),
who further promulgated the idea of shamanic flight[75] and valued women practitioners as teachers who bestowed esoteric revelations.[76] This was not a particularly new idea, as the fourth-century BCE *Chuang Tzu* had described the eccentric
and brilliant teaching of the sage Woman Crookback.[77] Among the immortals who
appeared to Yang Zi, giving him texts and instructions, was Wei Huacun (252–334),
who while on earth had received scriptures and oral teachings through her visions
of perfected beings. She is said to have ascended into heaven at the end of her life,
and an enduring cult to her was established.[78]

The Chinese had many ancient stories connected to magical flight, such as the
story of the two daughters of the legendary Emperor Yao, Nü Ying and O Huang,
both of whom were said to fly (discussed in the introduction to this book), as well
as ascension stories like that of the legendary Yellow Emperor, who was instructed
by female immortals such as the Simple Woman, the Colorful Woman, and the
Mysterious Woman,[79] and who learned the art of war from the Dark Lady, a woman
with a human head and a bird's body.[80] Catherine Despeux and Livia Kohn describe
the highest form of ascension known in Daoism, that of the goddess called the
Mother of the Dao[81] (Laozi's divinized mother) when she returned to heaven:

> After the Holy Mother Goddess had finished speaking, immortal officials and
> spirit attendants arrived with cloudy chariots and feathery canopies. Forest-
> like they assembled around her. She climbed into the chariot of the eight
> luminants and ascended to heaven in broad daylight.[82]

Commenting on this passage, Despeux and Kohn explain: "Receiving a summons
to office among the heavenly bureaucrats, the immortal readies himself or herself
and, on the day appointed, is formally met by a planet- or dragon-drawn cloudy
chariot and escorted to heaven by a large entourage of celestial guards, supernatural horsemen, and divine attendants."[83]

A well-known ascension story of a Daoist woman is that of He Xiangu, one of
the Eight Immortals and, again, the only woman among them. A popular story-
cycle about them began to be told during the Tang dynasty (618–907).[84] In one
story, she is the young servant of a tyrannical woman. One day, while the woman
is away, seven worn-out men beg her for some rice. Unknown to her, they are the
Seven Immortals, who have come to test her generosity. Overcoming fear of her
employer and the punishment she will receive, He Xiangu feeds them. The woman

returns, finds out what He Xiangu has done, and threatens to beat her unless she brings them back. He Xiangu runs after the men and they return with her. The woman makes the immortals vomit the food they have eaten and forces He Xiangu to eat the vomit. But as soon as her tongue touches it, "her body [begins] to float away."[85] The Immortals, too, rise over the house, and the last time the woman sees her servant she is in their midst, slowly disappearing into the sky. This story presents her ability to fly as a gift,[86] but Kwok Man Ho and Joanne O'Brien argue that she earned it through "her ascetic practices."[87] This possible revisionism continues in another story from this cycle, in which He Xiangu, after being an immortal for one hundred years, is humbled by an old man who turns out to be the legendary Yellow Emperor.[88] As shown in the story of Sun Bu'er, the Daoist idealization of the feminine principle was usually enacted through the patriarchal lens of Confucian society.[89] In a nineteenth-century text, He Xiangu is turned into a mouthpiece for Confucian values, expressing regret for her radical religious behavior and her missed opportunity for marriage.[90]

Daoist women sometimes "took flight" in the dual meaning of the phrase: both fleeing and flying. An example is the fourth-century Daoist woman known as the Tea Elder, who was imprisoned by a wicked official. She was about seventy years old, but the local people said her appearance had not changed in one hundred years. Every day she would go to the market and sell tea from a single bowl that was never emptied. When the local prefect, out of fear, tried to imprison her, she flew away with her magic bowl.[91] Yet another fleeing woman is an unnamed Han-dynasty princess who was married to a politician named Wang Gan. It was a time of political unrest, and she advised her husband to avoid politics and instead practice the Dao. But he chose worldly power, so she left him and retired to a hermitage in the mountains. With a change of government her husband lost favor and went looking for his wife, but she had already flown off to the clouds, leaving only her slippers behind.

Leaving a shoe or a slipper behind as they fly away is a fairly common motif in the lives of Daoist women as well as of Chinese Buddhist nuns.[92] This is an indication that they no longer need shoes, because they will no longer walk on the earth. The Holy Mother of Dongling (fourth century CE) had a very unpleasant husband, who was enraged by her abilities and practices, especially those that helped other people—so much so that he denounced her as lecherous and wicked, causing the magistrate to put her put in jail. The Holy Mother was a shape-shifter and could make herself invisible. She also could fly, so she flew out the window of her jail cell, leaving her shoes behind. After her disappearance, the local people set up shrines to the Holy Mother at which a bird would appear and respond to questions about stolen articles by flying toward the thief.[93] Once again, this is an example of the now-familiar association of birds and aerial women.

Not all Daoist women mystics had unhappy marriages. Thomas Cleary points out that "[f]or some Taoist practitioners, marriage itself was an outward cloak of an inner affinity, a miniature esoteric organization within which higher developmental practices could be carried out in private."[94] As an example, he tells the story of the Holy Mother's teacher, Fan Yunqiao, who was married to a fellow Daoist with whom she flew off to heaven. One of her poems captures the soaring freedom to be found in attaining the Dao and provides a fitting close to this discussion:

> What's the need to bow and pray
> To beg for long life?
> Clearly the original spirit
> Is thoroughly pure.
> Shatter space [attain the Dao] to become completely free.[95]

Fan Yunqiao has moved beyond the usual practices and attained the Dao—hence cause and effect are no longer valid.

BUDDHISM

Ancient Hindus and Buddhists, like so many other religious believers, accepted that supernatural powers could be acquired through ascetic practices. In India these ideas go back at least to the Vedic period (c. 1500–600 BCE) and to the belief in *riddhis*, or potencies uniquely expressed in all classes of beings—for example, the craft and skill by which a hunter captures game. More to the point here, *riddhi* gives birds the ability to fly.[96] Ascetic practices were thought to stimulate the *riddhis*, leading to supernatural power, including the ability to fly.

The belief in *riddhis* was absorbed into early Buddhism, where they are called *iddhis*, defined as fruits (*phala*)[97] of enlightenment that wreak havoc with the physical world, which Buddhists consider to be illusory and changeable.[98] Four of the ten *iddhis* on standardized lists describe aerial feats: to walk on water; to fly through the air; to touch the sun and moon; and to ascend into the highest heavens.[99] (As noted in chapter 6, the Buddha flew to heaven with his half-brother Nanda.)

A related idea is that such powers could be displayed at the time of death, as in the death of the first ordained Chinese Buddhist nun, Ching-chien (fourth century CE):

> At the end of the *sheng-p'ing* reign period (357–361) Ching-chien once again smelled the same fragrance (that had graced the ritual of her becoming a

nun), and she saw a red, misty cloud. Out of that cloud a woman holding a five-colored flower in her hands descended from the sky. Ching-chien was delighted to see her and said to the nuns [attending her], "Manage your affairs well in the future. I am taking leave of you now." Clasping their hands she bid them farewell and then rose up into the air. The path she travelled looked like a rainbow going straight up to heaven. At that time she was seventy years old.[100]

Human Ḍākinīs

The *mahāsiddhas* are especially well known for the power of *siddhi* (a variation on *iddhi*); they are the wandering Tantric *yogīs*, either Hindu or Buddhist, who were introduced in chapter 7 along with the divine *ḍākinīs* who frequently appeared to them. *Mahāsiddha* biographies reveal the magical powers these *siddhas* possessed, including, for many, the ability to fly. There is Maṇibhadrā, a young bride whose life is changed when she meets the *mahāsiddha* Kukkuripa while visiting her parents' home and who eventually becomes a *mahāsiddha* herself. When he asks her for alms, she challenges him, saying he should marry and not beg. He explains to her that he seeks enlightenment in this life, and that having a wife would be an impediment to reaching that goal. Maṇibhadrā is deeply impressed by his understanding of reality and asks him to teach her. He tells her to meet him in the cemetery around midnight. Although it was extremely difficult for a young woman to be out alone at night, she manages it and stays with him for several days, learning and practicing. Needless to say, when she returns home her parents are enraged, and they beat her—a common experience among female practitioners. She remains at home with her parents for a year, practicing as Kukkuripa has instructed. Then her husband comes to claim her and takes her to his home, where she does "the deeds and duties of the world as they are usually done"[101] and gives birth to three children. At the end of twelve years, she meets Kukkuripa again. Shortly after this meeting, she goes to draw water from the village well, but on the way home she trips and breaks her water pot. She stands fixed to that spot, staring. Eventually, her husband comes looking for her, which rouses her from her trance, but she refuses to return home. For her, the broken pot symbolizes the impermanent realm of being born, dying, and reincarnating again and again. She wants to be free of that cycle. Her realization is so great that she is able to rise into the air, where she instructs her fellow villagers for twenty-one days before leaving for the Land of the Ḍākas (a heaven).

Male *siddhas* constantly interacted with divine and human *ḍākinīs*, and almost all their biographies end with them ascending to the Land of the Ḍākas[102] in their

mortal bodies, by flying into the sky as Maṇibhadrā did. From about the tenth century, this became a common ending in the biographies of Tantric adepts, and later
biographies elaborate on this process. The biography of Mandāravā, a semi-legendary female Tantric practitioner believed to have lived in the eighth century, refers
to her as a ḍākinī because of her great spiritual accomplishment and states that she
announced her departure from this life by saying, "Now the time has come for me
to dissolve into the stainless dharmakaya."[103] The *dharmakāya* is the mystical realm
of Buddhist teachings. After this statement, her "body became a mass of swirling
light, and the entire sky filled with shimmering rainbows . . . . The *ḍākinī's* form
then seemed to fly like an arrow into space,"[104] as Mandāravā was transformed
into a Wisdom *Ḍākinī*,[105] a purely spiritual being. This process is often described
as "acquiring the rainbow body."[106] Rainbows symbolize a path between the earth
and sky realms, but the achievement of the rainbow body is a sign of the highest
spiritual accomplishment. Adepts leave behind just their hair and nails, or they
leave nothing at all and simply vanish in space.[107]

In addition to Maṇibhadrā and Mandāravā, a well-known, if somewhat legendary, human *ḍākinī* is Yeshe Tsogyel. She and Mandāravā were the Tantric consorts
of Padmasambhava (traditionally eighth century CE), but they both developed
into important and independent Tantric practitioners. Indeed, at the instruction of Padmasambhava, Yeshe Tsogyel took a male consort of her own.[108] Tantric
Buddhism can include sexual yoga (either actual or visualized) as a means of
achieving enlightenment, which (as was discussed in chapter 7) involves a union
of female and male attributes. Women who act as consorts, such as Mandāravā
and Yeshe Tsogyel, are sometimes referred to as *ḍākinīs*.

In a biography of Yeshe Tsogyel, she described the *siddhi*s she acquired, including flying, which she referred to as sky-dancing:

> My mundane *siddhi*s, in brief, are control of phenomena,
> Speed-walking, the eye-salve of omniscience, the healing pills of
>   everlasting life,
> And the *siddhi*s of sky-dancing, dancing through matter and the mystic
>   dance.[109]

Elsewhere she declares, "My body became a sky-dancing rainbow body."[110] Human
*ḍākinī*s, through their spiritual practices, can shape-shift, transforming their bodies into vehicles of flight.

The word *ḍākinī* comes from the Sanskrit root meaning "to fly." This was translated
into Tibetan as *khadoma* (mKha' 'gro ma), meaning "she who goes in the sky," often

glossed as "sky dancer." The latter resonates with other aerial females dancers discussed above: namely, *apsarās*, swan maidens, fairies, and shamans.

Yeshe Tsogyel utilizes avian and aerial imagery to describe her spiritual development:

> The fledgling Ḍākinī-bird nesting in a crag
> Could not conceive how easy was flight
> Until her skill in the six vehicles was perfected;
> But her potential realised, wings beating with hidden strength,
> Breaking the back of even the razor-edged wind,
> She arrived at whatever destination she chose.[111]

As is usual in the biographies of extraordinary practitioners, several pages of Yeshe Tsogyel's biography describe her death as an ascension and final transformation:

> As the first flicker of light dawned on the tenth day, a palanquin of the light of four Ḍākinīs in the form of an eight-petalled lotus descended like a shooting star before Tsogyel. . . . and Tsogyel mounted [it. She then speaks to her disciples.] . . . .
>
> When she had finished speaking, radiating blinding rainbow lights she dissolved into a sesame seed-pod-like sheath of shimmering blue light, and she vanished. The four Ḍākinī lotus petals began to move, and in a blaze of light the lotus ascended, higher and higher, until it vanished from sight.[112]

She conquered death and became a divine and eternal *ḍākinī*.

A fourth, also somewhat legendary, *ḍākinī* is Niguma (eleventh century).[113] We know her story and something about the teaching lineage she established through her Tibetan disciple, Kyungpo Naljor. While studying Tantra in India, he is repeatedly advised to meet her, but when he asks where she lives, he is told:

> If one's perception is pure, one can see her anywhere, whereas if one's perception is not pure she simply cannot be found; for she dwells on the pure stages and has achieved the holy rainbow body. However, when the dakinis gather to make tantric feasts in the great cemetery of the So-sa-ling forest, she sometimes physically appears.

Niguma has transcended corporeal reality, though she can choose to manifest physically.

Kyungpo Naljor's journey continues:

> Eventually he arrived in So-sa-ling Cemetery. Here he immediately had a
> vision of a dark brown dakini. She was dancing above him in the sky at the
> height of seven *tala* trees. . . . [S]he first was but one figure, then many, and
> then again but one, dancing in all directions.

Niguma eventually initiates him. Then,

> by means of the Dakini's magical ability, he was levitated into the sky, and
> found himself sitting on a small mound of gold dust with a host of dakinis
> circling in the sky above him.[114]

Machig Lapdron and Chod Practice

The most historically grounded example of a woman believed to have been both
a human *ḍākinī* and a divine *ḍākinī* is the great Tibetan teacher of the *chod* (gCod)
lineage, Machig Lapdron (Ma gcig la phyi sgron ma, 1055–1153).[115] Machig played
an integral role in the eleventh-century Tibetan Buddhist renaissance and also
founded a community of disciples.[116]

Her parents had auspicious dreams before her birth that predicted Machig
would be a great spiritual leader; when she was born there were many auspicious
signs and wonders, such as multiple rainbows appearing in the sky. As a child she
showed many signs of spiritual accomplishment. Her mother taught her to read,
and she became a particularly gifted reader of sacred texts. (The practice of reading
sacred texts aloud had great value in a preliterate society like medieval Tibet, and
people believed they acquired spiritual benefits when they hired readers for special
celebrations.[117]) Together with her mother and her sister, a nun who was sixteen
years her senior, she studied sacred scripture. Women, including her own daughter, were to remain important in Machig's lineage both as patrons and as disciples,
and to this day many nuns follow her practices.[118] Her main male guru, Phadampa
Sangye, also had several other women disciples.[119]

Machig Lapdron's life as a Tantric consort and her teachings express the sexual,
transcendent, cannibalistic, and death-defying aspects of the *ḍākinīs* and recall
the story of Padmasambhava being consumed by a *ḍākinī* (chapter 7). *Chod* literally means "to cut" and refers to the ritual practice—undertaken to destroy the
ego—of visualizing one's body being cut up and then offered to demons, ghouls,
and gods. Practitioners are called *chodpas*, and each begins by visualizing herself

as a *ḍākinī* while performing an elaborate sacred dance. During this visualization, the *chodpa* transforms her mind into a wrathful goddess who severs the *chodpa's* head, stretches it into cosmic proportions, and places the headless body in it, multiplying its parts endlessly to use as a food offering to the gathered spirits.[120] The expression "opening the door of the sky" (*nam mkha' sgo 'byed*)[121] is often used during the ritual to signify ascension to a state beyond consciousness, which is said to facilitate the realization that there is no enduring self. This practice's roots are in *jātaka* stories that tell of the Buddha offering his body to save other beings,[122] though it is also clearly connected to the cannibalistic stories associated with avian women in South Asia and to pre-Buddhist shamanic practices.

Chodpas live as wandering *yogīs* who frequent cemeteries. They literalize the practices of other aerial women, such as Valkyries, in that part of their practice is to remove dead bodies during epidemics.[123] Illness in general, but especially plague and other epidemics, is believed to be caused by low spiritual beings and demons who can be appeased by accomplished *chodpas*.

Even when guided by a guru, Machig's inner experiences are the driving force behind her spiritual development, which was considered so profound that she is credited with levitation and was reported to have flown on several occasions. Twice she flew to her son's meditation retreat to assist him in his practice, and she also flew to teach disciples in remote places.[124]

Ḍākinīs are frightening and powerful sexual beings who can transform themselves and, should they choose, transform male disciples, moving them beyond earthly constraints, including death, into the ultimate reality of enlightenment.

12

The Aviatrix: Nationalism, Women, and Heroism

AT THE DAWN of the twentieth century the human fascination with flight grew to a fever pitch.[1] Technology, capitalism, imagination, and warfare all combined to make the ancient dream of flight a reality[2]—and all too soon led to the tedium of twenty-first-century air travel. From the Wright Brothers at Kitty Hawk to the Zeppelin airships in Germany, flight rapidly became a reality for large numbers of people. Nevertheless, ancient beliefs that linked women with flying lingered, actualized by imaginary females like Wonder Woman (created in 1941), as well as real women, such as the American pilot Amelia Earhart (1897–1937) and the German Hanna Reitsch (1912–1979). This history of aerial women would not be complete without discussing these mythic and fully human women pilots.

WONDER WOMAN

Sexuality has been a key issue in the stories of many of the flying females we have discussed thus far, as has power. Some women have both, notably Lilith, but at the cost of being demonized. The same could be said of the European witches. Throughout this book I have been exploring whether women and female supernaturals can be both sexual and powerful.[3] In her early 1940s depiction, the comic book heroine Wonder Woman raises this question to another level. Although Wonder Woman appears not to be sexually active, and in spite of her love for US

Army pilot Steve Trevor, the fact that she was born (as Princess Diana) on Paradise Island—the mysterious home of the (in this telling, immortal) Amazons at the edge of the known world—signals a lesbian undertone that often rises to a crescendo in her relations with the Holliday College girls.[4] Wonder Woman's nom de guerre, Diana Prince—an inversion of her birth name, title, and gender—is but one example of her polymorphous sexuality.

Wonder Woman's sexuality consists of unsatisfied longing for army pilot Trevor (Amazon law forbids their union),[5] and scenes of girlish intimacy and fun with her female pals, while being a "hot babe" with a scantily clothed, curvaceous body that exudes sex and power.[6] Her physical power is unquestionable. She defeats all comers, except when it suits her purpose to be caught, which provides occasion for images of Wonder Woman being bound in countless ways, until she breaks free, reminding us of the escape of captive swan maidens. And she flies, mostly in her incredibly fast (two thousand miles per hour—very fast for the 1940s), invisible/transparent and therefore somewhat nonexistent plane,[7] often perched on its wing, like an eagle on a branch.[8] She can also leap high into the air or from tall buildings. She is part aviatrix and part warrior bird-woman, the member of a sisterhood (the Amazons, the Holliday College girls) like the Valkyries and swan maidens and, to a lesser degree, the *apsarās* and *ḍākinīs*.

Somewhat like Athena, Wonder Woman emerged from the head of a man, William Moulton Marston, the pen name of Charles Moulton (1893–1947), a Harvard-trained psychologist. Moulton was an extremely interesting man for his generation; there is no denying that he believed women to be superior to men, based in part on his belief in matriarchies that were or could be peace-loving societies.[9] Hence the name of Wonder Woman's matriarchal and manless home, Paradise Island, populated by goddess-worshiping Amazons. They hold Athena and Aphrodite as the highest deities and are especially devoted to the latter who, as the goddess of love, directly challenged Ares, the god of war, when he said, "My men shall rule with the sword!" by retorting, "My women shall conquer men with love!"[10] Marston actually wrote an issue predicting a peace-loving future matriarchy.[11] An enthusiastic American patriot, Marston has Aphrodite and Athena tell Wonder Woman's mother, Queen Hippolyte, that she must send her best Amazon to America to help with the war effort because America is "the last citadel of democracy, and of equal rights for women."[12] One cannot help but feel the irony of this given the failure to ratify the Equal Rights Amendment in America in 1982.

Wonder Woman first saw print in *All Star Comics* no. 8, which appeared in December 1941/January 1942, at the time of America's entrance into World War II.[13] It is not, therefore, irrelevant that her scanty costume is a red, white, and blue variant of the American flag: the dark blue field with white stars on her shorts or mini-culottes; the true red of her bustier and high-heeled boots; and the white stripe of her belt (Figure 12.1). Her involvement with World War II was deep: throughout the war, she fought German and Japanese spies in issues that frequently carried ads for war bonds.

Wonder Woman's story begins when she abandons her home and her immortality[14] out of love for pilot Steve Trevor, who has crashed his plane on her island. Once in the United States, she takes on two disguises: first as a nurse while Steve is hospitalized, and then as a secretary in the army intelligence office where he

FIGURE 12.1 Wonder Woman as she first appeared.
All Star Comics no. 8, December 1941/January 1942. © DC Comics.

works[15]—both perfectly respectful, non-heroic female occupations of the period. (The main element of her disguise is, like Clark Kent's, the eyeglasses she wears when not on superhero duty.)

Other touches to her costume that are worth mentioning include the eagle whose wings are spread across her chest, signifying her commitment to America and her shaman-like appropriation of the eagle's power of flight, to say nothing of the bird's ability to hunt down its prey. Her crown/headband holds back her long, loose hair; its lone red star on a gold field may signal another loyalty: her commitment to her homeland Paradise Island, or her commitment to her own singularity. Altogether, her superhero costume leaves her unencumbered, defines her as an American patriot, and exposes as much of her female flesh as the times allowed.

Her golden lasso is both an All-American cowgirl motif and a source of power similar to that of the Valkyries; once lassoed, Wonder Woman's captive has to truthfully answer her questions, recalling the Valkyries' ability to bind men to their will. Her mother, Queen Hippolyte, had the lasso made from links of her own magic girdle, which ensures the supremacy of the Amazons.[16] Long ago (remember, these Amazons are immortal), the queen had lost it to Hercules. When he could not defeat her in battle, he resorted to seduction and thus wooed it away from her, and with it, immediately enslaved all the Amazons.[17]

The legends of the Amazons pulse with sexuality shaped by the male fascination with women who reject heterosexuality (except for means of procreation). But Princess Diana does not have a father. In contrast to Athena, she is a totally female creation: her mother molded a statue of a little girl and then prayed to Aphrodite to bring it to life, which she did.[18] Wonder Woman exists outside definition through a male-based relationship to a father, husband, or son—she is completely independent of patriarchy.[19] Her bulletproof bracelets are a reminder of the time when the Amazons were slaves, after losing the war with Hercules, perhaps suggesting that Wonder Woman can be enslaved, as she is in *Sensation Comics* No. 4, April, 1942, when chains are welded to her bracelets and she loses her supernatural strength.[20]

Moulton created Wonder Woman to solve a major problem created by men: World War II. She is stronger and better than any man, having the strength of Hercules and the speed of Mercury, yet she is as beautiful as Aphrodite and as wise as Athena. Right from the start, she is the exceptional woman who saves what men try to destroy.[21] Moulton consciously created what he saw as a solution to the madness let loose on the world by men. As he wrote, "Into this tortured, upside-down world of men, torn by hatreds, war and destruction, comes Wonder Woman, a powerful being of light and happiness."[22]

After Moulton's death in 1947, Wonder Woman underwent rapid transformations in various comic-book series of the late 1940s and the 1950s.[23] With the rise of the women's movement she underwent various appropriations by heterosexual feminists, lesbian activists, and the television industry. She appeared on the cover of *Ms.* magazine three times (July 1972, Fall 2007, and Fall 2012) and continues as a gloss for a woman who can do it all and who "has it all." In 2011, she resurfaced in a new series of comic books.

Returning to Wonder Woman's sexuality: in his interactions with her, Steve Trevor is almost always injured and unconscious, as when he crashes his plane on Paradise Island. When we first see him, Wonder Woman is carrying his limp body to the hospital—an almost comic reversal of the hero carrying the fainting maiden![24] The fact of being unconscious helps him remain believably heroic, because, according to the mores of the day, it would have been considered emasculating for him to stand by impotently while she performed her extraordinary physical feats.

Then there are her female pals—her sorority sisters from Holliday College for Women.[25] What are we to make of this name? Is it a place where women are on holiday from the expectations of patriarchal society while they train in the martial arts? We first meet them when Wonder Woman needs their help to free Steve, who has been captured by enemy spies. Wonder Woman organizes one hundred of these college students to march on his captors and convince them to dance. The men, of course, agree, but on Wonder Woman's signal the girls knock the men down and handcuff them. Afterward, Wonder Woman gently carries the still-wounded Steve to a waiting car, which returns him to the hospital. From that issue on, the college girls rambunctiously, merrily, and fearlessly answer Wonder Woman's calls for assistance, replacing the sisterhood she left behind on Paradise Island.

Wonder Woman's lack of actual sexual contact can be read as a source of her power. She is the never-captured swan maiden, the celibate Christian mystic, Brunhilde before her rape, and the Nišan shaman before she was undone by rumors of having had a sexual relationship with her ritual assistant.

The two decades before Wonder Woman's creation were a high point for women aviators. Women's power and freedom to act, let alone fly, is reflected in quite interesting ways in the film *Christopher Strong* (1933), for example, in which Katharine Hepburn plays an aristocratic English aviator who gives an impassioned speech about her independence from love. But she has spoken too soon, as shortly thereafter she falls in love with a married man, gives up flying at his request, and finds herself pregnant. Rather than accept his reluctant offer to divorce his wife, she crashes her plane after having set a new record for altitude. She has flown as high as she could, and it has killed her. She, too, has her swan suit; in one scene, she is dressed for a costume party as a moth—prefiguring her own flaming death—in a shimmering silver gown and a close-fitting hat similar to those worn by pilots, but with antennae.[26] A subplot of the film involves her lover's daughter having a casual sexual affair—also with a married man—and then marrying her lover after his divorce; but other than this event, she is quite ordinary. So there is no critique of sexuality, or even of adultery, in the film, but Hepburn's character is heroic and thus held to different standards. The message is clear: to be exceptional and to remain powerful, a woman must repress her sexuality. Despite her many captivities, Wonder Woman remains strong because her love for Steve Trevor and even for the Holliday Girls is unconsummated. She was, after all, named Diana by the goddess Aphrodite in honor of the virgin goddess Artemis/Diana.

Wonder Woman was by no means the only famous woman aviator of her time, however.

AMELIA EARHART

The history of aviation is a history of men;[27] the women who have made significant contributions are too often lost in its hurrahs. They were almost always called "girls," no matter their age, and were frequently referred to as "ladybirds," "angels," and "sweethearts of the air." The wildly popular, nationally syndicated columnist and radio commentator Will Rogers called the Women's Air Derby of 1929—the first air race by women pilots—the Powder Puff Derby.[28] Amelia Earhart (1897–1939) came in third (Figure 12.2). Despite her piloting abilities and fame, she was always referred to as an "aviatrix" rather than an "aviator," the feminine form of the noun emphasizing that the category is male and the female aviator is an exception. This sexist language continued to be employed in the constant comparisons of her to Charles Lindbergh (1902–1974) as "Lady Lindy,"[29] while the media's reporting of women's aeronautical achievements revealed a preoccupation with the gender of heroism—tellingly, Lindbergh was never compared to Earhart. When men crashed planes, newspapers reported that the accidents were due to technical problems; when women crashed, it proved they were not fit to fly.[30] Earhart's earliest experience of this occurred during her first flying lesson, when her male instructor had another male pilot on board just in case her inherent female timidity caused her to panic and jump out. Her next lessons were with one of the leading female pilots of the day, Neta Snook (1896–1991), who taught the financially struggling Earhart on credit.[31]

Women fliers of the 1920s and 1930s were unperturbed by public opinion, as they described experiencing independence and freedom through flight. According to Louise Thaden (1905–1979), "Flying is the only real freedom we are privileged to possess." That sentiment finds an echo in the words of another early flier, Margery

FIGURE 12.2 Amelia Earhart, c. 1925.
Library of Congress Prints and Photographs Division, Washington, D.C.

Brown (1902–1961): "A woman who can find fulfillment in the skies will never again need to live her life in some man's spare moments." They were, however, all topped by the witty and rhyming Lady Mary Heath (1896–1939), who famously flew solo between South Africa and England: "Woman's place is in the home, but failing that the aerodrome."[32] Paradoxically, the prejudice against women fliers created opportunities for them; the perceived limitations of women pilots fostered the sales pitch that if a woman could fly then anyone could, furthering the perception of flying as safe. Negative views about female abilities opened doors for women as spokespersons, salespeople, demonstrators, and test pilots for the aviation industry. Women domesticated the skies—an inversion of the domestication of flying females like Brunhilde and swan maidens. Once the safety of flying was established, however, the doors were firmly shut against women, except as air hostesses, who, until the 1950s, had to be unmarried white women under the age of thirty-five.[33]

Amelia Earhart became the first woman to fly across the Atlantic Ocean in June 1928, and even though she flew merely as a passenger, she was catapulted to world fame.[34] Athletic,[35] slim, and attractive, Earhart was a natural at gaining public attention. Five years later, on the fifth anniversary of Lindbergh's historic solo flight across the Atlantic, Earhart became the first woman, and only the second person after Lindbergh, to fly solo across the Atlantic.[36] Her husband and promoter, George Putnam, selected the date for its publicity value. In fact, as soon as he met her in 1928 he became instrumental in getting her on board Lindbergh's second Atlantic flight, and he remained her chief supporter and publicist until her death.

Just before Lindbergh's 1928 flight, word got out that a woman was flying across the Atlantic and reporters went wild. Earhart had to respond to the claims of a Boston newspaper that she was doing it to recoup her family's fortune, when in fact she was receiving no compensation at all. She telegraphed instructions to Putnam:

> Please get the point across [to the reporters] that the only stake I win is the privilege of flying and the pleasure of having shared in a fine adventure well conducted whose success will be a real development and perhaps something of an inspiration for women.[37]

Earhart used her public image to promote the overall position of women and to encourage their achievements. As early as 1929, she and ninety-eight other women pilots founded the Ninety-Nines, an international organization of licensed women pilots.[38] As Susan Ware put it, "*She flew for women*."[39] It is of note that before she gained fame as a pilot, Earhart was a social worker in Boston;[40] helping others was a family tradition. Earhart believed her accomplishments represented the expanding opportunities available to women in the 1920s and 1930s.

Death and the Heroine

As we have seen, many flying females (such as Valkyries, *apsarās*, and goddesses of death and rebirth) have run ferry services of some kind or another to carry men to heaven or immortality; they do not primarily fly for their own pleasure, but rather to help others. Earhart redefined this pattern. The daughter of a formerly wealthy and prominent family, she began flying in the Midwest during the great barnstorming days of the 1920s and 1930s, taking her first flight in a plane when she was twenty-three.[41] A few days later, she was taking flying lessons, and six months later, after saving every penny from a series of odd jobs, she bought her own plane. At the end of World War I, the surplus of decommissioned planes brought their prices down,[42] but those military aircraft were subject to engine failures that killed many a pilot.[43] Earhart's first plane was a yellow Kinner Airster that, with her typical blend of self-deprecation and humor, she named "The Canary"—no soaring eagle here, but no caged bird either. Amelia Earhart had a high sense of fun, a love of freedom, and a joy in life.

Her husband, George Putnam, the wealthy and successful publisher of Charles Lindbergh's books, packaged Earhart, and he kept her in the news. Flying was and remains a very expensive sport, and Earhart needed to remain in the public's eye in order to support it.[44] Before becoming famous she had worked at innumerable odd jobs, including at the phone company, to support her flying. Until the financial crash of 1929 Putnam was wealthy, and even afterward he remained a powerful and influential man. As in the old myths, he had found Earhart's swan suit—a series of costly planes.[45] After her 1928 trans-Atlantic flight, Putnam bought her the plane that Lady Mary Heath had flown solo from South Africa to England. Earhart married him in 1931, but like a true swan maiden she made him promise to let her go in a year if they were not happy,[46] and, unusually for the time, she kept her maiden name and never wore her wedding ring.[47] They both worked hard and made good incomes, but their lavish lifestyle and the upkeep of planes quickly absorbed it all.

To improve their financial position, Earhart decided to become the first woman to fly around the world, at its widest point along the equator. Most of their financial resources were tied up in this venture; the plane was not even insured, because no insurer was willing to underwrite such a risky flight. This, in addition to her pride as a pilot, was likely a contributing factor in Earhart's decision to continue the flight despite her exhaustion and even after a crash on the initial takeoff from Honolulu. She and Putman made elaborate, expensive,[48] and technically detailed plans that involved Putnam gaining access to military maps and advisers. The United States government was already assisting Pan American Airlines in developing a route through the South Pacific, and these resources were made available to Earhart, including the all too appropriately named USS *Swan*[49] which, like the animal familiar of a shaman, was positioned halfway between Honolulu and Howland Island, the half-mile-wide, two-mile-long spit of land where Earhart was to refuel during her around-the-world flight. She never made it. Due to radio problems on her plane, those waiting on Howland Island in clear weather could only hear her communications; they could not respond to her requests for navigational assistance as she flew all but blind in cloudy weather, perhaps hundreds of miles off course. Flying her Lockheed Electra—a plane named after one of the most famous daughters in history—Earhart went down on July 2, 1937, close to Japanese-controlled waters, just before the start of World War II. Her disappearance instigated a $4 million search (the equivalent of $66 million today) by the United States Navy and Coast Guard that was personally authorized by President Franklin D. Roosevelt.[50] Earhart had been a frequent houseguest at the White House, and she and Eleanor Roosevelt were good friends.[51]

Earhart fulfilled the classical definition of female heroism by dying, but unlike the death of the classical heroine, hers was not private, indoors, or by her own hand.[52] Earhart's death was highly public, and it sparked a media frenzy. She is the female counter-hero defined by Maureen Fries:

> The[ir] adventurous paths . . . require the males who surround them to fill subordinate, non-protagonist roles in their stories. . . .[53] [T]he counter-hero possesses the hero's superior power of action without possessing his or her adherence to the dominant culture or capability of renewing its values. . . . [Instead,] the counter-hero violates them in some way.[54]

Earhart left behind a trail of conspiracy theories that still fascinate. Did she die in the plane crash? Did the Japanese capture her? Was she interrogated and then killed?[55] The widespread theory that she had purposely ditched her plane to give the United States government the opportunity to survey Japanese military strength in the South Pacific was supported by the 1949 RKO movie *Flight for Freedom*, in which Rosalind Russell stars as an intrepid female pilot who disappears over the Pacific while on a secret government mission. The grain of truth here is that the US Navy and Coast Guard did in fact gain extremely useful military information as they searched for Earhart.[56]

Like most of the aerial women surveyed thus far, she lived on, ever reinterpreted to suit changing ideologies. Indisputably, she has influenced the lives of innumerable women, many of whom have written about her. Judith Thurman, writing in *The New Yorker*, expressed this so well: "If Earhart became an 'icon,' it was, in part, because women who aspired to excel in any sphere, at a high altitude, looked upon her as their champion."[57] But her truest legacy, and one she would affirm, is that her feats helped pave the way for women pilots in World War II, for women's admission to the U.S. Air Force Academy, and for astronaut Sally Ride (1951–2012), another flying heroine.[58] Earhart had become a pacifist during World War I, when she served as a nurse's aide in Toronto and came to know death and the high human cost of war up close and personal.[59] Nonetheless, the future course of aviation was either in commercial or military professions. Inadvertently, she led the aerial women who came after her into war service, the inevitable domain of flying females.

HANNA REITSCH

Fourteen years younger than Earhart, Hanna Reitsch (1912–1979, Figure 12.3) was iron-willed[60] and fearless, even foolhardy. She began with gliders—she was the first woman to fly one over the Alps[61]—but her record-setting accomplishments

FIGURE 12.3 Hanna Reitsch.
Photographer: Scherl.

included powered planes, as well. She tested or flew everything Germany invented before and throughout World War II, including the first operational helicopter, which she demonstrated for Charles Lindbergh on one of his many trips to prewar Germany.[62] In a 1976 interview, Reitsch still exuded an effervescent enthusiasm for the thrill of flying the newest and most dangerous equipment, mixing a respect for the expense of the planes she tested with what seems to have been an innate skill for aeronautics. She described flying the rocket-powered Messerschmitt Me 163 as "thundering through the sky riding a cannonball."[63] At the very end of the war, she flew into Russian-occupied Berlin to join Adolf Hitler in his underground bunker, becoming part of the folklore of the final battle for Berlin.[64] She died of a heart attack at sixty-seven, having set a world record for distance flown in a glider just a few months earlier. In a parallel to Earhart, who is more famous for her disappearance than for her accomplishments as a pilot, Reitsch is better known for having witnessed the last days of the Third Reich than for her stupendous aeronautical feats. According to US Army captain Robert E. Work, who interrogated her on October 8, 1945, her account of the last days in Hitler's bunker "is probably as accurate a one as will be obtained."[65] Yet, if only because of the wide range of World War II–era German aircraft made available to her, she is without a doubt one of the greatest pilots, female or male, of the twentieth century.[66]

The daughter of a proud yet defeated nation, Hanna Reitsch had more limited options than Amelia Earhart when it came to aircraft. At the end of World War I, the Treaty of Versailles denied Germany the right to have an air force, which effectively denied it an aircraft industry, as well. When Reitsch wanted to learn to fly, the only planes available were relics from World War I, often missing their motors. German flying enthusiasts focused on gliders, thus turning the limitations of the Treaty of Versailles to their advantage by building ever more efficient and sophisticated gliders, and eventually becoming the leaders in international glider competitions. Reitsch had her first glider lesson when she was nineteen,[67] something she had longed to do since her childhood, when seeing birds in flight made her long to fly as they did, a longing that stayed with her into adulthood.[68] Reitsch said that she first attempted to fly when she was four by jumping off a balcony with her arms spread as wings—a practice she kept up for about four years, much to the chagrin of her parents.[69] While being taught how to guide a glider on the ground, she could not resist the temptation to become airborne; of course, she crashed—not for the last time—but she was unharmed. After further training, her first test was to stay airborne for ten minutes. As she caught the upwind, she was overcome by the beauty of it all—and then she saw

> two buzzards, gliding with motionless wings at the same height as myself. I knew that where these birds were flying the up-wind would be at its strongest. I decided to follow them . . . . They kept their heads turned toward me, their eyes fixed on the great, silent bird that was bearing me aloft. . . .
>
> Carried by the wind, still soaring, they rose in the air, I still striving to follow them. But they could do it better than I and suddenly I found them far above me. Again the game began. I flew after them, finding always a stronger up-wind where they had been. So, in every nerve I strained to imitate them, until my eye fell on my watch . . . . More than twenty minutes had passed.[70]

When she finally was given permission to fly for as long as she liked, she flew for five hours; upon landing, she learned that she had set a new world record.[71]

After completing her first glider course, she entered medical school in Berlin. Coming from a very religious family, Reitsch hoped to become a flying medical missionary, and so she began taking powered-flight lessons while she continued to fly gliders. After three years of flying, she broke several more records, including reaching a height of 9,750 feet in a glider, and she began to teach gliding as well. She was one of only a handful of female gliders, so all of her students were male. She became friends with one of them, Wernher von Braun, the future inventor of the rocket-propelled plane she later tested.[72] Fortunately, she became comfortable around men and boys because, unlike pilots in the United States, she would usually be the lone woman among fliers.

Reitsch's cultural situation eventually offered her an advantage over Earhart. Her life changed when Hitler became chancellor of Germany in 1933 and, among other things, repudiated the Treaty of Versailles and began training military pilots for what would become the Luftwaffe. Reitsch had accompanied an expedition to South America organized by Deutsche Forschungsinstitute für Segelflug (German Research Institute for Glider Flight, the DFS) to study air currents. The DFS received government support and was able to offer her a job; she accepted it and gave up medical school, which had not really held her interest. She gained experience flying experimental gliders and gained advanced pilot training available to very few men, let alone women. The DFS also allowed her to participate in foreign flying projects, which brought her international recognition.[73] She parlayed her success into permission from the Reich Air Ministry to attend the male-only Civil Airways Training School,[74] which was clandestinely training future military pilots. Unlike Earhart, she would continue to have access to the most advanced military aircraft, eventually becoming Germany's premier test pilot and flying the first rocket-propelled planes.[75]

In 1935 she returned to the DFS as a test pilot, not only flying gliders but, because of her developing technical knowledge, suggesting improvements and then retesting them, again and again.[76] She also continued to act as a German goodwill ambassador, training glider pilots in other countries. Her international fame was such that she was one of three pilots to perform daily during the Winter Olympics of 1936.[77] In 1937, she was given the honorary title of *Flugkapitan* (Flight Captain), and she met Hitler, whom she found disappointing.[78] Later that year, she was invited to join an elite group of military test pilots at Rechlin, near Berlin. Here she had the opportunity to test bigger and heavier planes. Reitsch was not only a woman in a man's field, but she had the most daring job in that field, and the one with the most glory.[79] Needless to say, her presence was not always appreciated by other pilots.[80] Her status was noted by the medals she acquired but undermined by the dark blue uniform she wore, one of her own design,[81] because she was not an official member of any military organization (her "Flight Captain" title was merely honorary). Even so, she was unique among women in Nazi Germany, with its slogan summarizing the proper place of women, *Kinder, Küche, und Kirche* (children, kitchen, and church), and its opposition to women in the military.[82]

As the war began to turn against Germany, she became involved in a scheme to establish a suicide squadron called the Leonidas Squadron: its pilots would crash their planes into the center of important Allied targets, thereby forcing the Allies to the table for peace talks before all of Germany was destroyed. But by the time she got approval and had trained seventy pilots, the Allies were so deeply entrenched on the Continent that the Leonidas Squadron pilots could not reach their targets before being shot down.[83] Regardless, Reitsch was prepared to die for the country she loved.[84]

When Hitler called Reitsch's old friend and mentor Robert Ritter von Greim[85] to his bunker in Berlin in April 1945, he decided to fly to Gatow Airport in Berlin in a small, fast plane with just enough room for himself and the pilot. Reitsch insisted on going along. Her diminutive size (she stood just over five feet tall) was an advantage as she rode in the cramped fuselage. Forty fighter planes flew cover for them, but they were still engaged by Russian aircraft throughout the flight.[86]

At Gatow they found every road blocked by either Russian troops or fleeing refugees, which meant the only way into the city was by air. Determined to get through, von Greim appropriated a single-engine plane. He piloted it because he had flown through enemy fire while Reitsch had not; she was not in the military, and even if she had been, German women were not allowed in combat. They were spotted and shot at by both air and ground fire. Von Greim was hit, shattering his right foot, and Reitsch leaned over his body to fly the plane, which was hit twice again before she brought it to a safe landing by the Brandenburg Gate. They were eventually picked up by a German truck that took them to the Reich Chancellery, under which lay Hitler's bunker, at about seven o'clock on the evening of April 26, 1945, four days before his suicide. Here Hitler lived out his last days with his mistress Eva Braun, his dog, loyal supporters such as Magda and Joseph Goebbels, and a staff of secretaries, domestics, medical personnel, and soldiers.

Hitler's bunker bore an eerie resemblance to the burial mounds of ancient Norse kings, who traditionally were buried with their clothing, furnishings, and companions. Moreover, Hitler and his companions actually thought of themselves as the old gods, and when they finally committed suicide they did it to the accompaniment of music from *Götterdämmerung* (*The Twilight of the Gods*),[87] the fourth and final opera in Wagner's Ring Cycle, which depicts the destruction of Valhalla.

A century of German and Scandinavian writing about the Norse past led up to that moment, beginning with Jacob Grimm's *Deutsche Mythologie,* published in 1835,[88] and the Romantic movement in Germanic philosophy, music, and art, which produced striking representations of Norse heroes such as Brunhilde. Apart from art, Romanticism was associated with a new sense of national pride that led various European scholars to explore their nations' ancient history and to romanticize it to greater or lesser degrees. This is not the place for a deep, sustained exploration of these complex studies. Suffice it to say that, beginning in the 1890s, but especially under National Socialism in Germany, scholarship about early Germany was put to a variety of uses. The Roman historian Tacitus's picture of ancient Germania as racially pure (*Germania,* Book IV) complemented early twentieth-century longings for a German utopia that found expression in the utilization of pre-Christian Germanic symbols such as swastikas and runes.[89] Heinrich Himmler was particularly obsessed with German Neopaganism, supporting the establishment of a learned society within the SS (the Schutzstaffel, "Protection Squadron") to promote Old Germanic learning.[90] The collars of SS uniforms, decorated with a double runic S that resembled twin lightning bolts, reflected this mythologized past. Hanna Reitsch fit perfectly into this mythology, filling the role of Hitler's protective Valkyrie.

In April 1945, under the continuous and encroaching Russian bombardment, all the residents of Hitler's bunker were resigned to their fate and awaited death. Then, on April 29, Hitler got word that Himmler was negotiating a peace settlement. This briefly put the fight back in him, although he remained delusional about his resources. He ordered Reitsch and the wounded von Greim, whose right foot had been completely smashed during his flight into Berlin, to fly back to Rechlin and organize Luftwaffe support for General Walther Wenck's troops, which Hitler thought were still advancing from the south. Unknown to the residents of the bunker, Wenck had created his own orders and was not rushing toward Berlin, but rather opening a corridor in the Russian line that enabled civilians and soldiers to escape the encircling Russian army.[91] Hitler's second instruction was that they find and arrest Himmler.[92]

Von Greim, whom Hitler had promoted to commander in chief of the all-but-defunct Luftwaffe, and Reitsch accepted their assignment and made it back to the Brandenburg Gate, where a pilot was waiting in a two-seater plane to fly them out. Reitsch once again rode in the fuselage, and again they came under heavy fire. Landing in Rechlin, von Greim ordered what was left of the Luftwaffe to defend Berlin, and then he and Reitsch flew north to Plön in pursuit of Himmler. This was also where the remains of the German high command had gathered, and where von Greim and Reitsch learned that Hitler was dead and that Wenck's army was defeated. The Third Reich was over, and the only military tactic left was to hold off the Russian army for as long as possible to enable civilians to flee westward toward Allied forces, which, hopefully, would be less vengeful.[93] They realized any further effort was useless and checked into a hospital on May 9, 1945, reporting to the American military authorities soon after they arrived.[94] Meanwhile, Reitsch's father, in fear of being returned to Russian-occupied territory (the family was from Silesia) shot his wife, his daughter Heidi, her three children, and then himself.[95]

Von Greim also committed suicide, leaving Reitsch as one of the few living witnesses of Hitler's last days, and therefore of vital importance to the Allies in establishing the details of Hitler's final days and death, and in the later war crimes trials against Nazi officials in Nuremberg. She was imprisoned until August 1946 but was not charged with any crime.[96] Upon her release, she wrote her memoirs and did some missionary work in Germany alongside two Catholic priests.[97] In 1951 the Allies eased their ban on gliding in Germany, and Reitsch once more took to the air, continuing to set records and teaching gliding all over the world until her death.

WOMEN, HEROISM, AND MILITARISM

In the aftermath of World War II, the Russians and Americans grabbed all the German rocket scientists they could in order to begin the next phase of aviation: the exploration of space.[98] In the United States, women were completely excluded from the nascent space program despite their aeronautical service during the war. In May 1941, before the United States entered World War II, it had created what would become the Air Transport Command of the US Army Air Force. (The US Air Force was not formed until after the war, on September 18, 1947.) The job of the all-male Air Transport pilots was to ferry airplanes from one place to another, especially much-needed bombers to England, a non-combat job that female pilots could do just as well. World War II was an air war and, even if only for a short time, intrepid women pilots were at its forefront.

Twenty-two-year-old Cornelia Fort (Figure 12.4) was giving a flying lesson over Honolulu on the morning of December 7, 1941, when she flew straight into the Japanese attack on Pearl Harbor. She took over the controls and safely landed her plane, followed by a hail of machine-gun fire as she and her student raced to the safety of the hanger.[99] After Pearl Harbor, the male ferry pilots were recalled for combat duty, leaving the United States in short supply of pilots. The suggestion that women pilots take over ferrying operations was rejected several times by the military, even though women in England were performing this duty,[100] until the spring of 1942, when the need became critical.[101] Fort was among the first twenty-eight women to join the Women's Auxiliary Ferry Squadron (WAFS) as civilian pilots working for the Army Air Corps. She was also the first American woman pilot to die during active military duty, in a crash over Texas on March 21, 1943, because a male pilot flew too close to her plane, severing one of its wings.[102] As a civilian she had none of the military benefits of insurance, burial subsidy, or honors. Nor would she be the last woman pilot to die while in service during World War II. Thirty-eight members of the short-lived WASPs (see below) died during the war.[103] And, even though they were better qualified than their male counterparts in education and training, they were paid less.[104]

The WAFS and a sister group, the Women's Flying Training Detachment, were merged in August 1943 into the Women Air Force Service Pilots (WASPs). WASP pilots began by flying small aircraft to their needed locations, sometimes

FIGURE 12.4 Cornelia Fort with a PT-19A.
Photograph: U.S. Air Force.

spending the night and then taking a train or a commercial flight back to their base. Male civilian pilots could hitch rides on military planes, but women pilots could not because the press tracked almost every move the women pilots made and the army was nervous about the possibility of scandal. In March 1943 the army briefly banned women from being copilots with men and grounded them while menstruating—women were just totally "other" to the male military establishment. Both restrictions, however, were rescinded in April of the same year.[105] These women broke ground for the women who followed, but the sexism they endured has hardly disappeared, as shown by the sexual harassment and assaults so common throughout the American military in the decades since.

Gradually, women pilots worked their way up to flying bigger, heavier bombers and cargo planes. In July 1943, they began towing targets for anti-aircraft and air-to-air gunnery practice, often with live ammunition.[106] All of these were domestic flights. Women never got to fly the famous B-17 bombers to England, though they flew them all over the United States (Figure 12.5). Two women pilots, Nancy Love and Betty Gillies, got as far as Greenland flying a B-17, before the final leg of their flight to Scotland was scuttled.[107]

The wings of women pilots were clipped when they, still listed as civilians, were prematurely deactivated shortly before Christmas 1944, as the need for pilots decreased and male pilots resisted being assigned to the infantry. It was not until 1977 that the United States Congress finally acknowledged that these women had been military personnel, declaring them veterans and issuing them honorable discharges.[108] Their abrupt deactivation in 1944 was part of the campaign to get women out of war jobs and back into the domestic realm.[109] Mainly, though, male pilots resented women pilots—many wanted flying to remain a boys' club, and they succeeded in keeping it so for a long time afterward.[110] (The very word "cockpit" sums up this attitude.) Women were not allowed to fly again for the American military, or for commercial airlines, until the 1970s. Needless to say, women were not considered for the early astronaut program of the 1960s, despite significant evidence that they were psychologically and physically better equipped than men to withstand the stress of space travel, and were lighter in weight—always a benefit since the earliest days of flying.[111] Although thirteen women had gone through and passed the initial Mercury Astronaut Candidate Testing Program, only male participants were actually allowed to travel into space.[112] Still in the 1960s, the

FIGURE 12.5 Four WASPs leaving a B-17 they just landed, Lockbourne Field, Ohio, 1944. Left to right: Frances Greene, Margaret "Peg" Kirshner (Stevenson), Ann Waldner, and Blanche Osborne. The nickname of the plane, "Pistol-Packin' Mama," can be seen on its nose.
Smithsonian: National Air and Space Museum.

prevalent view was that women could not fly while menstruating. As early as the 1930s, the US Air Commerce Bureau had considered grounding women for nine days while they were menstruating;[113] as mentioned, this idea resurfaced briefly during World War II, and was discussed again as a limitation for female astronauts in the 1960s. Somehow, the first female cosmonaut flew while menstruating without a problem, but ten years later Americans were still concerned about female astronauts menstruating.[114]

Russian women have a different history; they flew planes into battle. Liliia Vladimirovna Litviak (1921–1943) was the first woman fighter ace in history.[115] She was shot down and killed on August 1, 1943. The all-women 588th Night Bomber Air Regiment was nicknamed the Night Witches because of its pilots' terrifying technique of flying without lights, cutting their engines as they neared their targets, and gliding silently and invisibly as they dropped bombs.[116] They flew at night because darkness was their only protection they had for their cheaply constructed planes, which were usually unarmed and highly combustible. Nor did they have parachutes, and losses were consequently high.[117] Of course, the entire Russian population was mobilized to resist the German invasion—for the Russians it was a war of attrition and starvation, so everyone was to some extent cannon fodder. Nonetheless, the women's units were disbanded as soon as circumstances permitted,[118] just as the American and English women's units were.

Women were, however, part of the Soviet Union's space program. In 1957 the Russians launched the first space satellite and in 1963 the first female cosmonaut, Valentina Tereshkova (b. 1937). Tereshkova was not a trained aviator but rather a parachuting enthusiast. Russian spacecraft were more highly automated than American space shuttles, and a cosmonaut returning from space was ejected from the capsule and then parachuted to land or water.[119] So, rather than choosing from among proven women pilots, the Russians went through letters from women, including Tereshkova, who were asking to become cosmonauts, and they took candidates from flying and parachuting clubs. When chosen, Tereshkova was twenty-four years old and without higher education. She had worked in a textile factory, but she also had an excellent record as a leader in the communist youth group, the Komsomol, and was an inspiring public speaker. There were four other finalists, but Tereshkova's proletarian background may have been the deciding factor in her favor as the Soviet premier, Nikita Khrushchev, gave her the nod.[120]

It would take the United States another twenty years to send a woman into space: Sally Ride, a thirty-two-year-old astrophysicist, blasted off on June 18, 1983.[121] In 1995, Eileen Collins (b. 1956), the first woman to pilot an American spacecraft, carried the pilot's license of Evelyn Trout (1906–2003) into space. Trout had flown in the 1929 Women's Air Derby, and her pilot's license was signed by Orville Wright.[122] Thus far four women have died in the US space program: Judith Resnick (1949–1986) and schoolteacher Christa McAuliffe (1948–1986), both in the *Challenger* space shuttle disaster, and Laurel Clark (1961–2003) and Kalpana Chawla (1962–2003), who were both aboard the *Columbia* space shuttle. Chawla had been an avid birder and she left $300,000 in her will to the American Audubon Society for the protection of birds and the environment[123]—a gentle reminder of the inspiration to be found in a bird taking wing.

The Russian and American space programs are military and political competitions that reveal both the initial sexist exclusion of women and the completely opportunistic use of women when it made good media coverage.[124] History—and, hopefully, this book—show that while militarism and nationalism[125] initially offer women opportunities, neither is completely conducive to women's equality and autonomy, as the continuing sexual abuse of women in the military sadly illustrates.

Conclusion

FLIGHT UNITES THE female beings in this book: the ability to break free of the earth and to soar is a profound expression of freedom. A birdlike nature is shared by Paleolithic bird-headed women, winged goddesses, aerial mystics, swan maidens, and fairies, while bird imagery, wings, and feathers are important components of the costumes of Valkyries, shamans, Daoist mystics, and even Wonder Woman. Flight in the sense of fleeing has been a dominant theme in tales of swan maidens, Valkyries, and fairy brides, while mystics in various religious traditions aspired to rise above the limits of the flesh.

In almost all times and places, women's immanence and transcendence have been expressed primarily through a patriarchal lens that has been shaped to fit different environments and ideologies. No one group, religion, or ideology comes out of this study free of the tarnish of misogyny; in fact, the anti-woman commonalities across ethnic and religious boundaries have been staggering. The evidence does not merely lurk in dusty libraries; it leaps from the iconographic record and religious texts as well as from myths, legends, and popular culture (including films and comic books). What stuns the mind is the unanimity of views; the flying female is one thread that has unraveled a tapestry of gender conflict that continues to this day. The paradigm of aerial females reveals similarities that cross religious, national, and temporal boundaries, among others.

But, let's not forget how differently these stories could have been viewed by women, who may have felt trapped in patrilocal marriages, and men, whose alienating behavior toward women made them suspicious of the women in their beds (Circe comes to mind as an example of a personification of this sexual anxiety), who cooked their food and bore their children (thus, women had the power to poison their husbands, and to encourage their offspring to overthrow their fathers or to kill their children as an act of revenge). Indeed, this book has discussed a number of supernatural women who exacted such female revenge: Medea, Clytemnestra, Brunhilde, and Kriemhild. From the male point of view, how could women not secretly long to escape, while from the female point of view, how could such tales not remind them of the freedom, comfort, and familiarity of their long-lost birthplaces? In these stories women found an expression of their own longing; they found a sisterhood of feeling where there was none in their lives. The foreign woman, the outsider, has no allies except in her imagination.

These flighty women required rethinking, as did the religious and social categories that defined their lives. The freedom of swan maidens and fairies before their captivity was alluring. How else can we explain the proliferation of tales, images, and rituals of flying females, and the scarcity of males who fly? The actualization of these myths by female shamans and mystics as spiritual paths is only matched by the men who performed rituals to control and profit from aerial females such as *ḍākinīs* and *yoginīs*.

It is well understood that rape is about power, not sex. It is the worst expression of male power to deny women their autonomy and freedom, even their safety. Whether by conquering armies, abusive partners, individual men in all societies who maintain fear in women, predatory adults, or mythologies that reduce women into nameless objects (*hourīs*, *apsarās*), the message is the same: men have power and women do not. Even powerful goddesses (such as Isthar, and the Valkyries) and female warriors (including Brunhilde and aviators) are brought down by men who think of themselves, and not women, as heroes.

In the monstrous-feminine we see the demonization of aerial females and also the male need to make these independent beings into monsters and to destroy them, usually with the help of the male-identified, token goddess (such as Athena, patron of a great city-state exclusively and firmly ruled by men). It seems there is nothing more perverse and ugly than an independent woman.

Flying females arise in prehistory as richly ambiguous beings who can grant fertility or death, then evolve into individualized winged goddesses, only to crash against the rise of militarized states that support patriarchy—a point clearly articulated in Aeschylus's *Eumenides* when the court of the gods rule in favor of rule by the father, not the mother. After this, aerial females fly through increasingly constrained space, like indigenous people and endangered species whose environments are continually diminished. They evolve into their complete opposites: sleeping beauties or a swan maiden who commits suicide *to be with* her mortal lover. Their religious roles are diminished: shamans are encroached upon by patriarchal governments or male envy, female Christian mystics trying to escape the (patriarchal) world through communion with a male god only to see their bodily autonomy undermined. And, in the twentieth century, female aviators are falsely defined as incompetent pilots and denied flight by a military complex when menstruating—which is actually a sign of fertility and thus power, though it has been considered polluting and repugnant to men around the world.

There is something eerie about aerial females, something that cannot be pinned down. This is most evident in shape-shifters and divine or semi-divine females, but even human women who take flight are unnerving in their transcendence of gravity. Whether elusive, uncanny, awe-inspiring, frightening, or soothing—they stand apart.

THE EXCEPTIONAL WOMAN

The women in this study, through their exceptionalism (and often their punishments) offer conflicting roles and choices to women. Supernatural women are unrealistic models, but their punishments through humiliation, captivity, and rape are all too familiar to actual women. Here we should note the disproportionate number of women who were accused of witchcraft, tortured, burned alive, drowned, or hung until dead.

Individual women, through their exceptionality, have not always been good friends of other women, as Barbara Newman, in her final analysis of Hildegard of Bingen's statement that Christianity had entered an "effeminate age," brings out:

> In spite of her extensive feminine imagery for the church and priesthood, she not only assented to but actively supported the exclusion of women from the clergy and other forms of female subordination. . . . Her self-validation as a female prophet for an effeminate age only makes her *an exception to prove the rule*: women may continue to prophesy as long as the times remain womanish, but when they return to normal such exceptions will presumably be needless. It is significant that the sequence of apocalyptic ages prophesied in the *Scivias* and the *Activity of God* gives no hint of a coming era in which gender roles would be reversed or altered.[1]

While it has become somewhat fashionable to criticize Simone de Beauvoir, on whose shoulders we all stand, Toril Mori makes a telling point: "For Simone de Beauvoir, an exceptional woman is one who *is* a woman, but who also displays all the virtues normally associated with masculinity. In her own life, then, Beauvoir enjoyed all the advantages of being a token woman, as she herself candidly admit[ted]."[2]

This book has explored sisterhoods broken time and again in stories of the Valkyries and swan maidens, as well as aerial females who exist only to serve men—Valkyries, *apsarās*, *ḍākinīs*, and *yoginīs*—and females who require the protection or permission of men to support their aerial activities, such as medieval Christian mystics and modern women aviators.

The common element in the lives of aerial women is their uniqueness; they are the exceptional women, almost beyond mere mortals in their outstanding characteristics or abilities. They are women who have come close to rejecting the limitations not only of being female, but of being human. The rhetoric of sainthood in Christianity, Islam, Buddhism, and Daoism is masculine; therefore, female saints seem extraordinary and somewhat de-feminized. Their exceptionality can deny the all-too-real problems of ordinary women.

In the twenty-first century, what are we to think about these beliefs? The accomplishments of individual women still do not improve the overall situation of women, and their successes are very difficult to institutionalize for the benefit of others. Speaking of early twentieth-century women like Amelia Earhart (who did all she could to advance other women), Susan Ware notes, "[I]t proved very difficult to pass these highly fragile and historically specific gains on to the next generation."[3] Decisively, the various divine women discussed in this study never translated their power into a higher status for women in social reality because most religions disempower actual women while empowering imaginary ones. In effect, female imagery is used to conquer and control a fear of female power.[4]

The frequent captivity of aerial women highlights a power struggle between the sexes, one in which lies, betrayal, broken promises, and subterfuge have dominated. They were, for the most part, benevolent, toward men—who then sought to impose their will on females who grated against confinement and male definitions of their roles. Ancient Near Eastern goddesses, Valkyries, shamans, and even some fairies led men to some form of rebirth or immortality, yet in many cases they were punished. In the modern era women who risked life and limb in the service of their country were grounded and tossed aside when their services were no longer needed.

Much of the foregoing has dealt with women's bodies, illustrating the different relationships men and women have to their respective bodies. Female Christian mystics experienced union with God within and through their bodies, while male mystics did so through their intellects. Equally meaningful have been women's sexuality, fertility, and relationship to children. Time and again, aerial females' right to control their own sexuality has been challenged (in the cases of Isthar and the Nišan shaman), co-opted (for example, see the Valkyries, *hourīs*, *apsarās*, *ḍākinīs*, and *yoginīs*), denied (in the cases of Brunhilde and swan maidens), fantasized about (see witches, succubi, *hourīs*, and *apsarās*), or repressed (for example, see Wonder Woman and the Christian mystics). For many, sexuality was part of their downfall, which contradicts the ancient role of aerial females as those who bestow fertility and children.

WOMEN AND WAR

War has been connected to the erotic from ancient times to the present,[5] such as with the goddesses of both love and war, and the various celestial women given as war booty to dead warrior-heroes who had offered themselves as blood sacrifices to win eternal life and its many sensual pleasures. One story from an early Muslim collection tells us that a mother dedicated her son to *jihād* in the hope that as a martyr he would marry a *hourī*. She paid the dowry by buying weapons. Serving as witnesses to this marriage were Qur'ān reciters (*qurrā's*), who also fought in battle. Through one of these *qurrā'* the son sent her a message from the battle-field as he was dying: "Oh, mother your wish is fulfilled and your dowry accepted; I got married to the bride."[6] Such aspirations have continued, with contemporary jihadists likewise expecting sexual rewards in heaven, and have also devolved into the horrors of "comfort women" kidnapped by conquering armies to become sexual slaves. Women have disproportionately paid the price for wars started and maintained by men. Yet, as World War II shows, war has also provided women with opportunities to excel, that is, until the men come home. As discussed in the introduction, the male hero returns to conventional experience; the female heroine needs to be coerced back into it. Aerial women are wayward females, and we are better for knowing them.

This book has told the story of a single motif or trope in the human imagination—that of women not defined by the restrictive gravity of men's wishes or desires, but women whose ability to fly empowered them to impose conditions on men, or to escape roles they found constricting. They express female and male fantasies, although aerial women flew through an increasingly constrained space as the world changed and the male imagination came to dominate. Nowhere is this seen more clearly than in Brunhilde's evolving tale of declining power, culminating in tales of completely non-aerial, unconscious sleeping beauties, and in the mournful echoes that linger from the persecution of witches and the suppression of female shamanism.

This ancient concept of powerful winged women shape-shifts into many different forms over time and place; sometimes they lose one or more characteristics while at other times they gained additional ones. Whether human, divine, or mythic creature, men desire them, but not as they are. Rather, they want to clip their wings in order to hold them captive, controlling and constraining their freedom.

NOTES

ABBREVIATIONS

EOR: *Encyclopedia of Religion*, edited by Mircea Eliade, Macmillan, 1987.

ER&E: *Encyclopaedia of Religion and Ethics*, edited by James Hastings, Charles Scribner's Sons, 1922–1927.

EOW: *The Encyclopedia of Women and World Religion*, edited by Serinity Young, Macmillan, 1998.

OCD: *The Oxford Classical Dictionary*, edited by N. G. L. Hammond and H. H. Scullard, 2nd ed., Clarendon Press, 1970.

OED: *The Compact Edition of the Oxford Dictionary*, Oxford UP, 1971.

INTRODUCTION

1. Marina Warner discusses this sculpture and its placement in the Louvre in *Monuments and Maidens: The Allegory of the Female Form* 140–42. Charles Champoiseau excavated the statue on April 15, 1863, but it was not until 1875 that further archaeological investigations revealed that the complete sculpture placed Nike at the prow of a ship that served as its base. Her position on the ship, and within the ancient building where it was situated, privileged the three-quarters left view of the statue. The Louvre's website has a richly detailed analysis and description of the statue: see http://musee.louvre.fr/oal/victoiredesamothrace/victoiredesa-mothrace_acc_en.html. And Emory University has analyzed the site on Samothrace where Nike was found, with excellent diagrams, at http://www.samothrace.emory.edu.

2. Berger 7.

3. Hill 3.

4. Laufer, *The Prehistory of Aviation* 14–15, tells this story, which is contained in two ancient histories: the commentary on the *Bamboo Annals* (c. 296 BCE) and the *Suma Ch'ien* (c. 109–91 BCE), although it existed in oral form long before it was written down.

5. Anderson discusses the religious dimensions of dance and its role in rituals from prehistoric times to the present: see 6–7, 13–17, and 20. Orenstein briefly discusses the early relationship of ritual and theater, including dance, see 234, and 232–34, as does Talamantez 234–37, and Susan Pertel Jain 237–39. See also Hanna 69–74, 96–93, 97–114.

6. See Simone de Beauvoir's still-provocative discussion of transcendence as freedom and immanence as stagnation for women, xxviii–xxix, a theme that runs throughout her text. Iris Marion Young both summarizes and critiques de Beauvoir's position, 232–37. The essays in part III of this collection discuss de Beauvoir's philosophy more generally.

7. Wohl 31–36. The feminine ideal as a dying or dead woman is discussed by Gilbert and Gubar 24–27.

8. Wohl 35. Helen King has a fascinating study of female suicide by hanging in relation to ancient gynecological theory and also in relation to the cult of Artemis in Cameron and Kuhrt, eds., 113–25.

9. The classic study of the male hero is Joseph Campbell, *The Hero with a Thousand Faces*. See also Segal.

10. Fries 5–6. Carolyn G. Heilbrun makes a similar point in her study of narratives about women, which she finds do not follow male models but have an integrity of their own, see *Writing a Woman's Life*.

11. Gilbert and Gubar have suggested that this is simply knowledge based on women's point of view, not men's, 79.

12. See William Blake, *Lucia Carrying Dante in His Sleep*, Fogg Museum of Art, Harvard University.

13. Respectively, *Purgatorio* XV.53–54 and IX.50, in Paolo Milano, ed., *The Portable Dante* (Viking, 1947).

14. Mircea Eliade is quite expressive on this topic and brings together many examples from various times and places, *Myths, Dreams and Mysteries: The Encounter between Contemporary Faiths and Archaic Realities* 106–10. To mention Eliade is to raise a red flag among scholars of religion today, as he has come under a great of deal of criticism, some of which is quite valid and some of which is not. For a sample of the arguments, see Dudley. Obviously, I find many of his concepts highly evocative and therefore useful.

15. Eller, "Immanence and Transcendence" 465. See also Tedlock 72–73. Hollywood has a thought-provoking discussion of these issues, see 87–210.

16. Hollywood 139. Complementary discussions can be found in Scarry. For an Asian example, see Liz Wilson.

17. This is Charles Perrault's version. In the Grimm Brothers' tale, white birds that inhabit the tree that Cinderella (Aschenputtel) planted over her mother's grave help her go to the ball.

18. See Waller 895–897.

19. Gilbert and Gubar discuss the male construct of women as domestic angels or *outré* monsters, 20–44, as well as nineteenth-century women writers who utilized the female monster for their own ends and twentieth-century women poets who reinvented the female monster, ibid., 79 and 80, respectively.

20. Creed 3.

CHAPTER 1

1. Lewis-Williams has a clear analysis of the states of consciousness experienced by the Upper Paleolithic *Homo sapiens* with whom we share the same nervous system and therefore the potential to dream, hallucinate, and imagine alternative realities, see 126–35. He also specifically relates the somatic experiences and mental states that could define a three-tier division of the cosmos, ibid., 144–47. Mircea Eliade has popularized this idea in many of his books, see, e.g., *Shamanism: Archaic Techniques of Ecstasy* 259–74, and *The Sacred and the Profane: The Nature of Religion* 32–57. See also Wright. While a threefold division is a rich depiction of the universe, alternative cosmologies are equally meaningful, such as otherworlds located across water, and so on.

2. I wish to emphasize that this was not their only religious concern, but it is the one that is most germane to this book. Lewis-Williams persuasively argues that during the Upper Paleolithic those people who experienced visions were set apart from other people, 196.

3. This entire study details that evidence.

4. See Frits Staal's succinct discussion of sacrificial ritual involving the killing of an animal, and I would add a human being, versus rituals that are not sacrifices but that utilize other offerings, e.g., grain, *Rules Without Meaning: Ritual, Mantras and the Human Sciences* 69–70.

5. It was called the *Caturaśraśyenacit*, "resembling a falcon [constructed] from squares," Gaeffke 153.

6. Staal, *Rules Without Meaning* 116. See also Staal's magisterial study of this ritual, which he arranged to be performed and filmed in Kerala, India, April 12–24, 1975, *Agni: The Vedic Ritual of the Fire Altar* 1:85, and Knipe's discussion of this myth, 328–60.

7. Converse discusses the year-long rituals connected to the construction of this altar, 83, 85. See also Staal, *Agni* 1.xxii, as well as his later reflections on it, *Rules Without Meaning* 66–77.

8. Eggeling 10.1.4.14. See also Keith's discussion of this ritual, II.465–467.

9. Converse 83, 85. See also Staal, *Agni*, 1.xxii, and *Rules Without Meaning* 66–77.

10. Jamison 64.

11. Staal, *Agni* 1.87, quoting the *Śatapatha Brāhmaṇa* 10.1.4.13. Staal has an intriguing discussion of the structural similarities between mantras and bird song, *Rules Without Meaning*, 279–93.

12. Eliade, *Shamanism* 404, citing the *Taittirīya Saṃhitā* I, 7, 9. Mahony discusses this and similar rituals, "Flying Priests, Yogins, and Shamans in Early Hinduism and Buddhism" 22–49. See also Freedman's discussion of the *Taittirīya Upaniṣad* as a verbalized form of the *Agnicayana* to achieve the same end as the physical construction of such an altar, 330–331. Tull discusses this tomb, see 108–18. A less elaborate bird altar is also found in some South American tribes. See the illustration in Vitebsky 85.

13. White, *Kiss of the Yogini* 197. In general, this is an excellent source on magical flight in India. See also Eliade, *Yoga: Immortality and Freedom* 326–30.

14. Eliade, *Yoga* 104–05.

15. Aristophanes. It was first performed in 414 BCE.

16. Serinity Young, "Stars" 42–46.

17. Verdet 14.

18. Marshack 826–27, and Verdet 16. Useful chronologies of the Paleolithic and Neolithic are in Claudine Cohen 182–83. See also the works of Anthony F. Aveni on archaeoastronomy.

19. Lewis-Williams 54, 231, 235–36.

20. Following Korp, which has a good bibliography; Marshack 817; Tattersall 19–25; and Lewis-Williams, *The Mind in the Cave*.

21. It is hard to think of a major civilization that did not use astrology for divination; see, e.g., Barton; and Tester.

22. See also the religious ideas expressed by bridges in Edsman. Mahony presents a useful typology of mythic and religious ideas about flying in "Flight."

23. Eliade, *Myth, Dreams and Mysteries* 103–10. Eliade succinctly summarizes some of these descriptions, ibid., 99–115. Lewis-Williams analyzes the somatic experiences and mental states that could give rise to the experience of flying, *The Mind in the Cave* 144–47. Mahony's study offers a rich discussion of the somatic basis for the belief in magical flight and an analysis of the scholarly literature on magical flight, "Flying Priests" 1–20. See also Eliade, *Yoga* 326–30; Sutherland 139–140; and Mahony, "Flight." The phenomenon of flight is closely associated with shamans, discussed in chapter 9, but also with mystics and witches, discussed in chapters 7, 8, 10, and 11.

24. See Kuntz and Braver's discussion of ascent and descent in terms of Western iconography; and Hart 1–88, 193–210, 244–59.

25. See the discussion in Kugle 123–31, and its description in Qur'ān, Sūra 17:1 and 53:1–18. This will be discussed further in chapter 11.

26. See, e.g., Ettinghausen's discussion of a fourteenth-century series of Persian miniature paintings that have Muḥammad's face veiled, 360–78, though the veils may have been painted on at a later date, 367. He also discusses a fourteenth-century painting in which Muḥammad's face was later rubbed out, 378 and 379, figure 10. Interestingly, while Burāq is included in this series, Muḥammad is also shown being carried on the shoulders of Gabriel, figures 3, 4, 5, and 6. Additional discussions of this tradition include Séguy 21–24, and Rustomji 139.

27. Kendall et al. plate 42.

28. See Pearson's discussion of human attempts to transcend death, 142–45; Bloch and Parry 9–15; and Eliade, *Shamanism* 479–94.

29. Bulkeley has a sampling of flying dreams from several cultures, 67–75. See also Sukhu's discussion of the earliest recorded Chinese dreams, 145–53.

30. *OED*, respectively 1:1926, 1240 and 1239. See also Hartland 278–82.

31. *OED*, 1:1239.

32. O'Flaherty discusses women as skillful interpreters of dreams in ancient India, *Dreams, Illusion and Other Realities* 21. I have discussed the connections between women, dreams, and death in Serinity Young, *Dreaming in the Lotus* 160–62. Carol Schreier Rupprecht offers a useful presentation and integration of dream theory, dream data, feminist thought, and the differences between women's and men's dreams, 186–219.

33. Wolkstein and Kramer 74–75.

34. Sandars 64–65. Other second millennium BCE texts from Mesopotamia and Asia Minor confirm that dream interpreters were often women, though dream interpreters usually had low social standing, see Oppenheim, "Mantic Dreams in the Ancient Near East" 350.

35. E.g., Sandars 68.

36. Kagan has uncovered an analogous situation in sixteenth-century Spain, where male Catholic priests competed with low-status women for expertise in dream interpretation, 37.

37. Sukhu 65. See also his examples and discussion of flying and climbing dreams and the use of divination for their interpretation in the earliest Chinese poetry, ibid., 145–53. Schafer has an additional example of a prophetic dream flight, *Pacing the Void: T'ang Approaches to the Stars* 247.

38. Henningsen 196–97.

39. Betz spells nos. IV.2441–2621, VII.862–928, and XIV.1070–1077. Winkler discusses erotic spells in the Greek magical papyri and erotic dreams in the context of the second-century CE dream analyst Artemidorus's *Oneirocritica*, respectively, 71–98 and 17–44.

40. Crapanzano discusses the libidinous demoness 'A'isha Qandisha, who invades the dreams of Moroccan men, 145–59.

41. Stephen 72. See also Mary Beth Mills 250–65.

42. Serinity Young, *Dreaming in the Lotus* 149–52.

43. Bloom 119–22.

44. *Purgatorio* IX.50, in Milano. See Hart's discussion of flight in the *Divine Comedy*, 146–48, 253–56. (In chapter 10, we will see that several Christian women mystics fly to Purgatory.)

45. Milano xvii–xviii.

46. Milano xix.

47. *Athena Flying Her Owl*, c. 460 BCE. Metropolitan Museum of Art, New York.

48. Henry Fairfield Burton 84. This is a very ancient idea, see Eliade, *Myths, Dreams* 99–101.

49. Emperor Antoninus and Empress Faustina being carried to heaven by the winged figure of Eternity accompanied by eagles, base of the column of Antoninus Pius, c. 161 CE. Vatican Museum.

50. Lessing 9.

51. Laufer 18. Laufer also has several images of chariots drawn by flying dragons. For early Chinese concepts of the afterlife, see Yü.

52. British Museum, 1986, 0610.1. The hand of God figures in early representations of Christ's resurrection, e.g., an anonymous carving from the Bavarian National Museum, Munich, shown in Nesselrath 47, figure 4.

53. Musée d'Orsay, Paris. Warner, *Maidens and Monuments*, has a good discussion of the pagan aspects of Napoleon's memorial in Paris, 23–25.

54. See the example of the Holy Spirit as a dove in chapter 10 in this book, as when Hildegard of Bingen (1098–1179) refers to the Holy Spirit as a dove in her vision of the Trinity, *Scivias*, Book II, Vision 2 161–65. For her further eloquent elaboration on this doctrine see ibid., Book III, Vision 7 411–21. Catholic prayer cards continue to portray the Holy Spirit as a dove. See also Hart 12–13, 42–74.

55. See, for example, Angola Gaddi, *The Trinity*, c. 1390, Metropolitan Museum, New York. A fourteenth-century fresco from the Abbey of Vilbodone in Milan appears to have a woman representing the Holy Spirit, see the image and discussion in Caciola 57–60. Juliana of Norwich (fourteenth century) explains the Trinity as fatherhood, motherhood, and lordship, see *Revelations of Divine Love* chapter 58, 187.

56. Nilsson, *A History of Greek Religion* 17–18.

57. Nilsson, *The Minoan-Mycenaean Religion and Its Survival in Greek Religion* 330–40, 491.

58. Monier-Williams, 1046. Birds are also recognized as omens in *Rig Veda* XI.42–43.

59. Pease and Croon 356. See also Goodison's discussion of birth symbolism, 140–44.

60. Laufer, "Bird Divination among the Tibetans (Notes on Document Pelliot no. 3530, with a Study of Tibetan Phonology of the Ninth Century)" 2:483–632.

61. Budge, *Gods of the Egyptians* I:40–41.

62. Bailleul-LeSuer 16. In Budge, *Egyptian Book of the Dead* chap. xxvii, the dead fly away as falcons. Eliade discusses the widespread belief that the soul takes the form of a bird at death (and during life for shamans) and birds as psychopomps; see *Shamanism* 479–81.

63. Mahony, "Soul: Indian Concepts." This article problematizes the use of the term in an Indian context, 438–443.

64. Waugh 98–106, 107–21.

65. Harrison, *Prologomena to the Study of Greek Religion* 200–01.

66. In addition to the ancient Near East examples that follow, see also Schaeffer et al. 130–32, which excerpts documents excavated from Dun Huang depicting pre-Buddhist practices dating from c. the eighth century CE.

67. Budge, *Gods of the Egyptians* II:215.

68. Budge, *Gods of the Egyptians* II:871–72.

69. Goodison makes a tantalizing but uncited reference to Bronze Age "religious officiants dressing in bird clothing"; see p. 143. See also Kanaseki, though the accompanying sketches are really just stick figures, so there is no reason to assume they represent men dressed as birds rather than women. Nonetheless, it points to the early use of such costumes in conjunction with the introduction of rice cultivation in East Asia.

70. See the discussion of the spiritual uses of feathers in Rabineau 31–38, and Schafer, *The Golden Peaches of Samarkand* 110–15.

71. For example, see, a ceremonial vessel with a bird's head and a woman's breasts from Thera, c. sixteenth century BCE. National Archaeological Museum of Greece.

72. Eliade, *Myths, Dreams* 105.

73. Lewis-Williams punctures the idea that the Paleolithic visitors to these caves and the simple line figures are exclusively male; see *The Mind in the Cave* 18. He also reproduces a South African rock-art image of shamans with wings (figure 31) and another with the flight of birds (figure 32), as well as one from North American rock art (figure 43), ibid., and images of birds taken from Upper Paleolithic cave drawings, and refers to another, ibid., plates 28 and 231. He discusses the famous "birdman" of Lascaux, ibid., 264–65.

74. Friedrich, "An Avian and Aphrodisian Reading of Homer's *Odyssey*" 309–10.

75. Conversation with Claudine Cohen, April 2004. See also her *La femme des origins* for some beautiful early images, e.g., 123 and 130. See also Dexter 5. A debate by archaeologists on interpreting figurines is Hamilton.

76. Peter J. Ucko has several photographs of this image and a similar image from various angles in his *Anthropomorphic Figurines of Predynastic Egypt and Neolithic Crete with Comparative Material from the Prehistoric Near East and Mainland Greece*, 47, 48, 461–63. It can also be seen on the Brooklyn Museum's website along with similar figures at http://www.brooklynmuseum.org (search: 07.447.505 and 07.447.500).

77. Although his material is dated, as are some of his assumptions, see Edward A. Armstrong's chapter on prehistory, 1–24. More recently, see Hoppál's discussion of Siberian rock art, which includes images of bird-headed anthropomorphic figures dated to between the second and first millennium BCE, 135, figure 1, and 139, figures 4 and 5. Museums around the world abound with such figurines after the Neolithic period; see, e.g., cites in Dexter 194, n. 104. 113–132. Gimbutas has a chapter on bird goddesses in eastern Europe that contains many images, 112–51, as does Dexter 3–13 and 15–41. Cynthia Eller discusses Gimbutas's work and its controversies in *The Myth of Matriarchal Prehistory: Why an Invented Past Won't Give Women a Future* 36–53; see also Meskell; Hewitt; Ruth Tringham. Despite such criticism, Tedlock (31–32) reminds us that Gimbutas's work called much-needed attention to the androcentric bias of archaeology and led to the engendering of archaeology.

78. For the problems involved in analyzing early figurines, see Goodison and Morris, "Introduction. Exploring Female Divinity: From Modern Myths to Ancient Evidence" 6–21; and Tringham and Conkey, "Rethinking Figurines: A Critical View from Archaeology of Gimbutas, the 'Goddess' and Popular Culture" 22–45. The entire collection in which both of these essays are found is essential reading on this topic. See also Bailey, as well as Eller's summary of the scholarly and popular literature surrounding female images from the Paleolithic and Neolithic periods, 116–156. Dexter believes these figures had religious meaning—that they represented goddesses—and she sees them as the ancestors of the later, historical goddesses, 5–6, 12–13, which, of course, may be true in some but not all cases.

79. This is not to ignore Goodison and Morris's point that it is a rocky path from the Bronze Age to the Classical world; see "Beyond the 'Great Mother'" 131.

80. Westenholz thinks this may be a demonic form of Isthar, see 77–78.

81. Book III of the great Indian epic the *Mahābhārata* (c. dawn of the common era) lists many of them, per van Buitenen.

82. White, *Kiss of the Yogini* 35. White has a thorough discussion of these and related goddesses, ibid., 27–66.

83. David Kinsley has a good discussion of them, 151–60. He locates their earliest appearance in the later layers of the *Mahābhārata*, 151. The collections of the Mathura Museum (AMM 00.U.92; AMM 00.G.57) and Lucknow Museum (SML 60.168) include a significant number of Kushan-age bird-headed goddess images, including a series of five Mothers, all of whom have bird faces (AMM 33.2331), see Joshi 55–56.

84. White, *Kiss of the Yogini* 40.

85. White, *Kiss of the Yogini* 58.

86. See Carstairs.

87. Schafer, *The Golden Peaches of Samarkand* 113. See also Drewal and Thompson Drewal, who discuss the Yoruba belief that there is a secret society of powerful older women who can transform themselves into birds at night and are either benevolent or malevolent, xv, 17–19. Hanna also briefly discusses this ritual, 87–88. Similarly, in New Guinea men dance as the red bird of paradise, the preeminent form of spirit women, see Hanna 58.

88. On the ambiguous nature of Indian female divinities, see Pintchman 198–214.

89. Nilsson, *History of Greek Religion* 17–18.

90. Harrison, *Prologomena* 18–19.

91. Nilsson, *History of Greek Religion*, 28–29.

92. For relevant developments in ancient Greek religion, see Voyatzis.

CHAPTER 2

1. Budge, *Gods of the Egyptians* II:213; Fekri A. Hassan 98; and Hollis 1:487.

2. C. J. Bleeker, "Isis and Hathor: Two Ancient Egyptian Goddesses," 32.

3. Budge, *Gods of the Egyptians* II:215.

4. This sisterhood of attendants to the dead is reminiscent of the Valkyries, who carry dead warriors to Valhalla. The actions of Isis and Nephthys were imitated by women mourners, see Bleeker, "Isis and Nephthys as Wailing Women"

5. Bleeker, "Isis and Nephthys" 4.

6. Budge, quoting the "Hymn to Osiris" (c. 1500 BCE), *Gods of the Egyptians* II:150. See also Bleeker, "Isis and Hathor" 33, 35. In later Egyptian literature she is said to have shape-shifted into a kite and a goose, see Lichtheim III:149.

7. This story is told in Lichtheim II:81–84. It was inscribed on a limestone stele dating from the Eighteenth Dynasty (1567–1320 BCE).

8. Budge, *Gods of the Egyptians* II:208–11.

9. For general information see Frankfort, *Kingship and the Gods*.

10. Kozloff 63.

11. Budge, *Gods of the Egyptians* I:416–418.

12. Budge, *Gods of the Egyptians* I:40–41.

13. Scalf 36–39; Ikram 41–48.

14. The Oriental Institute of the University of Chicago has several examples of *ba* statues on its website.

15. Bailleul-LeSuer, "Introduction," 16, and catalog, 201. According to Budge, the dead fly away as falcons, see *Egyptian Book of the Dead* chap. xxvii.

16. Bailleul-LeSuer, catalog, 143–45.

17. Shonkwiler.

18. Bleeker, "Isis and Hathor" 29–30, 34–35; and "Isis and Nephthys," 1–17. General sources on women in the ancient Near East are Lesko; Capel and Markoe; and Seibert.

19. Bailleul-LeSuer, catalog, 210–211.

20. For her later development see Budge, *Gods of the Egyptians* II:216–221; Dexter 132–133; Bleeker, "Isis and Hathor," 36–40; and Hassan 99–100. Apuleius's novel *Metamorphoses* offers a detailed depiction of her cult in the Hellenistic period.

21. Eliade has an elegant discussion of cyclical time in *The Myth of the Eternal Return or, Cosmos and History*. Ann Grodzins Gold elucidates the theme of rebirth as a model for, and an antidote to, death in Hindu belief, 59ff.

22. See the discussion in Pearson 150–52.

23. See Louis-Vincent Thomas 5:456. For the use of red markings and the fetal position in Taiwanese burial practices, see Emily Martin 173. In general, see Pearson. As these examples suggest, prehistoric burial sites are rich in variants, but one must bear in mind that they exclude untraceable means of depositing the dead, such as cremation and burial at sea or in rivers. The Tibetan practice of sky burial is the most thorough: the flesh is stripped from the body and thrown to carrion birds and then the remaining bones are pounded to dust. For analyses of gendered burials, see, e.g., Pearson 95–123; Ehrenberg 118–39; and Pollack 372–79.

24. Pearson 105.

25. Bloch and Parry 11. See also Watson. For the Neolitihic skull cults in the Near East, see Verhoeven.

26. Pearson 151–55. In Western Europe, burials go back to the late Middle Paleolithic among Neanderthals, though earlier remains have been found along the migratory route of *Homo sapiens* out of Africa, per Lewis-Williams, *The Mind in the Cave*, 80–83.

27. Louis-Vincent Thomas 5:453.

28. Bloch. Emily Martin challenges some of these ideas with great subtlety, yet she offers evidence for similar beliefs in modern Taiwan. See also James L. Watson 173–174.

29. Watson 164.

30. Watson 162, 172–74.

31. Gail Holst-Warhaft has a rich typology of women's control of death rituals and the widespread opposition of male secular and religious authorities to that control, see "Mourning and Death Rites," *EOW*, vol. 1, pp. 682–85. See also Bloch's thoughtful analysis of gender tensions in mourning and funeral rites in Madagascar. For ancient Egyptian practices, see Bleeker, "Isis and Hathor" 34–35, and "Isis and Nephthys" 1–17. For ancient Greece, see Goodison 133–34. For South Asia see Storm 1:243–45; and Nabokov.

32. Bloch 226.

33. See Lefkowitz's discussion of Antigone.

34. Serinity Young, *Courtesans and Tantric Consorts* 172. The gender dynamic of this shamanic role is discussed in chapter 9.

35. Lincoln, *Death, War, and Sacrifice* 15. See also Jochelson, *Yukaghir* XIII, pt. 2, 198.

36. Lincoln, *Death, War* 78–80.

37. For a discussion of these associations and connections in the Hindu and Buddhist traditions, see O'Flaherty, *The Origins of Evil in Hindu Mythology* 27–35; and Storm, "Death." See also Bloch for African associations of sexuality and death, 221.

38. Additional examples of sexual promiscuity at funerals can be found in Metcalf and Huntington 57, 184.

39. Bloch and Parry 21. Metcalf and Huntington also discuss this ceremony, 113–30.

40. Bloch 227.

41. Sandars 29.

42. A broad discussion of Mesopotamian religion is Jacobsen, *The Treasures of Darkness: A History of Mesopotamian Religion*. Historical background can be found in Oppenheim, *Ancient Mesopotamia: Portrait of a Dead Civilization*.

43. Dexter 18. See also Wolkstein and Kramer xvi and Westenholz 71, 73.

44. See Wolkstein and Kramer 52–73. A similar story about Isthar is discussed below.

45. Jacobsen, "Mesopotamia" 214–16.

46. The popularity of her hymns to Inanna, written after she learned the Sumerian language, is attested to by the fact that they were listed in several of the literary catalogs of her time and they survive in nearly fifty different samples.

47. Dexter 22; and Fulco 7:145–46.

48. Dexter 19.

49. Rivkah Harris 270.

50. Westenholz 73, 204, n. 19. The definitive work on this subject is Samuel Noah Kramer. A more recent work includes Greece and Rome: Faraone and McClure. See also Jacobsen, "Mesopotamia" 214–16.

51. Westenholz 71–72.

52. Marglin, "Hierodouleia" 6:309.

53. Quoted by Rivkah Harris, see 271–72.

54. Pritchard 1:81–85. This is one of the texts from the library of Ashurbanipal (685–627 BCE), but one can safely presume that the text predates his reign.

55. Pritchard 1:232–33, italics in original.

56. Sandars 7–8; and Jastrow 198.

57. Sandars 59.

58. Moran 5:558.

59. There are innumerable laments about mortality in the Gilgamesh texts but they become more pronounced after the death of Enkidu, as Gilgamesh unsuccessfully searches for a way to avoid death.

60. Sandars 59, 114, respectively. Of course, these are all individual stories that are strung together. There is no single authorial voice.

61. Sandars 84–85.

62. Bolle 319–321.

63. Marglin, "Hierodouleia" 309.

64. Sandars 60–67.

65. Westenholz 76–77.

66. Pearson 168.

67. Voyatzis 133–47.

68. Harrison, *Prologomena* 18–19; and Nilsson, *A History of Greek Religion* 28–29.

69. Pollard 116–29, 155–61.

70. Nilsson, *Minoan-Mycenaean Religion*; and Pollard 149–54. Burkert discusses this background and changing scholarly opinions about it, see 19–53.

71. Eva Keuls is elegant on this point.

72. Nilsson, *Greek Religion* 25–27, and *Minoan-Mycenaean Religion*, 489–91. See also Rose and Robertson, "Athena" 138–39; and Burkert 139–43.

73. Luyster 144.

74. Respectively, Nilsson, *Greek Religion* 129; and Voyatzis 135–41.

75. On this point see Luyster 139.

76. Hesiod, and even more Homer, shaped regionally diverse beliefs into what we now think of as Greek religion. See Burkert on this point, 120–25.

77. See also Harrison's remarks on this genesis, *Prolegomena* 302–03. Luyster argues for the early link between Athena's warlike nature and her powers of fertility.

78. See the brief discussion of the monstrous-feminine in the introduction to this book. Burkert has a short discussion of her *aegis*, 140.

79. Eva Keuls 38–40. See also Warner's discussion of this statue, especially the *aegis*, as well as vase paintings of Athena, *Monuments and Maidens*, 107–26.

80. See the discussion in Nilsson of Athena's long development and many manifestations, *Minoan-Mycenaean Religion* 488–501; and also Voyatzis 135–41 and 144–45.

81. Nilsson points out that her protection of certain heroes continued with their sons (see *Minoan-Mycenaean Religion* 501), a trait we will see among the Valkyries, discussed in chapter 3.

82. George M. A. Hanfmann and John R. T. Pollard, "Gorgo or Medusa," *OCD*, p. 472.

83. Eva Hanfmann and Pollard, "Gorgo or Medusa," *OCD*, p. 472. See Garber and Vickers for a collection of stories about and interpretations of Medusa from ancient to modern time. The vase is held by the Metropolitan Museum of Art, New York.

84. Luyster 137, 147. He further discusses Medusa in detail, 157–62.

85. Hanfmann and Pollard, "Gorgo or Medusa," *OCD*, p. 472, and Warner, *Monuments and Maidens* 109–12. See also Creed's discussion of the Medusa and the *vagina dentata*, 105–11.

86. The riddle is never stated in Sophocles' famous play *Oedipus Rex* and comes down to us in various versions through later Greek writers.

87. Harrison, *Prolegomena*, 211–12.

88. George M. A. Hanfmann and John R. T. Pollard, "Sphinx," *OCD*, p. 1009.

89. Iphigeneia's sacrifice is assumed in Greek literature but never actually depicted in Homer or elsewhere. A post-Homeric epic, the *Kypria*, is the first to assert that Artemis carried her away, as does a fragment of Hesiod. In Pindar she is sacrificed, but in Aeschylus's *Agamemnon* he stops short of the sacrifice itself. The dramatic point of Euripides' play is that her relatives

believe she has been killed; see Euripides, *Iphigeneia in Tauris* 8. Dowden discusses the earliest sources of her legend, see especially 9–47.

90. Herbert Jennings Rose, "Erīnyes" 406–07; Geffcken; and Finkelstein. Klinger contextualizes their role in archaic Greek religion, see 366–67.

91. Aristotle believed that females provide the body of the fetus but males provide the soul because the soul is potentially contained in semen, which is pure, and not in menstrual blood, which is impure, *The Generation of Animals*, II:3 and 4.

92. Aeschylus, *The Eumenides by Aeschylus* 58.

93. Aeschylus, *The Eumenides by Aeschylus* 60.

94. Bernal brings out the critical representations of Clytemnestra in Attic vase paintings beginning in the fifth century BCE.

95. The Eumenides and Erīnyes are both earth deities, though the former are more benevolent bestowers of fertility. We perhaps see here a division of labor among ancient chthonic deities. Rose, "Erīnyes," 406–07.

96. Euripides, *Iphigeneia in Tauris*, 45, ll.946–949.

97. Finley 187.

98. Friedrich, "An Avian and Aphrodisian Reading of Homer's *Odyssey*" 307. Nilsson discusses her several avian forms, see *Minoan-Mycenaean Religion* 491–96.

99. Luyster 151.

100. Luyster discusses these various forms, see 151–54.

101. Harrison discusses her winged and wingless depictions in Greek art, see *Prolegomena*, 306–07.

102. Nilsson, *Minoan-Mycenaean Religion* 500.

103. The enumeration of Medea's many services to Jason became a set-piece in later versions of her tale. See Bessone 575.

104. Flying chariots are often the vehicles of divinities. This scene continues to be popular as in the second century CE. Roman sarcophagus held by the Pergamon Museum, Berlin, and a fifteenth-century illuminated manuscript of Ovid, *Heriodes*, Episode 12, folio 49v, *Death of the Sons of Medea*, held by Harvard University, Houghton Library.

105. Jane Ellen Harrison, "Harpies" 517–19.

106. Gaster 78. Marilyn Arthur has a pertinent analysis of Hesiod's theological agenda and later Greek mythologizing, see 80–84.

107. Harrison, *Prolegomena*, 214–15. See also her discussion of the Harpies' role in Aeschylus' plays, 217–39.

108. Held by the J. Paul Getty Museum, Los Angeles.

109. Herbert Jennings Rose and Charles Martin Robertson, "Harpyiae, Harpies" 488–89. This, despite the fact that Aeschylus described them neither as like women nor as having wings; see *Eumenides* 48–52. See Cecil Smith's discussion.

110. Herbert Jennings Rose, "Phineus" 825, offers various other versions of his offense. See also Harrison, "Harpies" 518.

111. Hanfmann and Pollard, "Sirens" 993.

112. Friedrich, "An Avian and Aphrodisian Reading of Homer's *Odyssey*" 311. Harrison discusses their role in the *Odyssey* and elsewhere, *Prolegomena* 198–206.

113. Harrison, *Prolegomena* 199.

114. Terra-cotta vase in the form of a Siren, c. 550–500 BCE, from Rhodes held by the Metropolitan Museum of Art.

115. Detienne 111–112.

116. Johnston, "Aphrodite (Venus)" 48.

117. Boedeker 40–42. Paul Friedrich discusses Aphrodite's multiple origins, *The Meaning of Aphrodite* 9–54.

118. Friedrich summarizes her tenuous connections to war, *Meaning of Aphrodite* 95–97.

119. Harrison, *Prolegomena*, 307–08. See also Friedrich, "An Avian and Aphrodisian Reading of Homer's *Odyssey*" 312; and Walton.

120. Burkert 52, 152–53, and 155.

121. For example, see Pietro Vannucci's, known as Perugino, fresco *Lord with Prophets and Sibyls*, 1496–1507, part of which shows Aphrodite/Venus in her chariot drawn by doves. College Del Cambio, Perugia, Italy.

122. Friedrich discusses these and other of her avian associations; see *Meaning of Aphrodite* 76–77.

123. See e.g., Hans Peter Duerr's depiction of her evolution and variations, 12–39.

124. Barnstone 70.

125. Friedrich has a lengthy discussion of Sappho's poetry and influence on beliefs about Aphrodite; see *Meaning of Aphrodite* 107–28.

126. Boedeker discusses her erotic nature, see 32–36. See also Friedrich, *Meaning of Aphrodite* 141–46; Walton 80; Johnston, "Aphrodite (Venus)" 47; MacLachlan; and Burkert 152.

127. Friedrich, *Meaning of Aphrodite* 143–44.

128. Friedrich, *Meaning of Aphrodite* 136–37. Salomon analyzes the first such statue of Aphrodite; and Beth Cohen adds to the discussion.

129. Beth Cohen 70.

130. Salomon lists many additional examples in Western art (see 197), and carefully unpacks the multiple narratives provoked by this statue (see 197–219).

131. Friedrich discusses her powers of fertility in *Meaning of Aphrodite* 93–95.

132. Hanfmann and Pollard, "Nike" 735.

133. Hanfmann and Pollard, "Nike" 735.

134. Sikes 281. This brief article describes the evolution of Nike and carefully separates her from Athena Nike at Athens, who, he argues, was a later development.

135. Warner, *Monuments and Maidens* 80, 128–29.

136. Sikes.

137. Walter Burkert briefly discusses this mystery cult, see 282–85. See also Susan Guettel Cole.

138. Hanfmann and Pollard, "Nike" 735.

139. Rose, "Victoria." Stefan Weinstock discusses her development, temples, and divine and imperial associations in Rome. He does go astray in his comparison of Victoria to Nike when he says Nike had no cult or temples in Greece (218), both of which were documented by Pausanias 5.14.8.

140. Warner, *Monuments and Maidens* 130.

141. Berefelt, *A Study on the Winged Angel: The Origin of a Motif* 32–39. See also Peers 25–27.

142. Peers 257; Berefelt 21–56; and Warner, *Monuments and Maidens* 137.

CHAPTER 3

1. The sagas often speak of women possessing wisdom and foresight; frequently they are important counselors to their husbands. See Byock, which offers abundant examples of this in addition to Brunhilde: e.g., Hjordis, 52, Kostbera, 97, and Signy throughout her entire episode,

but especially 39. There were also itinerant female seers, *völvas*, who predicted the fortunes of individuals and whole communities. See Allan 104–05. It is a *völva* who tells the god Odin the story of the beginning of the world and predicts its future destruction and eventual renewal in the *Völspá* (*The Prophecy of the Völva*) in Bellows I:3ff.

2. There are connections to be made between them and the *apsarās*, discussed in chapter 6. *Houris*, the celestial maidens of the Muslim paradise who are the reward of all faithful male believers, seem to have played a similar role in that they are first mentioned in the context of warfare. See the discussion in chapter 4.

3. The Alaisiagae were daughters of Týr, the god replaced by Odin/Wotan. Krappe, 56–57, 72–73. Of some interest, they were worshiped by the elite cavalry of the Roman army, the *equites singulare*, a unit made up of men from all corners of the Empire but especially Celts and the Germanic tribesmen. The Latinized Celtic name of these goddesses was *campestres*, and they were believed to protect cavalrymen on the practice field and in battle; see Irby-Massie. Krappe discusses additional influences in the development of the Valkyries and offers comparisons of them in other religious traditions; see 55–73.

4. Ellis Davidson, *Gods and Myths of Northern Europe* 61–66.

5. Andersson is eloquent on this point; see 241–49.

6. Byock discusses the development of this text, and lists its sources, respectively, 3–4 and 123–24. Andersson, focusing as he does on Brunhilde, analyzes this text and the earlier and later sources relating to it, 22. In addition to contextualizing the text, Tom Shippey also problematizes the text given its remarkable survival (it was found in an unknown Icelandic farmhouse in the seventh century), xiii.

7. Byock 115, n. 36.

8. Dexter quotes a story of uncertain provenance that describes Odin's punishment of Brunhilde as provoked by a king who stole her swan suit. Consequently, being under his control, she is forced to kill the son of Odin, for which reason he punishes her. Dexter also claims that Freyja is the first Valkyrie, 104.

9. See Acker for a discussion of these and other images of Sigurd and Fafnir. An eleventh-century example of such a memorial stone was raised by a woman named Sigrid; see Rosedahl 171. Many runic stones were raised by women and for women; see Rosedahl 59.

10. See, e.g., a wood portal from Hillestad, Norway, at the Museum of Cultural History, Oslo, C4321.

11. Andersson's analysis of the oldest sources concludes that the poems were all about Brunhilde, not Sigurd; see 78.

12. Shippey notes that heroes are silent, mutely expressing their code of self-control in the face of defeat, while heroines, equally committed to a heroic death, have speech privileges and use words as privileges, xviii. For a fuller discussion of women's speech in Eddic poetry, see Fridriksdóttir.

13. That knowing the language of birds leads to wisdom and prophecy can be found in ancient Greece as well; see Luyster 147.

14. Krappe discusses their swan forms; see 65.

15. The belief that Viking helmets had horns or wings was a nineteenth-century invention of the Romantic movement.

16. Ellis, *The Road to Hel* 151–97 and 146, respectively.

17. Jenny Jochens problematizes this dialogue by suggesting it occurred with another Valkyrie, Sigrdrífa, in an earlier version of the *Volsungs Saga*, making it highly likely she and

Brunhilde are one and the same, see 92–93. See also Andersson on this point, 81–84, 104, 115–16, and Fridriksdóttir 118.

18. Fridriksdóttir 119.

19. Jochens discusses the textual lacunas of the *Volsungs*, 163–67.

20. See Byock's short discussion of this, 10–11. Jochens discusses this topic at great length, see 132–58. Richard Wagner used this theme for his own ends in the incestuous unions of brothers and sisters; see Catherine Clément 160–61.

21. This is also the case in the oldest Brunhilde poem; see Andersson 26.

22. Andersson 26.

23. See, e.g., Jacob Grimm's discussion of Norns, 1.405–17, and his comparison of them to Valkyries, fays, and other such female predictors of fate, 1.425–26. See also MacCulloch 238–47 on the Norns, and 248–57 on the Valkyries.

24. Valkyries are often depicted weaving. Weaving and then tearing the cloth to pieces is a powerful motif in Norse legends, as can be seen in a dream/vision from *Njal's Saga*.

25. Jochens 62.

26. Gunnar's younger brother's murder of Sigurd is contained in the oldest versions of this tale, Andersson 26–30.

27. This act suggests several meanings. It may be a reference to the occasional practice among Norse people of sacrificing human and animal companions to serve a dead king, a practice Brunhilde, too, soon enacts. It was also a frequent choice in warrior societies where a blood-debt required killing a man's sons, as well as the man himself, because upon reaching adulthood the children would be obligated to revenge their father.

28. Ellis, *The Road to Hel*, 73–98. There are several variants on Brunhilde's death in the oldest materials; see Andersson 109–110, 114.

29. This is also reminiscent of the famous account of a Viking funeral in Russia by Ibn Fadlan, an Arab diplomat (traveled 920–921), which describes how a slave girl volunteers to follow her lord in death. She is stabbed and strangled at the same time, in a sacred ritual associated with Odin, and then placed with the dead man on a ship that is set on fire and pushed out to sea. See Ellis Davidson, "The Ship of the Dead" 80–82. Cohat has a long quote from Ibn Fadlan's account, see 152–55.

30. Damico 189, n. 6. Jochens also briefly discusses their possible connection, 100, 107–12. In *The Saga of the Volsungs* Gudrun fights beside her brothers, and Signy's sustained heroic quest for vengeance takes her beyond the human. Of course, Brunhilde, too, fights in the early sections of the *Nibelungenlied*.

31. Saxo Grammaticus, Book VIII, 310–11.

32. Ellis Davidson, *Gods and Myths*, 61.

33. Krappe 55.

34. Byock discusses these episodes; see 11–26.

35. Following Gregory of Tours, *History of the Franks*, cited by Byock 24–25. Jochens also briefly discusses their possible connection, see 173.

36. Ellis, *The Road to Hel* 136. See also Jochens 47–48, 78–83, and 117–31, for the declining status of women in Norse religion.

37. Munch 33.

38. Ellis Davidson, *Gods and Myths* 61. See also Grimm 1:423–425.

39. See Ellis, *The Road to Hel*.

40. Good sources on Norse religion include Ellis Davidson, *Gods and Myths*; Dumézil, *Gods of the Ancient Northmen*; and Polomé, "Germanic Religion." A classic in the field is de Vries, *Altergermanische Religionsgeschichte*. Especially relevant for the study of divine and heroic women in Norse religion is Jochens, *Old Norse Images*. Two good overviews of Viking history and migrations are Gwyn Jones, *A History of the Vikings*, and Fitzhugh and Ward, editors, *Vikings: The North Atlantic Saga*.

41. A recent study suggests the stones could be even earlier and that they followed templates; see Laila Kitzler Åhfeldt, "3D Scanning of Gotland Picture Stones with Supplementary Material: Digital Catalogue of 3D Data" 55–65. See, e.g., a similar stone carving from Kirkastigen, Ed, Uppland, Sweden, Gwyn Jones figure 17.

42. Wilson and Klindt-Jensen 80.

43. Ellis Davidson, *Viking and Norse Mythology* 40–41; and Wilson and Klindt-Jensen plate XXIV.

44. Ellis, *The Road to Hel* 77.

45. See Damico 177–80, and Ellis, *The Road to Hel* 69–73, 77.

46. See *The Lay of Helgi*, discussed below and in Ellis Davidson, *Gods and Myths* 61.

47. Ellis, *The Road to Hel* 134–35.

48. Hreinsson 2:27.

49. Hreinsson 2:42. It is interesting to compare this dream to those Maher Jarrar found in his study of *hourī* motifs in the early literature on *jihād* (87–107). See the discussion in chapter 4. Of some interest, the tale of Janshan is a basic swan maiden tale, but the woman in question is called a *hourī*, in Burton vol. 5, night 509, 346, and night 514, 354. The conflation of *hourīs* with swan maidens circles back to Valkyries, who are also conflated with swan maidens. The connections between these and other aerial females show a common and widespread understanding of their nature, no matter what they are called.

50. Damico 181 makes this point, as does Andersson 5.

51. Jochens 139. Andersson discusses some of this earlier material, see 24–27.

52. Byock 69.

53. O'Flaherty has an extremely rich discussion of the mare goddess, see *Women, Androgynes, and Other Mythical Beasts* 149–280.

54. Grimm 1:421.

55. Ellis, *The Road to Hel* 66. See also Ellis Davidson, *Gods and Myths* 114–24, and Grimm 1:304–306.

56. Ellis Davidson, *Gods and Myths* 117.

57. Eliade, *Shamanism* 386, n. 39.

58. Bellows I:175.

59. Ellis, *The Road to Hel* 138. Hamayon makes a similar point about the supernatural wives of Siberian shamans who were inherited from generation to generation, 84.

60. Ellis Davidson does not make this connection, but she does discuss women going to Valhalla; see *Gods and Myths* 150–51.

61. Andersson 114–15.

62. MacCulloch; and Munch 126. This tale is discussed further in chapter 4, below.

63. Hatto, *Nibelungenlied* 7. See the discussion of its sources, ibid., 370–95. Andersson provides a history of *Nibelungenlied* scholarship (15–23 and 205–22) as well as a provocative discussion of its earlier sources (151–204).

64. Clément (163) makes this point about Wagner's use of invisibility, but it is equally valid here.

65. Andersson (26–29) presents a reconstruction of this Norse poem and then briefly analyzes it in relation to equally early sources.

66. See Jochens 26–27, 140, and 143.

67. Joachim Köhler has written expressively about the uniqueness of the *Ring* operas, especially 314ff.

68. Byock (26–29) has a brief discussion on Wagner's textual sources.

69. Köhler describes the theme of incest in Wagner's own family and in his work, 408–468.

70. Wagner 12. I have somewhat modified the translation. This scene takes place in act 2.

71. Quoted in Köhler 351.

72. Wagner 16–17. There is another interesting connection here between Valkyries and *hourīs*. Utilizing an eighth-century source, Jarrar finds several motifs about *hourīs*, one of which said that they encourage warriors in battle but the warriors cannot see them until they face heroic death; see "The Martyrdom of Passionate Lovers," 96 and 106; see also 101 and 102.

73. Wagner 19.

74. Wagner 19.

75. Clément (167) reads this as a ploy to preserve herself and her youthfulness until Siegfried has grown up.

76. Clément 157.

77. See Köhler.

78. Patrick Carnegy describes the ideas behind the Bayreuth theater and Wagner's staging of the *Ring*, see 69–106.

79. Carnegy 82–84.

80. Frank 675.

81. Wagner, London recording libretto, 10–11.

CHAPTER 4

1. Most of us know this story through Hans Christian Andersen's popularization of the ancient tale. For more of the mythology of the swan, see Dunnigan; and Charbonneau-Lassay 243–57.

2. Barbara Fass Leavy finds it to be such a template that she uses it as a point of reference throughout her study of animal brides and demon lovers, see esp. 34. Leach 1091–92.

3. O'Flaherty, *The Rig Veda* 10.95ff., 253–54, and Keith I.183. The beginning is explained and elaborated upon in later texts, see the discussion below.

4. I have chosen to use the scholarly convention of transliterating *apsarāsas* as *apsarā*.

5. Monier-Williams 59, col. a.

6. For example, Shastri 7.56, 542–544; Kālidāsa, *Vikramorvaśī: An Indian Drama*; Gitomer 204; and Dimmitt and van Buitenen 271.

7. O'Flaherty, *Rig Veda* v. 3, 253.

8. This text romanticizes the basic tale of the captured swan-wife, Eggeling XLIV:68–74. Handique quotes it at length, integrating it with the original verses from the *Rig Veda*, *Apsarases in Indian Literature* 75–76. See also Gitomer 349–50.

9. Leavy discusses the role of sisterhood in various swan maiden tales, 40–46.

10. O'Flaherty, *Rig Veda* v. 5, 253, see also vv. 11 and 13. In the *Śatapatha Brāhmaṇa*, when Urvaśī marries Purūravas she says, "Thrice a day shalt thou embrace me; but do not lie with me against my will, and let me not see thee naked," X.5.1.

11. In the *Viṣṇu Purāṇa* she has seven children with Purūravas, see Dimmitt and van Buitenen 272. O'Flaherty briefly discusses this myth and broadly contextualizes it within Indo-European mythology, *Women* 180–84.

12. O'Flaherty, *Rig Veda* 245.

13. In addition to *apsarā*s, other kinds of female beings shape-shift into swan maidens, or are conflated with them, such as Valkyries, who carry fallen warriors up to Valhalla, and fairies, who to this day are believed to marry mortal men and then flee, see Krappe 65–67. See also the discussion of variants in the swan maiden tales in Tawney, a translation and rearrangement of Somadeva's *Kathāsaritsāgara*, appendix 1, 213–234; and Hatto's three types of this tale, "Swan-Maiden" 324.

14. Silver has an interesting discussion of Victorian uses of and understandings about such tales, 89–116.

15. Leavy 2. Leavy has a nuanced discussion of the role of gender in the shaping, telling, and gathering of tales. See also Mills.

16. Quoted in Leavy 53. Unfortunately her citation does not lead to the original source on this tale. For further examples, see ibid. 50–63. See Harva 501–02 for a Siberian variant of a captured swan maiden forced to marry.

17. Hatto, "Swan-Maiden" 336.

18. Hatto, "Swan-Maiden" 337.

19. Plato 84E, 1:469–470. For more on this belief, see Charbonneau-Lassay 249–50. Dunnigan briefly discusses the swan's association with song in various cultures, "Swans" 14:188.

20. Charbonneau-Lassay 250–51.

21. Hatto, "Swan-Maiden" 334.

22. Hatto, "Swan-Maiden" 333–34. See also Leavy 2.

23. See, e.g., Purūravas's struggle, discussed below; Eberhard 43–44; Zong 21–25; Ralston 44–74; and Kleivan 29. Leavy discusses some others, e.g. 245–76.

24. E.g., in ancient Egypt and the shamanic religions of northern Asia; see Dunnigan, 14:188.

25. For more on Christ's association with swans, see Charbonneau-Lassay 247–53.

26. Handique; Gitomer 348–51; and Tawney II:34–36 and 245–59.

27. E.g., Kālidāsa, *Vikramorvaśī*, and the *Viṣṇu Purāṇa*, in Dimmitt and van Buitenen 271.

28. E.g., Kālidāsa, *Vikramorvaśī*; Eggeling, *Śatapatha Brāhmaṇa* XI.5.12; and the *Viṣṇu Purāṇa*, in Dimmitt and van Buitenen 272–73.

29. See Gitomer's discussion of the various versions of this play and whether or not they were composed by Kālidāsa (344–48), as well as Winternitz III:244–48.

30. In South Asian cosmology there is an ongoing battle between the gods and demons (*asuras*); see, e.g., Dimmitt and van Buitenen 232–39. Somadeva also has Urvaśī fall in love with Purūravas, but without the threat of demons; see Tawney II:34.

31. Kālidāsa act 3, scene 1, 42–43. In the *Kathāsaritsāgara*, Urvaśī and Purūravas are cursed to be separated by the heavenly dance master when Purūravas laughs at the performance of another *apsarā*, but they are eventually reunited by Purūravas's penance; see Tawney II:35–36.

32. Somadeva's *Kathāsaritsāgara* also makes avian allusions to her and Purūravas, see Tawney II:36.

33. In Somadeva's *Kathāsaritsāgara*, another *apsarā*, while swimming in a lake, is captured when a man takes her clothes; see Tawney VIII:58.

34. Monier-Williams 1286, col. a. See also Armstrong on geese and swans, though he needs to be read with caution, 25–61; as well as Leavy 33.

35. See, for example a crystal goose (*haṃsa*) reliquary from first-century CE India held by the British Museum, 1867,0427.2.

36. Monier-Williams 1286, col. a.

37. See entry on "*Haṃsa*" in Stutley and Stutley 108.

38. MacCulloch II:262.

39. According to Grimm, "the swan was considered a bird *augury*," 1:427.

40. MacCulloch II:259.

41. Bellows II:255.

42. MacCulloch II:260.

43. MacCulloch II:260.

44. Translated by Miller, 55–86.

45. In addition to *Swan Lake* (1877) and *La Sylphide* (1832), some leading examples are "The Ballet of the Nuns" from *Robert le Diable* (1831), *Giselle* (1841), *The Dying Swan* (1905), and *Les Sylphides* (1909). See Anderson 75–92.

46. Hanna references the worldwide use of female dancers as objects of male desire, see 56, 59–72, 103–06, and 124–26, although she avows that the women may have understood themselves as artists, see 64.

47. Anderson 57–58, 85–86, 97–98, and 110. Hanna has numerous references to the worldwide association between dance and prostitution, 47, 54, 56–57, 60–62, 64–69, 103–06, and 124–26.

48. Hanna briefly discusses Taglioni's technique and influence, see 125.

49. Wiley reproduces engravings from the 1877 production, see figures 7 and 8, as does Beaumont, along with a later photograph, see 1–17 and 20–21. See also 61.

50. Ko has an intriguing discussion of the development of Chinese foot binding in relation to dancing. Tang dynasty records reveal that these dancers, too, hoped to emulate the flight of birds or the appearance of dancing on clouds, see 35–44, discussed below.

51. Jaini 533–34, 555–56.

52. Senart I.xi–xii.

53. A translation of this tale that appears in the fourteenth-century Tibetan *Kangyur* (*bKa' 'gyur*) emphasizes the romantic theme, see Ralston 44–74. It was probably taken from the *Divyāvadāna* version of her story. Both texts are discussed below.

54. This is an elaboration on the story that Yaśodharā's father required the Buddha to pass tests of manly skill before he would agree to the marriage; see, e.g., Senart II:73–77.

55. Jaini 539.

56. Ralston 54. This is a Tibetan version of the *Divyāvadāna*.

57. She also gives the hunter this jewel in the *Divyāvadāna* and in two other redactions, see Jaini 540. These and additional differences indicate that while the *Mahāvastu* and the *Divyāvadāna* may have had a common, now lost, source, they did not borrow from each other. See Jaini's discussion of this point, especially 550, but see also 552.

58. These events also occur in the *Divyāvadāna* and in two other redactions; see Jaini 541.

59. Ralston 62.

60. Masaharu Anesaki discusses Japanese swan maiden tales; *Japanese Mythology* 8.261–67, as well as *The Bamboo-Cutter's Daughter* that was translated by Dickins.

61. Miller (78) points out that a feather robe is part of the imperial enthronement ceremony.

62. Waley, *The Nō Plays of Japan* 223. Anesaki has also translated this play, *Japanese Mythology* 8.259–60, as have Pound and Fenollosa, see 98–104. Schafer has a brief but interesting discussion of this story's relation to an earlier Chinese story, *The Golden Peaches of Samarkand* 114–15. *Tennin* often carried the connotation of a fairy. Time and again we will see the conflation of these beings. Miller cites an even earlier Japanese tale and others not included here, respectively, 68 and 76.

63. Schafer has a brief discussion of this dance, *Golden Peaches* 114–15.

64. Ko 39–40.

65. Ko 40.

66. Nijo 229.

67. Rabineau 31–38; and Schafer, *Golden Peaches* 110–15.

68. Schafer, *Golden Peaches* 110–115.

69. The demand for feathers in Europe and America, especially for women's hats, became *de rigueur* for nineteenth-century middle-class women; see Doughty 2. I am grateful to the Costume Institute of the Metropolitan Museum of Art for allowing me to look through their Woodman-Thompson collection of advertisements for women's hats throughout the nineteenth century. See also Jennifer Price 58–60 and its illustrations.

70. Waley, *Ballads and Stories* 236.

71. Hatto, "Swan Maiden" has an interesting discussion of this story, but I cannot agree that it predates the *Rig Veda* tale of Urvaśī; see 328–31. He also discusses additional and interesting Asian swan maiden tales.

72. Waley, *Ballads and Stories* 149–55.

73. Dorson 226.

74. Dorson 226–27.

75. Haddawy xiv–xvi; and Tuczay 272.

76. Haddawy refers to these encounters as marriages, see 14–15, but Malti-Douglas does not, see 20.

77. Haddawy 14–15 and 20–23.

78. Malti-Douglas 11. Malti-Douglas has a rich and provocative discussion of Scheherazade's role and it analyses by multiple Middle Eastern and Western writers, 11–28.

79. Haddawy 14–15.

80. Burton 8:7, n. 1. Haddawy critiques Burton's translation but admits it is "as full and complete as possible," xix. Haddawy and Burton were using different compilations.

81. This is reminiscent of the marriage problems in Brunhilde's stories.

82. She is finally named toward the end of the story, when Hasan reaches her land, per Burton 8:97.

83. This tale is told in vol. 5 of Burton.

84. Solomon was said to know the language of birds in Sūra 27:15 of the Qur'ān.

85. See also night 514, 354. On night 510, the king of the birds says they are jinns, 348.

86. See Séguy's commentaries on plates 31, 43, and 44. This fifteenth-century manuscript was created in Herat in present-day Afghanistan. The text was translated into Turkish from an Arabic original and written in the Uighur script by the poet Mīr Haydar. The original manuscript is in the Bibliothèque nationale in Paris (Supplément Turc 190).

87. Rustomji 136.

88. For more on Islamic beliefs about paradise see Rustomji; Jarrar 87–107; and Jane I. Smith, "Paradise" 2:758–759. For the historical development of the *hourī*s, see Gibb et al. 3.581–82, and Rustomji 94–96 and 111–114. *Hourī*s are often conflated with *jinnī*s and *parī*s.

89. Gibb 2.449 and 3.582.

90. Jarrar 88, n. 4.

91. Rustomji 15 and 16–17.

92. Jarrar 94. For the development of the *hourī* motif, see ibid.

93. Jarrar, 96 and 106; see also 101 and 102.

94. Hatto, "Swan Maiden" 335.

95. See, e.g., Hatto, "Swan Maiden," 341–44 and 351–52, and chapter 9 of this book.

CHAPTER 5

1. See Berefelt's analysis and history of angels in Western art; and David Albert Jones 16–36.

2. Clara Erskine Clement lists the appearances of angels in scripture (158–200) along with their representations in art, and their appearances in legend (207–61). See also Rees 3–14.

3. I Corinthians 11:10.

4. Rees discusses these traditions, as well as Classical and Hellenistic pagan ideas about similar beings.

5. See, for example, King, *Hippocrates' Woman*; Cadden; and Furth.

6. Peers provides a nuanced introduction to angelology in all its complexity, see 1–11, and especially to the challenges of representing them iconographically, see 13–193. Dyan Elliott discusses changing Christian views about the substantiality of angels' bodies in *Fallen Bodies: Pollution, Sexuality, and Demonology in the Middle Ages* 128–42.

7. Berefelt 13, and David Albert Jones 16–18. Nonetheless, cherubim are described as a decoration for the Ark of the Covenant (Exodus 25:20).

8. Peers 23–36 and 59–60. Sannibale and Liverani accept the Classical origins of angel iconography while emphasizing that "no figure in classical culture has the spiritual significance and functions that an angel has in Judeo-Christian religion," 62. Nesselrath discusses the history of the Christian depiction of angels, saying they were originally wingless and rejecting Victory as a model for winged angels primarily because of her sex and a quibble about wings, "Wrestling with Angels," 44–61. It is notable that this entire volume does not contain one image of a female angel, although they are discussed.

9. Ringrose 143–62; and Berefelt 30.

10. See William Smith's succinct, if rather Christian-oriented, history of angels in his Bible dictionary (36–37); and Hart 52–88.

11. They are not all male despite, e.g., Qur'ān, Sūra 53:28.

12. Commentary on plate 33, Séguy.

13. Glassé 42–43.

14. Gibb, respectively, 2.547–50 and 3.581. Islam has a rich assortment of spirits, see Rees 90–91. Sūra 72 of the Qur'ān is named *The Jinn*.

15. Cozad 2:939.

16. Waugh 94. See also Rees's discussion of the appearances of angels in the Qur'ān, 14.

17. Waugh, 131, and more generally, 127–50.

18. Cole and Christian 36.

19. Caciola 38, 39.

20. Qur'ān, Sūra 2:96. Trachtenberg 21–22, 24, and 69–77.

21. Sannibale and Liverani 62–63; Cagni 98.

22. See Coudert 1:282–286; and Rees 4, 104–18.

23. Trachtenberg, 77.

24. Trachtenberg 69–77; and David Albert Jones 7. An additional influence came from the pagan Roman belief that each individual was allotted a *genius* at birth that influenced a person's character and their good or bad fortunes; see Rees 90, 172–94.

25. Berefelt 113; and David Albert Jones 18. Male angels and/or cherubs appear in later Muslim art; for examples see the Mughal art of India and Persian art.

26. Sannibale and Liverani also credit the influence of the winged Etruscan goddess Vanith, who guided souls to the afterlife, see 64, figure 5, and 65. See also the winged female figures on a third-century BCE Etruscan funerary urn, 67, figure 9, and catalog numbers 17 to 22.

27. Berefelt 17, 16–20, and Warner, *Monuments and Maidens* 138–39. Nesselrath puts forth a counterargument, 44–46.

28. Warner, *Monuments and Maidens* 139.

29. Berefelt 1; and Rees 205.

30. Peers 25–27. Berefelt discusses at length the influence of Victory iconography on that of Christian angels, see 21–65 and 96–104. David Albert Jones has a brief but thorough discussion of angel iconography, including issues of gender, see 16–36.

31. See catalog numbers 27 to 32, in Durston and Nesselrath.

32. Peers 25–27. See also Berefelt 32–39, and for his discussion of the Erotes on sarcophagi, 57–66.

33. Peers 26.

34. Berefelt 96–111. This is not to deny the Christian medieval elaboration of the heavenly host, e.g., archangels (the only angels with names), seraphim, cherubim, and so on; see Clement 15–19. Rees briefly discusses the rise of the *putti*, see 116.

35. Berefelt 107.

36. Berefelt 110.

37. David Albert Jones 36.

38. A similar image is an Italian poster from World War I, *Vittoria e Pace*, University of Minnesota Libraries, Collection of War Posters.

39. David Albert Jones 36.

40. Langland 296.

41. Peterson 677.

42. Langland 297.

43. Peterson 679.

44. Shannon Forbes describes this struggle in Woolf's novel, especially through Mrs. Ramsey, who is the self-sacrificing angel in the house.

45. Woolf 58–59.

46. Cole and Christian 36, 42.

47. Caciola 162. See also the discussion, ibid., 161–75.

48. Steinberg.

49. See, e.g., a fresco by Giovanni da Modena, c. 1420, from the Church of San Petronius in Bologna, in Caciola 138, figure 7, and the discussion, ibid., 137–39.

50. See Caciola 164–74.

51. Caciola 251–56.

52. See, e.g., Briggs, *Dictionary of Fairies*; and Evans-Wentz.

53. E.g., Briggs, *The Fairies in Tradition and Literature* 30–47; and Squire 244. See also Grimm, who remarks that "the connection of valkyries with fays [fairies] is placed beyond doubt," 1.41; and Krappe 65–67.

54. Squire 245; Briggs, *The Fairies in Tradition and Literature* 171, 179–80; Silver 28–31; and Evans-Wentz xxvi, 256–57.

55. Briggs, *The Fairies in Tradition and Literature* 18–22, 62–65, 169–71, and 179–80. See also Silver 172–74, 178–83; and Leach, *Funk & Wagnalls Standard Dictionary of Folklore* 363.

56. Briggs, *The Fairies in Tradition and Literature* 11–13, 169–79. Silver has a good discussion of various views of fairies based on, but developed outside, the folk tradition by early nineteenth-century British scientists, writers, and artists, see 9–31 and 37–57.

57. Grimm Brothers 226–32.

58. Nicolas Kiessling, *The Incubus in English Literature: Provenance and Progeny*, Washington State UP, 1977, 48.

59. Briggs, *The Fairies in Tradition and Literature* 31.

60. Mircea Eliade, "Some Observations on European Witchcraft" 160.

61. Henningsen.

62. Silver.

63. Bourke 90, 201.

64. Cozad 2:939.

65. See the discussion of Morgan as Arthur's sister in Paton 136–44.

66. Grimm II.456, 460–61, 463–66. Silver has a chapter on their frightening aspects dating from the Victorian era, see 149–83.

67. Cited in Paton 165, n. 1.

68. Paton conveniently lists passages in the major sources and their dates, see 7–8, n. 1, and 255–58.

69. Ackerman is a good introduction to the social and religious background of this literature. Mac Cana 85–99 succinctly presents this process.

70. For more information on the status of pre-medieval northern European women, see Chance; Damico and Hennessey; and Davies.

71. See Sklar's analysis of Malory's influence.

72. Fries 5–6.

73. Malory 137–52. An analysis of this edition as well as a discussion of modern scholarship on Malory can be found in Brewer.

74. Malory 10. Malory claims that Morgan was sent to school in a nunnery. It is interesting to try to get behind Malory's text and to speculate how the oral tradition described Morgan's education in an all-female environment, especially one where Malory relates that she became skilled in necromancy, an ability not usually associated with nuns.

75. Malory 151.

76. Malory 142. The Irish princess Isolde/Iseult is another royal woman healer in the Arthurian story cycle.

77. Stephens 53.

78. Newall 5:246. See also Grimm's discussion of their connection with the Norns, I.405–417; and MacCulloch 245–46.

79. Paton 148–66.

80. Serinity Young, "Stars" 43.

81. See, for example, Queen Medb in the *Tain*, translated by Kinsella.

82. Loomis 127.

83. Lincoln, *Death, War, and Sacrifice*, respectively 67 and 74, n. 27.

84. Lincoln, *Death, War, and Sacrifice* 74, n. 27.

85. Evans-Wentz 353.

86. See, for example, W. T. H. Jackson 88–100.

87. Davis 179.

88. Davis 181, citing Lecky 2:12–44.

89. Briggs, *The Fairies in Tradition and Literature* 10, 53; Squire 245–46; and Kiessling, *The Incubus* 45.

90. See the discussion in chapter 3 and also in Hartland 9–11.

91. Briggs writes that, "as early as the seventeenth century 'fairy' was used as a synonym for a lady of easy virtue" (*The Fairies in Tradition and Literature* 132). Edmund Spenser brings out fairies' erotic side in *The Faerie Queene* (published 1590s).

92. Briggs, *The Fairies in Tradition and Literature* 151; and Silver 178–83.

93. Mason 62–76.

94. Paton 2.

95. Briggs, *The Fairies in Tradition and Literature*, especially 123–26.

96. Silver 93.

97. Silver 73, 167–72; and Grimm II.466–69.

98. Silver discusses some of the medical symptoms of such changelings, see especially 74–77.

99. Silver has a chapter on changelings (see 59–87), and Bourke's book is the study of a single case. See also Hartland 91–134.

100. Grimm Brothers 226–32.

101. Snyder.

102. Christie 75; and Anesaki 8.256–57 and 266 ff.

103. Christie 105. See also Schafer, *Pacing the Void* 132–42.

104. Anesaki 8.264–65, and Hartland 161–264.

105. Chinese did not use many linguistic gender markers until the twentieth century. In the stories that follow I have looked for other signifiers of gender. If I do not specify gender, the fairies could be male or female, as is the case in this story. Victorian translators notoriously added gender markers, which were absent in Chinese, where they fit with their own Victorian understanding of the world. For example, they classified many Chinese stories as "fairy tales" when, as suggested above, the Chinese had a more complex spirit world than did earlier Western translators.

106. Eberhard 97–98.

107. Bedford has a wonderful article on this festival and its attendant legends. In some versions of the tale Chang'e, called Chang'O, is said to have been banished to the moon for drinking the elixir.

108. Schafer, *Pacing the Void* 131–42.

109. See, for example, Van Over 98–99.

110. Van Over 45–51.

111. Gale 111–24.

112. Anesaki 8.261. Waley, *The Nō Plays of Japan* 223. Schafer has a brief but interesting discussion of this story's relation to an earlier Chinese story, see *The Golden Peaches of Samarkand* 114–15.

113. Anesaki 8.261.

114. I have abbreviated this complex tale written sometime before the tenth century, but Schafer translates it in full, see *Pacing the Void* 139–42.

CHAPTER 6

1. Monier-Williams 59, col. c. I have chosen to follow scholarly convention and use *apsarā* for the singular form of the noun, pluralizing it as *apsarās* to avoid the cumbersome plural, *apsarāsas*.

2. See the story of Urvaśī, the swan maiden/*apsarā*, in chapter 4. The Buddhist *Saṃgāmāvacara Jātaka* (no. 182) refers to them as dove-footed (*kakuṭa-pādiniyo*), Fausbøll II:93. They could also change the shape of others, as when the *apasarā* Kalavati shrunk her human husband to fit inside a lotus she wore as an ornament. In this way she was able to smuggle him into heaven, Tawney IX:21.

3. Chalier-Visuvalingam depicts an aspect of this process.

4. Konarak and Bhuvaneshwar are additional sites in India that have *apsarā* images.

5. O'Flaherty, *Rig Veda* 10.95.1ff.

6. Cited by White, *Kiss* 35. Additional examples are briefly discussed in Krishnamorthy 15.

7. In Buddhist literature they travel in golden chariots, *Alambusā Jātaka* (no. 523), Cowell V:83, discussed further below.

8. There are several terms for these structures based on religious and regional differences. See Settar and Sontheimer, "Preface." The earliest ones, called *caityas*, dating back to the third century BCE, were erected by Buddhists to commemorate their dead saints. See also Rao, who uncovered seventeen hero stones in Andhra Pradesh dating from the tenth to fifteenth centuries. Ten of these depict pairs of *apsarās* escorting the hero to heaven. See plates 16.2, 16.3, 16.4, and 16.5, and the discussion, 166–69. Sengupta discusses hero stones found in Eastern India.

9. See especially S. Rajasekhara 227–30.

10. Sircar, "The Maukharis and the Later Guptas" 70, fns. 4 and 5.

11. Cited in Ronald Davidson 87–88.

12. White, *Kiss* 282, n. 48. Harlan (114–20) discusses them as *kuldevīs*, goddesses who are the source of a Rajput warrior's power in battle and much more. A *kuldevī* protects the family lineage and is typically a kite, a bird that screeches and circles the battlefield in search of bloody flesh. In other words, heroes' bodies become carrion for goddesses appearing as kites or vultures. After death, Rajput heroes cease to be reborn and go instead to a heaven called Virgati, the "Goal of Heroes," where they will spend eternity enjoying wine, women, and song, including dancing girls.

13. O'Flaherty, "Indra" 7:215.

14. Van Buitenen, *The Mahābhārata* 1:203, 396–397. The same story is told about the *apsarā* Tilottamā, ibid.

15. These images are discussed in Zimmer 103–04, and plates 541 and 544. They are also represented at Konarak and Bhuvaneshwar.

16. Basham 315; and Hopkins 164.

17. *The Ramayana of Valmiki* I:125. The *Rāmāyaṇa*, *Mahābhārata*, and *Purāṇas* are the living repositories of the best-known Hindu stories and important means of communicating the religious and social values of Hinduism. I shall refer to them frequently in this chapter.

18. *Ramayana* I:1256. This is revealing of the tensions between sages and gods.

19. Van Buitenen, *The Mahābhārata* 1:162–163. This multivolume epic was composed over several centuries around the dawn of the common era, with additions made over the following centuries.

20. Śakuntalā's and her mother's stories are contained in van Buitenen, *The Mahābhārata* 1:155–171, and was retold by the great Indian playwright, Kālidāsa (c. fourth century CE), see 1–74.

21. Dimmitt and van Buitenen 259.

22. This story is translated in Dimmitt and van Buitenen 258–62.

23. This is a characteristic of swan maidens and fairies, as well; see chapters 4 and 5.

24. Van Buitenen, *The Mahābhārata* 3:658. See also White, *Kiss* 48; Hopkins 164; and O'Flaherty, *Women* 135.

25. See Coomaraswamy on the fertility-granting powers of *apsarās*, *Yaksas* part II, 33–34.

26. Most of these hymns can be found in Bloomfield's translation. White discusses the ambivalent nature of the *apsarās*, *Kiss* 34.

27. See Sontheimer's discussion of the hero and the *yogī*, 273–74.

28. I:4b, Olivelle, *Upaniṣads* 204.

29. Van Buitenen, *The Mahābhārata* 2:310.

30. See, for example, Garimella. Marglin discusses some of these stories, *Wives of the God-King* 100–101, as does O'Flaherty, citing some Buddhist sources, among others, in *Asceticism and Eroticism in the Mythology of Śiva* 42–52. See also O'Flaherty's Index of Motifs, no. 21ea, *Asceticism and Eroticism in the Mythology of Śiva* 377.

31. Tawney II:97.

32. See Basham 184. Dehejia, "The Very Idea of a Portrait," has traced aristocratic identifications with divinities in depictions of kings and queens, as well as of saints as divinities.

33. Courtesans were also thought to be as heartless as the *apsarās*; see Serinity Young, *Courtesans and Tantric Consorts* 105–19.

34. Marglin, *Wives of the God-King* 101–08. See also the discussion of *devadāsīs* in Young, *Courtesans and Tantric Consorts* 108–11.

35. See, for example, Garimella. Marglin discusses some of these stories in *Wives of the God-King*, as does O'Flaherty in *Asceticism and Eroticism* 42–52.

36. Marglin, *Wives of the God-King* 91, 145.

37. See the brief discussion of the auspicious powers of female figures and *apsarās* in Desai, *Khajuraho: Monumental Legacy* 31–32.

38. Marglin, *Wives of the God-King*, and Serenity Young, *Courtesans and Tantric Consorts*, 107–12.

39. Stutley and Stutley 90–91; and Hopkins 159–64.

40. Winternitz I:134–35.

41. Bloomfield 536.

42. *Viṣṇu Purāṇa*, in Dimmitt and van Buitenen 94–98.

43. Valmiki, *Ramayana*, vol. 1, bk. 1, chap. 45, p. 95.

44. Valmiki, *Ramayana*, vol. 3, bk. 7, chap. 26, p. 465.

45. Valmiki *Ramayana*, vol. 1, bk. 1, chap. 73, p. 146.

46. Handique 15.

47. O'Flaherty, *Rig Veda* 245.

48. One of the earliest fragments of Buddhist drama, from the first century CE, has a courtesan as a character; see Winternitz III:199.

49. See, e.g., the Buddha's biographies, discussed below, and two sculpted panels at Bhārhut, described in Zimmer 70 and 193, plates 36a and 32a. See also Dehejia, *Discourse in Early Buddhist Art: Visual Narratives of India* 46, figure 35.

50. For example, in Vaidya 255–57.

51. Frédéric 269–70.

52. E.g., American Museum of Natural History 70.0/6863, 70.0/6867, 70.0/6944, 70.0/7202, and 70.0/7204.

53. E.g., American Museum of Natural History 70.0/6914.

54. Frédéric 270.

55. Their popularity in East Asian Buddhist art would seem to be connected to ancient Chinese beliefs about magical flight, such as the aerial abilities of Emperor Yao's daughters discussed in the introduction to this book, and in legends about Daoist sages (see chapter 10).

56. See, e.g., vol. I of Whitfield. Fan Xingru shows the large number of *apsarā* images at this site. Unfortunately, the images are poorly reproduced.

57. Bandaranayaka discusses the history of the interpretation of these images. See also Coomaraswamy, *Medieval Sinhalese Art*; and Joanna Williams.

58. Bandaranayaka 122.

59. Serenity Young, *Courtesans and Tantric Consorts* 87–91. See also Aśvaghoṣa, *Saundarānanda Mahākāvya of Ācārya Aśvaghoṣa with Tibetan and Hindi Translations*, translated by Ācārya Shri L. Jamspal, Central Institute of Higher Tibetan Studies, 1999, VII:24–46, discussed below.

60. For some of these stories see Serinity Young, *Courtesans and Tantric Consorts* 87–88.

61. Aśvaghoṣa II:28ff, IV:26 and V:69.

62. See also iii:65 and v:45.

63. Aśvaghoṣa IV:29ff. Udāyin also debated with the Buddha, berating him for not enjoying women, IV:62ff.

64. Mieke Bal has written about the function of such namelessness or anonymity, which "eliminates them [the nameless ones] from the historic narrative as utterly forgettable," (1).

65. It was an extremely popular text throughout the Mahāyāna world, where it was recited at temple festivals and copied as a means of generating merit. Its hero, the lay bodhisattva Vimalakīrti, was often the subject of painting and sculpture (Paul 222).

66. Robert Thurman 37–39.

67. Cowell, *Jātaka* no. 523.

68. For a discussion of several of these stories from the point of view of the women abandoned by their husbands, see Serinity Young, *Courtesans and Tantric Consorts* 87–91.

69. Cowell V:80.

70. Per Cowell, *Valāhassa Jātaka* (no. 196) is an excellent example of the destructive nature of women's wiles, as discussed in Serinity Young, *Courtesans and Tantric Consorts* 212–14.

71. See, for example, Serinity Young, *Courtesans and Tantric Consorts*; and Liz Wilson, *Charming Cadavers*.

72. This story is also told in Cowell, *Saṁgāmāvacara Jātaka* (no. 182).

73. There is an English translation by E. H. Johnston, *The Saundarānanda or Nanda the Fair*, (Oxford UP, 1932) See Dieter Schlingloff for textual and iconographic versions of this story, 50; and Grey 265–66. This story is also discussed in Winternitz II:263ff, as are some of its Pali sources, II:263, n. 1. Waley has translated a brief version of it from a text found at Dun Huang, which confuses the Buddha's cousin and favorite disciple, Ānanda, with his brother, Nanda (207–09).

74. This is a variation on the Buddha's abandonment of his wife. For a discussion of this practice among monks in early Buddhism, see Serinity Young, *Courtesans and Tantric Consorts* 83–98.

75. Aśvaghoṣa, *Saundarānanda* X.36–42. I have slightly modified the translation.

CHAPTER 7

1. Vidya Dehejia offers a telling example of how these two terms were often used interchangeably, citing a Hindu story told in two different texts, one calling them *ḍākinīs* and the

other *yoginīs*, in *Yoginī Cult and Temples: A Tantric Tradition* 15–16. Similarly, *nāths*, *siddhas*, and *yogīs* are also used somewhat interchangeably. See also Herrmann-Pfandt, "The Good Woman's Shadow: Some Aspects of the Dark Nature of *Ḍākinīs* and *Śākinīs* in Hinduism" 43–44; and White, *Kiss* 62.

2. See, for example, Dasgupta 7–23, for his discussion of the roots of Tantra, as well as Ronald M. Davidson, *Indian Esoteric Buddhism*. For more on Tantra see David Gordon White, *Tantra in Practice*; for women in Tantra, see Serinity Young, "Tantra" 2:956–959, and *Courtesans and Tantric Consorts*; Shaw; and Denton.

3. Hugh Urban unpacks the complexities of tribal practices and Tantra in "The Womb of the Goddess: Goddesses, Tribals and Kings in Assam." See also Ronald M. Davidson, *Indian Esoteric Buddhism* 224–34.

4. Neumann.

5. Ronald M. Davidson, *Indian Esoteric Buddhism* 118, 369, n. 18. See also Samuels 40–42. Synonymous terms for *yoginī tantras* are *ḍākinī tantras* and *prajñā* (wisdom) *tantras*; see Lessing and Wayman 251. They are the basis for a large part of the Tibetan Buddhist corpus and are considered the highest teachings. See the discussion in Roger R. Jackson, *Tantric Treasures: Three Collections of Mystical Verse from Buddhist India* 10–42.

6. Luczanits discusses the iconography of *mahāsiddhas* in cemeteries. See also Neumann 42–50.

7. Ronald M. Davidson describes this for the Buddhist *yoginī tantras*; see *Indian Esoteric Buddhism* 223–24, 238.

8. See, e.g., Sircar, *Śākta Pīṭhas*; and Shastri.

9. See, e.g., Robert Linrothe's discussion of Śrīśailam in South India as a meeting place of Hindu and Buddhist *siddhas*, "Siddhas and Śrīśailam, 'Where All Wise People Go'" (124–43) and his discussion of Sikh and Ṣūfī *siddhas*, "Hindu, Sikh, and Ṣūfī Siddhas in India and Nepal" (386–421); and Bangdel's discussion of Jñānadākinī as a Buddhist and Hindu deity in the Kathmandu Valley.

10. Dehejia, *Yoginī* 11–37. More generally, see also Hausner; and McDaniel.

11. Dehejia, *Yoginī* 7. A Jain text translated by Paul Dundas associated the cult of the sixty-four *yoginīs* with specific northern Indian cities, such as Delhi, which the text calls "the city of *yoginīs*," as well as Ajmer, Ujjain, and Broach, "The Jain Monk Jinapti Sūri Gets the Better of a Nāth Yogī," in White, *Tantra in Practice* 234. See also the essays in Keul.

12. Dehejia, *Yoginī* 7.

13. See Keul's discussion of ongoing beliefs about *yoginīs* in Orissa 5–7, and von Stietencron's vivid description of his visit to Hirapur in 1965 and his 1971 visit to the *yoginī* temple near Ranipur-Jharial in Keul 70–72.

14. Diamond, *Yoga: The Art of Transformation* 124. See also Ernst 62.

15. See, for example, the fully clothed *Yogini with Mynah* in the Chester Beatty Library, Dublin. This painting, along with other paintings of *yoginīs*, was commissioned by Ibrahim 'Adil Shah II (reigned 1579–1627); Diamond, *Yoga* 124; but see also Diamond, "Occult Science and Bijapur's Yoginis," where she reviews the art-historical literature in which the *yoginīs* are consistently interpreted as images of mortal ascetics or princesses in yogic masquerade (1–9).

16. Dehejia, *Yoginī* 1–5.

17. On the secrecy of this cult see Dehejia, *Yoginī* ix–x; on the Hirapur Temple, see ibid. 95–109; Keul 5–7; and von Stietencron 70–71, 76–81.

18. See Dehejia, *Yoginī*. She discusses the Bheraghat temple, ibid. 125–140. Davidson takes exception to some of her research, *Indian Esoteric Buddhism* 179–83. See also Keul 1–17; and Bisschop.

19. Michell, *The Penguin Guide to the Monuments of India* 67–70, and *The Hindu Temple: An Introduction to Its Meaning and Forms* 86–93 as well as Stella Kramrisch, *The Hindu Temple*, 1946, reprint, Motilal Barnarsidass, 1976, 21ff., but see also Kramrisch's discussion of other open to the sky temples, such as Buddhist *stūpas*, 197ff. See also Dehejia's detailed discussion of their unique features, *Yoginī* 39–43. This is not to ignore the singular early tenth-century *rectangular yoginī* temple at Khajuraho, see Desai, "The Goddess Hinghalāja of the Yoginī Temple at Khajuraho" 109–16.

20. The "subtle body" is a psycho-spiritual body believed to exist within the physical human body. It is frequently conflated with other terms, such as the "rainbow body," the "illusory body," and even the "astral body." The *yoginīs* are believed to preside over each of the seven chakras of the subtle body, see Dehejia, *Yoginī* 17–18, 42–52. A similar idea exists in Buddhism regarding the *ḍākinīs*; see Herrmann-Pfandt, "Ḍākinīs in Indo-Tibetan Tantric Buddhism: Some Results of Recent Research" 49.

21. Rabe 439.

22. Davidson, *Indian Esoteric Buddhism* 294–300. See also Dehejia's brief discussion and image of *yoginī cakras* (circles) that were drawn on paper, *Yoginī* 2.

23. George Michell and John Huntington have suggested that it may have been constructed as late as the eleventh century, see Lopez y Royo 229. Keul (3–5) has documented the multi-functional uses of the possibly oldest, and newly restored, *yoginī* temple (ninth to eleventh centuries) at Hirapur, Orissa, which include worship, performance, and a place for family outings; it also functions as a museum.

24. Von Stietencron 76. Other discussions of this temple include Keul 1–17; and Lopez y Royo 226–34. White discusses *yoginī* temples as mainly sundials, *Kiss* 62–63.

25. Bisschop 59–63.

26. Bisschop 50–51.

27. Dehejia discusses this temple, *Yoginī* 125–40.

28. Michael Rabe, "Sexual Imagery on the 'Phantasmagorical Castles' at Khajuraho," *International Journal of Tantric Studies*, vol. 2, no. 2, Nov. 1996, at asiatica.org/ijts/vol2_no02/sexual-imagery-phantasmagorical-castles-khajuraho/. Dehejia also mentions that the *yoginīs* could confer military success, see *Yoginī* 51, 56; and Bisschop (52–54) attributes patronage of early medieval *yoginī* temples to royal support, for which military matters were paramount. Chitgopekar presents epigraphic evidence to support this view, as does Ferrari.

29. See Davidson for the social-political environment in which Tantra arose and flourished, *Indian Esoteric Buddhism*.

30. Rabe 442.

31. For today see Keul 5–14; Bisschop 55–56; and Humes 158.

32. Haksar xv.

33. Dehejia, *Yoginī* 194–99. See also her comments on these lists, 187–93. McDaniel (139) also refers to this grouping as *yoginīs*.

34. Edgerton 165, l. 2 of the Brief Recension.

35. White, *Kiss* 194. He has a thorough discussion of the relationship of kingship and *yoginīs*, ibid., 123–47. Dehejia also briefly discusses this story in *Yoginī* 114. Two additional stories of a royal boy being given sovereignty by the *yoginīs* are in Bisschop, see 53–54.

36. Gyatso has a short discussion of this role, *Apparitions of the Self: The Secret Autobiographies of a Tibetan Visionary* 243–46. See also June Campbell's assessment, *Traveller in Space: In Search of Female Identity in Tibetan Buddhism,* especially 131.

37. I have argued these points at greater length in *Dreaming in the Lotus,* 147–62. Katz has an interesting discussion of *ḍākinīs* as guides, "Anima and mKha'-'gro-ma: A Critical Comparative Study of Jung and Tibetan Buddhism."

38. Gyatso, too, connects this sexual role with the gendered constructions of South Asia and Tibet, *Apparitions,* 248–49. See also Serinity Young, *Courtesans and Tantric Consorts,* chapters 8, 9, and 10.

39. This greatly oversimplifies the complexity of Hindu Tantra. David Gordon White extensively treats the sexual symbolism of Hindu Tantra, in *The Alchemical Body: Siddha Traditions in Medieval India.*

40. See Dasgupta 28.

41. Dehejia, *Yoginī.* Of course, the term "possession" is highly problematic. Through reading early Śaiva texts, Törzsök provides a more nuanced discussion of possession in the *yoginī* cult, while Saraogi questions the appropriateness of using the term through her study of the *Jayadrathayāmala.*

42. White, *Kiss* 113–14.

43. But see Sanderson's brief discussion of Kāpālika influence on some Tantric forms of Buddhism that involved the *yoginīs* and the dissemination of *yoginī tantras,* 146–47. Davidson takes exception to some of this in *Indian Esoteric Buddhism,* 202ff. and 386, n. 105.

44. I have simplified this quite complex practice. David White has a good discussion of the practice from the Hindu perspective in *The Alchemical Body* 199–202. See also Marglin, "Types of Sexual Union and their Implicit Meanings"; and Dasgupta 87–107. Buddhist practices are discussed below.

45. White, *Kiss* 114.

46. Sanderson 148.

47. White, *Kiss* 215–18.

48. Dehejia, *Yoginī* 185–86.

49. Bisschop 47–60.

50. Lorenzen briefly discusses this play, 50, 56–57; as does Davidson, *Indian Esoteric Buddhism* 203.

51. Bhavabhūti V.3–4.

52. White, *Kiss* 212. This belief is shared by Buddhists, see, e.g., *Hevajra Tantra,* I:11.11.

53. Somadeva VIII:59. Tawney connects this story with the swan maiden motif and related Indian stories, see Appendix 2 VIII:213ff.

54. Dehejia, *Yoginī* 13–15, 57.

55. Herrmann-Pfandt discusses several of these stories, see "The Good Woman," 55–63.

56. Dehejia, *Yoginī* 13–15, 57. O'Flaherty offers examples of the human *yoginī* as "a dangerous, phallic woman"—e.g., Ambā, who became an ascetic in order to gain the power to kill her abductor, see *Women* 307.

57. Von Stietencron 72. He retells several stories about them, see 72–74. While speaking of medieval Bengal, McDaniel (134) notes that *yoginīs* give *siddhis* to devotees during daytime worship and punish their enemies during night worship.

58. Dehejia, *Yoginī* 57–61.

59. White, *Kiss* 204.

60. White, *Kiss* 207.

61. White, *Kiss* 207.

62. Sanderson 138–40. Dehejia has documented textual evidence that Śiva was regarded as the leader of the *yoginīs* and that he is usually the central deity of these temples, *Yoginī* 11–35, 40.

63. Shastri xxxi, xlvii, 53. See also Urban, "The Path of Power: Impurity, Kingship, and Sacrifice in Assamese Tantra" 789. This belief is shared by some contemporary *tantrikas* in Orissa, see Keul 6.

64. Kinsley has a good discussion of them, see 151–60. He locates their earliest appearance in the later layers of the *Mahābhārata*, see 151.

65. Von Stietencron 70–81; Kaimal 99, 104–06; and Dehejia, *Yoginī* xii.

66. Dehejia, *Yoginī* 1–2. See also Kinsley 197–211; Keul 5–7; and Chitgopekar 62.

67. For example, Desai, "The Goddess Hiṅghalāja" 109–16; and Ferrari.

68. For instance, the above-mentioned articles in Keul that deal with the *yoginī* cult in Śaivite literature: Törzsök 179–97; Saraogi 198–212; Chitgopekar 61–69; Bisschop 47–60; and Hatley 21–31.

69. For Hindu examples, see Sanderson 157–72. For Buddhist examples, see Davidson, *Indian Esoteric Buddhism*, especially 252. See also Chalier-Visuvalingam 253–301.

70. Dundas 236–237. Dehejia discusses similar Jain stories as an indication of the widespread belief of the power of the *yoginīs*, *Yoginī* 76–77.

71. Sanderson 139; Vijaisri.

72. See Dehejia, *Yoginī* 13; Bennett 261–308.

73. Monier-Williams cites a reference to them in Pāṇini, the fourth-century BCE grammarian, see 430, col. b. Herrmann-Pfandt has done groundbreaking work on *ḍākinīs*; see *Ḍākinīs: Zur Stellung und Symbolik des Weiblichen im Tantrischen Buddhismus*. See also her article "Ḍākinīs" 46–49, where she discusses the early history of the word *ḍākinī*; as well as Gyatso's discussion of *ḍākinīs* in *Apparitions* 243–64; Edou 100–05; and Willis, "Ḍākinī: Some Comments on Its Nature and Meaning."

74. Dehejia, *Yoginī* 13–17. Here she groups together *śākinīs* (witches) with *ḍākinīs* and *yoginīs*.

75. Roy 193. Babb 148, 203–05; Levine 263; Carstairs 15–16; and Thalith 892.

76. Nudity plays a prominent role in magic and religious rituals; see Sharma.

77. Dowman 258. For the story of the male *mahāsiddha* Kambala, who successfully battled witch-*ḍākinīs*, see Abhayadatta 117–20.

78. Roy discusses the history of this term, see 186–87. The same holds true for Madhya Pradesh, though the Hindi term for witch is *tonhi*, a feminine noun, see Babb 204, 227–28.

79. Denton 226–27.

80. White, *Kiss* 207. He discusses it further, ibid. 139, with the Sanskrit text on 321, n. 69.

81. Nebesky-Wojkowitz 488.

82. Gtsaṅ smyon He ru ka, *Mi la'i mGur 'Bum* 88–89.

83. Templeman 144.

84. White, citing "The circa ninth-century *Yogaratnamāla* of Kaṇha, one of the few extant Sanskrit commentaries on the *Hevajra Tantra* (2.3.3)," *Kiss* 204–05.

85. Klein 79.

86. Abhayadatta. Another well-known list of eighty-five *yogīs*, by Vajāsana, includes no women, see Linrothe, *Holy Madness* 278. See also Tāranātha for his account of fifty-nine *siddhas* and their lineages. Ray offers an excellent, brief overview of them, while White's *The Alchemical Body* is a study of the Hindu *siddha* tradition and its interaction with Buddhism and Jainism that offers fresh insights. See also Davidson's three chapters on them, *Indian Esoteric Buddhism*, 169–335. Rob Linrothe's *Holy Madness* is especially to be noted for its combination of visual and textual evidence in the excellent essays by noted scholars.

87. Interestingly, a much better known heaven is that of the *ḍākinīs*. See Young, *Courtesans and Tantric Consorts* 223–26.

88. Abhayadatta 28, 23, 128–29.

89. Interestingly, she is named Vajrayoginī ("the adamantine *yoginī*"), not Vajraḍākinī. Vajrayoginī is a divine practitioner of yoga who has the status of a divine *ḍākinī*.

90. Examples of her appearances occur in Tāranātha on 2, 11, 15, 18, 23, 67, 69, 70–72, 84, 93, and 100. See also the biographies of the Karmapas in Douglas and White 46, 55, and 102; and Gyatso's discussion of their role in Jigme Lingpa's (1730–1798) life, *Apparitions* 243–64.

91. Herrmann-Pfandt has a good discussion of the animal side of the *ḍākinī*, especially that drawn from chapter 8 of the third-century CE *Laṅkāvatārasūtra,* which criticizes the meat-eating associated with them, "The Good Woman" 51–63. As we have seen, some *yoginīs* also have animal heads.

92. Herrmann-Pfandt, "Ḍākinīs" 49; and Evans-Wentz, *The Tibetan Book of the Dead* 128, n. 2. A similar idea exists in Hinduism regarding the *yoginīs*, Dehejia, *Yoginī* 17–18.

93. Douglas and Bays Canto 22 I.142–43. This text also contains portraits of Padmasambhava that depict such biographical events, in this case, 199.

94. Douglas and Bays Canto 34, I.220–21. A depiction of this event is contained ibid., in the painting on 203. This is reminiscent of the *chod* practice of Machig Lapdron discussed in chapter 11.

95. For more on *termas*, see Gyatso, *Apparitions*; Aris; Germano; and Dargyay.

96. See the discussion of sexual yoga and treasure discoverers in Young, *Courtesans and Tantric Consorts* 155; and in Gyatso, *Apparitions* 255–56.

97. Gyatso has a short discussion of this role, see *Apparitions* 243–46. See also Campbell's assessment, especially 131.

98. See p. 283, n. 38.

99. I discuss some of these images in *Courtesans and Tantric Consorts* 133–39. See also Adelheid Herrmann-Pfandt, "Yab Yum Iconography and the Role of Women in Tibetan Tantric Buddhism."

100. Buddhist Tantric metaphysics developed, in large part, from the *prajñāpāramitā sutras,* in which a feminine noun, the abstract and quiescent concept of wisdom, is said to manifest in women. See the discussion in Snellgrove, *Buddhist Himalaya: Travels and Studies in Quest of the Origins and Nature of Tibetan Religion* 81–82.

101. See Dasgupta 28. These are often also referred to respectively as emptiness (*śunyatā*) and compassion (*karuna*). See the discussion in Dowman 10–11; and Cabezón. Robert Thurman 17–19.

102. There are stories about both Kṛṣṇa and Śiva not ejaculating during sex, see Marglin, *Wives of the God-King* 201–02, 214.

103. Shaw's brief explanation of these drops is informative, 157–58 and nn. 81 and 82, 249–50.

104. I have simplified this highly complex practice. For more details about Buddhist practice, see Cozort 69ff.; Snellgrove, *Indo-Tibetan Buddhism* 170–76, 257–70; Guenther 76–78, with the Tibetan text on 262–63; and Dasgupta 87–107. White, *The Alchemical Body* 199–202, has a good discussion of the practice from the Hindu perspective. See also O'Flaherty, *Women*; and Marglin, "Types of Sexual Union" 298–315.

105. E.g., they are said to have appeared at the birth of the second Karmapa (1204–1283), Douglas and White 41.

106. E.g., prior to the birth of Machig, Edou 122–24. For further examples see Young, *Dreaming in the Lotus* 75–85.

107. See Gtsaṅ smyon He ru ka, *The Life of Milarepa* 177ff.; and the discussion of Yeshe Tsogyel's death in chapter 11. Templeman elaborates on their role in the lives of Buddhist saints.

108. Many such encounters are recorded in Milarepa's collection of songs, Gtsaṅ smyon He ru ka, *Mi la'i mGur 'Bum*. See examples in songs nos. 2, 3, 7, 8, 9, 17, 23, 24, 25, and 47.

109. Gtsaṅ smyon He ru ka, *Life of Milarepa*, respectively, 9–11 and 177–78.

110. Herrmann-Pfandt, "Ḍākinīs" 51.

111. Herrmann-Pfandt, citing the second *bar do* of the *Bar do thos grol* (*The Tibetan Book of the Dead*), "Ḍākinīs," 55, though all the peaceful and wrathful deities appear during this forty-nine day transition between death and either liberation or rebirth. See Evans-Wentz 127–28, 130, 199, and 201.

112. Songs nos. 27–31 all deal with Seringma, Gtsaṅ smyon He ru ka, *Mi la'i mGur 'Bum*.

113. Nebesky-Wojkowitz goes on to list their attributes and names as found in various texts, see 178–81.

114. Gtsaṅ smyon He ru ka, *The Hundred Thousand Songs of Milarepa* I:297.

115. Nebesky-Wojkowitz 177.

116. Kapstein 119.

117. Gtsaṅ smyon He ru ka, *The Hundred Thousand Songs of Milarepa* I:301–02. Nonetheless *ḍākinīs* can also *cause* illness, see Parfionovitch et al. See also song no. 30, Gtsaṅ smyon He ru ka, *The Hundred Thousand Songs of Milarepa*.

118. Gtsaṅ smyon He ru ka, *The Hundred Thousand Songs of Milarepa* I:322–23.

119. Huber 134. This story is also contained in song no. 30, Gtsaṅ smyon He ru ka, *The Hundred Thousand Songs of Milarepa*. Interestingly, a beautiful young *ḍākinī* rushes Milarepa to Seringma's side via a flying blanket, I:334.

120. See, e.g., Dalton; and, for a particular female example, Gyatso, "Down with the Demoness: Reflections on a Feminine Ground in Tibet."

121. Herrmann-Pfandt, "Ḍākinīs" 46. See also Gyatso's discussion of the term *ḍākinī*, *Apparitions* 243–64.

122. Edou 102.

123. Chonam and Khandro.

124. Germano and Gyatso. This is a fascinating translation of a document that reveals the interactions of a Tantric community of women and men with divine *ḍākinīs*.

125. Buddhists have classified *ḍākinīs* as both those still in the world and those out of the world, see Das 180. See also Gyatso's brief discussion of their various manifestations, *Apparitions* 247–48, and Herrmann-Pfandt, "Dakinis" 49–50. Edou (103–04) summarizes some of the literature according to a threefold division: field-born, mantra-born, and co-emergent *ḍākinīs*.

CHAPTER 8

1. See Culianu's succinct summary of (1) the ever-changing interaction of ecclesiastical and secular law; and (2) the diversity of persecution from one European country to another. As is generally known, the word "witch" derives from the Old English words *wicca* and *wicce*, referring respectively to a male witch and a female witch; these words in turn are derived from the verb *wiccian*, meaning "to cast a spell," see Russell and Alexander 12.

2. Larner 84–85.

3. See Levine 265. In ancient Babylonia, witches were usually depicted as women, especially foreign women or socially marginal women. Rollin (37–40) has a useful discussion of the five categories of Mesopotamian witchcraft in which women dominate four of the categories; see also Abusch, "The Demonic Image of the Witch in Standard Babylonian Literature: The Reworking of Popular Conceptions by Learned Exorcists" 31, as well as his discussion of the use of gendered grammatical forms in witchcraft texts, in which the feminine is used for a living witch and the masculine for dead witches, whether female or male, *Mesopotamian Witchcraft: Toward a History and Understanding of Babylonian Witchcraft Beliefs and Literature* 226–27.

4. This is not to say that other classical treatments of Medea are without interest. Ovid greatly added to Medea's gruesome image in his *Metamorphoses* (187–200). Apollonius of Rhodes's third-century BCE *Argonautica* added a distinctly malevolent coloration to her character, while Seneca the Younger's first-century CE *Medea* greatly expanded her magical powers. See the list of sources in Rose and Robertson, "Medea."

5. Ovid, in the *Metamorphoses,* has this vow take place before the altar of Hekate.

6. See Johnston, *Hekate Soteira: A Study of Hekate's Roles in the Chaldean Oracles and Related Literature*, for a discussion of Hekate's role in malevolent and benevolent magic, and chapter 2 herein.

7. Euripides, *Euripides: Medea and Other Plays* 29.

8. Euripides, *Medea* 58. See also Ovid, who makes frequent references to this chariot, *Metamorphoses* 193–94, 197–200.

9. See, e.g., Pausanias's description of ancient Corinth, I.138–39.

10. Ovid, who added greatly to her gruesome image, particularly brings out this aspect, *Metamorphoses* 187–200.

11. Homer 172.

12. See, e.g., Hart 232.

13. *Amores* I.8.1-15, cited by Cohn, *Europe's Inner Demons: The Demonization of Christians in Medieval Christendom* 163; and Hart 232–33

14. Cited by Cohn, *Europe's Inner Demons* 163.

15. Apuleius 68–69. She is called a witch, see 28.

16. Civil et al. I.190.

17. Frankfort 56. Raphael Patai has a good discussion of Lilith's development over time in *The Hebrew Goddess* 221–54.

18. For some legends about Lilith, see Ginzberg I:64–66.

19. Trachtenberg 37. For Jewish sources on Lilith, see ibid., n. 33, 277.

20. Patai 224–29, 236–41.

21. On Jewish amulets in general, see Trachtenberg 132–52; for specific practices to protect mother and child from Lilith, see ibid. 169, and Patai 224–29.

22. Howard Schwartz (8–10) briefly retells Lilith's story and has collected several stories about her or about seductive female demons that share her characteristics. See also Patai 223–24.

23. Trachtenberg 37–43.

24. Cohn discusses some of the early European evidence for the belief in night-flying women, *Europe's Inner Demons*, 164–80; as does Ginzburg, "Deciphering the Witches' Sabbath" 126, 132, and *Ecstasies: Deciphering the Witches' Sabbath* 90–133. See also Baroja, *The World of the Witches* 60–61, 24–27; Ankarloo 288–90; and Duerr 4–5, 7–15, 34–39.

25. Ovid, VI, ll. 131–168.

26. Hesiod, *Theogony*. The eighth- to seventh-century BCE "Hymn to Demeter" noted her role in the primary myth of Demeter and Persephone and its later rituals of death and rebirth, as it is only Hekate and the Sun who hear Persephone's cries for help when Hades kidnaps her. When Hades allows Persephone to return to the earth he gives her a pomegranate seed to eat, so that she will only be able to remain there for part of each year. Hekate greets her upon her return: "And from that day on that lady [Hekate] precedes and follows Persephone" (Boer 130).

27. Lea summarizes the history of Christian beliefs in and stories about succubi and incubi (I:145–62). Kiessling, while interested in the male incubi, comments on the presence of female succubi in the ancient world up to nineteenth-century Europe, 21–28, 36–42. Jones lists other European terms for them, *On the Nightmare* 82.

28. See Trachtenberg on the nocturnal power of demons, 46–47.

29. Elliott, *Fallen Bodies* 29–34. See also Newman, who discusses several cases of demonic possession by incubi, "Possessed by the Spirit: Devout Women, Demoniacs, and the Apostolic Life in the Thirteenth Century" 740, 743–45, and 751. Walter Stephens discusses the multitude of witchcraft treatises that began to proliferate in the thirteenth century in terms of a crisis of faith in spirits, *Demon Lovers*, discussed below.

30. Trachtenberg (52–54) describes at length a seventeenth-century lawsuit in which a female demon fought for the inheritance rights of her offspring from a man. Schwartz also tells this story in greater detail (166–74), as well as many other stories of female demons seducing human men (8–10).

31. See Ernest Jones e.g., 77, 82–97; Kilborne 490–91; and Elliott, who discusses attitudes toward sexual dreams in early and medieval Christianity, *Fallen Bodies* 14–34. A similar Chinese belief is discussed in terms of female "fox fairies," Despeux and Kohn 10.

32. Ernest Jones 82–83, and Serenity Young, *Dreaming in the Lotus* 21–24, 75–85, 152–53.

33. See, e.g., Obeyesekere 138–42.

34. Cohn discusses some of the early European evidence for the belief in night-flying women, *Europe's Inner Demons* 164–10; as does Ginzburg, "Deciphering the Witches' Sabbath" 126, 132, and *Ecstasies*, 90–133. See also Baroja, *The World of the Witches* 60–61, 24–27, 198, n. 62; Ankarloo 288–90; Hart 233–34; and Duerr 4–5, 7–15, and 34–39. Eliade provides interesting information about the cult of Diana in Romania, which appears not to have been so heavily filtered through a Christian lens as in other parts of Europe; see "Some Observations on European Witchcraft" 149–72.

35. See Cohn, *Europe's Inner Demons* 203–09. Klaits (128–58) discusses the role of torture in eliciting confessions.

36. Cohn discusses the evolving processes that developed into the papal Inquisition in *Europe's Inner Demons* 41–50. See also Boswell 269–302.

37. See, e.g., Muchembled 139. Oster suggests that colder temperatures, and thus crop failures, coincided with the most active period of witchcraft trials.

38. See Thomas 40–47. See also the evidence for medieval Estonia, Kahk 275.

39. See, for instance, one of the early trials for witchcraft, that of Joan of Arc (1412–1431), Barstow; and Marina Warner, *Joan of Arc: Reality and Myth*. See also Carlo Ginzburg, *Night Battles: Witchcraft and Agrarian Cults in the Sixteenth and Seventeenth Centuries*; and Ruggiero. See Duerr 136–37 on Hungarian covens. Klaits provides a succinct overview and well documents the historical rise of the witch trials, see 59–65.

40. Baroja summarized some of this thinking in "Witchcraft and Catholic Theology," see 23.

41. Cohn, *Europe's Inner Demons* 202–10.

42. For example, Guillaume Adeline (c. 1400–1455), a professor of theology at the Sorbonne, was put on trial for preaching that witches' sabbaths were not real events; see Cohn, *Europe's Inner Demons* 207.

43. Neave 4; Marrow and Shestack 114; and St. Clare https://shareok.org/handle/11244/34591.

44. Prior to this, the accuser could be liable for punishment if the charges were dropped, so both parties were at risk, per Cohn, *Europe's Inner Demons* 214–17. Beginning in the seventeenth century, changes in the judiciary system effectively brought the witch trails to an end; see, e.g., Klaits 62–164, 171.

45. Muchembled 153–55. See also Boswell 269–302, who discusses social changes, such as increasing urbanization and the rise of absolute monarchies, that contributed to the criminalization of many formerly unquestioned practices.

46. Stephens is particularly persuasive in marking 1400 as the year when witchcraft ceased to be an imaginary crime.

47. This text was once thought to date back to the Council of Ancyra in 314 CE, but Stephens (126–27) dates it from the mid-ninth century, because it reflects pre-Christian beliefs that survived alongside Catholicism in Carolingian Europe. It was incorporated into a standard reference work on canon law by Gratian in about 1140.

48. Baroja, *The World of the Witches* 24–26, 168.

49. Quoted in Kors and Peters 29–31. The Spanish Inquisition remained faithful to this passage, which spared the lives of a number of accused witches. See Henningsen 194 for evidence that it was a dream cult, at least in Sicily.

50. I have adopted Stephens's use of the term "witchcraft theorists" as a convenient means of grouping together judges, inquisitors, interrogators, and theologians who, as we shall see, shaped much of the ideology of witchcraft, see 9.

51. Stephens thoroughly traces this history, see 125–44.

52. Hart 232.

53. Cohn, *Europe's Inner Demons*, 202–09.

54. See, e.g., Klaits, who summarizes much of the literature on this subject, 86–90.

55. E.g., Cohn, *Europe's Inner Demons*, 164–255. Ginzburg argues briefly for its basis in folk beliefs in "Deciphering the Witches' Sabbath" 121–37, and at length in *Ecstasies*. See also Henningsen, who discusses a fairy dream cult that involved flying.

56. Henningsen offers meaningful counterexamples in which folk beliefs were not, to use his term, "diabolized."

57. Newman, "Possessed by the Spirit" 741–44, 754–55.

58. See, e.g., Michel de Certeau for a public, two-year-long exorcism of seventeen nuns, *The Possession at Loudun*. Klaits discusses the role of the possessed as accusers of witches, 113–27.

59. Caciola 225. See also Stephens's highly nuanced reading of exorcism and possession, 322–42.

60. Caciola 251–52. In medieval Judaism, too, women were thought to be more vulnerable to possession than men, which was believed to make them more prone to sorcery as well. See Trachtenberg 50–51; and Fishbane.

61. Muchembled 150–51.

62. See Rudolph M. Bell 151–79. Caroline Walker Bynum also mentions Catherine of Siena and Lidwina of Schiedam, *Holy Feast* 316, n. 46.

63. Bynum, *Holy Feast* 23.

64. Though this seems not to have been the case in Scandinavia. See Ankarloo 310–11; Madar 266–67; Heikkinen and Kervinen 321–22; and Hastrup 386–88.

65. Larner 84–88.

66. Ankarloo 316–17. In general, see Stuart Clark for a discussion of the dichotomous and hierarchical thinking that dominated during the witch-hunting period. See also Baroja, *World of the Witches* 50–51.

67. See Klaits's summary of accusations against older women, especially poor, older, and unmarried women dependent on the charity of others, 94–95, 101–03.

68. Here I have elaborated upon Klaits's subtle reading of the period, 65–75, and that of Larner 84–88.

69. Translated in Kors and Peters 107–12. See the discussions of it in Stephens 55–57, and Baroja, "Witchcraft and Catholic Theology" 30–31.

70. Elliott has a thoughtful discussion of this important text, *Fallen Bodies*, as does Stephens 32–57. Stephens attributes a greater influence to Kramer, 377, n. 3.

71. See the discussion of this iconography in Stephens 106–24.

72. On this point see Stephens 61.

73. Kramer and Sprenger part I, question 6, 47.

74. Stephens 46.

75. Stephens 50. This is in an early draft of the *Malleus Maleficarum*.

76. See Elliott, *Fallen Bodies* 35–60.

77. Klaits is particularly good at bringing this out; see chapter 3.

78. Kramer and Sprenger part I, question 6, 46. Medea as a sorceress is frequently represented in late medieval and Renaissance art, see, e.g., Pinson 950.

79. Stephens 200, 241–56. Of course, this charge had also been leveled against medieval Jews; see Boswell 273. Cohn has shown that the belief in cannibalistic witches existed by at least the sixth century CE among Germanic people, *Europe's Inner Demons* 164–65.

80. Stephens 249–51.

81. Stephens offers many examples of this belief, see 288–89.

82. Cohn, *Europe's Inner Demons* 202–10. Cohn goes on to argue that where the authorities believed such flight occurred, witch-hunting proliferated, ibid. 180. See also Stephens 125–44.

83. Duerr, n. 25, 147.

84. Cohn, *Europe's Inner Demons*, 143, 205.

85. Rowland 168.

86. Neave 4; Marrow and Shestack 114; and St. Clare. Hieronymus Bosch used flying witches and the witches' sabbath in his *Temptation of Saint Anthony* (c. 1505–1506), although it is shown mainly as detail. See the discussion in Pinson 953. Although Goya painted important images of witches, the witch trials had subsided by Goya's time, and he used these images to highlight the vices and social abuses of his own age.

87. For further discussion see Pinson; and Strauss 38.

88. Neave 6.

89. Marrow and Shestack 14–15; and Neave 5–7, discuss his images of witches.

90. For a fascinating discussion of these ointments and flying witches from different cultures, see Duerr 1–11, 76–88. Some of the ointments were psychotropic; see Harner; and Stephens 145–68. The effects of these drugs were questioned even during the period of the trials; see Baroja, *The World of the Witches* 180–89.

91. See, e.g., Pinson 52, and Jane P. Davidson plates 20, 27, and 28.

92. Duerr 1–2.

93. Duerr 4. See also Jane P. Davidson's many images of flying witches. Ginzburg cites the confession of a Scottish witch flying to a witches' sabbath; see "Deciphering the Witches' Sabbath" 128.

94. Kramer and Sprenger part II, question 1, chapter 3, 107.

95. Kramer and Sprenger part II, question 1, chapter 3, 107–08.

96. Kramer and Sprenger part II, question 1, chapter 3, 108.

97. See the literature discussed in Duerr 1–11; and Harner.

98. Duerr 4–7.

99. Respectively, Cohn, *Europe's Inner Demons* 180; and Klaits 58–59.

100. William Monter has a brief, useful discussion and table of figures, see 213–16. See also Muchembled on the English trials, as well as the similar experiences in Denmark and Sweden.

101. Stephens 102–06.

102. See Keith Thomas, *Religion and the Decline of Magic* 40–47.

103. See Ruggiero's discussion of Christian prayer and how it was seen by church authorities as crossing over into magical incantation, 103–05. See also Muchembled 152.

104. For example, *Malleus Maleficarum* justifies the use of torture in Kramer and Sprenger part I, question 1, 6. See also Cohn, *Europe's Inner Demons*, 203–10, 230.

105. This is not to deny ongoing witchcraft accusations, especially in Africa, that often lead to the death of the accused.

106. See the discussion in chapter 2 of the Greek defeat of earlier religious practices.

CHAPTER 9

1. Humphrey and Onon 12, 64, n. 4. See also Tedlock's discussion of words used for shamans, 24–25.

2. Anthropology has a long history of using non-Western words (e.g., "taboo," "mana," and "totem," to name just a few) to encompass multiple indigenous practices or concepts. See Laufer's discussion in "Origin of the Word Shaman." As it turns out, in Siberia there are multiple terms for what are considered shamanic activities. Humphrey delineates many of these terms in Humphrey and Onon.

3. See Vitebsky 26–51; and Kendall, *Shamans, Housewives, and Other Restless Spirits* 28–29. For an overview of the pros and cons of different methodologies in the study of shamanism, see Atkinson. A good introduction to the academic study of (and indeed, creation of the academic discipline of) shamanism and various methodologies is Price, "An Archaeology of Altered States: Shamanism and Material Culture Studies." Eliade's *Shamanism*, a classic in the study of shamanism, brings together many different sources, but see critiques of his work by Humphrey, "Shamanic Practices and the State in Northern Asia" 191–92; and Thomas and Humphrey 1–4.

4. In emphasizing women's shamanic flight, I disagree with Susan Starr Sered's contention (186) that soul flight "is not a feature of religious specialist roles in women's religions." Her position seems to have developed out of her disagreement with Lewis's work, but the evidence gathered here indicates that flight is part of female shamanic experience. Tedlock summarizes the thinking behind Sered's position, 72–73.

5. A. V. Grebenshchikov collected three written copies of the text between 1908 and 1913, although it was still in circulation as a popular oral tale in northern Manchuria; Nowak and Durrant 35–36. Durrant translated the 1913 version, which is the most complete text, ibid., 36. Caroline Humphrey discusses more recent versions among the Daur; Humphrey and Onon

305–12. See also a brief version collected in Shi; and Stary's translation and discussion of the same text, i–xiii.

6. Nowak has a good discussion of the function of water in this epic in Nowak and Durrant 110–13.

7. Humphrey, "Shamanic Practices and the State in Northern Asia" 195. The Manchurian imperial court in Beijing used shamans of a different sort and in different capacities, see Humphrey, "Shamanic Practices" 211, which seems to be suggested in the epic of the Nišan shaman that begins with statements about the inadequacy of other shamans.

8. See Humphrey's subtle analysis of the historical ups and downs of the relationship of the state to shamanism, "Shamanic Practices."

9. Durrant 340, 347.

10. Nowak and Durrant 54.

11. Nowak and Durrant 57.

12. See, e.g., Lewis 50–56 and the discussion below.

13. Nowak and Durrant 56. The Daur version relates that she herself died—that is, became temporally dead in order to enter the Land of the Dead; Humphrey and Onon 307.

14. For the significance of the rooster and the dog, see Nowak and Durrant 58, fns. 15 and 16. Eliade also briefly discusses dogs in shamanism, *Shamanism* 466–67. See also Taksami.

15. Nowak and Durrant 61. Nowak follows and elaborates upon Lévi-Strauss's analysis of Manchu kinship, in which he suggests there may have been a transition from matrilineal to patrilineal descent, ibid., 102–06.

16. Nowak and Durrant 95–98, 105–06, 108–09.

17. Hamayon 78–81.

18. Nowak and Durrant 68–70.

19. Nowak and Durrant 73.

20. Durrant 347.

21. Nowak and Durrant 74.

22. In another version, she only became a shaman after her husband's death; see Stary ii.

23. Tedlock has found that in many parts of the world pregnancy is believed to enhance shamanic powers (see 205–08), though the Chukchi of northeastern Siberia believed that women's trances were inferior to those of men because childbearing weakened their powers; see Bogoras vol. xi, 415, 421.

24. This episode is very similar to the experiences of Tibetan *delogs*—*yogīs*, mostly women, who have shamanic death experiences, journey to hell, and return to report on how sins are punished there. For the story a famous female *delog*, see Serinity Young, *Courtesans and Tantric Consorts* 169–75. Eliade briefly discusses other Siberian tales of descent to the underworld and witnessing the punishment of sins in *Shamanism*, 213–14.

25. Humphrey and Onon 286–312.

26. Incense is used to call the spirit into the shaman, and then to call the shaman back into her own body, through the powerful pull of the olfactory organ. Both the human spirit and spirits of other worlds are believed to be attracted by fragrance and repelled by unpleasant odors.

27. Nowak and Durrant 87. This is reminiscent of Isis fanning Osiris with her wings in order to bring him back to life (chapter 2).

28. This coda is not part of two other redactions of the text; see Nowak and Durrant 36 and 109. Humphrey and Onon discuss the Daur version of the story, which also does not

contain the coda; they see it as an assertion of Daur values in contradistinction to those of the Manchus (305–12). Nonetheless, the coda does exist in the three versions collected in 1961; see Stary vii.

29. Nowak and Durrant 88. Nowak, however, discusses the acceptability of this relationship within Manchu morality, ibid. 105.

30. Nowak and Durrant 90. In a shorter version, the emperor orders that she be killed, but later realizes her great power and repents, decreeing that offerings be made to her whenever they are made to other deities; see Shi 228; and Stary iii.

31. Nowak discusses this in Nowak and Durrant 31–34 and 94–110.

32. Humphrey makes this point in Humphrey and Onon (310). Recent research reveals the revitalization of shamanism among the Manchu; see Shi 223–24.

33. For a discussion of shamanism in various kinds of modern societies, see Kendall, *The Life and Hard Times of a Korean Shaman: Of Tales and the Telling of Tales*; Kendall, "Korean Shamans and the Spirit of Capitalism"; Thomas and Humphrey; Humphrey, "Shamans in the City"; Balzer, "Healing Failed Faith?: Contemporary Siberian Shamanism"; and Choi.

34. Lewis-Williams analyzes the source of altered states of consciousness in *Homo sapiens* in support of his argument that shamans existed in the Upper Paleolithic, *The Mind in the Cave* 121–35.

35. Shamanic journeys to the Land of the Dead are often recorded in legends and folktales, see, e.g. Eliade, *Shamanism* 213–14. Korean shamans study various versions of "Princess Pari," in part because it contains the chants to the gods to be sung in the Land of the Dead; *Princess Pari*, translated by Myung Hee Kim, unpublished manuscript. This text is discussed below. A Tibetan folk drama, *Nangsa*, is named after a woman believed to have lived in the eleventh century who is said to have been dead for seven days, during which time she went to the Land of the Dead and, like the Nišan shaman, was taught about the punishment of sins. I discuss this text in *Courtesans and Tantric Consorts* 169–75.

36. Lewis (146–50) discusses ceremonies among both the Akawaio of British Guyana and the Inuit in which the shaman encourages public confessions from people who have created discord or broken taboos. Kendall discusses the role of shamanism in healing through the resolution of painful family histories in *Shamans, Housewives* 89–92, and in "Initiating Performance: The Story of Chini, a Korean Shaman."

37. On this point see Hamayon.

38. Tedlock 3–4, 28–30; Devlet 51, figure 3.8, 52.

39. Stary iv.

40. See Walraven's thoughtful discussion of this in the context of Korean history.

41. Harva discusses examples of both (496–99), as does Eliade, *Shamanism* 13–109. See also Czaplicka 172–78.

42. For example, Kendall, *Shamans, Housewives* 57–65; Taksami; Rex L. Jones, "Limbu Spirit Possession and Shamanism" 47; and Shirley Kurz Jones, "Limbu Spirit Possession—A Case Study."

43. For a discussion of the use of hallucinogens in shamanic practice, see La Barre, "Old and New World Narcotics: A Statistical Question and an Ethnological Reply"; and Tedlock 142–70.

44. Balzer, "Flights of the Sacred: Symbolism and Theory in Siberian Shamanism."

45. Desjarlais, "Presence," and "Healing Through Images: The Magical Flight and Healing Geography of Nepali Shamans." See also David Holmberg 48.

46. See Eliade, *Shamanism* 477–82; Peters and Price-Williams; Lewis-Williams, "Southern African Shamanistic Rock Art in Its Social and Cognitive Contexts"; and for Australia, Lommel 99–100.

47. Eliade, *Shamanism* 98. He also points out that "magic" and "song," especially that of birds, are often expressed by the same word in several languages, ibid., 98 and n. 114. See also Sukhu 145.

48. Humphrey and Onon 297.

49. Devlet.

50. Eliade, *Shamanism* 145. See Humphrey's discussion of the Daur shaman costume, which also incorporates political and military imagery, Humphrey and Onon 202–09; Dolgikh; Djakonova; and Czaplicka 203–27.

51. Devlet 44. See also, ibid., figures 3.2–3.5, discussed 45–46.

52. Jochelson, *Yukaghir* 174–75, 183–84; and *The Yakut* 107–18. Eliade provides examples of the pervasiveness of bird feathers on shamanic costumes throughout the world, see *Shamanism* 176–80. See also Rex L. Jones, "Limbu Spirit Possession and Shamanism" 34–35; and Sagant 87–88.

53. Jochelson, *Yukaghir* 169. The Yukaghir terms have been deleted. He makes additional references to avian imagery in shaman costumes, 173–82. Harva describes other bird suits (4:514–16), with several illustrations of these, see plates LVIII, LX, and LXI and figures 22, 23, and 24. See also Balzer, "Flights of the Sacred" 306, 315, n. 5.

54. Discussed by Jochelson, *Yukaghir* 184. See also Devlet 50.

55. Jochelson, *Yakut* 111.

56. Eliade, *Shamanism* 147–48.

57. Jochelson alludes to this in the sad context of a shaman selling his costume, see *Yukaghir* 170–71.

58. Jochelson, *Yukaghir* 196, and *The Yakut* 121; and Waida 224–25. Eliade elaborates on the relationship of shamans and their spirit animals, see *Shamanism* 92–95. Siberian shamans may also mimic the act of riding a horse or reindeer while imitating the sounds of those animals, but then change into a bird; see Žornickaja 129–30.

59. Faure 307.

60. Eliade discusses this ritual in *Shamanism* 190–97. See also 117–27 for additional rituals involving tree climbing.

61. Uno Holmberg plate XLVI. Balzer has a photograph of wooden birds with outstretched wings on a pole slanted skyward in "Flights of the Sacred," figure 2, 308.

62. Kendall and Lee; Eliade, *Shamanism* 231, 242, 252, 338, 443; Blacker 22, 290; and Žornickaja 127–34.

63. Eliade describes a Carib ritual that involved swinging and several other forms of shamanic ascent in *Shamanism*, respectively, 129–31,132–44, 426–65, 487–94. Blacker has an appendix on a sword-climbing rite in Japan, 317–20, and a photo, plate 17. See also Desjarlais, "Healing through Images" 292–93; and Rex L. Jones, "Limbu Spirit Possession and Shamanism" 36–37.

64. Furst, "Shamanism: South American Shamanism" 219. See also Tedlock's discussion of the drum as inducement to trance, 80–83. See also Uno Holmberg's discussion of the shaman's drum and its use, *Finno-Ugric Mythology* 287–92; Harva 519–22, plates XLVIII, XLIX, LII; Potapov; Czaplicka 203–27; and Jones, "Limbu Spirit Possession and Shamanism" 35.

65. Devlet 47, and see figures 3.1–3.6, 3.9, and 3.10, 44–54.

66. Eliade describes several examples of choosing the tree, see *Shamanism*, 169–70. He also propagated the universal applicability of the idea of the *axis mundi* and three levels of the cosmos in many of his works, see, e.g., ibid., 259–74. (As mentioned in chapter 1, while this is a rich depiction of the universe, alternative cosmologies are equally meaningful.) Humphrey contextualizes this concept for Siberia in Humphrey and Onon 191–268.

67. For examples, see Balzer, "Flights of the Sacred" 306–07, 313. In the same way that shamans cross between the separate realms of the living and the dead, through shape-shifting they cross from the human to the animal realm. As will be shown below, some can also shape-shift between genders.

68. Harva 498. For some examples of the use of bird imagery, see ibid., 508–22. Balzer discusses the three souls of Sakha shamanism, "Flights of the Sacred" 308–09. For more on the placement of dead shamans, see Humphrey and Onon, 27, 129–30, 212.

69. Harva 501. Balzer confirms the enduring sacredness of the eagle and the fear of killing one among Sakhas today, see "Flights of the Sacred" 305–18.

70. Messerschmidt, "Ethnographic Observations," 210.

71. Harva 504–06; and Eliade, *Shamanism* 37–69. Eliade presents additional stories about the first shaman, *Shamanism*, 68–77. See also Rex L. Jones, "Limbu Spirit Possession and Shamanism" 32–33.

72. Balzer, "Flights of the Sacred" 308. Humphrey and Onon discuss Siberian beliefs about new souls nesting in a celestial tree to await rebirth, see Humphrey and Onon 286–312. See also Tedlock 222.

73. Lewis-Williams, *The Mind in the Cave* 135, 205–26; Eliade, *Shamanism,* especially 502–07; Jochelson, *Yakut,* 107; and La Barre, *The Ghost Dance: The Origins of Religion* 352. Hoppál discusses the evidence of Siberian rock art from between the second and first millenniums BCE. Devlet also discusses the Siberian rock art of shamans, while Lewis-Williams discusses that of Southern Africa, "Southern African Shamanistic Rock Art," and of North America, *The Mind in the Cave,* 136–79.

74. Johnson.

75. See Bogoras 413–14; and Jochelson, *Yukaghir,* 194–95.

76. Atkinson, "Shaminisms Today" 317–19. Vitebsky has a nuanced reading of gender in shamanism. See also Tedlock.

77. Hawkes. Sukhu's recent translation and interpretation of this text sheds further light on the shamanic elements in these poems. See also Schafer, *The Divine Woman* 11–15.

78. Blacker 28. Blacker also discusses the *mikos,* female shamans of Japan, 104–26, and ancient women shamans, 113–15. See also Ruch 521–25.

79. Bogoras 415, 421. Tedlock 205–08. Lewis argues for woman's greater susceptibility to possession.

80. Rex L. Jones, "Limbu Spirit Possession and Shamanism" 49; Sagant 70–72; and Tedlock 5–6, 22, 185–188, 276.

81. Eliade, *Shamanism,* e.g., 351–52, 448–49.

82. La Barre, *The Ghost Dance* 93–120, especially 107.

83. In addition to the examples in Lewis, see, e.g., Humphrey, "Shamanic Practices," 211–14, and the discussion below.

84. Lewis actually contrasts the male shaman with the female medium, which does not hold up in wider contexts; see Kendall, "Shamanism." See also Tedlock's discussion of mythic battles in which men take shamanic power from women, 55–59.

85. Humphrey has suggested a more fluid model of the relationship between Buddhism and shamanism, at least in the Inner Asian states, in "Shamanic Practices" 195, 198. See also Faure on the expulsion of female shamans from mountain cults in Japan, 219–49.

86. For a brief discussion of the Confucian government's persecution of shamanism in Korea during the Yi Dynasty (1392–1910), see Youngsook Kim Harvey 3, 10; and Walraven. For Manchuria and China, see Humphrey, "Shamanic Practices" 191–228.

87. Lewis 86–87, 92–93ff.

88. Jochelson, *Yukaghir* 162, 680–733.

89. Kendall, *Shamans, Housewives* 24–25, and "Shamanism"; and Holmberg.

90. Bacigalupo. See also Hamayon 86; Atkinson 317–18; Caldwell, esp. n. 23, 222–23.

91. Tedlock.

92. See van Genep; and Lincoln, *Emerging from the Chrysalis: Studies in Rituals of Women's Initiation*.

93. An exception, though, is Balzer, "Rituals of Gender Identity: Markers of Siberian Khanty Ethnicity, Status, and Belief."

94. Humphrey and Onon 168–78, 286–312.

95. Hollimon 123; and Sutherland 135–36.

96. Peter Knecht summarizes some of the issues involved in analyzing shamans as a third sex, 20–22. Hollimon summarizes a wide range of studies on the existence of a third gender, 124–25, 128–29. See also Herdt.

97. Bogoras 449–56. See also Jochelson, *Yakut* 52–54.

98. Halifax 22–28, who also has examples of women who dressed and lived as men, and Walter L. Williams 19, 35–36. See also the examples and discussion in Czaplicka 248–55; and Linn.

99. Eliade, *Shamanism*, 351–54.

100. Bacigalupo.

101. Kendall, *Shamans, Housewives* 27. Now that shamanism has increased in status there are more male shamans. This may also have been the case in Japan; see Ruch 522.

102. Caldwell 199; and Moreno 110. See also my discussion of *hijrās*, men (some of whom have emasculated themselves) who dress as women and worship a goddess, in Serinity Young, *Courtesans and Tantric Consorts* 111–13.

103. Hanna 58.

104. Jochelson, *Yukaghir* 194–95; see also 169, 170, 174, 185–86, 196. See also Eliade on this point, *Shamanism* 351–52.

105. Jochelson, *Yakut*, 118, 53, n. 3.

106. Marjorie Mandelstam Balzer, "Sacred Genders in Siberia: Shamans, Bear Festivals, and Androgyny" 248. See also Grabmo 107. Grabmo finds evidence of male shamans/magicians dressing as women in medieval and perhaps earlier Norse culture. See also Basilov.

107. Tedlock 247. She goes on to describe the more fluid sense of gender in other cultures, particularly in relation to shamanism, see 248–54; as does Hollimon 126–27.

108. See Sukhu's highly nuanced reading of this phenomena, 79–81.

109. Balzer, "Sacred Genders" 254. See also Halifax 22–28; and Linn, 495, 499. Linn's article is actually about transvestism and transsexuality in various religious traditions.

110. See Poole.

111. Sorensen 403, n. 1.

112. Kim 15.

113. Her story is contained in the biography of Tibet's first legendary doctor, Yuthog, translated by Rechung Rinpoche in *Tibetan Medicine* 153–63.

114. Sukhu 77–81. See also Schafer, *The Divine Woman* 12; and Kohn 83–84.

115. Jochelson, *Yukaghir* 194, 197–200; and Uno Holmberg 292–93. Roseman; see also Uno Holmberg 291; and Eliade, *Shamanism* 128.

116. Blacker 27. Itinerant female shamans may also have worked as prostitutes, see Ruch 522, 524–25. Indeed, an active slave trade in young girls fed the ranks of shamans, prostitutes, and entertainers, Ruch 525.

117. Jochelson, *Yukaghir* 198, n. 4.

118. Oosten 124–25.

119. For the Amazon, see Furst 219; for Siberia, see Bogoras 452–54, and Eliade, who discounts their importance as part of his argument against Leo Sternberg (see below). Nonetheless, he mentions several other instances of this practice, see *Shamanism* 71–75, 421–24, 463–64. Blacker discusses the marriage of blind female shamans of Japan to male spirits, 146–47; and Vitebsky mentions the marriage of female Sora (India) shamans to male spirits, 40, 56–57. In general, see Lewis 50–56. See also Tedlock's discussion of spirit marriages among the K'iche' Maya (85–102), and the role of sexuality in shamanism and its physiological relationship to trance (150–51). The presence of spirit assistants of the opposite sex is echoed in the human male assistant of the Nišan shaman.

120. Spiro (205) notes that only about 3 to 4 percent of shamans are male. Their numbers seem to be increasing, especially in urban areas. See Merrison.

121. Spiro describes such a wedding and its expense, 212–17.

122. Spiro 208–09.

123. Spiro 209. This is also the case for predominantly female Korean shamans, though this is changing in the early twenty-first century.

124. Spiro 222. When possessed by male deities, female Korean shamans similarly dress in male costumes and act like men.

125. Spiro 220. Despite the dominance of female shamans, they do not escape male supervision. At the Taugbyon, a national festival that lasts a full week, there is a hereditary male custodian who appoints a man as chief shaman over all the shamans in Burma and below him four principle female shamans and four male shamans, see Spiro 113–17. The Taugbyon occurs just after the planting season, which is also the period of Buddhist Lent, when ordinary human weddings are prohibited but when most *nat* weddings occur, see Spiro 213, 222.

126. Merrison.

127. See also the sexual dreams of Australian shamans discussed by Lommel 99–100; and those of Nepali shamans, Sagant 63–64.

128. Sternberg 477.

129. See, e.g., Blacker on this point, 15–123. Of course, one has to tread lightly in taking folklore as documentary evidence for religious practice.

130. Sternberg 479.

131. Sternberg 481.

CHAPTER 10

1. For a thoughtful discussion of Thomas de Cantimpré's hagiographic writings on women saints, see Elliott, *Proving Woman* 52–58, 65–84; and Hollywood, who also discusses Christina's life, 241–47.

2. Hollywood 347, n. 17.

3. His statement opens the prologue to de Cantimpré (11–12), and he himself included details of her in his prologue to the *Life of Marie of Oignies* (1176–1213), written c. 1213. For an insightful analysis of the *Life of Christina*, see Stern, especially chapter 4, 136–68, which deals with the miraculous incidents that follow.

4. De Cantimpré 12.

5. When she finally did die, she once again returned to life in order to answer the questions of a nun, and she was said to foretell the future. See de Cantimpré 45–46, 32–35, and 39, respectively.

6. For example, Ida of Louvain; see Caciola 31, 37–38, 45–46, and 69–70.

7. Lozanno 26–33; and Rese and Gray: 141. See also the discussion below of Hadewijch's vision of climbing a tree. During the famous demonic possession of the Ursuline nuns of Loudon, a witness claimed that they ran on the convent roofs and perched on the very end of tree branches for days, in rain and frost, without eating; de Certeau 32.

8. De Cantimpré 20 and 26.

9. See Bynum's discussion of women's bodies as food, *Holy Feast* 169–276.

10. See also Elliott's discussion of Christina as functioning between the living and the dead in her assumption of purgatorial penances, *Proving Woman* 75–76.

11. De Cantimpré 15–16, 24; see also 27, 41, and 21, where she walks on water.

12. See Hollywood's discussion of how Christina and other medieval female mystics understood their experiences and how those experiences were represented by male hagiographers, 246–66. Teresa of Ávila stands out, as her autobiography was written after her two male spiritual directors told her she was being deluded by the devil and they insisted she write down her experiences for their judgment. From this evolved her exquisite *Life*.

13. Newman, "Possessed by the Spirit" 766–67.

14. See the discussion of illness and medieval female visionaries in Petroff 37–44.

15. Stern 166.

16. De Cantimpré 22, 32, 36; Stern 156.

17. Clara Erskine Clement 73. One depiction of this is Bernardino Luini's fresco, *Burial of St. Catherine*, 1521–1523, in the Pinacoteca di Brera, Milan.

18. Leroy 33–34.

19. Leroy 35–36. Leroy lists more female saints who are said to have levitated, (44–135), and he questions most of these events, as he does that of male saints (148–68). He does not mention Ss. Irene of Chrysobalanton, Elisabeth of Schönau, Ursula, or Hadewijch, all discussed below.

20. Elliot, *Proving Woman* 183.

21. Petroff 169, 172.

22. Teresa describes her experiences of rising above the ground in chapter 20 of her *Life*, which is devoted to the subject of ecstasy and levitation, and also in chapters 38 to 40, which are devoted to her visionary and auditory experiences. See also one nun's report of Teresa's levitation, Leroy 72.

23. Respectively, Bynum, *Holy Feast* 204; and McDonnell 354–55.

24. One depiction of this is Nicolas Poussin's *The Miraculous Translation of Saint Rita de Cascia*, c. 1633, held at the Dulwich Picture Gallery, London.

25. "Our Lady of the Pillar" https://udayton.edu/imri/mary/o/our-lady-of-the-pillar.php.

26. McNamara 493.

27. Jan Olof Rosenqvist has translated and edited the original Greek in one edition; see xliii. See also Rapp's discussion of the uses and audiences for Byzantine hagiographies, 313, 335–44, and, regarding the possibility of a female author for Irene's *Life*, 322.

28. A good overview of Eastern Orthodoxy is Timothy Ware.

29. Rosenqvist 63, n. 14.

30. Rosenqvist 77. For additional cases of levitation in the Eastern Orthodox tradition, see 77, n. 4.

31. Kazhdan and Maguire 5.

32. Shoemaker has prepared a thoroughgoing analysis of Mary's Assumption.

33. Hart, *Images of Flight*, 1–52 and the accompanying images.

34. See, e.g., Hildegard of Bingen, vision 12, 517.

35. Her life is discussed and some of her writings are excerpted in Petroff 140–42, 159–70, and in Thiébaux 349–84. See especially Anne Clark's penetrating study.

36. Anne Clark 79.

37. Elisabeth of Schönau.

38. Petroff 161, from *Visions* II.7; Thiébaux 364; and Anne Clark 78, vision 37.

39. Petroff 59, from *Visions* II.1.

40. Letter 49, cited by Caciola 14, and Newman 3. For similar male perceptions of the age and later negative male interpretations, see Newman, respectively, 55–57, 274–77. Newman has a thorough analysis of this phrase (238–49), which she translates as a "womanish age."

41. Anne Clark 1. Clark discusses their one meeting and elaborates on Hildegard's influence on the younger Elisabeth as well as on their differences, e.g., 34–36, as does Newman 36–41.

42. Anne Clark 87.

43. Anne Clark 87.

44. Visions 16 and 17, Clark 87. Teresa of Ávila also described her mystical experiences as raptures, 144–45.

45. Anne Clark 88.

46. See the discussion in Anne Clark 12–13,88–89; and Petroff 141.

47. Apocalyptic expectation had been popular since the tenth century, see Cohn, *The Pursuit of the Millennium*. Hildegard of Bingen's *Scivias* concludes with a vision of the Apocalypse, see book 3, vision 11, 493–511, and one of the Day of Judgment, book 3, vision 12, 513–21. See also Hadewijch's vision, discussed below.

48. Anne Clark 21, 31.

49. Anne Clark 4–5, 11; for a detailed discussion of the writing process, see 28–67 and 130–33; for the *De Obitu Elisabeth*, 43–45; and for transmission of her works, 137–45.

50. Anne Clark 81, 88.

51. Visions 15, 16, 44, and 45, Anne Clark 103.

52. Petroff 141.

53. Petroff 169–70, from *Visions* II.31, and Thiébaux 352.

54. Warner discusses the development of ideas about and iconography of Mary's Assumption, *Alone of All Her Sex: The Myth and the Cult of the Virgin Mary* 81–102. But see also Shoemaker's more thorough coverage of this topic.

55. Accordingly, Elisabeth corrected the Assumption's date to September 23 from August 15, the latter being the presumed date of her death. She had some regional success in this, but it did not last; the assumption is celebrated on August 15 in both Roman Catholicism and Eastern Orthodoxy. See Anne Clark 109.

56. Petroff 169, from *Visions* II.31.

57. Petroff 169, from *Visions* II.31.

58. Warner, *Alone of All Her Sex* 89–90. Anne Clark discusses the dissemination and availability of her works, 2, 6, 25–28, and of the Assumption text in particular, 40–41.

59. Thiébaux 352; the text is translated on 366–82. See also Anne Clark 37.

60. Thiébaux 354. See also Poncelet.

61. Thiébaux 353–54. The existence of several sets of life-cycle paintings of Ursula indicate the popularity of her legend, though none depict an ascension; see de Tervarent.

62. Thiébaux 355.

63. The vision itself is translated in Thiébaux 367. See Anne Clark and her discussion of Elisabeth's role in the development of this legend 37–40. Baring-Gould outlines the legend's history, or lack thereof, before Elisabeth and speculates on its roots in European paganism, 318–40.

64. Visions 60–61, translated in Thiébaux 361–64, and discussed by Anne Clark, 103–07.

65. Thiébaux 362. Hildegard of Bingen also associated women with Christ's humanity, which may have influenced Elisabeth; see Bynum, *Fragmentation and Redemption: Essays on Gender and the Human Body in Medieval Religion* 210. For a more generalized discussion of women symbolizing humanity in the later Middle Ages, see Bynum, *Holy Feast* 264ff.

66. Thiébaux 363–64.

67. Bynum opened up the study of the somatic experiences of medieval female mystics, *Fragmentation and Redemption* 60, and especially 181–238; *Holy Feast*; and *Jesus as Mother: Studies in the Spirituality of the High Middle Ages.* For the levitations of male saints, see Hart 193–210. See also Rudolph M. Bell; and Elliott, *Proving Woman*, e.g., 144–48.

68. Bynum, *Holy Feast* 77. Elliott mentions several other female saints who levitated, *Proving Woman* 183. See also those mentioned above.

69. In general, see Weinstein and Bell's comparison of male and female saints; McGinn; and Hollywood 6–13, 113–70.

70. Bynum, *Fragmentation and Redemption* 162.

71. See McDonnell; and Bowie.

72. Bynum, *Holy Feast* 24; and Petroff 171–74.

73. Caciola 15, 54–63, 75, 214–15.

74. As Caciola (214–15) shows, elaborate physiological theories placed the Holy Spirit in the heart and demons in the bowels or womb—a distinction that was not helpful in the discernment of spirits,.

75. Caciola 32–33.

76. Kramer and Sprenger part I, question 6. See also the discussion in Caciola 34–54, 70–71, 77.

77. Newman 34. Elisabeth of Schönau also expressed her fear of such an accusation, Newman 35.

78. Hildegard of Bingen book 1, vision 4, 113–14.

79. Caciola (140–58) explores the medical depiction of women, as well as the notion that women's bodies are more "open" than men's.

80. Caciola 14–19.

81. Slade 9–10, and quoting the *Directorium Inquisitorum.* Slade further discusses the Spanish Inquisition, see 10–11.

82. Caciola 35. See three case histories, 87–125.

83. Caciola 76.

84. Bynum, *Holy Feast*, 316, n. 46. She discusses these saints further in chapters 4 and 5. See also Rudolph M. Bell on the accusations against Catherine of Siena (27–29), Columba Rieti (155–58), Catherine of Racconigi (159–61), and Domenica dal Paradiso (165–66).

85. Bynum, *Holy Feast* 23.

86. See, for example, Bynum, *Fragmentation and Redemption* 190–91; and Thiébaux 385–412.

87. Petroff 5, 32–35. Her introduction (3–59) is invaluable for understanding medieval female visionary experience. For further discussions of the role of female celibacy as a source of power and freedom, see Schüssler Fiorenza; and Ruether.

88. See Bynum's discussion of medieval women's use of fasting to both control their sexuality (*Holy Feast* 214–16) and manipulate their bodies (*Holy Feast* 200–01). For the overall complexity of fasting and women, see Bynum, *Holy Feast*; and Rudolph M. Bell. Fasting is a technique known worldwide for achieving alternative states of consciousness, e.g., see chapter 11 herein.

89. Flying by Daoist mystics is well documented; they tried to achieve levitation, in part, through what they did and did not eat, see Laufer, *Prehistory of Aviation* 28–30; and the discussion in chapter 11.

90. Bynum, *Holy Feast* 195; and Demos 164–65.

91. Rudolph M. Bell 27.

92. See Bynum's discussion of female devotion to the Eucharist in the thirteenth century, *Fragmentation and Redemption* 119–50.

93. Bynum, *Fragmentation and Redemption* 134ff.

94. Caciola 63.

95. Petroff has a useful overview of illness in the lives of medieval female visionaries, see 37–44.

96. Thiébaux (390) focuses on the works of Mechthild of Magdeburg (c. 1212–c.1282) and Beatrijs of Nazareth (c. 1200–1268).

97. Thiébaux 385–386.

98. Thiébaux 398, quoting her poem, *The Flowing Light of the Godhead*, book I.xv.

99. Thiébaux 407–408, quoting her *The Seven Manners of Holy Minne*.

100. Hildegard of Bingen, book 1, vision 4, 112.

101. Hadewijch of Brabant 102, 290.

102. Teresa of Ávila 144–45.

103. Teresa of Ávila 286.

104. Visions 15, 16, 44, and 45, Anne Clark 103.

105. Anne Clark (68–80) provides a good historical overview of the situation.

106. Anne Clark 72.

107. Anne Clark 72–73.

108. The defining work on them is McDonnell. See also Petroff 51–65.

109. Shea 68–69.

110. Bowie 11–21. Shea discusses the changing tenor of that time, see 63–64.

111. See the introduction to Hadewijch (1); and Petroff 176–77, which also contains visions 7, 10, and 11. Vanderauwera discusses ways in which her writings survived and resurfaced, see 190–92.

112. Several images of her are available online, although none of them have any historical validity.

113. Vanderauwera (186–87) presents the evidence for her residing in Brabant, Antwerp, or Brussels.

114. Shea discusses the life of noblewomen and of women religious in thirteenth- to fourteenth-century northern Europe, 36–43, 45–47. Additional studies of Hadewijch include Milhaven; Walters, who discusses her in comparison with four other twelfth- and thirteenth-century mystics; and Vanderauwera.

115. Hadewijch 4–5; and Bowie 96. Hildegard of Bingen had similar problems with her sister nuns and with outsiders, see Newman 34–35. See also Petroff's discussion of Hadewijch's poems on *Minne* 182–203; and Vanderauwera.

116. Shea 73, 79–81.

117. Visions 3, 6, and 7 also occur after she has received the Eucharist.

118. Hadewijch 22–24.

119. Hadewijch 266. See Hart's reading of this vision, xi–xii, 24–25.

120. Hadewijch 276. Other examples include Visions 6–8 and 10–13.

121. Hadewijch 297. Hildegard also describes God with wings, see Newman 18.

122. See Hadewijch, Visions 5 (276), 10 (281), and 20 (287, 293–96). Teresa of Ávila also experienced being carried through the air by an eagle, 136.

123. Hadewijch 102, 290.

124. Hart (193–210) devotes a chapter to him, but virtually ignores the aerial female saints.

125. To my knowledge, the only other male saints to levitate are John of the Cross—who, however, did so in the company of Teresa of Ávila (Hart 194–95)—and Francis of Assisi. For levitation of male saints, see Hart, who adds Philip Neri and Dominic of Jesus-Mary to the list of male levitators, 193–210; and Leroy 32–135. Leroy dismisses many of these levitations, but not that of St. Joseph of Copertino, 148–68.

126. Hart 196.

127. Hart 199.

CHAPTER 11

1. Schimmel 14–15. For a traditional discussion see Kalābādhī 5–12.

2. Schimmel 23–97, 228–58.

3. The exact dating of Rābi'ah is problematic; see Helms.

4. Margaret Smith, *Rabi'a the Mystic and Her Fellow-Saints in Islam* 74–76, 87. Helms has a helpful critique of this well-known study of Rābi'ah, see 2–3, 10–11.

5. Smith, *Rabia'a* 25.

6. Helms (15–16) discusses this and other incidents as her "direct, interactive relation with God."

7. Smith, *Rabia'a* 8.

8. Smith, *Rabia'a* 55–57, 69–70.

9. Annemarie Schimmel discusses her enduring influence on Ṣūfīs, e.g., 36–41, 53. See also Kalābādhī, who includes a verse on love attributed to her, 113 and n. 2, as well as other comments she made, e.g., 91–92, 103, and 175; and Smith, *Rabia'a* 96–110.

10. Paraphrasing Smith, *Rabia'a* 98.

11. Helms discusses 'Attar's presentation of Rābi'ah and his text in general, 1–2, 12–14, 47–53, n. 3.

12. Smith, *Rabia'a* 4. In addition to Smith, studies of women and Islam include Beck and Keddie; Betteridge; Fernea and Fernea; and Stowasser. Helms lists additional sources on Rābi'ah, see 62, fns. 5 and 6.

13. Helms discusses 'Attar's statement as neither denigrating womanhood nor adulating manhood, "Rābi'ah as Mystic," 39–40.

14. Smith, *Rabia'a*, 13–14, and Helms, "Rābi'ah as Mystic," 55–57, n. 4.

15. Attar 45.

16. For example, Attar 38, 83–84, 122; Shah, *Tales of the Dervishes* 84–85; and Smith, *Rabia'a* 187.

17. Arberry translates Abū Bakr al-Kalābādhī's discussion of the miracles saints could perform, 62–66; and Nicholson describes some miracles performed by Ṣūfīs, though his early twentieth-century orientalism is very heavy-handed; see 133–46. Shah, *The Sufis*, adds to the discussion, 367–88.

18. Muḥammad's flight is alluded to in the Qur'ān, Sūras 17:1 and 53:1–18. Rustomji discusses it at length, see 26–36. Waugh discusses additional sources for the *Mi'rāj*, see 25–38, as well as the flight itself, though only in terms of its symbolism, see 40–69. He makes the point that "because of the unity and singularity of God, Islam required symbols capable of formalizing the immediate relationship with God without compromising the latter; transcendent-type images could provide means of relating with God in a personal manner without being committed to literalness—the symbol could bear the presence of God without the restrictions of definition," iii. The *Mi'rāj* is also commemorated as a national holiday in several Middle Eastern countries, respectively, 67 and 40, n. 2. The flying horse is a frequent motif in *The Arabian Nights*, Tuczay 281, and thus part of Arabic folk belief; see, e.g., the tale of Hasan of Basra in chapter 4.

19. Rustomji discusses its reception and the problems some Muslims experienced with it, 30–31. See also Séguy's commentary on a fifteenth-century Turkish manuscript, 7–30.

20. Awliya 314.

21. This story was embellished by poets and depicted by Persian and Mughal artists, Schimmel 220, 226. See Rustomji's brief discussion of its evolution as a story and in iconography, respectively, 26–28 and 139–148; and Woodward for a sampling of various versions of this story, 191–97. Unfortunately, his citations are poor.

22. Rustomji 27.

23. Schimmel 27, 41, 48, 94, 218–219, 255, 303. Kugle has a thought-provoking analysis of the relationship of Muḥammad's ascension to Ṣūfī beliefs about the integration of body and spirit in mystical experience, 123–80, while Schimmel comments that abstaining "from food as much as possible" is required for experiencing spiritual ascension (255), something we have seen above in the case of Christian women mystics. Waugh traces the development of levitation theory in Ṣūfī circles, see 31–38, 70–92, and 151–54.

24. Smith, *Rabi'a*, and *Readings from the Mystics of Islam* 195–98.

25. Schimmel has a good discussion of the history of and arguments for and against the legitimacy of dancing and listening to music as mystical states, 179–86. Studies of the Mevlevis include Shah, *The Sufis* 294–346; and Trimingham.

26. Seeking the state of ecstasy was not limited to the Mevlevis; many Ṣūfīs aspired to this state, see Kalābādhī for Arberry's discussion of ecstasy or intoxication, 121–23; and Nicholson 59–67.

27. Glassé 268–69.

28. Schimmel, respectively, 185, 181.

29. Kugle 103–04.

30. See the discussion of female Ṣūfī saints in Kugle 81–121.

31. Austin 1–16.

32. Ibn 'Arabī 154.

33. Ibn 'Arabī 154–55.

34. In many parts of the Muslim world there are trees sacred to saints that share in their miraculous powers, such as curing illness, protecting children, and so on, see Smith, *Rabia'a* 200.

35. Smith, *Rabia'a* 188–89.

36. The current romanization is *Zhuangzi*

37. Translated by Schafer, *Pacing the Void* 243.

38. Wong xvii–xxiii. Daoist sexual practices are remarkably similar to those of Tantric Buddhism, discussed in chapter 7, especially in the way men are told to avoid ejaculation as a way to gain energy (*qi*) from their sexual partners; see Despeux and Kohn 9–10. See also Despeux and Kohn's discussion of alchemy, 19–21, 177–243. Robson presents a few texts on sexual practices, 623–26.

Introductions to Daoism include Boltz; and Welch. A useful, rich anthology of Daoist texts is Robson, though he does not include Sun Bu'er.

39. Ho and O'Brien 12–22. For more information on Daoist flight, see Kohn 81–86, 90–95, 112–14; and Kaltemark, especially 8–13. Schafer, *Pacing the Void* has a good discussion of the early roots of the Daoist belief in self-propelled human flight and of later beliefs, as well as the expression of those beliefs in poetry, 234–69.

40. See Birrell's discussion of evolving ideas about longevity and immortality, 181–82, 187–88.

41. Kaltemark.

42. Kaltemark 8–9.

43. Robson 380–82.

44. Cleary 56. In addition to the women discussed below, Despeux and Kohn list other women who have ascended to heaven, 87–88, 92–93, 124–25.

45. See the Chinese dancers discussed in chapter 4.

46. The pinyin system of transliteration has replaced the earlier Wade-Giles system. Dao is in pinyin, Tao in Wade-Giles. The sources I have consulted use both systems.

47. Wong xvi–xxiii.

48. Wong 54–59; and Despeux and Kohn 18. There are many examples of women disfiguring themselves in order to pursue a spiritual path, e.g., the Japanese Zen nun Ryōnen Genso (1646–1711), see Serinity Young, *An Anthology of Sacred Texts By and About Women* 325–26. As will be shown below, pretending to be insane seems to have been a common ploy among Daoist women who wanted to escape difficult husbands or domestic constraints in order to pursue the spiritual path.

49. There is some evidence that certain Daoists performed sexual practices in public, see Ho and O'Brien 21. Kohn (81) notes the shamanic influence on Daoism, and it will be recalled that shamanism often involved sexual activities; see chapter 9.

50. Wong 120–21. See also Despeux and Kohn 11.

51. Despeux and Kohn 18. Her monastic school of Complete Perfection remains dominant in China today, ibid., 140. For a list of sources on her from the Daoist Canon and other texts see ibid., 143–44, n. 4.

52. Despeux and Kohn 143. I have discussed the importance of conception dreams in the biographies of several Buddhist figures, *Dreaming in the Lotus*, 21–24, 75–85.

53. Despeux and Kohn 142–47.

54. Innumerable translations of the *Dao De Jing*, or *Tao Te Ching*, are available. Frequently used translations and discussion of the text include Blakney; Lau; and Waley. For recent discussions of Laozi's life and dating, see Henricks; and LaFargue. Robson gives fair warning about several "versions" of the *Dao De Jing* presented as translations by enthusiastic westerners, most notably Ezra Pound, 740–41.

55. Lau, *Tao Te Ching*, e.g., chapters 6 and 15. Zhuangzi also emphasizes the female nature of the sage, 27–28. See Despeux and Kohn's discussion of women and female imagery, 6–8, and their discussion of yin, 8–10, 36–40.

56. Despeux and Kohn 21. See their detailed discussion of this, 177–243.

57. James R. Ware 57–58.

58. James R. Ware 194.

59. Giles (35) believes this story to have been written down by 30 BCE. Despeux and Kohn discuss both these stories in connection with Daoist practices, 87–79.

60. Burton Watson, story I:13, 33–34.

61. Kohn 92–95. See also Kroll's translation of and comments on one important example, 156–65.

62. Some studies of women in Daoism include Ahern; Chen; Cleary; Despeux and Kohn; Kirkland; and Reed.

63. Despeux and Kohn 17–18.

64. Schafer, *The Golden Peaches of Samarkand* 113. A similar feather cape is worn by another female sage in a painting on silk at the Freer Gallery of Art, accession number F1916.46. Waterbury discusses an 8.2 cm high bronze figure of a human being wearing a bird mask and a feather garment that dates from the late Zhou dynasty, 92–93, shown in plate XXII and held by the Brooklyn Museum, accession number L 49.4.82

65. Despeux and Kohn 84.

66. Schafer, *The Golden Peaches of Samarkand* 113.

67. Kaltemark 10–11.

68. Despeux and Kohn 75, quoting the *Yunji qiqian* 31.10b, 11b.

69. Despeux and Kohn 74. Schafer, *Pacing the Void* has a good discussion of these star women, 131–48.

70. Kohn 84.

71. Robson 61.

72. Translated by Schafer, *Pacing the Void* 237. There were far-roving hats as well, ibid., 236.

73. Kohn 86.

74. Kohn (91) lists further similarities, as do Despeux and Kohn 85. See their general discussion of the Immortals and their techniques, 83–98.

75. Kohn 108; for some of their practices see ibid., 113–14. See also Schipper's translation of and comments on two poems from Yang Zi's collection, 402–04.

76. Despeux and Kohn 6, 13–16, 110–18.

77. Watson 78–79.

78. Despeux and Kohn 13–14. For additional examples of Daoist women teachers see ibid. 129–74. Robson has a short biography of her, 396–98.

79. Despeux and Kohn 14. See also Kohn 86.

80. Birrell 137. This combination of birds and war is suggestive of Valkyries and *apsarās*. For a brief account of this myth cycle, see 130–37.

81. Despeux and Kohn discuss this complex deity, 48–63.

82. Despeux and Kohn 60–61, quoting the *Youngceng jixian lu* 1.8b.

83. Despeux and Kohn 61, quoting Sima Qian's *Shiji* (*Records of the Historian*). This is reminiscent of the story of the Bamboo Cutter's Daughter translated by Dickins as *The Old Bamboo-Hewer's Story*.

84. Ho and O'Brien 23; the telling of the story cycle continues to this day, Despeux and Kohn 35.

85. Ho and O'Brien 132.

86. Cleary briefly discusses her as having received this ability as a gift, 11, 13.

87. Ho and O'Brien 30.

88. Ho and O'Brien 133–36.

89. See Despeux and Kohn's discussion of these two points of view regarding women, 1–5, and their discussion of Confucianism's influence, and lack of influence, on the roles of Daoist women, 14–15, 21–22.

90. Despeux and Kohn 135. In a 1907 Buddhist text, she takes the opposite position, see 137.

91. Cleary 12–13; Despeux and Kohn 101.

92. The connection with the Cinderella story-cycle is of interest. Dorothy Ko dates the earliest version of the Cinderella story, whose heroine is called Yexian, to ninth century China. The story predates the Qin dynasty (221–206 BCE), see 25–28.

93. Cleary 10–11. Campany translates her story, 146–47. A text entitled the *Holy Mother Manuscript* was anonymously composed in 793 to record the renovation of her temple near Yangzhou and was inscribed on a stele in 1088. A rubbing of this is at the Freer Gallery of Art, accession number F1998.41.

94. Cleary 13. See also Despeux and Kohn 99–100. Campany also comments on relations between several Daoist married couples, 139–48.

95. Cleary 72–73.

96. Rhys Davids and Stede 120, col. b. See also Dehejia's discussion of the *aṣṭamahāsiddhi*s (the eight great *siddhi*s), *Yoginī Cult and Temples* 53–54, and Mahony, "Flying Priests" 51–52, 69–71.

97. Rhys Davids and Carpenter, *Dīgha Nikāya*, I:ii.86.

98. See the discussion in Katz, *Buddhist Images of Human Perfection* 106–17. Mahony compares Buddhist practices to those of Hindu *yogī*s and of shamans, respectively, "Flying Priests" 86–105 and 106–49.

99. Rhys Davids and Stede 120, col. b.

100. Tsai 19.

101. Robinson 210.

102. See p. 285, n. 87.

103. Chonam and Kandro 188.

104. Chonam and Kandro 191.

105. Chonam and Kandro 193.

106. See the discussion of the subtle body in chapter 7.

107. Chonam and Kandro 22, n. 15.

108. Discussed in Young, *Courtesans and Tantric Consorts* 151–53.

109. Dowman 96.

110. Dowman 94.

111. Dowman 160.

112. Dowman 178–80. Examples of other women who flew up to the sky and did not leave bodies behind appear in Dan Martin 60.

113. For more information on her, see the history of her lineage in book 9 of *The Blue Annals* 728–52. Jamgon Kongtrul refers to her as Sukāsiddhī, 93, 210; and Mullin.

114. Mullin 96–97.

115. Janet Gyatso briefly discusses her problematic dating, "The Development of the Gcod Tradition," 330 and n. 38. Herrmann-Pfandt dates her death to 1149, "On a Previous Birth Story of Ma gcig Lab sgron ma," 19. The biography of another female *chodpa*, A-Yu Kadro, appears in Allione 233–64.

116. Edou 116.

117. Allione 144–45.

118. Heather Stoddard, lecture, Tibet House, New York City, April 2, 2001.

119. Edou 137. See also the biography of A-Yu Khandro, who initially studied with her aunt, practiced with other female *chodpas*, and had many female disciples, Allione 233–64.

120. Evans-Wentz, *Tibetan Yoga* 311–12. Orofino summarizes Western literature on *gCod* and its Tibetan sources, 396–97, 411–12, and her summary of its history and basic premises is helpful, 398–410.

121. Orofino 404. Herrmann-Pfandt has an interesting discussion of this practice in rela-tion to a past-life story about Machig, "On a Previous Birth Story," 19–22. Two important *gCod* manuscripts are translated and discussed in Evans-Wentz, *Tibetan Yoga*, 277–334.

122. See, for instance "The Story of the Tigress," in Āryaśūra 1–8.

123. Allione 149, see also 246–47, where *chodpas* take care of a dead body, and 253, where one cures an epidemic among livestock.

124. Mullin 186. Unfortunately, Mullin does not offer any citation other than a vague refer-ence to Machig's biography.

CHAPTER 12

1. This had been preceded by an equally fevered interest in ballooning, beginning in the late eighteenth century, in which women played a prominent role, especially Sophie Blanchard (1778–1819), who received formal aeronautical positions from both Napoleon and the restored Louis XVIII. In the late nineteenth century, Englishwomen performed various aeronauti-cal feats, such as acrobatics (often in scanty costumes), parachute jumps, and the like, see Holmes, respectively, 40–46, 305–09.

2. Berg has a brief description of this history, *Lindbergh* 60–62, to which must be added Holmes. See Laufer, *The Prehistory of Aviation*, for a deeper history. For the role of women in early aviation, see Ware 60–89; Boase; and Deborah C. Douglas. An index of women in aviation is available in Egan, http://www.ctie.monash.edu.au/hargrave/pioneers.html.

3. See the discussion in Pomeroy, e.g., 8–15.

4. Harmon has a rather glib play on this, 185–86.

5. See, e.g., *Wonder Woman* No. 1, Summer 1942, in Marston and Peter 1:171.

6. As Goldstein notes: "This mix of sex-object and power figure recurs in the Amazon genre," 19.

7. The plane is introduced in *Sensation Comics* No. 2, January 1942. It is said to be transpar-ent and invisible, Marston and Peter 1:18 and 28. After her creator Marston's death, she was given a new history and the ability to fly, *Wonder Woman* No. 105, April 1959. See Robinson's discussion of this, 79.

8. It cannot be ignored that this is reminiscent of the daredevil women "wing walkers," who stood on wings of airborne planes and performed even more daring feats at flying circuses; see the discussion in Boase 21–26.

9. See, e.g., Eller, *The Myth of Matriarchal Prehistory*. Lepore has written a fascinating pro-file of Marston, his complexities, and his surprising relationships, such as a ménage à trois in which one of the women, Olive Byrne, was Margaret Sanger's niece, 64–73.

10. *Wonder Woman* No. 1, Summer 1942, in Marston and Peter 1:147.

11. *Wonder Woman Comics* No. 7, Winter 1942, cited by Robinson 36.

12. Marston and Peter 1:15.

13. Marston and Peter 1:8–16.

14. Robinson discusses Wonder Woman's immortality being changed to longevity, 34–37. Aging would definitely have presented a problem to her heroic stature.

15. She begins as a nurse in *Sensation Comics* No. 1, January 1942, but in No. 3, March 1942, when Steve Trevor is well enough to leave the hospital, she begs him to get her a job as a secretary in his office, which he does. Both in Marston and Peter vol. 1. Although she is still a nurse in No. 9, September 1942, the issue also refers to her as a stenographer, 1:134.

16. *Wonder Woman* No. 1, Summer 1942, in Marston and Peter 1:157. This lasso is elaborated upon in *Sensation Comics* No. 6, June 1942, ibid., 1:93–94.

17. These and many more details about Wonder Woman's origins and homeland are in *Wonder Woman* No. 1, Summer 1942, in Marston and Peter 1:143–48, which is an expansion of her introduction in *Introducing Wonder Woman*, ibid., 1:8–16.

18. This is told in the No. 1, Summer 1942, issue, in Marston and Peter 1:143–58.

19. In traditional societies, women are often referred to by their son's name, and many women throughout the world abandon their own (maiden) name to be called Mrs. So-and-So.

20. In Marston and Peter 1:69.

21. Marston and Peter 1:9.

22. *Sensation Comics* No. 2, February 1942, in Marston and Peter 1:32.

23. Robinson delineates some of that history, 78–88, 130–33. See also Daniels; Edgar; and Lepore.

24. Marston and Peter 1:9.

25. They are introduced in *Sensation Comics* No. 2, February 1942, in Marston and Peter 1:31–44.

26. Dorothy Arzner, director, *Christopher Strong*, 1933, distributed by RKO Radio Pictures, Inc. Katharine Hepburn saw the film's character as similar to Amelia Earhart, whom she greatly admired, Berg, *Kate Remembered* 141–43. Several types of planes from this period were variously called Gipsy Moth, Puss Moth, Moth Major, Tiger Moth, etc., see Boase 32, 91, so the moth allusion in the film is doubly appropriate.

27. Susan Ware 60–89.

28. Susan Ware 81; and Butler 230. The camaraderie of the participants led to the establishment of the Ninety-Nines, the first organization for female pilots, Butler 232–33.

29. Lindbergh's biographer, Berg, suggests she was "coiffed and costumed to look a little too much like Lindbergh," *Lindbergh* 278. See also Lovell 95, 107–108, 111, 122, etc.; and Earhart's initial comments on this comparison, 115–16. Susan Ware offers a thoughtful reading of the comparison, 16–24.

30. Susan Ware 78–82; and Corn 79–80. Earhart also spoke out in defense of female pilots who crashed, e.g., Butler 136–37. Rickman, "The Female Pilots We Betrayed," writes that Cornelia Fort crashed and was killed because another (male) pilot flew too close to her plane, severing off one of her wings. See also Rickman, *WASP of the Ferry Command*.

31. Butler 94–97; see 97ff for more about their complicated relationship.

32. All cited by Susan Ware 62 and 63. Boase discusses them at greater length, especially Lady Heath, as well as other early international female pilots. Additional books by early female aviators include Lindbergh, *North to the Orient*, and *Listen, the Wind!*; and Markham, to name only a few.

33. Joseph J. Corn; and Kolm.

34. Lovell (103) discusses this flight and its sources. Earhart's later record-setting flights were as a pilot, e.g., as the first woman to fly solo across the United States from the Atlantic to Pacific coast, to make the return flight, etc., ibid., 136–37. See also Earhart's own book about that flight, *20 Hrs.*; and the *Amelia Earhart Papers*, Schlesinger Library, Radcliffe College.

35. Butler discusses her precocious athleticism, 39–40, 43–44, 49–50, etc.

36. Earhart ix.

37. Butler 179, quoting the *New York Times*, June 4, 1928.

38. Butler 232–33, ninety-nine being the number of women pilots who applied to fly in the "Powder Puff Derby." The organization is still in existence; see ninety-nines.org.

39. Susan Ware 24, emphasis in the original. See also ibid., 43–44, 57–59; as well as the chapter on women and aviation that Earhart included in *20 Hrs.*, 137–44.

40. Butler 125–31.

41. Lovell 32–33; and Earhart 10–13.

42. Brooks-Pazmany 4.

43. Butler 92–93.

44. Susan Ware has a chapter on the financial aspects of Earhart's career, 90–116; see also 206–09, 213.

45. Susan Ware 48.

46. She did this in a letter she gave to Putnam moments before they were married on February 7, 1931. The letter is reproduced in Lovell 165–66; photographs of this extraordinary document appear, ibid., before 199. Susan Ware also quotes and discusses it, 50–54; as does Butler 251–52.

47. Susan Ware 49.

48. Lovell 248–54. See also Susan Ware 212, 218–19.

49. Lovell 242, 271. The USS *Swann* was a reconfigured minesweeper that could carry light aircraft. It had been in the best position on her first attempt but, unfortunately, not on the second.

50. Lovell 292ff. In 1964, Jerrie Mock (1925–2014) became the first woman to fly solo around the world. It is some measure of how little things had changed for women that she was never inducted into the National Aviation Hall of Fame, and during a television appearance she was asked who cleaned the house for her husband while she was away for twenty-nine days, see Weber.

51. Lovell 216–17, 233ff; and Susan Ware 69–70.

52. Lovell examines the various theories and rightly concludes that Earhart died when her plane ran out of fuel because she and/or Noonan had miscalculated their position and missed Howland Island, see 354–60. See also Butler, who examined the evidence of Japanese researchers, 417–19. More recently, the International Group for Historic Aircraft Recovery announced having found evidence that Earhart may have survived on Gardner Island, now named Nikumaroro, and is undertaking a search operation, Mendelsohn. See also "The Earhart Project," tighar.org/Projects/Earhart/AEdescr.html.

53. See the discussion of the heroine in the introduction to this book.

54. Though Earhart's husband has been viewed in many different ways, he seemingly fulfilled this role in her life, e.g., Susan Ware 131–39.

55. Fries 6.

56. Lovell 321; and Susan Ware 225–26. Two other Hollywood films about her are *Amelia*, starring Hilary Swank, 2009, and *Amelia Earhart: The Final Flight*, starring Diane Keaton, 1994, originally made for television. There are also several documentaries of varying veracity.

57. Judith Thurman.

58. See Stiehm; and Susan Ware, who puts her in the forefront of feminist figures of the twentieth century and thus looks at Earhart's contributions to the position of women in a broader context.

59. Lovell 26–27; Earhart xii–xiii, 3–8; and Susan Ware 120.

60. For example, her persistence through a grueling eight-month-long recovery from a rocket crash in order to once again be a test pilot, Reitsch, *Reminiscences of Hanna Reitsch* 23–28.

61. Piszkiewicz 34; and Lomax 49.

62. Piszkiewicz 37; and Berg, *Lindbergh* 368, which mentions the test but does not name the pilot. Reitsch discusses this flight, *Flying Is My Life* 130–40, and comments on Lindbergh, Piszkiewicz, 132. For interesting photographs and links, see Egan, http://www.ctie.monash. edu.au/hargrave/reitsch.html. Her papers are held in the Deutsches Museum in Munich and for the most part are still closed. In spring 2014, I was unable to receive permission to examine them for this project.

63. WVradioman. "Hanna Reitsch--test-pilot Interview (1976). https://www.youtube.com/ watch?v=ykre9XCoXac.

64. This is portrayed in the British film *Hitler: The Last Ten Days* (1973). The folklore about the fall of Berlin suggests that she convinced Hitler to fly out of Berlin with her and that he remained alive, see Beevor 399.

65. *United States Army Interrogation of Hanna Reitsch*, October 8, 1945. National Archives, Ref. No. AIU/IS/1, College Park, Maryland, 1, and Lomax 120–38.

66. Boase (197) is alone in granting Reitsch her due.

67. Piszkiewicz 11.

68. Reitsch, *Flying* 3.

69. Reitsch, *Reminiscences* 1; and Lomax 31. Lomax describes Reitsch's early flying experiences, see 6, 8, 12–25.

70. Reitsch, *Flying* 22. Her biography is peppered with bird imagery.

71. Reitsch, *Flying* 24.

72. Lomax 13.

73. Piszkiewicz 29, 39, 124–25.

74. Lomax 27; and Reitsch, *Flying* 86–92.

75. The American film *Operation Crossbow* (1965) depicts her testing a rocket-propelled plane.

76. Reitsch, *Flying* 109–20; and Reitsch, *Reminiscences* 16–20.

77. Lomax 37 and 39.

78. Lomax makes the case that Reitsch only gave the appearance of idolizing Hitler and kept her disappointment to herself, see 60–70.

79. Piszkiewicz describes many of her test flights, e.g., 40–45. Two other German female test pilots at the time were Melitta Schiller and Beate Koestlin, see Sigmund 13–14.

80. E.g., Piszkiewicz 52–53; and Lomax, e.g., 54–55.

81. Piszkiewicz 64.

82. For a thorough discussion of the role of women during the Third Reich, see Koonz. D'Ann Campbell discusses the military roles of German women and the German attitude toward enemy female combatants. See also Sigmund 9–20.

83. Piszkiewicz 65–66, 72–82; Lomax 87, 94–101; and Reitsch, *Flying Is My Life* 207–19. Beevor (237–38) reports incidents of German pilots crashing into Russian bombers in the spring of 1945 and a group of *Selbstopfereinsatz*, suicide-mission pilots, who crashed into bridges the Russians built across the Oder River. In his 2004 novel *Ordinary Lives* (85), Josef Skvorecky describes Germany in the spring of 1945 when everyone knew the war was lost, despite the rumor that a female suicide pilot, who was madly in love with Hitler, was going to crash a V-3 rocket into New York City. In his notes, Skvorecky identifies her as Hanna Reitsch and describes her many aeronautical feats, see 222.

84. She makes this clear in discussing the suicidal V-1 rocket, see Reitsch, *Reminiscences* 32–33.

85. There has been much speculation, though little evidence, that they were lovers. Beevor coolly refers to her as von Greim's mistress without providing any supporting evidence, see 322. Lomax refutes this, see 107.

86. See *United States Army Interrogation*, 2–3; Reitsch, *Flying* 223–37; and Lomax 107–09.

87. Clément 158.

88. See Jochens's analysis of this period, 234–38.

89. See Mees's excellent essay on this period, sydney.edu.au/arts/medieval/saga/pdf/316-mees.pdf, 318.

90. Mees 325.

91. Beevor 285, 395–96.

92. *United States Army Interrogation* 11.

93. Piszkiewicz 109.

94. *United States Army Interrogation* 14–15. Reitsch had little to say about her internment, except that it should have been more comfortable, *Flying* 238–39.

95. Lomax 122–23.

96. Piszkiewicz 120; and Cook.

97. Reitsch wrote several memoirs; see Lomax 151–53.

98. Beevor has tracked quite thoroughly the Russian moves to capture German atomic scientists, equipment, and supplies of uranium ahead of the other Allies, see 138–39, 210, 232, 324–25.

99. Rickman, *The Originals* 153–61. For her moving account of that morning and her experience ferrying planes for the US Army, see Fort, originally published in *Woman's Home Companion*, July 1943, 19.

100. See, e.g., Whittell. Boase discusses these pilots, see 177–95. Twenty-five American women pilots joined them, serving until they were recalled for duty in the United States, see Jean Hascall Cole 2. This is a series of interviews with and photographs of thirty-five women who, along with Cole, were members of a 1944 graduating class of the WASP training program, as is Elizabeth S. Bell.

101. Rickman, *The Originals* 11–12. Deborah C. Douglas has a good history of American women flyers.

102. Rickman also discusses that female pilots lacked death benefits and honors, which was almost righted when WASPs earned veterans' status in 1977 and then in 2002, when the army granted them military funeral honors and the right to be buried in Arlington Cemetery—a right that, horrifyingly, was rescinded in 2015 and that, at this writing, is up for review, see "The Female Pilots We Betrayed." See also Rickman, *The Originals* 274; and Jean Hascall Cole 1, on the number of WASPs killed during World War II.

103. Jean Hascall Cole, dedication, 123. Landdeck (193) discusses the uneven treatment of their bodies.

104. Landdeck 170.

105. Rickman, *The Originals* 165–66. At roughly the same time, the United States government sponsored Civilian Pilot Training Programs at universities in which women were allowed to participate, but at a one-to-ten or one-to-fifteen ratio with men, see Jean Hascall Cole 11; and Deborah C. Douglas 6–7. Jean Hascall Cole lists the many indignities and details the harsh treatment the women received without complaint. African American women were excluded from the WASPs on grounds of race, see, e.g., Bragg and Kriz.

106. Rickman, *The Originals* 185; and Jean Hascall Cole xvii.

107. Landdeck 175.

108. Jean Hascall Cole x, xix, 4.

109. Landdeck elaborates on this point, see 167–68, 182–95. She also has an excellent analysis of the literature about World War II female pilots and interviews with surviving WASPs.

110. Jean Hascall Cole 135–38.

111. Kevles 7–11.

112. McCullough; and Sanborn.

113. Joseph J. Corn 563, 568–69. Earhart fought against this, see Butler 337–38.

114. Kevles 6, 12–13, 30, 32–33, 47–48, 65, 73.

115. Shephard 7. For more information on Russian women pilots, see Pennington. Shepitko's heartfelt 1966 film *Wings* movingly depicts the sorrowful life of a Russian woman fighter pilot twenty years after the war. Although the film has few aerial images, toward the end it includes some beautiful and moving aerial footage as the pilot recalls following her lover's shot-up plane in its slow, inevitable descent, hovering above it and moving from side to side with the grace of a mother bird watching over her offspring's first flight. There is an incredible femaleness in her flying. The kicker is that since the war she has been grounded. She is a national heroine, and all the male pilots know her when she visits the aerodrome—one even offers her a ride. Produced by Mosfilm, *Wings* is available as a DVD in the Eclipse series of the Criterion Collection (2008).

116. Kevles 21; and D'Ann Campbell 13.

117. Goldstein 66–68.

118. Goldstein 22, 64–70.

119. Kevles 24, 26.

120. Kevles 29.

121. A short biography and discussion of Ride's training is covered in Sanborn 45–52, 87–88.

122. Douglas Martin.

123. *India Abroad*, November 7, 2003. Two birding companions recall their friendship with Chawla; see Tuthill and Conley.

124. Kevles.

125. McClintock put it succinctly: "In the chronicles of male nationalism, women . . . are all too often figured as mere scenic backdrops to the big-brass business of masculine armies and uprisings," 104.

CONCLUSION

1. Newman 247. Emphasis added.

2. Mori, *Simone de Beauvoir* 137.

3. Susan Ware 139.

4. Bennett (261–308) makes this point in relation to male worship and propitiation of fierce female deities in Nepal. See also Herrmann-Pfandt specifically on the role of ḍākinīs, "Ḍākinīs" 56–58.

5. Jarrar cites discussions in Denis de Rougemont, *Passion and Society*, translated by Montgomery Belgion (Faber and Faber, 1956) 243ff.; and Georges Bataille, *Erotism: Death and Sexuality*, translated by Mary Dalwood (City Lights Books, 1986) 71ff. See also J. H. Marks and R. M. Good, editors, *Love and Death in the Ancient Near East: Essays in Honor of Marvin H. Pope* (Four Quarters Publishing, 1987).

6. Jarrar 103.

WORKS CONSULTED

PRIMARY SOURCES

Abhayadatta. *Caturaśīta-siddha-pravṛtti*. Translated by James B. Robinson as *Buddha's Lions: The Lives of the Eighty-Four Siddhas, with the Tibetan text, Grub thob brgyad cu rtsa bzhi'i lo rgyus*, Dharma Publishing, 1979.

Aeschylus. *The Eumenides by Aeschylus*. Translated by Hugh Lloyd-Jones, Prentice-Hall, 1970.

Allione, Tsultrim. *Women of Wisdom*. Routledge, 1984.

Amelia Earhart Papers. Schlesinger Library, Radcliffe College.

Apuleius. *Metamorphoses*. Translated by Robert Graves as *The Golden Ass*, Farrar, Straus & Giroux, 1951.

Aristophanes. *Five Comedies of Aristophanes*. Translated by Benjamin Bickley Rogers, Doubleday, 1955.

Āryaśūra. *The Jātakamālā*. 1895. Translated by J. S. Speyer, Motilal Banarsidass, 1982.

Aśvaghoṣa. *Saundarānanda Mahākāvya of Ācārya Aśvaghoṣa with Tibetan and Hindi Translations*. Translated by Ācārya Shri L. Jamspal, Central Institute of Higher Tibetan Studies, 1999; *The Saundarānanda or Nanda the Fair*. Edited by E. H. Johnston, Oxford UP, 1932.

Attar, Farid al-Din. *Muslim Saints and Mystics: Episodes from the Tadhkirat al-Auliya' ('Memorial of the Saints') by Farid al-Din Attar*. Translated by Arthur John Arberry, Arkana, 1990.

Awliya, Nizam ad-din. *Nizam ad-din Awliya: Morals for the Heart*. Translated by Bruce B. Lawrence, Paulist Press, 1992.

Barnstone, Willis, translator. *Greek Lyric Poetry*. Bantam Books, 1962.

Bellows, Henry Adams, translator. *The Poetic Edda*. 1923. 2 vols, Princeton UP, 1936.

Betz, Hans Dieter, editor. *The Greek Magical Papyri in Translation, Including the Demotic Spells*. 2nd ed., 2 vols. U of Chicago P, 1992.

Bhavabhūti. *Mālatīmādhavam*. Edited and translated by C. R. Devadhar and N. G. Suru, C. R. Devadhar and N. G. Suru, 1935.

Blakney, R. B., translator. *The Way of Life—Lao Tzu*. New American Library, 1955.

Bloomfield, Maurice, translator. *Hymns of the Atharva-Veda*. 1897. Reprint, Motilal Banarsidass, 1979.

Boer, Charles, translator. *The Homeric Hymns*. The Swallow Press, 1970.

Boltz, Judith M. *A Survey of Taoist Literature: Tenth to Seventeenth Centuries*. Institute of East Asian Studies, U of California, 1987.

Bragg, Janet, and Marjorie M. Kriz. *Soaring Above Setbacks: The Autobiography of Janet Harmon Bragg, African American Aviator*. Smithsonian Institution P, 1996.

Budge, E. A., translator. *The Egyptian Book of the Dead: The Papyrus of Ani in the British Museum*. 1895. Reprint, Dover Publications, 1967.

Buitenen, J. A. B. van, editor and translator. *The Mahābhārata*. U of Chicago P, 1975.

Burton, Richard F., translator. *The Book of the Thousand Nights and a Night: A Plain and Literal Translation of the Arabian Nights Entertainments*. 10 vols. The Burton Club, 1885–1886 [approximate].

Byock, Jesse L., translator. *The Saga of the Volsungs: The Norse Epic of Sigurd the Dragon Slayer*. U of California P, 1990.

Charbonneau-Lassay, Louis. *The Bestiary of Christ*. Translated and abridged by D. M. Dooling, Parabola Books, 1940.

Chonam, Lama, and Sangye Khandro, translators. *The Lives and Liberation of Princess Mandarava*. Wisdom Publications, 1998.

Chuang Tzu. *Chuang Tzu: Basic Writings*. Translated by Burton Watson. New York: Columbia UP, 1964.

Civil, Miguel, et al., editors. *The Assyrian Dictionary of the Oriental Institute of the University of Chicago*. Oriental Institute, 1973.

Cleary, Thomas, translator and editor. *Immortal Sisters: Secrets of Taoist Women*. Shambhala, 1989.

Cowell, E. B., editor. *The Jātaka*. 1895. 6 vols. Reprint, Pali Text Society, 1973.

Dante Alighieri. *The Portable Dante*. Edited by Paolo Milano, Viking P, 1947.

Das, Sarat Chandra. *Tibetan-English Dictionary*. 1902. Reprint, Gaurav Publishing House, 1985.

de Cantimpré, Thomas. *The Life of Christina the Astonishing*. 2nd ed. Translated by Margot H. King, Peregrina Publishing, 1999.

Dickins, F. Victor, translator. *The Old Bamboo-Hewer's Story*. Trübner & Co., Ludgate Hills, 1888.

Dimmitt, Cornelia, and J. A. B. van Buitenen. *Classical Hindu Mythology: A Reader in the Sanskrit Purāṇas*. Temple UP, 1978.

Douglas, Kenneth, and Gwendolyn Bays, translators. *The Life and Liberation of Padmasambhava*. Dharma Publishing, 1978.

Dorson, Richard M. *Folk Legends of Japan*. Charles E. Tuttle, 1962.

Dowman, Keith, translator. *Sky Dancer: The Secret Life and Songs of the Lady Yeshe Tsogyel*. Routledge, 1984.

Earhart, Amelia. *20 Hrs., 40 Min.: Our Flight in the* Friendship. 1928. Reprint, National Geographic, 2003.

Eberhard, Wolfram, editor. *Folktales of China*. 1937. Rev. ed., Routledge, 1965.

Edgerton, Franklin, editor and translator. *Vikrama's Adventures; or, The Thirty-two Tales of the Throne*. Harvard Oriental Series, vol. 27. Harvard UP, 1926.

Eggeling, Julius, translator. *The Śatapatha Brāhmaṇa*. Sacred Books of the East, vol. 44. Oxford University Press, 1900.

Elisabeth of Schönau. *Poem on the Assumption*. Edited by J. D. Strachey. Cambridge Anglo-Norman Texts, no. xxviii. Cambridge UP, 1924.

Euripides. *Euripides: Medea and Other Plays*. Translated by Philip Vellacott, Penguin Books, 1963.

Euripides. *Iphigeneia in Tauris*. Translated by Richard Lattimore, Oxford UP, 1973.

Evans-Wentz, W. Y., translator. *The Tibetan Book of the Dead*. 1960. Reprint, Oxford UP, 1969.

Evans-Wentz, W. Y., translator. *Tibetan Yoga and Secret Doctrines*. Oxford UP, 1967.

Fausbøll, V., editor. *The Jātaka Together with Its Commentary*. 6 vols. Trübner, 1887.

Fort, Cornelia. "At Twilight's Last Gleaming." 1943. *The 99 News*, November 1985, p. 13.

Gale, James, S., translator. *Korean Folk Tales: Imps, Ghosts and Fairies*. Dutton, 1913.

Giles, Lionel, translator. *A Gallery of Chinese Immortals*. John Murray, 1948.

Ginzberg, Louis. *Legends of the Jews*. Translated by Henrietta Szold. 7 vols. The Jewish Publication Society of America, 1909.

Grimm Brothers. *Grimms' Fairy Tales*. Translated by Edgar Taylor. 1823–1826. Reprint, Penguin Books, 1996.

Grimm, Jacob. *Teutonic Mythology*. Translated from the 4th ed. by James Steven Stallybrass. 3 vols. George Bell & Sons, 1883.

Gtsaṅ smyon He ru ka. *The Hundred Thousand Songs of Milarepa*. Translated by Garma C. C. Chang, Shambhala, 1977.

Gtsaṅ smyon He ru ka. *The Life of Milarepa*. Edited by J. W. de Jong. Translated by Lobsang P. Lhalungpa, Shambala, 1984.

Gtsaṅ smyon He ru ka. *Mi la'i mGur 'Bum*. Sherab Gyaltsen, 1983.

Guenther, Herbert V., translator. *The Life and Teaching of Nāropa*. Oxford UP, 1963.

Haddawy, Husain, translator. *The Arabian Nights*. Norton, 1990.

Hadewijch of Brabant. *Hadewijch: The Complete Works*. Translated by Columba Hart, Paulist P, 1980.

Haksar, A. N. D., translator. *Simhāsana Dvātriṃsīkā: Thirty-Two Tales of the Throne of Vikramaditya*. Penguin Books India, 1998.

Hatto, A. T., translator. *The Nibelungenlied*. Penguin Group, 1965.

Hawkes, David, translator. *Ch'u Tz'u: The Songs of the South: An Ancient Chinese Anthology*. Clarendon P, 1959.

Henricks, Robert G. *Lau Tzu's Tao Te Ching: A Translation of the Startling New Documents Found at Guodian*. Columbia UP, 2000.

Hildegard of Bingen. *Scivias*. Translated by Mother Columba Hart and Jane Bishop, Paulist Press, 1990.

Ho, Kwok Man, and Joanne O'Brien, translators and editors. *The Eight Immortals of Taoism: Legends and Fables of Popular Taoism*. Penguin Books, 1991.

Homer. *The Odyssey*. Translated by Robert Fitzgerald, Doubleday, 1961.

Hreinsson, Vidar, translator. *The Complete Sagas of Icelanders, Including 49 Tales*. Leifur Eriksson Publishing, 1997.

Ibn Al'Arabī. *The Bezels of Wisdom*. Translated by R. W. J. Austin, Paulist P, 1980.

Ibn 'Arabī, Muhyiddin. *Sufis of Andalusia: The Rūḥ al-quds and al-Durrat al-fākhirah of Ibn 'Arabī*. Translated by R. W. J. Austin, U of California P, 1977.

Juliana of Norwich. *Revelations of Divine Love*. Translated by M. L. del Mastro, Image Books, 1977.

Kalābādhī, Abū Bakr al. *The Doctrine of the Ṣūfīs*. 1935. Translated by Arthur John Arberry, Reprint, Sh. Muhammad Ashraf, 1976.

Kālidāsa. *Śakuntalā*. Translated by P. Lal as *Great Sanskrit Plays*, New Directions, 1957, pp. 11–74.

Kālidāsa. *Vikramorvaśī: An Indian Drama*. Translated by E. B. Cowell, Stephen Austin, 1851.

Kaltemark, Max, translator. *Le Lie-Sien Tchouan (Biographies legendaires des Immortels toaistes de l'antiguite)*. Publications du Centre d'etudes sinologiques de Pekin, 1953.

Kim, Myung Hee, translator. *Princess Pari*. Unpublished manuscript.

Kinsella, Thomas, translator. *The Tain*. Oxford UP, 1969.

Kongrul, Jamgon. *Jamgon Kongrul's Retreat Manual*. Translated by Ngawang Zangpo, Snow Lion, 1994.

Kramer, Heinrich, and Jakob Sprenger. *The Malleus Maleficarum*. 1928. Translated by Rev. Montague Summers, reprint, Dover Publications, 1971.

Lau, D. C., translator. *Tao Te Ching*. Penguin Books, 1963.

Leach, Maria, editor. *Funk and Wagnalls Standard Dictionary of Folklore, Mythology and Legend*. 2 vols. Funk and Wagnalls, 1949.

Lichtheim, Miriam, editor. *Ancient Egyptian Literature: A Book of Readings*. 3 vols. University of California Press, 1976.

Lindbergh, Anne Morrow. *Listen, the Wind!* Harcourt, Brace and Company, 1938.

Lindbergh, Anne Morrow. *North to the Orient*. Harcourt, Brace and Company, 1935.

Markham, Beryl. *West with the Night*. 1942. Reprint, Farrar, Straus and Giroux, 1995.

Malory, Sir Thomas. *The Works of Sir Thomas Malory*. Edited and translated by Eugène Vinaver, Clarendon P, 1947.

Marston, William Moulton, and H. G. Peter. *Wonder Woman Archives*. DC Comics, 1998.

Monier-Williams, Sir M. *Sanskrit-English Dictionary*. 1899. Reprint, Oxford UP, 1976.

Müller, F. Max, editor. *Sacred Books of the Buddhists*. Oxford UP, 1899.

Mullin, Glenn H., editor and translator. *Selected Works of the Dalai Lama II: The Tantric Yogas of Sister Niguma*. Snow Lion, 1985.

Nijo, Lady. *The Confessions of Lady Nijō*. Translated by Karen Brazell, Stanford UP, 1976.

Nowak, Margaret, and Stephen Durrant. *The Tale of the Nišan Shamaness: A Manchu Folk Epic*. U of Washington P, 1977.

O'Flaherty, Wendy Doniger, translator. *The Rig Veda*. Penguin Books, 1981.

Olivelle, Patrick, translator. *Upaniṣads*. Oxford UP, 1996.

Ovid. *Metamorphoses*. Translated by Horace Gregory, Viking P, 1958.

Pausanias. *Guide to Greece*. Translated by Peter Levi, Penguin Books, 1971.

Petroff, Elizabeth Alvilda, editor. *Medieval Women's Visionary Literature*. Oxford UP, 1986.

Plato. "Phaedo." *The Dialogues of Plato*. 1892. 2 vols. Translated by B. Jowett, reprint, Random House, 1937.

Pound, Ezra, and Ernest Fenollosa. *The Classic Noh Theatre of Japan*. 1917. Reprint, New Directions, 1959.

Pritchard, James B., editor. *The Ancient Near East: An Anthology of Texts and Pictures*. 2 vols. Princeton UP, 1958.

Ralston, William Ralston Shedden. *Tibetan Tales Derived from Indian Sources*. N.p., 1882.

Reitsch, Hanna. *Flying Is My Life*. Translated by Lawrence Wilson. Putnam, 1954.

Reitsch, Hanna. *Reminiscences of Hanna Reitsch: Oral History, 1960*. Aviation Oral History Project. Columbia U, 1960.

Rhys Davids, T. W., and J. Estlin Carpenter, editors. *Dīgha Nikāya*. 3 vols. London, 1949. An English translation is in *Sacred Books of the Buddhists*. Ed. F. Max Müller, London, 1899.

Rhys Davids, T. W., and William Stede. *Pali-English Dictionary*. 1921–1925. Reprint, Motilal Banarsidass, 1993.

Roerich, George N., translator. *The Blue Annals*. 1949. 2nd ed., Motilal Banarsidass, 1976.

Rosenqvist, Jan Olof, editor and translator. *The Life of St. Irene, Abbess of Chrysobalanton: A Critical Edition with Introduction, Translation, Notes and Indices*. Uppsala U, 1986.

Sandars, N. K., translator. *The Epic of Gilgamesh*. Penguin Books, 1960.

Saxo Grammaticus. *History of the Danes*. Translated by Peter Fisher and edited by Hilda Ellis Davidson, Rowman and Littlefield, 1979–1980.

Senart, É., editor. *Le Mahāvastu*. 3 vols. L'Imprimerie nationale, 1890.

Shastri, Biswanarayan, editor. *Yoginī Tantra*. Bharatiya Vidya Prakashan, 1982.

Smith, William. *Smith's Bible Dictionary*. 1863. Reprint, Jove Publications, 1977.

Somadeva. *Kathāsaritsāgara*. 8 vols. Edited by Jagadish Lal Sastri, Motilal Banarsidass, 1970.

Spenser, Edmund. *The Faerie Queene*. Edited by Thomas P. Roche Jr., Penguin Books, 1978.

Stary, Giovanni. *Three Unedited Manuscripts of the Manchu Epic Tale 'Nišan Saman-I Bithe'*. Kommissionsverlag Otto Harrassowitz, 1985.

Tāranātha, Jo Nang. *The Seven Instruction Lineages*. Translated by David Templeman, Library of Tibetan Works and Archives, 1983.

Tawney, C. H., translator. *The Ocean of Story*. 10 vols. Translation and rearrangement of Somadeva's *Kathāsaritsāgara*. Chas. J. Sawyer, 1924.

Teresa of Ávila. *The Life of St. Teresa of Ávila by Herself*. Translated by J. M. Cohen, Penguin Books, 1957.

Thiébaux, Marcelle, editor. *The Writings of Medieval Women: An Anthology*. 2nd ed. Garland Publishing, 1994.

Thurman, Robert A. F., translator. *The Holy Teaching of Vimalakīrti: A Mahāyāna Scripture*. The Pennsylvania State UP, 1976.

Tsai, Kathryn Ann. *Lives of the Nuns: Biographies of Chinese Buddhist Nuns from the Fourth to Sixth Centuries*. U of Hawaii P, 1994.

United States Army Interrogation of Hanna Reitsch, October 8, 1945. National Archives, Ref. No. AIU/IS/1, College Park, Maryland.

Vaidya, P. L., editor. *Lalitavistara*. Mithila Institute, 1958.

Valmiki. *The Ramayana of Valmiki*. 3 vols. Translated by Hari Prasad Shastri, Shanti Sadan, 1959.

Van Over, Raymond. *Taoist Tales*. New American Library, 1973.

Wagner, Richard. *Die Walküre*. Translated by Stewart Robb, G. Schirmer, 1960.

Waley, Arthur. *Ballads and Stories from Tun-Huang: An Anthology*. George Allen & Unwin, 1960.

Waley, Arthur. *The Nō Plays of Japan*. Alfred A. Knopf, 1922.

Waley, Arthur. *The Way and Its Power: A Study of the Tao Te Ching*. Grove P, 1958.

Watson, Burton, translator. *Record of Miraculous Events in Japan: The Nihon ryōiki*. Columbia UP, 2013.

Wolkstein, Diane, and Samuel Noah Kramer. *Inanna Queen of Heaven and Earth: Her Stories and Hymns from Sumer*. Rider and Company, 1984.

Wong, Eva, translator. *Seven Taoist Masters: A Folk Novel of China*. Shambhala, 1990.

Woolf, Virginia. *Virginia Woolf: Women and Writing*. Edited by Michèle Barrett, The Women's P, 1979.

Zong, In-Sob, translator. *Folk Tales from Korea*. Hollym Publishers, 1970.

SECONDARY SOURCES

Abusch, Tzvi. "The Demonic Image of the Witch in Standard Babylonia Literature: The Reworking of Popular Conceptions by Learned Exorcists." *Religion, Science, and Magic*, edited by Jacob Neusner et al., Oxford UP, 1989, pp. 27–58.

Abusch, Tzvi. *Mesopotamian Witchcraft: Toward a History and Understanding of Babylonian Witchcraft Beliefs and Literature*. Brill, 2002.

Acker, Paul. "Dragons in the Eddas and in Early Nordic Art." *Revisiting the Poetic Edda*, edited by Paul Acker and Carolyne Larrington, Routledge, 2013, pp. 53–75.

Acker, Paul, and Carolyne Larrington, editors. *Revisiting the Poetic Edda: Essays on Old Norse Heroic Legend*. Routledge, 2013.

Ackerman, Robert W. *Background in Medieval English Literature*. Random House, 1966.

Ahern, Emily M. "The Power and Pollution of Chinese Women." *Women in Chinese Society*, edited by Margery Wolf and Roxane Witke, Stanford UP, 1975, pp. 193–214.

Åhfeldt, Laila Kitzler. "3D Scanning of Gotland Picture Stones with Supplementary Material: Digital Catalogue of 3D Data." *Journal of Nordic Archaeological Sciences*, vol. 18, 2013, pp. 55–65.

Allan, Tony. *Vikings: The Battle at the End of Time*. Duncan Baird, 2002.

Anderson, Jack. *Ballet & Modern Dance: A Concise History*. 1986. 2nd ed., Princeton Book Company, 1992.

Andersson, Theodore M. *The Legend of Brynhild*. Cornell UP, 1980.

Anesaki, Masaharu. *Japanese Mythology. The Mythology of all Races*, vol. 8, edited by Louis Herbert Gray, Marshall Jones Company, 1916–32, pp. 207–387.

Ankarloo, Bengt. "Sweden: The Mass Burnings (1668–76)." *Early Modern European Witchcraft: Centres and Peripheries*, edited by Bengt Ankarloo and Gustav Henningsen,Clarendon P, 1993, pp. 285–317.

Ankarloo, Bengt, and Gustav Henningsen, editors. *Early Modern European Witchcraft: Centres and Peripheries*. Clarendon P, 1993.

Aris, Michael. *Hidden Treasures and Secret Lives: A Study of Pemalingpa (1450–1521) and the Sixth Dalai Lama (1683–1706)*. Indian Institute of Advanced Study, 1988.

Armstrong, Edward A. *The Folklore of Birds: An Enquiry into the Origin and Distribution of some Magico-Religious Traditions*. Collins, 1958.

Arthur, Marilyn. "From Medusa to Cleopatra: Women in the Ancient World." *Becoming Visible: Women in European History*, edited by Renate Bridenthal, et al., Houghton Mifflin, 1987, pp. 79–105.

Arzner, Dorothy, director. *Christopher Strong*. 1933. RKO Radio Pictures, Inc.

Atkinson, Jane Monig. "Shamanisms Today." *Annual Review of Anthropology*, vol. 21, 1992, pp. 307–30.

Austin, R. W. J. "Introduction." *The Bezels of Wisdom* by Ibn Al'Arabi, Paulist P, 1980.

Babb, Lawrence A. *The Divine Hierarchy: Popular Hinduism in Central India*. Columbia UP, 1975.

Bacigalupo, Ana Mariella. "The Mapuche Man Who Became a Woman Shaman: Selfhood, Gender Transgression, and Competing Cultural Norms." *American Ethnologist*, vol. 31, no. 3, 2004, pp. 440–57.

Bailey, Douglass W. "Reading Prehistoric Figurines as Individuals." *World Archaeology*, vol. 25, no. 3, 1994, pp. 321–31.

Bailleul-LeSuer, Rozenn, editor. *Between Heaven and Earth: Birds in Ancient Egypt*. The Oriental Institute of the U of Chicago, 2012.

Bal, Mieke. "The Rape of Narrative and the Narrative of Rape." *Literature and the Body: Essays on Populations and Persons*, edited by Elaine Scarry, Johns Hopkins UP, 1988, pp. 1–32.

Balzer, Majorie Mandelstam. "Flights of the Sacred: Symbolism and Theory in Siberian Shamanism." *American Anthropologist*, vol. 98, no. 2, 1996, pp. 305–18.

Balzer, Majorie Mandelstam. "Healing Failed Faith?: Contemporary Siberian Shamanism." *Anthropology and Humanism Quarterly*, vol. 26, no. 2, 2001, pp. 134–49.

Balzer, Majorie Mandelstam. "Rituals of Gender Identity: Markers of Siberian Khanty Ethnicity, Status, and Belief." *American Anthropologist*, vol. 83, no. 4, Dec. 1981, pp. 850–67.

Balzer, Majorie Mandelstam. "Sacred Genders in Siberia: Shamans, Bear Festivals, and Androgyny." *Shamanism: A Reader,* edited by Graham Harvey, Routledge, 2003, pp. 242–61.

Bandaranayaka, Senaka. "Sigiriya." *The Cultural Triangle,* UNECSO, 1993, pp. 112–35.

Bangdel, Dina. "Goddess of the Periphery, Goddess of the Centre: Iconology of Jnanadakini in Newar Buddhism." *Orientations*, vol. 33, no. 10, 2002, pp. 42–50.

Bapat, Jayant Bhalchandra, and Ian Mabbet. *The Iconic Female: Goddesses of India, Nepal and Tibet*. Monash UP, 2008.

Baring-Gould, Sabine. *Curious Myths of the Middle Ages*. Little, Brown, 1904.

Baroja, Julio Caro. "Witchcraft and Catholic Theology." *Early Modern European Witchcraft: Centres and Peripheries*, edited by Bengt Ankarloo and Gustav Henningsen, Clarendon P, 1993, pp. 19–43.

Baroja, Julio Caro. *The World of the Witches*. Translated by O. N. V. Glendinning, U of Chicago P, 1965.

Barstow, Anne Llewellyn. *Joan of Arc: Heretic, Mystic, Shaman*. The Edwin Mellen P, 1986.

Barton, Tamsyn. *Ancient Astrology*. Routledge, 1994.

Basham, A. L. *The Wonder That Was India*. 1954. Grove P, 1959.

Basilov, V. N. "Vestiges of Transvestism in Central-Asian Shamanism." *Shamanism in Siberia*, edited by Vilmos Diószegi and Mihály Hoppál. Translated by S. Simon, Akadémiai Kiadó, 1996, pp. 118–26.

Beaumont, Cyril W. *The Ballet Called Swan Lake*. 1952. Reprint, Dance Horizons, 1982.

Beauvoir, Simone de. *The Second Sex*. 1949. Translated and edited by Howard M. Parshley, reprint, Bantam Books, 1961.

Beck, Lois, and Nikki Keddie, editors. *Women in the Muslim World*. Harvard UP, 1978.

Bedford, Elizabeth. "Moon Cakes and the Chinese Mid-Autumn Festival: A Matter of Habitus." *Asian Material Culture*, edited by Marianne Hulsbosh et al., Amsterdam UP, 2009, pp. 17–36.

Beevor, Antony. *The Fall of Berlin 1945*. Penguin, 2002.

Bell, Elizabeth S. *Sisters of the Wind: Voices of Early Women Aviators*. Trilogy Books, 1994.

Bell, Rudolph M. *Holy Anorexia*. U of Chicago P, 1985.

Benard, Elisabeth, and Beverly Moon, editors. *Goddesses Who Rule*. Oxford UP, 2000.

Bennett, Lynn. *Dangerous Wives and Sacred Sisters: Social and Symbolic Roles of High-Caste Women in Nepal*. Columbia UP, 1983.

Berefelt, Gunnar. *A Study on the Winged Angel: The Origin of a Motif*. Almqvist & Wiksell, 1968.

Berg, A. Scott. *Kate Remembered*. G. P. Putnam's Sons, 2003.

Berg, A. Scott. *Lindbergh*. 1998. Berkley Books, 1999.

Berger, John. *Ways of Seeing*. Penguin Books, 1972.

Bernal, Francine Viret. "When Painters Execute a Murderess: The Representation of Clytemnestra on Attic Vases." *Naked Truths: Women, Sexuality, and Gender in Classical Art and Archaeology*, edited by Ann Olga Koloski-Ostrow and Claire L. Lyons, Routledge, 1997, pp. 93–107.

Bessone, Federica. "Medea's Response to Catullus: Ovid, *Heroides* 12.23-4 and Catullus 76.1-6." *The Classical Quarterly*, vol. 45, no. 2, 1995, pp. 575–78.

Betteridge, Anne H. "Domestic Observances: Muslim Practices." *EOR*, vol. 4, 1987, pp. 404–407.

Bilinkoff, Jodi. *The Avila of St. Teresa: Religious Reform in a Sixteenth-Century City*. Cornell UP, 1989.

Birrell, Anne. *Chinese Mythology: An Introduction*. Johns Hopkins UP, 1993.

Bisschop, Peter. "The Abode of the Pañchamurdrās: A Yoginī Temple in Early Medieval Vārāṇasī." *"Yogini" in South Asia: Interdisciplinary Approaches*, edited by István Keul, Routledge, 2013, pp. 47–60.

Blacker, Carmen. *The Catalpa Bow: A Study of Shamanistic Practices in Japan*. Allen & Unwin, 1975.

Bleeker, C. J. "Isis and Hathor: Two Ancient Egyptian Goddesses." *The Book of the Goddess: Past and Present*, edited by Carl Olson, Crossroad Publishing Company, 1989, pp. 29–48.

Bleeker, C. J. "Isis and Nephthys as Wailing Women." *Numen*, vol. 5, no. 1, Jan. 1958, 1–17.

Bloch, Maurice. "Death, Women and Power." *Death and the Regeneration of Life*, edited by Maurice Bloch and Jonathan Parry, Cambridge UP, 1982, pp. 211–30.

Bloch, Maurice, and Jonathan Parry, editors. *Death and the Regeneration of Life*. Cambridge UP, 1982.

Bloch, Maurice, and Jonathan Parry. "Introduction." *Death and the Regeneration of Life*, edited by Maurice Bloch and Jonathan Parry, Cambridge UP, 1982, pp. 1–44.

Bloom, Harold. *Omen of the Millennium: The Gnosis of Angels, Dreams, and Resurrection*. Riverhead Books, 1996.

Boase, Wendy. *The Sky's the Limit: Women Pioneers in Aviation*. Macmillan, 1979.

Boedeker, Deborah. *Aphrodite's Entry into Greek Epic*. Brill, 1974.

Bogoras, W. *The Chukchee Religion*. Memoirs of the American Museum of Natural History, vol. xi. American Museum of Natural History, 1907.

Bolle, Kees W. "Hieros Gamos." *EOR*, vol. 6, 1987, pp. 317–21.

Boswell, John. *Christianity, Social Tolerance, and Homosexuality: Gay People in Western Europe from the Beginning of the Christian Era to the Fourteenth Century*. U of Chicago P, 1980.

Bottigheimer, Ruth B. "Tale Spinners: Submerged Voices in Grimms' Fairy Tales." *New German Critique*, vol. 27, Fall 1982, pp. 141–50.

Bourke, Angela. *The Burning of Bridget Cleary: A True Story*. 1999. Reprint, Penguin Group, 2001.

Bowden, Ross. "Sorcery, Illness and Social Control in Kwoma Society." *Sorcerer and Witch in Melanesia*, edited by Michele Stephen, Rutgers UP, 1987, pp. 193–204.

Bowie, Fiona, editor. *Beguine Spirituality*. Crossroad, 1990.

Brewer, D. S. "The Present Study of Malory." *Arthurian Romance: Seven Essays*, edited by D. D. R. Owen, Barnes and Noble Books, 1970, pp. 83–97.

Bridenthal, Renate, et al., editors. *Becoming Visible: Women in European History*. 2nd ed. Houghton Mifflin, 1987.

Briggs, Katharine. *A Dictionary of Fairies*. Penguin Books, 1976.

Briggs, Katharine. *The Fairies in Tradition and Literature*. Routledge, 2002.

Brooks-Pazmany, Kathleen. *United States Women in Aviation 1919–1929*. Smithsonian Studies in Air and Space, no. 5. Smithsonian Institution P, 1983.

Budge, E. A. Wallis. *The Gods of the Egyptians: Studies in Egyptian Mythology*. 2 vols. 1904. Reprint, Dover, 1969.

Bulkeley, Kelly. *Spiritual Dreaming: A Cross-Cultural and Historical Journey*. Paulist P, 1995.

Burkert, Walter. *Greek Religion*. Translated by John Raffan, Harvard UP, 1985.

Burton, Henry Fairfield. "The Worship of the Roman Emperors." *The Biblical World*, vol. 40, no. 2, 1912, pp. 80–91.

Butler, Susan. *East to the Dawn: The Life of Amelia Earhart*. Da Capo P, 1999.

Bynum, Caroline Walker. *Fragmentation and Redemption: Essays on Gender and the Human Body in Medieval Religion*. Zone Books, 1992.

Bynum, Caroline Walker. *Holy Feast and Holy Fast: The Religious Significance of Food to Medieval Women*. U of California P, 1987.

Bynum, Caroline Walker. *Jesus as Mother: Studies in the Spirituality of the High Middle Ages*. U of California P, 1982.

Cabezón, José Ignacio. "Mother Wisdom, Father Love: Gender-based Imagery in Mahāyāna Buddhist Thought." *Buddhism, Sexuality, and Gender*, edited by José Ignacio Cabezón, State U of New York P, 1992, pp. 181–99.

Caciola, Nancy. *Discerning Spirits: Divine and Demonic Possession in the Middle Ages*. Cornell UP, 2003.

Cadden, Joan. *Meanings of Sex Difference in the Middle Ages: Medicine, Science and Culture*. Cambridge UP, 1993.

Cagni, Luigi. "Winged Genius." *Angels from the Vatican: The Invisible Made Visible*, edited by Allen Duston and Arnold Nesselrath, Art Services International, 1998, pp. 95–101.

Cahill, Suzanne. *Transcendence and Divine Passion: The Queen Mother of the West in Medieval China*. Stanford UP, 1993.

Caldwell, Sarah. "Bhagavati: Ball of Fire." *Devī: Goddesses of India*, edited by John Stratton Hawley and Donna Marie Wulff, U of California P, 1996, pp. 195–226.

Cameron, Averil, and Amélie Kuhrt, editors. *Images of Women in Antiquity*. Croom Helm, 1983.

Campany, Robert Ford. *To Live as Long as Heaven and Earth: A Translation and Study of Ge Hong's Traditions of Divine Transcendents*. U of California P, 2002.

Campbell, D'Ann, "Women in Combat: The World War Two Experience in the United States, Great Britain, Germany and the Soviet Union." *Journal of Military History*, vol. 57, April 1993, pp. 301–23.

Campbell, Joseph. *The Hero With A Thousand Faces*. 1949. Reprint, The World Publishing Company, 1956.

Campbell, June. *Traveller in Space: In Search of Female Identity in Tibetan Buddhism*. George Braziller, 1996.

Capel, Anne K., and Glenn E. Markoe, editors. *Mistress of the House, Mistress of Heaven: Women in Ancient Egypt*. Hudson Hills P, 1996.

Carnegy, Patrick. *Wagner and the Art of the Theatre*. Yale UP, 2006.

Carstairs, G. Morris. *Death of a Witch: A Village in North India 1950–1981*. Hutchinson, 1983.

Certeau, Michel de. *The Possession at Loudun*. Translated by Michael B. Smith, U of Chicago P, 1996.

Chalier-Visuvalingam, Elizabeth. "Bhairava and the Goddess: Tradition, Gender and Transgression." *Wild Goddesses in India and Nepal*, edited by Axel Michaels et al., Peter Lang, 1996, pp. 253–301.

Chance, Jane. *Woman as Hero in Old English Literature*. Syracuse UP, 1986.

Chen, Ellen Marie. "Tao as the Great Mother and the Influence of Motherly Love in the Shaping of Chinese Philosophy." *History of Religions*, vol. 14, no. 1, 1974, pp. 51–64.

Chitgopekar, Nilima. "Yoginīs in Madhya Pradesh: An Epigraphic Study." *"Yogini" in South Asia: Interdisciplinary Approaches*, edited by István Keul, Routledge, 2013, pp. 61–69.

Choi, Chungmoo. "Nami Ch'ae and Oksun: Superstar Shamans in Korea." *Shamans of the Twentieth Century*, edited by Ruth-Inge Heine, Irvington Publications, 1991, pp. 51–61.

Christie, Anthony. *Chinese Mythology*. Paul Hamlyn, 1968.

Cixous, Hélène. "The Laugh of the Medusa." *Signs: Journal of Women in Culture and Society*, vol. 1, no. 4, Summer 1976, pp. 875–93.

Clark, Anne L. *Elisabeth of Schönau: A Twelfth-Century Visionary*. U of Pennsylvania P, 1992.

Clark, Stuart. "Inversion, Misrule and the Meaning of Witchcraft." *Past and Present*, vol. 87, 1980, pp. 98–127.

Clément, Catherine. *Opera, or the Undoing of Women*. U of Minnesota P, 1988.

Clement, Clara Erskine. *Angels in Art*. L. C. Page, 1898.

Cohat, Yves. *The Vikings: Lords of the Sea*. H. N. Abrams, 1992.

Cohen, Beth. "Divesting the Female Breast of Clothes in Classical Sculpture." *Naked Truths: Women, Sexuality, and Gender in Classical Art and Archaeology*, edited by Ann Olga Koloski-Ostrow and Claire L. Lyons, Routledge, 1997, pp. 66–92.

Cohen, Claudine. *La femme des origines: Images de la femme dans la préhistoire occidentale*. Éditions Herscher, 2003.

Cohn, Norman. *Europe's Inner Demons: The Demonization of Christians in Medieval Christendom*. 1993. Rev. ed., U of Chicago P, 2000.

Cohn, Norman. *The Pursuit of the Millennium*. 1957. Reprint, Oxford UP, 1980.

Cole, Basil, and Robert Christian. "Angels and the World of Spirits." *Angels from the Vatican: The Invisible Made Visible*, edited by Allen Duston and Arnold Nesselrath, Art Services International, 1998, pp. 34–43.

Cole, Jean Hascall. *Women Pilots of World War II*. U of Utah P, 1992.

Cole, Susan Guettel. *Theoi Megaloi: The Cult of the Great Gods at Samothrace*. Brill, 1984.

Converse, Hyla Stuntz. "The Agnicayana Rite: Indigenous Origin?" *History of Religions*, vol. 14, no. 2, 1974, pp. 81–95.

Cook, Joan. "Hanna Reitsch, 67: A Top German Pilot." *New York Times*, Aug. 31, 1979.

Coomaraswamy, Ananda K. *Medieval Sinhalese Art*. Essex House P, 1908.

Coomaraswamy, Ananda K. *Yaksas*. 1928–1931. Munshiram Manoharlal, 2001.

Corn, Joseph J. "Making Flying 'Thinkable': Women Pilots and the Selling of Aviation, 1927–1940." *American Quarterly*, vol. 31, no. 4, Autumn 1979, pp. 556–71.

Corn, Joseph J. *Winged Gospel: America's Romance with Aviation*. Oxford UP, 1983.

Coudert, Allison. "Angels." *EOR*, vol. 1, 1987, 282–86.

Cozad, Laurie. "Spirits." *EOW*, vol. 2, 1998, 938–41.

Cozort, Daniel. *Highest Yoga Tantra: An Introduction to the Esoteric Buddhism of Tibet*. Snow Lion Publications, 1986.

Crapanzano, Vincent. "Saints, Jinn, and Dreams: An Essay in Moroccan Ethnopsychology." *Psychiatry: Journal for the Study of Interpersonal Processes*, vol. 2, no. 38, May 1975, 145–59.

Creed, Barbara. *The Monstrous-Feminine: Film, Feminism, Psychoanalysis*. Routledge, 1993.

Culianu, Ioan Petru. "Sacrilege." *EOR*, vol. 12, 1987, pp. 557–63.

Czaplicka, M. A. *Aboriginal Siberia: A Study in Social Anthropology*. Oxford UP, 1914.

Dalton, Jacob P. *The Taming of the Demons: Violence and Liberation in Tibetan Buddhism*. Yale UP, 2011.

Damico, Helen. "The Valkyrie Reflex in Old English Literature." *New Readings on Women in Old English Literature*, edited by Helen Damico and Alexandra Hennessey Olsen, Indiana UP, 1990, pp. 176–90.

Damico, Helen, and Alexandra Hennessey Olsen. *New Readings on Women in Old English Literature*. Indiana UP, 1990.

Daniels, Les. *Wonder Woman: The Life and Times of the Amazon Princess: The Complete History.* Chronicle Books, 2000.

Dargyay, Eva M. *The Rise of Esoteric Buddhism in Tibet.* Motilal Banarisdass, 1977.

Dasgupta, Shashibhushan. *Obscure Religious Cults.* 1946. 2nd ed., Firma K. L. Mukhopadhyay, 1962.

Davidson, Jane P. *The Witch in Northern European Art: 1470–1750.* Luca, 1987.

Davidson, Ronald M. *Indian Esoteric Buddhism: A Social History of the Tantric Movement.* Columbia UP, 2002.

Davies, Wendy. "Celtic Women in the Early Middle Ages." *Images of Women in Antiquity*, edited by Averil Cameron and Amélie Kuhrt, Routledge, 1983, pp. 145–66.

Davis, Natalie Zemon. "Women on Top: Symbolic Sexual Inversion and Political Disorder in Early Modern Europe." *The Reversible World: Symbolic Inversion in Art and Society*, edited by Barbara A. Babcock, Cornell UP, 1978, pp. 147–90.

Dehejia, Vidya. *Discourse in Early Buddhist Art: Visual Narratives of India.* Munshiram Manoharlal 1997.

Dehejia, Vidya. "The Very Idea of a Portrait." *Ars Orientalis*, vol. 28, 1998, pp. 40–48.

Dehejia, Vidya. *Yoginī Cult and Temples: A Tantric Tradition.* National Museum, 1986.

Demos, John Putnam. *Entertaining Satan: Witchcraft and the Culture of Early New England.* Oxford UP, 1982.

Denton, Lynn Teskey. "Varieties of Hindu Female Asceticism." *Roles and Rituals for Hindu Women*, edited by Julia Leslie, Motilal Banarsidass, 1992, pp. 211–31.

Desai, Devangana. "The Goddess Hinghalāja of the Yoginī Temple at Khajuraho." *"Yoginī" in South Asia: Interdisciplinary Approaches*, edited by István Keul, Routledge, 2013, pp. 109–16.

Desai, Devangana. *Khajuraho: Monumental Legacy.* Oxford UP, 2000.

Desjarlais, Robert R. "Healing Through Images: The Magical Flight and Healing Geography of Nepali Shamans." *Ethos*, vol. 17, no. 3, Sept. 1989, 289–307.

Desjarlais, Robert R. "Presence." *The Performance of Healing*, edited by Carol Laderman and Marina Roseman, Routledge, 1996, pp. 143–64.

Despeux, Catherine, and Livia Kohn. *Women in Daoism.* Three Pines P, 2003.

Detienne, Marcel. "Orpheus," *EOR*, vol. 11, 1987, pp. 111–14.

Devlet, Ekaterina. "Rock Art and the Material Culture of Siberian and Central Asian Shamanism." *The Archaeology of Shamanism*, edited by Neil Price, Routledge, 2001, pp. 43–55.

Dexter, Miriam Robbins. *Whence the Goddesses: A Source Book.* Pergamon P, 1990.

Diamond, Debra. "Occult Science and Bijapur's Yoginis." *Indian Painting: Theme, History and Interpretations (Essays in Honour of B. N. Goswang)*, edited by Mahesh Sharma, Mapin Publishing, 2013, pp. 1–9.

Diamond, Debra. *Yoga: The Art of Transformation.* Freer Gallery of Art, 2013.

Di Castro, Angelo Andrea. "Archaeology of the Goddess: An Indian Paradox." *The Iconic Female: Goddesses of India, Nepal, and Tibet*, edited by Jayant Bhalchandra Bapat and Ian Mabbet, Monash UP, 2008, pp. 21–41.

Diószegi, Vilmos, and Mihály Hoppál. *Shamanism in Siberia.* Translated by S. Simon, Akadémiai Kiadó, 1996.

Djakonova, V. P. "The Vestments and Paraphernalia of a Tuva Shamaness." *Shamanism in Siberia*, edited by Vilmos Diószegi and Mihály Hoppál. Translated by S. Simon, Akadémiai Kiadó, 1996, pp. 21–41.

Dolgikh, B. O. "Nganasan Shaman Drums and Costumes." *Shamanism in Siberia*, edited by Vilmos Diószegi and Mihály Hoppál. Translated by S. Simon, Akadémiai Kiadó, 1996, pp. 68–78.

Doughty, Robin. *Feather Fashions and Bird Preservation*. U of California P, 1975.

Douglas, Deborah C. *United States Women in Aviation: 1940–1985*. Smithsonian Institution P, 1990.

Douglas, Nik, and Meryl White. *Karmapa: The Black Hat Lama of Tibet*. Luzac & Company, 1976.

Dowden, Ken. *Death and the Maiden: Girls' Initiation Rites in Greek Mythology*. Routledge, 1989.

Drewal, Henry John, and Margaret Thompson Drewal. *Gelede: Art and Female Power among the Yoruba*. Indiana UP, 1990.

Dudley, Guilford. *Religion on Trial: Mircea Eliade and His Critics*. Temple UP, 1977.

Duerr, Hans Peter. *Dreamtime: Concerning the Boundary between Wilderness and Civilization*. 1978. Translated by Felicitas Goodman, Basil Blackwell Inc., 1987.

Dumézil, Georges. *Gods of the Ancient Northmen*. 1959. U of California P, 1977.

Dundas, Paul. "The Jain Monk Jinapti Sūri Gets the Better of a Nāth Yogī." *Tantra in Practice*, edited by David Gordon White, Princeton UP, 2000, pp. 231–38.

Dunnigan, Ann. "Swans," *EOR*, vol. 14, 1987, pp. 188–89.

Durrant, Stephen W. "The Nisan Shaman Caught in Cultural Contradiction." *Signs*, vol. 5, no. 2, 1979, pp. 338–47.

Durston, Allen, and Arnold Nesselrath, editors. *Angels from the Vatican: The Invisible Made Visible*. Art Services International, 1998.

Edgar, Joanne. "Wonder Woman Revisited." *Ms.*, July 1972, pp. 50–53.

Edou, Jérôme. *Machig Labrön and the Foundations of Chöd*. Snow Lion Publications, 1996.

Edsman, Carl-Martin. "Bridges," *EOR*, vol. 2, 1987, pp. 310–14.

Ehrenberg, Margaret. *Women in Prehistory*. U of Oklahoma P, 1989.

Eliade, Mircea. *The Myth of the Eternal Return or, Cosmos and History*. 1949. Reprint, Princeton UP, 1971.

Eliade, Mircea. *Myths, Dreams and Mysteries: The Encounter between Contemporary Faiths and Archaic Realities*. 1957. Translated by Philip Mairet, Harper & Row, 1967.

Eliade, Mircea. *Patterns in Comparative Religion*. 1958. Translated by Rosemary Sheed. Reprint, New American Library, 1974.

Eliade, Mircea. *The Sacred and the Profane: The Nature of Religion*. Translated by William R. Trask, Harcourt, Brace & World, 1959.

Eliade, Mircea. *Shamanism: Archaic Techniques of Ecstasy*. 1951. Reprint, Princeton UP, 1972.

Eliade, Mircea. "Some Observations on European Witchcraft." *History of Religions*, vol. 14, no. 3, 1975, pp. 149–72.

Eliade, Mircea. *Yoga: Immortality and Freedom*. Translated by Willard R. Trask, Princeton UP, 1969.

Eller, Cynthia. "Immanence and Transcendence." *EOW*, vol. 1, 1998, pp. 465–66.

Eller, Cynthia. *The Myth of Matriarchal Prehistory: Why an Invented Past Won't Give Women a Future*. Beacon P, 2000.

Elliott, Dyan. *Fallen Bodies: Pollution, Sexuality, and Demonology in the Middle Ages*. U of Pennsylvania P, 1999.

Elliott, Dyan. *Proving Woman: Female Spirituality and Inquisitional Culture in the Later Middle Ages*. Princeton UP, 2004.

Ellis (Davidson), Hilda Roderick. *The Road to Hel*. Cambridge UP, 1943.

Ellis Davidson, H. R. *God and Myths of Northern Europe*. 1964. Reprint, Penguin Books, 1990.

Ellis Davidson, H. R. "The Ship of the Dead." *The Journey to the Other World*, edited by H. R. Ellis Davidson, Rowman and Littlefield, 1975, pp. 73–89.

Ellis Davidson, H. R. *Viking and Norse Mythology*. Barnes and Noble, 1969.

Ernst, Carl W. "Muslim Interpreters of Yoga." *Yoga: The Art of Transformation*, edited by Debra Diamond. Freer Gallery of Art, 2013, pp. 59–67.

Ettinghausen, Richard. "Persian Ascension Miniatures of the Fourteenth Century." *Islamic Art and Archaeology*, 1984, pp. 360–83.

Evans-Wentz, W. Y. *The Fairy-Faith in Celtic Countries*. 1911. Reprint, Humanities P, 1977.

Fan, Xingru. *Flying Apsaras in Dunhuang*. Duhuang Literature and Arts Publishing House, 1994.

Faraone, Christopher A., and Laura K. McClure, editors. *Prostitutes and Courtesans in the Ancient World*. U of Wisconsin P, 2006.

Faure, Bernard. *The Power of Denial: Buddhism, Purity, and Gender*. Princeton UP, 2003.

Fernea, Robert A., and Elizabeth W. Fernea. "Variation in Religious Observance among Islamic Women." *Scholars, Saints, and Sufis: Muslim Religious Institutions in the Middle East since 1500*, edited by Nikki R. Keddie, U of California P, 1972, pp. 385–401.

Ferrari, Fabrizio M. "Alternative Yoginīs with Alternative Powers: Singing the Blues in the Causaṭṭī Yoginī Devī Mandir of Vārāṇasī." *"Yoginī" in South Asia: Interdisciplinary Approaches*, edited by István Keul, Routledge, 2013, pp. 148–162.

Finkelstein, Naomi. "Furies." *EOW*, vol. 1, 1998, pp. 356–57.

Finley, M. I. *The Ancient Greeks*. 1963. Reprint, Peregrine Books, 1987.

Fishbane, Simcha. "'Most Women Engage in Sorcery': An Analysis of Sorceresses in the Babylonian Talmud." *Jewish History*, vol. 7, no. 1, 1993, pp. 27–42.

Fitzhugh, William W., and Elisabeth I. Ward, editors. *Vikings: The North Atlantic Saga*. Smithsonian Institution P, 2000.

Forbes, Shannon. "'When Sometimes She Imagined Herself Like Her Mother': The Contrasting Responses of Cam and Mrs. Ramsay to the Role of the Angel in the House." *Studies in the Novel*, vol. 32, no. 4, Winter 2000, pp. 464–87.

Frank, Roberta. "Wagner's Ring, North-by-Northwest." *University of Toronto Quarterly*, vol. 74, no. 2, Spring 2005, pp. 671–76.

Frankfort, Henri. *Art and Architecture of the Ancient Orient*. Penguin Books, 1954.

Frankfort, Henri. *Kingship and the Gods: A Study of Ancient Near Eastern Religions as the Integration of Society and Nature*. U of Chicago P, 1948.

Frédéric, Louis. *Buddhism*. Flammarion, 1995.

Freedman, Yitzhak. "Altar of Words: Text and Ritual in Taittirīya Upaniṣad 2." *Numen*, vol. 59, 2012, pp. 322–43.

Fridriksdóttir, Jóhanna Katrín. "'Gerðit hon . . . sem konor aðrar': Women and Subversion in Eddic Heroic Poetry." *Revisiting the Poetic Edda: Essays on Old Norse Heroic Legend*, edited by Paul Acker and Carolyne Larrington, Routledge, 2013, pp. 117–35.

Friedrich, Paul. "An Avian and Aphrodisian Reading of Homer's Odyssey." *American Anthropologist*, vol. 99, no. 2, 1997, pp. 306–20.

Friedrich, Paul. *The Meaning of Aphrodite*. U of Chicago P, 1978.

Fries, Maureen. "Female Heroes, Heroines, and Counter-Heroes: Images of Women in Arthurian Tradition." *Popular Arthurian Traditions*, edited by Sally K. Slocum, Bowling Green State U Popular P, 1992, pp. 5–17.

Fulco, William J. "Inanna." *EOR*, vol. 7, 1987, pp. 145–46.

Furst, Peter T., editor. *The Flesh of the Gods: The Ritual Use of Hallucinogens*. Reprint, Waveland P, 1990.

Furst, Peter T. "Shamanism: South American Shamanism." *EOR*, vol. 13, 1987, pp. 219–23.

Furth, Charlotte. *A Flourishing Yin: Gender in China's Medical History, 960–1665*. U of California P, 1999.

Gaeffke, Peter. "Maṇḍalas: Hindu Maṇḍalas." *EOR*, vol. 1, 1987, p. 153.

Garber, Marjorie, and Nancy J. Vickers, editors. *The Medusa Reader*. Routledge, 2003.

Garimella, Annnapurna. "Apsaras." *EOW*, vol. 1, 1998, pp. 48–50.

Gaster, Theodor H. "Monsters." *EOR*, vol. 10, 1998, pp. 76–80.

Geffcken, J. "Eumenides, Erinyes." *ER&E*, vol. 5, 1922–27, pp. 573–75.

Genep, Arnold van. *The Rites of Passage*. Translated by Monika B. Vizedom and Gabrielle L. Caffee, U of Chicago P, 1960.

Germano, David. "Re-membering the Dismembered Body of Tibet: Contemporary Tibetan Visionary Movements in the People's Republic of China." *Buddhism in Contemporary Tibet: Religious Revival and Cultural Identity*, edited by Melvyn C. Goldstein and Matthew T. Kapstein, U of California P, 1998, pp. 53–94.

Germano, David, and Janet Gyatso. "Longchenpa and the Possession of the Ḍākinī." *Tantra in Practice*, edited by David Gordon White, Princeton UP, 2000, pp. 239–65.

Gero, Joan M., and Margaret W. Conkey, editors. *Engendering Archaeology: Women and Prehistory*. Basil Blackwell, 1991.

Gibb, H. A. R., et al., editors. *The Encyclopaedia of Islam: New Edition*. 4 vols. Brill, 1965.

Gilbert, Sandra M., and Susan Gubar. *The Madwoman in the Attic: The Woman Writer and the Nineteenth Century Literary Imagination*. Yale UP, 1979.

Gimbutas, Marija. *The Goddesses and Gods of Old Europe: Myths and Cult Images*. U of California P, 1982.

Ginzburg, Carlo. "Deciphering the Witches' Sabbath." *Early Modern European Witchcraft: Centres and Peripheries*, edited by Bengt Ankarloo and Gustav Henningsen, Clarendon P, 1993, pp. 121–37.

Ginzburg, Carlo. *Ecstasies: Deciphering the Witches' Sabbath*. Translated by Raymond Rosenthal, Penguin Books, 1992.

Ginzburg, Carlo. *Night Battles: Witchcraft and Agrarian Cults in the Sixteenth and Seventeenth Centuries*. Translated by John and Anne Tedeschi, Penguin Books, 1985.

Gitomer, David. "Urvaśī Won by Valor." *Theater of Memory: The Plays of Kālidāsa*, edited by Barbara Stoler Miller, Columbia UP, 1984, pp. 177–251 and 344–67.

Glassé, Cyril. *The Concise Encyclopedia of Islam*. 1989. Harper Collins, 1991.

Gold, Ann Grodzins. *Fruitful Journeys: The Ways of Rajasthani Pilgrims*. U of California P, 1988.

Goldstein, Joshua S. *War and Gender: How Gender Shapes the War System and Vice Versa*. Cambridge UP, 2001.

Goodison, Lucy. *Death, Women and the Sun: Symbolism of Regeneration in Early Aegean Religion*. Bulletin Supplement 53. Institute of Classical Studies, 1989.

Goodison, Lucy, and Christine Morris, editors. *Ancient Goddesses: The Myths and the Evidence*. U of Wisconsin P, 1998.

Goodison, Lucy, and Christine Morris. "Beyond the 'Great Mother': The Sacred World of the Minoans." *Ancient Goddesses*, edited by Lucy Goodison and Christine Morris, U of Wisconsin P, 1999, pp. 113–32.

Goodison, Lucy, and Christine Morris. "Introduction. Exploring Female Divinity: From Modern Myths to Ancient Evidence." *Ancient Goddesses*, edited by Lucy Goodison and Christine Morris, U of Wisconsin P, 1999, pp. 6–21.

Goodrich, Norma Lorre. *King Arthur*. Harper & Row, 1986.

Grabmo, Ronald. "Unmanliness and Seidr: Problems Concerning the Change of Sex." *Shamanism: Past and Present, Part I*, edited by Mihály Hoppál and Otto von Sadovsky, Ethnographic Institute, 1989, pp. 103–13.

Graceva, G. N. "A Nganasan Shaman Costume." *Shamanism in Siberia*, edited by Vilmos Diószegi and Mihály Hoppál. Translated by S. Simon, Akadémiai Kiadó, 1996, pp. 79–87.

Grey, Leslie. *Concordance of Buddhist Birth Stories.* Pali Text Society, 1994.

Grunebaum, G. E. von, and Robert Caillois, editors. *The Dream and Human Societies.* U of California P, 1966.

Gyatso, Janet. *Apparitions of the Self: The Secret Autobiographies of a Tibetan Visionary.* Princeton UP, 1998.

Gyatso, Janet. "The Development of the Gcod Tradition." *Soundings in Tibetan Civilization,* edited by Barbara Aziz and Matthew Kapstein, Manohar, 1985, pp. 320–41.

Gyatso, Janet. "Down with the Demoness: Reflections on a Feminine Ground in Tibet." *Feminine Ground: Essays on Women and Tibet,* edited by Janice D. Willis, Snow Lion Publications, 1989, pp. 33–51.

Halifax, Joan. *Shamanic Voices: A Survey of Visionary Narratives.* Dutton, 1979.

Hamayon, Roberte N. "Shamanism in Siberia: From Partnership in Supernature to Counter-power in Society." *Shamanism, History and the State,* edited by Nicholas Thomas and Caroline Humphrey, U of Michigan P, 1994, pp. 76–89.

Hamilton, Naomi. "Viewpoint: Can We Interpret Figurines?" *Cambridge Archaeological Journal,* vol. 6, no. 2, Oct. 1996, pp. 281–307.

Handique, Krishnakanta. *Apsarases in Indian Literature.* Decent Books, 2001.

Hanfmann, George M. A., and John R. T. Pollard. "Gorgo or Medusa." *OCD,* 1970, p. 472.

Hanfmann, George M. A., and John R. T. Pollard. "Nike." *OCD,* 1970, p. 735.

Hanfmann, George M. A., and John R. T. Pollard. "Sirens." *OCD,* 1970, p. 993.

Hanfmann, George M. A., and John R. T. Pollard. "Sphinx." *OCD,* 1970, p. 1009.

Hanna, Judith Lynne. *Dance, Sex and Gender: Sign of Identity, Dominance, Defiance, and Desire.* U of Chicago P, 1988.

Harlan, Lindsey. *Goddesses' Henchmen: Gender in Indian Hero Worship.* Oxford UP, 2003.

Harmon, Jim. "A Swell Bunch of Guys." *All in Color for a Dime,* edited by Dick Lupoff and Don Thompson, Krause Publications, 1997, pp. 167–90.

Harner, Michael J. "The Role of Hallucinogenic Plants in European Witchcraft." *Hallucinogens and Shamanism,* edited by Michael J. Harner, Oxford UP, 1973, pp. 125–49.

Harris, Rivkah. "Inanna-Ishtar as Paradox and a Coincidence of Opposites." *History of Religions,* vol. 30, no. 3, Feb. 1991, pp. 261–78.

Harrison, Jane Ellen. "Harpies." *ER&E,* vol. 6, 1922–27, pp. 517–19.

Harrison, Jane Ellen. *Prolegomena to the Study of Greek Religion.* 1922. 3rd ed. Reprint, Princeton UP, 1991.

Hart, Clive. *Images of Flight.* U of California P, 1988.

Hartland, Edwin Sidney. *The Science of Fairy Tales: An Inquiry into Fairy Mythology.* Charles Scribner's Sons, 1911.

Harva, Uno. *Siberian Mythology. Mythology of All Races,* vol. 10, edited by Louis Herbert Gray, Marshall Jones Company, 1927.

Harvey, Graham. *Shamanism: A Reader.* Routledge, 2002.

Harvey, Youngsook Kim. *Six Korean Women: The Socialization of Shamans.* West Publishing Co., 1979.

Hassan, Fekri A. "The Earliest Goddesses of Egypt: Divine Mothers and Cosmic Bodies." *Ancient Goddesses: The Myths and the Evidence,* edited by Lucy Goodison and Christine Morris, U of Wisconsin P, 1998, pp. 98–112.

Hastrup, Kirsten. "Iceland: Sorcerers and Paganism." *Early Modern European Witchcraft: Centres and Peripheries,* edited by Bengt Ankarloo and Gustav Henningsen, Clarendon P, 1993, pp. 383–401.

Hatley, Shaman. "What is a Yoginī? Towards a Polythetic Definition." *"Yoginī" in South Asia: Interdisciplinary Approaches,* edited by István Keul, Routledge, 2013, pp. 21–31.

Hatto, A. T. "The Swan Maiden: A Folk-Tale of North Eurasian Origin?" *Bulletin of the School of Oriental and African Studies*, vol. 24, no. 2, 1961, pp. 326–52.

Hausner, Sondra. "The Category of the Yoginī as a Gendered Practitioner." *"Yoginī" in South Asia: Interdisciplinary Approaches*, edited by István Keul, Routledge, 2013, pp. 32–43.

Heikkinen, Antero, and Timo Kervinen. "Finland: The Male Domination." *Early Modern European Witchcraft: Centres and Peripheries*, edited by Bengt Ankarloo and Gustav Henningsen, Clarendon P, 1993, pp. 319–38.

Heilbrun, Carolyn G. *Writing a Woman's Life*. Ballantine Books, 1988.

Helms, Barbara Lois. "Rābi'ah as Mystic, Muslim and Woman." *The Annual Review of Women in World Religions*, vol. 3, 1994, pp. 1–87.

Henningsen, Gustav. "'The Ladies from Outside': An Archaic Pattern of the Witches' Sabbath." *Early Modern European Witchcraft: Centres and Peripheries*, edited by Bengt Ankarloo and Gustav Henningsen, Clarendon P, 1993, pp. 191–215.

Herdt, Gilbert, editor. *Third Sex, Third Gender: Beyond Sexual Dimorphism in Culture and History*. Zone Books, 1994.

Herrmann-Pfandt, Adelheid. "Ḍākinīs in Indo-Tibetan Tantric Buddhism: Some Results of Recent Research." *Journal of the Seminar for Buddhist Studies*, vol. 5, no. 6, 1992–1993, pp. 46–63.

Herrmann-Pfandt, Adelheid. *Ḍākinīs: Zur Stellung und Symbolik des Weiblichen im Tantrischen Buddhismus*. Indica et Tibetica Verlag, 1992.

Herrmann-Pfandt, Adelheid. "The Good Woman's Shadow: Some Aspects of the Dark Nature of Ḍākinīs and Śākinīs in Hinduism." *Wild Goddesses in India and Nepal*, edited by Axel Michaels et al., Peter Lang 1996, pp. 39–70.

Herrmann-Pfandt, Adelheid. "On a Previous Birth Story of Ma gcig Lab sgron ma." *The Tibet Journal*, vol. 25, no. 3, Autumn 2000, pp. 19–31.

Herrmann-Pfandt, Adelheid. "Yab Yum Iconography and the Role of Women in Tibetan Tantric Buddhism." *Tibet Journal*, vol. xxii, no. 1, Spring 1997, pp. 12–34.

Hewitt, Marsha. "Marija Gimbutas." *EOW*, vol. 1, 1998, p. 370.

Hill, Christopher. "Introduction." *Crisis in Europe: 1560–1660*. 1965. Edited by Trevor Aston. Reprint, Routledge, 2011, pp. 1–3.

Hollimon, Sandra E. "The Gendered Peopling of North America: Addressing the Antiquity of Systems of Multiple Genders." *The Archaeology of Shamanism*, edited by Neil Price, Routledge, 2001, pp. 123–34.

Hollis, Susan Tower. "Isis." *EOW*, vol. 1, 1998, p. 487–88.

Hollywood, Amy. *Sensible Ecstasy: Mysticism, Sexual Difference, and the Demands of History*. U of Chicago P, 2002.

Holmberg, David. "Shamanic Soundings: Femaleness in the Tamang Ritual Structure." *Signs*, vol. 9, no. 1, Autumn 1983, pp. 40–58.

Holmberg, Uno. *Finno-Ugric Mythology*. Vol. 4 in *The Mythology of All Races*, edited by J. A. MacCulloch. Marshall Jones Company, 1927.

Holmes, Richard. *Falling Upwards: How We Took to the Air*. Vintage Books, 2014.

Holst-Warhaft, Gail. "Mourning and Death Rites." *EOW*, vol. 1, 1998, p. 682–85.

Hopkins, E. Washburn. *Epic Mythology*. 1915. Reprint, Motilal Banarasidass, 1974.

Hoppál, Mihály. "On the Origin of Shamanism and the Siberian Rock Art." *Studies on Shamanism*, edited by Anna-Leena Siikala and Mihály Hoppál, Finnish Anthropological Society, 1992, pp. 132–49.

Hoppál, Mihály, and Otto von Sadovsky, editors. *Shamanism: Past and Present, Part I*. Ethnographic Institute, 1989.

Huber, Tony. "Guidebook to Lapchi." *Religions of Tibet in Practice*, edited by Donald S. Lopez, Jr., Princeton UP, 1997, pp. 103–19.

Humes, Cynthia Ann. "Wrestling with Kali: South Asian and British Constructions of the Dark Goddess." *Encountering Kālī: In the Margins, at the Center, in the West*, edited by Rachel Fell McDermott and Jeffrey J. Kripal, U of California P, 2003, pp. 145–68.

Humphrey, Caroline. "Shamanic Practices and the State in Northern Asia: Views from the Center and Periphery." *Shamanism, History, and the State*, edited by Nicholas Thomas and Caroline Humphrey, U of Michigan P, 1994, pp. 191–228.

Humphrey, Caroline. "Shamans in the City." *Anthropology Today*, vol. 15, no. 3, June 1999, pp. 3–10.

Humphrey, Caroline, with Urgunge Onon. *Shamans and Elders: Experience, Knowledge, and Power Among the Daur Mongols*. Oxford UP, 1996.

Ikram, Salima. "An Eternal Aviary: Bird Mummies from Ancient Egypt." *Between Heaven and Earth*, edited by Rozenn Bailleul-LeSuer, Oriental Institute of the U of Chicago, 2012, pp. 41–48.

Irby-Massie, Georgia L. "The Roman Army and the Cult of the *Campestres*." *Zeitschrift für Papyrologie und Epigraphik*, vol. 113, 1996, pp. 293–300.

Jackson, Roger R. *Tantric Treasures: Three Collections of Mystical Verse from Buddhist India*. Oxford UP, 2004.

Jackson, W. T. H. *The Literature of the Middle Ages*. Columbia UP, 1960.

Jacobsen, Thorkild. "Mesopotamia." *Before Philosophy: The Intellectual Adventure of Ancient Man*. 1946. Edited by Henri Frankfort et al., reprint, Penguin Books, 1971, pp. 137–234.

Jacobsen, Thorkild. *The Treasures of Darkness: A History of Mesopotamian Religion*. Yale UP, 1976.

Jain, Susan Pertel. "Dance: In Asian Traditions." *EOW*, vol. 1, 1998, pp. 234–37.

Jaini, Padmanabh S. "The Story of Sudhana and Manoharā: An Analysis of the Texts and the Borobudur Reliefs." *Bulletin of the School of Oriental and African Studies, University of London*, vol. 29, no. 3, 1966, pp. 533–58.

Jamison, Stephanie W. *Sacrificed Wife, Sacrificer's Wife: Women, Ritual, and Hospitality in Ancient India*. Oxford UP, 1996.

Jamgon Kongtrul. *Jamgon Kongrul's Retreat Manual*. Translated by Ngawang Zangpo, Snow Lion, 1994.

Jarrar, Maher. "The Martyrdom of Passionate Lovers: Holy War as a Sacred Wedding." *Myths, Historical Archetypes, and Symbolic Figures in Arabic Literature: Towards a New Hermeneutic Approach*, edited by Angelika Neuwirth et al., Franz Steiner Verlag, 1999, pp. 87–107.

Jastrow, Morris, Jr. "Adam and Eve in Babylonian Literature." *The American Journal of Semitic Languages and Literatures*, vol. 15, no. 4, July 1899, pp. 193–214.

Jochens, Jenny. *Old Norse Images of Women*. U of Pennsylvania P, 1996.

Jochelson, Waldemar. *The Yakut*. American Museum of Natural History, 1933.

Jochelson, Waldemar. *The Yukaghir and the Yukaghirized Tungus*. Memoirs of the American Museum of Natural History, vol. XIII, pt. 2. G. E. Stechert, 1924.

Johnson, Paul C. "Shamanism from Ecuador to Chicago: A Case Study in New Age Ritual Appropriation." *Shamanism: A Reader*, edited by Graham Harvey, Routledge, 2002, pp. 334–48.

Johnston, Sarah Iles. "Aphrodite (Venus)." *EOW*, vol. 1, 1998, pp. 47–48.

Johnston, Sarah Iles. *Hekate Soteira: A Study of Hekate's Roles in the Chaldean Oracles and Related Literature*. Scholars Press, 1990.

Jones, David Albert. *Angels: A History*. Oxford UP, 2010.

Jones, Ernest. *On the Nightmare*. Liveright, 1971.

Jones, Gywn. *A History of the Vikings*. Oxford UP, 1973.

Jones, Rex L. "Limbu Spirit Possession and Shamanism." *Spirit Possession in the Nepal Himalayas*, edited by John T. Hitchcock and Rex L. Jones, Vikas, 1996, pp. 29–55.

Jones, Shirley Kurz. "Limbu Spirit Possession—A Case Study." *Spirit Possession the Nepal Himalayas*, edited by John T. Hitchcock and Rex L. Jones, Vikas, 1996, pp. 22–28.

Joshi, N. P. *Catalogue of the Brahmanical Sculptures in the State Museum, Lucknow (Part I)*. State Museum Lucknow, 1972.

Kagan, Richard L. *Lucrecia's Dreams: Politics and Prophecy in Sixteenth-Century Spain*. U of California P, 1990.

Kahk, Juhan. "Estonia II: The Crusade against Idolatry." *Early Modern European Witchcraft: Centres and Peripheries*, edited by Bengt Ankarloo and Gustav Henningsen, Clarendon P, 1993, pp. 273–84.

Kaimal, Padma. "Yoginīs in Stone: Auspicious and Inauspicious Power." *"Yoginī" in South Asia: Interdisciplinary Approaches*, edited by István Keul, Routledge, 2013, pp. 97–108.

Kanaseki, Hiroshi. "Folk Masquerading as Birds." *Proceedings of the International Conference on Anthropology and the Museum*, edited by Tsong-yuan Lin, Taiwan Museum, 1995, pp. 219–25.

Kapstein, Matthew. "The Guide to the Crystal Peak." *Religions of Tibet in Practice*, edited by Donald S. Lopez Jr., Princeton UP, 1997, pp. 103–19.

Katz, Nathan. "Anima and mKha'-'gro-ma: A Critical Comparative Study of Jung and Tibetan Buddhism." *Tibet Journal*, vol. 2, no. 3, 1977, pp. 113–43.

Katz, Nathan. *Buddhist Images of Human Perfection*. Motilal Barnarsidas, 1982.

Kazhdan, Alexander, and Henry Maguire. "Byzantine Hagiographical Texts as Sources on Art." *Dumbarton Oaks Papers*, vol. 45, 1991, pp. 1–22.

Keith, Arthur Berriedale. *The Religion and Philosophy of the Veda and Upanishads*. 2 vols. Motilal Banarsidass, 1970.

Kendall, Laurel. "Initiating Performance: The Story of Chini, a Korean Shaman." *The Performance of Healing*, edited by Carol Laderman and Marina Roseman, Routledge, 1996, pp. 17–58.

Kendall, Laurel. "Korean Shamans and the Spirit of Capitalism." *American Anthropologist*, vol. 98, no. 3, 1996, 512–27.

Kendall, Laurel. *The Life and Hard Times of a Korean Shaman: Of Tales and the Telling of Tales*. U of Hawai'i P, 1988.

Kendall, Laurel. "Shamanism." *EOW*, vol. 2, 1998, pp. 892–95.

Kendall, Laurel. *Shamans, Housewives, and Other Restless Spirits: Women in Korean Ritual Life*. U of Hawai'i P, 1985.

Kendall, Laurel, et al. *Drawing Shadows to Stone: The Photography of the Jesup North Pacific Expedition, 1897–1902*. American Museum of Natural History, 1997.

Kendall, Laurel, and Diana S. Lee. *An Initiation "Kut" for a Korean Shaman*. Video. Distributed by U of Hawai'i, 1991.

Keul, István. "Introduction." *"Yoginī" in South Asia: Interdisciplinary Approaches*, edited by István Keul, Routledge, 2013, pp. 1–17.

Keuls, Eva C. *The Reign of the Phallus: Sexual Politics in Ancient Athens*. Harper & Row, 1985.

Kevles, Bettyann Holtzman. *Almost Heaven: The Story of Women in Space*. Basic Books, 2003.

Kiessling, Nicolas. *The Incubus in English Literature: Provenance and Progeny*. Washington State UP, 1977.

Kilborne, Benjamin. "Dreams," *EOR*, vol. 4, 1987, pp. 482–92.

King, Helen. "Bound to Bleed: Artemis and Greek Women." *Images of Women in Antiquity*, edited by Averil Cameron and Amélie Kuhrt, Croom Helm, 1983, pp. 109–27.

King, Helen. *Hippocrates' Woman: Reading the Female Body in Ancient Greece*. Routledge, 1998.

Kinsley, David. *Hindu Goddesses: Visions of the Divine Feminine in the Hindu Religious Tradition*. U of California P, 1986.

Kirkland, Russell. "Taoism: An Overview." *EOW*, vol. 2, 1997, pp. 959–64.

Klaits, Joseph. *Servants of Satan: The Age of the Witch Hunts*. Indiana UP, 1985.

Klaniczay, Gábor. "Hungary: The Accusations and the Universe of Popular Magic." *Early Modern European Witchcraft: Centres and Peripheries*, edited by Bengt Ankarloo and Gustav Henningsen, Clarendon P, 1993, pp. 219–55.

Klein, Anne Carolyn. "Nondualism and the Great Bliss Queen." *Journal of Feminist Studies in Religion*, vol. 1, no. 1, 1985, pp. 73–98.

Kleivan, Inge. "The Swan Maiden Myth among the Eskimo." *Acta*, vol. 13, 1962, pp. 15–49.

Klinger, Elmar. "Revenge & Retribution." *EOR*, vol. 12, 1987, pp. 362–68.

Knecht, Peter. "Introduction." *Shamans in Asia*, edited by Clark Chilson and Peter Knecht, RoutledgeCurzon, 2003, pp. 1–30.

Knipe, David M. "The Heroic Theft: Myths from R̥igveda IV and the Ancient Near East." *History of Religions*, vol. 6, no. 4, May 1967, pp. 328–60.

Ko, Dorothy. *Every Step a Lotus: Shoes for Bound Feet*. U of California P, 2001.

Köhler, Joachim. *Richard Wagner: The Last of the Titans*. Translated by Stewart Spencer, Yale UP, 2004.

Kohn, Livia. *Early Chinese Mysticism: Philosophy and Soteriology in the Taoist Tradition*. Princeton UP, 1992.

Kolm, Suzanne L. "'Who Says It's a Man's World?': Women's Work and Travel in the First Decades of Flight." *The Airplane in American Culture*, edited by Dominick Pisano, U of Michigan P, 2003, pp. 147–64.

Koloski-Ostrow, Ann Olga, and Claire L. Lyons, editors. *Naked Truths: Women, Sexuality, and Gender in Classical Art and Archaeology*. Routledge, 1997.

Koonz, Claudia. *Mothers in the Fatherland: Women, the Family and Nazi Politics*. St. Martin's P, 1987.

Korp, Maureen. "Prehistoric Religions: Pre-Agricultural People." *EOW*, vol. 2, 1998, pp. 795–800.

Kors, Alan C., and Edward Peters. *Witchcraft in Europe 1100–1700: A Documentary History*. U of Pennsylvania P, 1972.

Kozloff, Arielle P. "Pharaoh Was a Good Egg, but Whose Egg Was He?" *Between Heaven and Earth: Birds in Ancient Egypt*, edited by Rozenn Bailleul-LeSuer, Oriental Institute of the U of Chicago, 2012, pp. 59–64.

Kramer, Heinrich, and Jakob Sprenger. *Malleus Maleficarum*. 1928. Translated by Rev. Montague Summers. Reprint, Dover, 1971.

Kramer, Samuel Noah. *The Sacred Marriage Rite*. Indiana UP, 1969.

Kramrisch, Stella. *The Hindu Temple*. 1946. Reprint, Motilal Banarsidass, 1976.

Krappe, Alexander Haggerty. "The Valkyries." *The Modern Language Review*, vol. 1, 1926, pp. 55–73.

Krishnamorthy, K. "Hero: Death: Commemoration, as reflected in Sanskrit literature–A Study." *Memorial Stones: A Study of their Origin, Significance and Variety*, edited by S. Settar and G. Sontheimer, South Asia Institute, U of Heidelberg, 1982, pp. 9–20.

Kroll, Paul W. "An Early Poem of Mystical Excursion." *Religions of China in Practice*, edited by Donald S. Lopez Jr., Princeton UP, 1996, pp. 156–65.

Kugle, Scott. *Sufis & Saints' Bodies: Mysticism, Corporeality, & Sacred Power in Islam*. U of North Carolina P, 2007.

Kuntz, Paul Grimley, and Lee Braver. "Ascent/Descent." *Encyclopedia of Comparative Iconography: Themes Depicted in Works of Art*, vol. 1, edited by Helene E. Roberts, Fitzroy Dearborn, 1998, pp. 69–81.

La Barre, Weston. *The Ghost Dance: The Origins of Religion*. Dell, 1972.

La Barre, Weston. "Old and New World Narcotics: A Statistical Question and an Ethnological Reply." *Economic Botany*, vol. 24, 1970, pp. 73–80.

Laderman, Carol, and Marina Roseman, editors. *The Performance of Healing*. Routledge, 1996.

LaFargue, Michael. *The Tao of the Tao-te-ching*. State U of New York P, 1992.

Landdeck, Katherine Sharp. "Experiment in the Cockpit: The Women Airforce Service Pilots of World War II." *The Airplane in American Culture*, edited by Dominick Pisano, U of Michigan P, 2003, pp. 165–98.

Langland, Elizabeth. "Nobody's Angels: Domestic Ideology and Middle-Class Women in the Victorian Novel." *PMLA*, vol. 107, no. 2, 1992, 290–304.

Larner, Christina. *Witchcraft and Religion: The Politics of Popular Belief*. Basil Blackwell, 1984.

Laufer, Berthold. "Bird Divination Among the Tibetans (Notes on Document Pelliot no. 3530, with a Study of Tibetan Phonology of the Ninth Century)." *Sino-Tibetan Studies: Selected Papers on the Art, Folklore, History, Linguistics and Prehistory of Sciences in China and Tibet*, vol. 2, collected by Hartmut Walravens, Rakesh Goel, 1987, pp. 483–632.

Laufer, Berthold. "Origin of the Word Shaman." *American Anthropologist*, vol. 19, 1917, pp. 261–71.

Laufer, Berthold. *The Prehistory of Aviation*. Chicago Natural History Museum, 1928.

Lea, Henry Charles. *Materials Toward a History of Witchcraft*. 1939. Edited by Arthur C. Howland. Reprint, Thomas Yoseloff, 1957.

Leavy, Barbara Fass. *In Search of the Swan Maiden: A Narrative on Folklore and Gender*. New York UP, 1994.

Lecky, W. E. H. *A History of Ireland in the Eighteenth Century*. D. Appleton, 1893.

Lefkowitz, Mary R. "Influential Women." In *Images of Women in Antiquity*, edited by Averil Cameron and Amélie Kuhrt, 49–64.

Lepore, Jill. "The Last Amazon: Wonder Woman Returns." *New Yorker*, September 22, 2014, pp. 64–73.

Leroy, Olivier. *Levitation: An Examination of the Evidence and Explanations*. Oates & Washbourne, 1928.

Lesko, Barbara S. *Women's Earliest Records: From Ancient Egypt and Western Asia*. Proceedings of the Conference on Women in the Ancient Near East, Brown University, November 5–7, 1987. Scholars Press, 1989.

Lessing, Ferdinand. *Yung-ho-kung, an Iconography of the Lamaist Cathedral in Peking, With Notes on Lamaist Mythology and Cult*, vol. 1. N.p., 1942.

Lessing, Ferdinand, and Alex Wayman. *Introduction to the Buddhist Tantric Systems*. 1968. 2nd ed., Samuel Weiser, Inc., 1980.

Levine, Nancy E. "Belief and Explanation in Nyinba Women's Witchcraft." *Man*, vol. 17, no. 2, 1982, pp. 259–74.

Lewis, I. M. *Ecstatic Religion: A Study of Shamanism and Spirit Possession*. 1971. Reprint, Routledge, 1989.

Lewis-Williams, J. David. *The Mind in the Cave: Consciousness and the Origins of Art*. Thames and Hudson, 2002.

Lewis-Williams, J. David. "Southern African Shamanistic Rock Art in its Social and Cognitive Contexts." *The Archaeology of Shamanism*, edited by Neil S. Price, Routledge, 2001, pp. 17–39.

Lincoln, Bruce. *Authority: Construction and Corrosion*. U of Chicago P, 1994.

Lincoln, Bruce. *Death, War, and Sacrifice: Studies in Ideology and Practice*. U of Chicago P, 1991.

Lincoln, Bruce. *Emerging from the Chrysalis: Studies in Rituals of Women's Initiation*. Harvard UP, 1981.

Linn, Priscilla Rachun. "Gender Roles." *EOR*, vol. 5, 1987, pp. 495–502.

Linrothe, Robert. "Hindu, Sikh, and Sūfī Siddhas in India and Nepal." *Holy Madness: Portraits of Tantric Siddhas*, edited by Robert Linrothe, Serindia Publications, 2006, pp. 386–421.

Linrothe, Robert. "Siddhas and Śrīśailam, 'Where All Wise People Go.'" *Holy Madness: Portraits of Tantric Siddhas*, edited by Robert Linrothe, Serindia Publications, 2006, pp. 124–43.

Linrothe, Robert, editor. *Holy Madness: Portraits of Tantric Siddhas*. Serindia Publications, 2006.

Lomax, Judy. *Hanna Reitsch: Flying for the Fatherland*. John Murray, 1988.

Lommel, Andras, *Shamanism: The Beginnings of Art*. Translated by Michael Bullock, McGraw-Hill, 1967.

Loomis, Roger Sherman. *Wales and the Arthurian Tradition*. U of Wales P, 1956.

Lopez, Donald S., Jr., editor. *Religions of China in Practice*. Princeton UP, 1996.

Lopez, Donald S., Jr., editor. *Religions of Tibet in Practice*. Princeton UP, 1997.

Lopez y Royo, Alessandra. "Performing Hirapur: Dancing the Śakti Rūpa Yoginī." *"Yoginī" in South Asia: Interdisciplinary Approaches*, edited by István Keul, Routledge, 2013, pp. 226–34.

Lorenzen, David N. *The Kāpālikas and Kālāmukhas: Two Lost Saivite Sects*. 2nd rev. ed. Motilal Banarsidass, 1991.

Lovell, Mary S. *The Sound of Wings: The Life of Amelia Earhart*. St. Martin's P, 1989.

Lozanno, Juan Manuel. "Eremitism." *EOR*, vol. 5, 1987, p. 141.

Luczanits, Christian. "The Eight Great Siddhas in Early Tibetan Painting." *Holy Madness: Portraits of Tantric Siddhas*, edited by Robert Linrothe, Serindia Publications, 2006, pp. 88–91.

Luyster, Robert. "Symbolic Elements in the Cult of Athena." *History of Religions*, vol. 5, no. 1, Summer 1965, pp. 133–63.

MacCana, Proinsias. "Celtic Goddesses of Sovereignty." *Goddesses Who Rule*, edited by Elisabeth Benard and Beverly Moon, Oxford UP, 2000, pp. 85–99.

MacCulloch, John Arnott. *Eddic, The Mythology of All Races*. 2 vols. Marshall Jones Company, 1930.

MacLachlan, Bonnie. "Sacred Prostitution and Aphrodite." *Studies in Religion*, vol. 21, no. 12, 1992, pp. 145–62.

Madar, Maia. "Estonia I: Werewolves and Poisoners." *Early Modern European Witchcraft: Centres and Peripheries*, edited by Bengt Ankarloo and Gustav Henningsen, Clarendon P, 1993, pp. 257–72.

Mahony, William K. "Flight." *EOR*, vol. 5, 1987, pp. 349–53.

Mahony, William K. "Flying Priests, Yogins, and Shamans in Early Hinduism and Buddhism." Dissertation, University of Chicago, 1982.

Mahony, William K. "Soul: Indian Concepts." *EOR*, vol. 13, 1987, pp. 438–43.

Malti-Douglas, Fedwa. *Woman's Body, Woman's Word: Gender and Discourse in Arabo-Islamic Writing*. Princeton UP, 1991.

Marglin, Frédérique Apffel. "Hierodouleia." *EOR*, vol. 6, 1987, pp. 309–13.

Marglin, Frédérique Apffel. "Types of Sexual Union and their Implicit Meanings." *The Divine Consort: Rādhā and the Goddesses of India*, edited by John Stratton Hawley and Donna Marie Wulff, Beacon P, 1986, pp. 298–315.

Marglin, Frédérique Apffel. *Wives of the God-King*. Oxford UP, 1985.

Marrow, James H., and Alan Shestack, editors. *Hans Baldung Grien: Prints and Drawings*. Yale U Art Gallery, 1981.

Marshack, Alexander. "Upper Paleolithic Notation and Symbol." *Science* (New Series), vol. 178, no. 4063, Nov. 24, 1972, pp. 817–28.

Martin, Dan. "The Woman Illusion? Research into the Lives of Spiritually Accomplished Women Leaders of the 11th and 12th Centuries." *Women in Tibet*, edited by Janet Gyatso and Hanna Havnevik, Columbia UP, 2005, pp. 49–82.

Martin, Douglas. "Evelyn Trout, Record-Setting Flier, Dies at 97." *New York Times*, Feb. 2, 2003.

Martin, Emily. "Gender and Ideological Differences in Representations of Life and Death." *Death Ritual in Late Imperial and Modern China*, edited by James L. Watson and Evelyn S. Rawski, U of California P, 1988, pp. 164–79.

Mason, Eugene. *The Lays of Marie de France and Other French Legends*. J. M. Dent & Sons, 1911.

McClintock, Anne. "'No Longer in a Future Heaven': Women and Nationalism in South Africa." *Transition*, no. 51, 1991, pp. 104–23.

McCullough, Joan. "The 13 Astronauts Who Were Left Behind." *Ms.*, vol. 2, no. 3, Sept. 1973, pp. 41–45.

McDaniel, June. "Yoginīs in Bengali Religious Traditions: Tribal, Tantric and Bhakti Influences."*"Yogini" in South Asia: Interdisciplinary Approaches*, edited by István Keul, Routledge, 2013, pp. 133–47.

McDonnell, Ernest. *The Beguines and Beghards in Medieval Culture, with Special Emphasis on the Belgian Scene*. Rutgers UP, 1954.

McGinn, Bernard. *The Flowering of Mysticism: Men and Women in the New Mysticism, 1200–1250*. Crossroad, 1998.

McNamara, Jo Ann Kay. *Sisters in Arms: Catholic Nuns through Two Millennia*. Harvard UP, 1996.

Mendelsohn, Jane. "Amelia Earhart, Found and Lost." *New York Times*, June 10, 2012.

Merrison, Lindsey, producer and director. *Friends in High Places: The Art of Survival in Modern Day Burma*. Documentary Education Resources, 2001.

Meskell, Lynn. "Goddesses, Gimbutas and 'New Age' Archaeology." *Antiquity*, vol. 69, no. 262, March 1995, pp. 74–86.

Messereschmidt, Donald A. "Ethnographic Observations of Gurung Shamanism in Lamjung District." *Spirit Possession the Nepal Himalayas*, edited by John T. Hitchcock and Rex L. Jones, Vikas, 1996, pp. 197–216.

Messerschmidt, Donald A. *The Gurung of Nepal: Conflict and Change in a Village Society*. Aris and Phillips, 1976

Metcalf, Peter, and Richard Huntington. *Celebrations of Death: The Anthropology of Mortuary Ritual*. 1979. 2nd ed., Cambridge UP, 1991.

Michaels, Axel, Cornelia Vogelsanger, and Annette Wilke, editors. *Wild Goddesses in India and Nepal*. Peter Lang, 1996.

Michell, George. *The Hindu Temple: An Introduction to Its Meaning and Forms*. U of Chicago P, 1988.

Michell, George. *The Penguin Guide to the Monuments of India: Volume I: Buddhist, Jain, Hindu*. Penguin Books, 1990.

Milhaven, John Giles. *Hadewijch and Her Sisters: Other Ways of Loving and Knowing*. State U of New York P, 1993.

Miller, Alan L. "The Swan-Maiden Revisited: Religious Significance of 'Divine-Wife' Folktales with Special Reference to Japan." *Asian Folklore Studies*, vol. 46, no. 1, 1987, pp. 55–86.

Mills, Margaret. "Sex Role Reversals, Sex Changes, and Transvestite Disguise in the Oral Tradition of a Conservative Muslim Community in Afghanistan." *Women's Folklore, Women's Culture*, edited by Rosan A. Jordan and Susan J. Kalčik, U of Pennsylvania P, 1985, pp. 125–45.

Mills, Mary Beth. "Attack of the Widow Ghosts: Gender, Death, and Modernity in Northeast Thailand." *Bewitching Women, Pious Men: Gender and Body Politics in Southeast Asia*, edited by Aihwa Ong and Michael G. Peletz, U of California P, 1995, pp. 244–73.

Monter, William. "Protestant Wives, Catholic Saints, and the Devil's Handmaid: Women in the Age of Reformations." *Becoming Visible: Women in European History*, edited by Renate Bridenthal et al., 2nd ed. Houghton Mifflin, 1987, pp. 203–19.

Moran, William L. "Gilgamesh." *EOR*, vol. 5, 1987, pp. 557–60.

Moreno, Manuel. "God's Forceful Call: Possession as a Divine Strategy." *Gods of Flesh, Gods of Stone: The Embodiment of Divinity in India*, edited by Joanne Punzo Waghorne and Norman Cutler, Columbia UP, 1985, pp. 103–20.

Mori, Toril. *Simone de Beauvoir: The Making of an Intellectual Woman*. Blackwell, 1994.

Muchembled, Robert. "Satanic Myths and Cultural Reality." *Early Modern European Witchcraft: Centres and Peripheries*, edited by Bengt Ankarloo and Gustav Henningsen, Clarendon P, 1993, pp. 139–60.

Mullin, Glenn H. *The Flying Mystics of Tibetan Buddhism*. Serindia Publications, 2006.

Munch, Peter Andreas. *Norse Mythology: Legends of Gods and Heroes*. Translated by Sigurd Bernard Hustvedt, American-Scandinavian Foundation, 1954.

Nabokov, Isabelle. "Lament." *South Asian Folklore: An Encyclopedia*, edited by Margaret A. Mills et al., Routledge, 2003, pp. 350–51.

Neave, Dorinda. "The Witch in Early 16th-Century German Art." *Woman's Art Journal*, vol. 9, no. 1, 1988, pp. 3–9.

Nebesky-Wojkowitz, René de. *Oracles and Demons of Tibet: The Cult and Iconography of the Tibetan Protective Deities*. Akademische Druck-u.Verlagsanstalt, 1975.

Nesselrath, Arnold. "Wrestling with Angels: The Invisible Made Visible." *Angels from the Vatican: The Invisible Made Visible*, edited by Allen Durston and Arnold Nesselrath, Art Services International, 1998, pp. 44–61.

Neumann, Helmut F. "Cremation Grounds in Early Tibetan Mandalas." *Orientations*, vol. 33, no. 10, 2002, pp. 42–50.

Neusner, Jacob, et al. *Religion, Science and Magic: In Concert and in Conflict*. Oxford UP, 1989.

Newall, Venetia. "Fairies." *EOR*, vol. 5, 1987, pp. 246–50.

Newman, Barbara. "Possessed by the Spirit: Devout Women, Demoniacs, and the Apostolic Life in the Thirteenth Century." *Speculum*, vol. 73, no. 3, July 1998, pp. 763–68.

Newman, Barbara. *Sister of Wisdom: St. Hildegard's Theology of the Feminine*. U of California P, 1997.

Nicholson, Reynold A. *The Mystics of Islam*. 1914. Reprint, Routledge, 1979.

Nilsson, Martin P. *A History of Greek Religion*. 1925. Translated by F. J Fielden, 2nd rev. ed., Norton, 1964.

Nilsson, Martin P. *The Minoan-Mycenaean Religion and Its Survival in Greek Religion*. 2nd rev. ed., Biblo and Tannen, 1971.

Obeyesekere, Gananath. *Medusa's Hair: An Essay on Personal Symbols and Religious Experience*. U of Chicago P, 1981.

O'Flaherty, Wendy Doniger. *Asceticism and Eroticism in the Mythology of Śiva*. Oxford UP, 1975.

O'Flaherty, Wendy Doniger. *Dreams, Illusion and Other Realities*. U of Chicago P, 1985.

O'Flaherty, Wendy Doniger. "Indra." *EOR*, vol. 7, 1987, p. 215.

O'Flaherty, Wendy Doniger. *The Origins of Evil in Hindu Mythology*. U of California P, 1976.

O'Flaherty, Wendy Doniger. *Women, Androgynes, and Other Mythical Beasts*. U of Chicago P, 1980.

Oosten, Jaarich G. "Male and Female in Inuit Shamanism." *Études Inuit*, vol. 10, nos. 1–2, 1986, pp. 115–31.

Oppenheim, A. Leo. *Ancient Mesopotamia: Portrait of a Dead Civilization*. 1964. Rev. ed., U of Chicago P, 1977.

Oppenheim, A. Leo. "Mantic Dreams in the Ancient Near East." *The Dream and Human Societies*, edited by G. E. von Grunebaum and Robert Caillois, U of California P, 1966, pp. 341–50.

Orenstein, Claudia. "Dance and Drama: An Overview." *EOW*, vol. 1, 1998, pp. 232–34.

Orofino, Giacomella. "The Great Wisdom Mother and the Gcod Tradition." *Tantra in Practice*, edited by David Gordon White, Princeton UP, 2000, pp. 396–416.

Oster, Emily. "Witchcraft, Weather and Economic Growth in Renaissance Europe." *Journal of Economic Perspectives*, vol. 18, no. 1, Winter 2004, pp. 215–28.

Parfionovitch, Yuri, et al., translators. *Tibetan Medical Paintings*. Harry N. Abrams, 1992.

Patai, Raphael. *The Hebrew Goddess*. 3rd ed. Wayne State UP, 1990.

Paton, Lucy Allen. *Studies in the Fairy Mythology of Arthurian Romance*. 1903. Reprint, Burt Franklin, 1960.

Paul, Diana. *Women in Buddhism: Images of the Feminine in the Mahāyāna Tradition*. 2nd ed. U of California P, 1985.

Pease, Arthur Stanley, and Johan Harm Croon. "Divination." *OCD*, 1970, pp. 356–57.

Pearson, Mike Parker. *The Archaeology of Death and Burial*. Texas A&M UP, 1999.

Peers, Glenn. *Subtle Bodies: Representing Angels in Byzantium*. U of California P, 2001.

Pennington, Reina. *Wings, Women and War: Soviet Airwomen in World War Two Combat*. UP of Kansas, 2001.

Peters, Larry G., and Douglass Price-Williams. "Towards an Experiential Analysis of Shamanism." *American Ethnologist*, vol. 7, no. 3, August 1980, pp. 397–413.

Peterson, M. Jeanne. "No Angels in the House: The Victorian Myth and the Paget Women." *The American Historical Review*, vol. 89, no. 3, June 1984, pp. 677–708.

Pinson, Yona. "Witchcraft/Sorcery." *Encyclopedia of Comparative Iconography: Themes Depicted in Works of Art*, vol. 1, edited by Helene E. Roberts, Fitzroy Dearborn, 1998, pp. 947–56.

Pintchman, Tracy. *The Rise of the Goddess in the Hindu Tradition*. State U of New York P, 1994.

Pisano, Dominick, editor. *The Airplane in American Culture*. U of Michigan P, 2003.

Piszkiewicz, Dennis. *From Nazi Test Pilot to Hitler's Bunker: The Fantastic Flights of Hanna Reitsch*. Praeger, 1997.

Pollack, Susan. "Women in a Men's World: Images of Sumerian Women." *Engendering Archaeology: Women and Prehistory*, edited by Joan M. Gero and Margaret W. Conkey, Basil Blackwell, 1991, pp. 366–87.

Pollard, John. *Birds in Greek Life and Myth*. Thames and Hudson, 1977.

Polomé, Edgar C. "Germanic Religion." *EOR*, vol. 5, 1987, pp. 520–36.

Pomeroy, Sarah B. *Goddesses, Whores, Wives, and Slaves: Women in Classical Antiquity*. Schocken Books, 1975.

Poole, Fitz John Porter. "Transforming 'Natural' Woman: Female Ritual Leaders and Gender Ideology among Bimin-Kuskusmin." *Sexual Meanings: The Cultural Construction of Gender and Sexuality*, edited by Sherry B. Ortner and Harriet Whitehead, Cambridge UP, 1981, pp. 116–65.

Potapov, L. P. "The Shaman Drum as a Source of Ethnographical History." *Shamanism in Siberia*, edited by Vilmos Diószegi and Mihály Hoppál. Translated by S. Simon, Akadémiai Kiadó, 1996, pp. 107–17.

Price, Jennifer. *Flight Maps: Adventures with Nature in Modern America*. Basic Books, 1999.

Price, Neil S. "An Archaeology of Altered States: Shamanism and Material Culture Studies." *The Archaeology of Shamanism*, edited by Neil Price, Routledge, 2001, pp. 3–16.

Price, Neil S., editor. *The Archaeology of Shamanism*. Routledge, 2001.

Rabe, Michael. "Secret Yantras and Erotic Display for Hindu Temples." *Tantra in Practice*, edited by David Gordon White, Princeton UP, 2000, pp. 434–46.

Rabineau, Phyllis. *Feather Arts: Beauty, Wealth, and Spirit from Five Continents*. Field Museum of Natural History, 1979.

Rajasekhara, S. "Rāstrakuta Hero-stones: A Study." *Memorial Stones: A Study of their Origin, Significance and Variety*, edited by S. Settar and G. Sontheimer, South Asia Institute, U of Heidelberg, 1982, pp. 227–30.

Rank, Otto. "The Myth of the Birth of the Hero. *In Quest of the Hero*, edited by Robert A. Segal, Princeton UP, 1990, 3–87.

Rao, D. Hanumantha. "Hero-Stones at Pushpagiri." *Studies on Art, Archaeology and Indology: Papers Presented in Memory of Dr. Haribishnu Sarkar*, vol. 1, edited by Arundhati Banerji, Kaveri Books, 2006, pp. 164–70.

Rapp, Claudia. "Figures of Female Sanctity: Byzantine Edifying Manuscripts and Their Audience." *Dumbarton Oaks*, vol. 50, 1996, pp. 313–33, 335–44.

Ray, Reginald A. "Mahāsiddhas." *EOR*, vol. 9, 1987, pp. 122–26.

Reed, Barbara. "Taoism." *Women in World Religions*, edited by Arvind Sharma, State U of New York P, 1987, pp. 161–81.

Rees, Valery. *From Gabriel to Lucifer: A Cultural History of Angels*. I. B. Tauris, 2013.

Rese, Pamela R., and S. J. M. Gray. "Trees." *EOR*, 15, 1987, pp. 26–33.

Rhie, Marylin M., and Robert A. F. Thurman. *Wisdom and Compassion: The Sacred Art of Tibet*. Expanded ed., Harry N. Abrams, 2000.

Rickman, Sarah Byrn. "The Female Pilots We Betrayed." *New York Times*, February 21, 2016.

Rickman, Sarah Byrn. *The Originals: The Women's Auxiliary Ferrying Squadron of World War II*. Disc-Us Books, 2001.

Rickman, Sarah Byrn. *WASP of the Ferry Command: Women Pilots, Uncommon Deeds*. U of North Texas P, 2017.

Ringrose, Kathryn M. *The Perfect Servant: Eunuchs and the Social Construction of Gender in Byzantium*. U of Chicago P, 2004.

Rechung Rinpoche. *Tibetan Medicine*. U of California P, 1976.

Roberts, Helene E. *Encyclopedia of Comparative Iconography: Themes Depicted in Works of Art*. Fitzroy Dearborn, 1998.

Robinson, Lillian S. *Wonder Women: Feminisms and Superheroes*. Routledge, 2004.

Robson, James, editor. *Daoism*. Norton, 2015.

Rollin, Sue. "Women and Witchcraft in Ancient Assyria (c. 900–600 BC)." *Images of Women in Antiquity*, edited by Averil Cameron and Amélie Kuhrt, Croom Helm, 1983, pp. 34–45.

Rose, Herbert Jennings. "Erīnyes." *OCD*, 1970, pp. 406–07.

Rose, Herbert Jennings. "Phineus." *OCD*, 1970, p. 825.

Rose, Herbert Jennings. "Victoria." *OCD*, 1970, p. 1120.

Rose, Herbert Jennings, and Charles Martin Robertson. "Athena." *OCD*, 1970, pp. 138–39.

Rose, Herbert Jennings, and Charles Martin Robertson. "Harpyiae, Harpies." *OCD*, 1970, pp. 488–89.

Rose, Herbert Jennings, and Charles Martin Robertson. "Medea." *OCD*, 1970, p. 660.

Rosedahl, Else. *The Vikings*. 1991. Translated by Susan M. Margeson and Kirsten Williams. Rev. ed., Penguin Books, 1998.

Roseman, Marina. "'Pure Products Go Crazy': Rainforest Healing in a Nation-State." *The Performance of Healing*, edited by Carol Laderman and Marina Roseman, Routledge, 1996, pp. 233–70.

Rowe, Karen E. "To Spin a Yarn: The Female Voice in Folklore and Fairy Tale." *Fairy Tales and Society: Illusion, Allusion, and Paradigm*, edited by Ruth B. Bottigheimer, U of Pennsylvania P, 1986, pp. 141–50.

Rowland, Robert. "'Fantasticall and Devilishe Persons': European Witch-beliefs in Comparative Perspective." *Early Modern European Witchcraft: Centres and Peripheries*, edited by Bengt Ankarloo and Gustav Henningsen, Clarendon P, 1993, pp. 161–90.

Roy, Satindra Narayan. "The Witches of Orissa." *The Journal of the Anthropological Society of Bombay*, vol. 14, no. 2, 1929, pp. 185–200.

Ruch, Barbara. "The Other Side of Culture." *The Cambridge History of Japan*, vol. 3, edited by Kozo Yamamura, Cambridge UP, 1990, pp. 500–43.

Ruether, Rosemary. "Mothers of the Church: Ascetic Women in the Late Patristic Age." *Women of Spirit: Female Leadership in the Jewish and Christian Traditions*, edited by Rosemary Ruether and Eleanor McLaughlin, Simon and Schuster, 1979, pp. 71–98.

Ruether, Rosemary, and Eleanor McLaughlin, editors. *Women of Spirit: Female Leadership in the Jewish and Christian Traditions*. Simon and Schuster, 1979.

Ruggiero, Guido. *Binding Passion: Tales of Magic, Marriage, and Power at the End of the Renaissance*. Oxford UP, 1993.

Rupprecht, Carol. "Women's Dreams: Mind and Body." *Feminist Archetypal Theory: Interdisciplinary Re-Visions of Jungian Thought*, edited by Estella Lauter and Carol Schreier Rupprecht, U of Tennessee P, 1985, pp. 186–219.

Russell, Jeffrey B., and Brooks Alexander. *A History of Witchcraft: Sorcerers, Heretics, and Pagans*. Thames and Hudson, 2007.

Rustomji, Nerina. *The Garden and the Fire: Heaven and Hell in Islamic Culture*. Columbia UP, 2009.

Sagant, Philippe. "Becoming a Limbu Priest: Ethnographic Notes." *Spirit Possession in the Nepal Himalayas*, edited by John T. Hitchcock and Rex L. Jones, Vikas, 1996, pp. 56–99.

Salomon, Nanette. "Making a World of Difference: Gender, Asymmetry, and the Greek Nude." *Naked Truths: Women, Sexuality, and Gender in Classical Art and Archaeology*, edited by Ann Olga Koloski-Ostrow and Claire L. Lyons, Routledge, 1997, pp. 197–212.

Samuels, Geoffrey. "The Siddha as a Cultural Category." *Holy Madness: Portraits of Tantric Siddhas*, edited by Robert Linrothe, Serindia Publications, 2006, pp. 37–47.

Sanborn, Sara. "Sally Ride, Astronaut: The World Is Watching." *Ms.*, Jan. 1983, pp. 45–46.

Sanderson, Alexis. "Śaivism and the Tantric Traditions." *The World's Religions: The Religions of Asia*, edited by Friedhelm Hardy, Routledge, 1990, pp. 128–72.

Sannibale, Maurizio, and Paolo Liverani. "The Classical Origins of Angel Iconography." *Angels from the Vatican: The Invisible Made Visible*, edited by Allen Duston and Arnold Nesselrath, Art Services International, 1998, pp. 62–71.

Saraogi, Olga Serbaeva. "Can Encounters with Yoginīs in the *Jayadrathayāmala* be Described as Possession?" *"Yoginī" in South Asia: Interdisciplinary Approaches*, edited by István Keul, Routledge, 2013, pp. 198–212.

Scalf, Foy. "The Role of Birds within the Religious Landscape of Ancient Egypt." *Between Heaven and Earth*, edited by Rozenn Bailleul-LeSuer, Oriental Institute of the U of Chicago, 2012, pp. 33–40.

Scarry, Elaine, editor. *Literature and the Body: Essays on Populations and Persons.* Johns Hopkins UP, 1990.

Schaeffer, Kurtis R., et al., editors. *Sources of Tibetan Tradition.* Columbia UP, 2013.

Schafer, Edward H. *The Divine Woman: Dragon Ladies and Rain Maidens.* North Point Press, 1980.

Schafer, Edward H. *The Golden Peaches of Samarkand: Study of T'ang Exotics.* U of California P, 1963.

Schafer, Edward H. *Pacing the Void: T'ang Approaches to the Stars.* U of California P, 1977.

Schimmel, Annemarie. *Mystical Dimensions of Islam.* U of North Carolina P, 1975.

Schipper, Kristofer. "The *Five Sentiments of Gratitude.*" *Sources of Chinese Tradition*, vol. 1, 2nd ed., edited by Wm. Theodore de Bary and Irene Bloom, Columbia UP, 1999, pp. 402–04.

Schlingloff, Dieter. *Studies in Ajanta Paintings: Identifications and Interpretations.* Ajanta Publications, 1987.

Schüssler Fiorenza, Elisabeth. "Word, Spirit and Power: Women in Early Christian Communities." *Women of Spirit: Female Leadership in the Jewish and Christian Traditions*, edited by Rosemary Radford Ruether and Eleanor McLaughlin, Simon and Schuster, 1979, pp. 29–70.

Schwartz, Howard. *Lilith's Cave: Jewish Tales of the Supernatural.* Oxford UP, 1988.

Segal, Robert A., editor. *In Quest of the Hero.* Princeton UP, 1990.

Séguy, Marie-Rose. *The Miraculous Journey of Mahomet: Mirâj Nâmeh.* Translated by Richard Pevear, George Braziller, 1977.

Seibert, Ilse. *Women in the Ancient Near East.* Translated by Marianne Herzfeld, Abner Schram, 1974.

Sengupta, Gautam. "Hero-stone of West Bengal: A Preliminary Study." *Journal of Bengal Art*, vol. 4, 1999, pp. 77–97.

Sered, Susan Starr. *Priestess, Mother, Sacred Sister: Religions Dominated by Women.* Oxford UP, 1994.

Settar, S., and Gunther D. Sontheimer, editors. *Memorial Stones: A Study of Their Origin, Significance and Variety.* South Asia Institute, U of Heidelberg, 1982.

Shah, Idries. *The Sufis.* Doubleday, 1964.

Shah, Idries. *Tales of the Dervishes: Teaching-Stories of the Sufi Masters over the Past Thousand Years.* E. P. Dutton, 1970.

Sharma, Arvind. "Nudity." *EOR*, vol. 11, 1987, pp. 7–10.

Sharrock, Peter. "The Yoginīs of the Bayon." *"Yoginī" in South Asia: Interdisciplinary Approaches*, edited by István Keul, Routledge, 2013, pp. 117–29.

Shaw, Miranda. *Passionate Enlightenment: Women in Tantric Buddhism.* Princeton UP, 1994.

Shea, Mary Lou. *Medieval Women on Sin and Salvation: Hadewijch of Antwerp, Beatrice of Nazareth, Margaret Ebner, and Julian of Norwich.* American University Studies VII: Theology and Religion, vol. 304. Peter Lang, 2010.

Shephard, Ben. "Flyers But Not Fighters." *Times Literary Supplement*, May 24, 2002.

Shepitko, Larisa, director. *Wings.* 1966. Available as a DVD in the Eclipse series of the Criterion Collection, 2008.

Shi, Kun. "Ny Dan the Manchu Shamaness." *Religions of China in Practice*, edited by Donald S. Lopez, Jr., Princeton UP, 1999, pp. 223–28.

Shippey, Tom. "Foreword." *Revisiting the Poetic Edda: Essays on Old Norse Heroic Legend*, edited by Paul Acker and Carolyne Larrington, Routledge, 2013, pp. xiii-xix.

Shoemaker, Stephen J. *Ancient Traditions of the Virgin Mary's Dormition and Assumption.* Oxford UP, 2002.

Shonkwiler, Randy. "Sheltering Wings: Birds as Symbols of Protection in Ancient Egypt." *Between Heaven and Earth: Birds in Ancient Egypt*, edited by Rozenn Bailleul-LeSuer, Oriental Institute of the U of Chicago, 2012, pp. 49–57.

Sigmund, Anna Maria. *Women of the Third Reich*. NDE Publishing, 2000.

Sikes, E. E. "Nike and Athena Nike." *The Classical Review*, vol. 9, no. 5, June 1895, pp. 280–83.

Silver, Carole G. *Strange and Secret Peoples: Fairies and Victorian Consciousness*. Oxford UP, 1999.

Sircar, Dines Chandra. "The Maukharis and the Later Guptas." *Journal of the Royal Asiatic Society of Bengal, Letters*, vol. XI, no. 2, 1945, 69–74.

Sircar, Dines Chandra. *Śākta Pīṭhas*. 1973. Reprint, Motilal Banarsidass, 1998.

Sklar, Elizabeth S. "Thoroughly Modern Morgan: Morgan le Fey in Twentieth-Century Popular Arthuriana." *Popular Arthurian Traditions*, edited by Sally K. Slocum, Bowling Green State U Popular P, 1992, pp. 24–35.

Skvorecky, Josef. *Ordinary Lives*. Translated by Paul Wilson. Key Porter Books, 2008.

Slade, Carole. *St. Teresa of Avila: Author of a Heroic Life*. U of California P, 1995.

Slocum, Sally K., editor. *Popular Arthurian Traditions*. Bowling Green State U Popular P, 1992.

Smith, Cecil. "Harpies in Greek Art." *The Journal of Hellenic Studies*, vol. 13, 1892–1893, pp. 103–14.

Smith, Jane I. "Islam." *Women in World Religions*, edited by Arvind Sharma, State U of New York P, 1987, pp. 235–50.

Smith, Jane I. "Paradise." *EOW*, vol. 2, 1998, pp. 758–59.

Smith, Margaret. *Rabi'a the Mystic and Her Fellow-Saints in Islam*. Cambridge UP, 1928.

Smith, Margaret. *Readings from the Mystics of Islam*. Luzac & Company, 1950.

Snellgrove, David L. *Buddhist Himalaya: Travels and Studies in Quest of the Origins and Nature of Tibetan Religion*. Philosophical Library, 1957.

Snellgrove, David L. *Indo-Tibetan Buddhism: Indian Buddhists and Their Tibetan Successors*. Serindia Publications, 1987.

Snyder, Gary. "Foreword." *The Divine Woman: Dragon Ladies and Rain Maidens*, edited by Edward H. Schafer, North Point Press, 1980, xi–xvi.

Sontheimer, Gunther. "Hero and Sati-stones of Maharashtra." *Memorial Stones: A Study of Their Origin, Significance and Variety*, edited by S. Settar and Gunther D. Sontheimer, South Asia Institute, U of Heidelberg, 1982, pp. 270–76.

Sorensen, Clark W. "The Myth of Princess Pari and the Self Image of Korean Women." *Anthropos*, vol. 83, 1988, pp. 403–19.

Spiro, Melford E. *Burmese Supernaturalism: Expanded Edition*. Transaction, 1996.

Squire, Charles. *Celtic Myth and Legend*. 1905. Reprint, Newcastle Publishing, 1975.

Staal, Frits, et al. *Agni: The Vedic Ritual of the Fire Altar*. Asian Humanities Press, 1983.

Staal, Frits. *Rules Without Meaning: Ritual, Mantras and the Human Sciences*. Peter Lang, 1989.

Steinberg, Leo. *The Sexuality of Christ in Renaissance Art and in Modern Oblivion*. Pantheon Books, 1983.

Stephen, Michele. "Master of Souls." *Sorcerer and Witch in Melanesia*, edited by Michele Stephen, Rutgers UP, 1987, pp. 41–75.

Stephens, Walter. *Demon Lovers*. U of Chicago P, 2002.

Stern, Christina. "At the Crossroads of Male Anxiety and Aspiration: Marvels, Movement, and Marginality in the Vita of Christina Mirabilis, a Thirteenth-Century Holy Woman of Saint-Trond." Dissertation, New York University, 2003.

Sternberg, Leo. "Divine Election in Primitive Religion." *Congrés International des Américanistes, Compte-Rendu de la XXIe*, Pt. 2, 1924. Göteborg Museum, 1925, pp. 472–512.

Stiehm, Judith. *Bring Me Men and Women: Mandated Change at the United States Air Force Academy*. U of California P, 1981.

Stietencron, Heinrich von. "Cosmographic Buildings of India: The Circles of The Yoginīs." *"Yoginī" in South Asia: Interdisciplinary Approaches*, edited by István Keul, Routledge, 2013, pp. 70–83.

Stoddard, Heather. Lecture, Tibet House, New York City, April 2, 2001.

Storm, Mary. "Death." *EOW*, vol. 1, 1998, pp. 243–45.

Stowasser, Barbara Freyer. "The Status of Women in Early Islam." *Muslim Women*, edited by Freda Hussain, St. Martin's P, 1984, pp. 11–43.

Strauss, Walter L., editor. *The Complete Engravings, Etchings and Drypoints of Albrecht Dürer*. Dover, 1972.

Stutley, Margaret and James Stutley. *Harper's Dictionary of Hinduism: Its Mythology, Folklore, Philosophy, Literature, and History*. Harper & Row, 1984.

Sukhu, Gopal. *The Shaman and the Heresiarch: A New Interpretation of the* Li Sao. State U of New York P, 2012.

Sutherland, Patricia D. "Shamanism and the Iconography of Palaeo-Eskimo Art." *The Archaeology of Shamanism*, edited by Neil Price, Routledge, 2001, pp. 135–45.

Taksami, C. N. "The Story of a Nivkhi Shamaness as Told by Herself." *Shamanism in Siberia*, edited by Vilmos Diószegi and Mihály Hoppál. Translated by S. Simon, Akadémiai Kiadó, 1996, pp. 102–06.

Talamantez, Ines M. "Dance: In Microhistorical Traditions." *EOW*, vol. 1, 1998, pp. 237–39.

Tattersall, Ian. *The Origin of the Human Capacity*. American Museum of Natural History, 1998.

Tedlock, Barbara. *The Woman in the Shaman's Body: Reclaiming the Feminine in Religion and Medicine*. Bantam Books, 2006.

Templeman, David. "The Ḍākinī in Tibetan Hagiography." *The Iconic Female: Goddesses of India, Nepal, and Tibet*, edited by Jayant Bhalchandra Bapat and Ian Mabbet, Monash UP, 2008, pp. 133–47.

Tervarent, Guy de. *La Légende de Sainte Ursule: Dans la Littérature et l'Art du Moyen Age*. 2 vols. Les Éditions G. van Oest, 1932.

Tester, Jim. *A History of Western Astrology*. Ballantine Books, 1987.

Thalith, Joseph. "Witchcraft and Witches in Central India." *Anthropos*, vol. 41, no. 4/6, 1946/1949, pp. 892–93.

Thomas, Keith. *Religion and the Decline of Magic*. Charles Schribner's Sons, 1971.

Thomas, Louis-Vincent. "Funeral Rites." *EOR*, vol. 5, 1987, p. 456.

Thomas, Nicholas, and Caroline Humphrey, editors. *Shamanism, History, and the State*. U of Michigan P, 1994.

Thurman, Judith. "Missing Woman: Amelia Earhart's Flight." *The New Yorker*, September 14, 2009, pp. 103–08.

Törzsök, Judit. "Yoginī and Goddess Possession in Early Śaiva Tantras." *"Yoginī" in South Asia: Interdisciplinary Approaches*, edited by István Keul, Routledge, 2013, pp. 179–97.

Trachtenberg, Joshua. *Jewish Magic and Superstition: A Study in Folk Religion*. 1939. Reprint, Atheneum, n.d.

Trimingham, J. Spencer. *The Sufi Orders in Islam*. Clarendon P, 1971.

Tringham, Ruth. "The Civilization of the Goddess: The World of Old Europe." *American Anthropologist*, vol. 95, no. 1, March 1993, pp. 196–97.

Tringham, Ruth, and Margaret Conkey. "Rethinking Figurines: A Critical View from Archaeology of Gimbutas, the 'Goddess' and Popular Culture." *Ancient Goddesses: The Myths and the Evidence*, edited by Lucy Goodison and Christine Morris, U of Wisconsin P, 1998, pp. 22–45.

Tuczay, Christa A. "Motifs in *The Arabian Nights* and in Ancient and Medieval European Literature: A Comparison." *Folklore* vol. 116, Dec. 2005, pp. 272–91.

Tull, Herman W. *The Vedic Origins of Karma: Cosmos as Man in Ancient Indian Myth and Ritual*. State U of New York P, 1989.

Tuthill, Cynthia, and Carolynn Conley. "Birding with Kalpana." *Birding*, Oct. 2003, pp. 530–34.

Ucko, Peter J. *Anthropomorphic Figurines of Predynastic Egypt and Neolithic Crete with Comparative Material from the Prehistoric Near East and Mainland Greece*. Royal Anthropological Institute, Occasional Paper No. 24. London, 1968.

Upton, Charles. *Doorkeeper of the Heart: Versions of Rabi'a*. Threshold Books, 1988.

Urban, Hugh. "The Path of Power: Impurity, Kingship, and Sacrifice in Assamese Tantra." *Journal of the American Academy of Religion*, vol. 69, no. 4, Dec. 2001, pp. 777–816.

Urban, Hugh. "The Womb of Tantra: Goddesses, Tribals and Kings in Assam." *The Journal of Hindu Studies*, vol. 4, 2011, pp. 231–47.

Vanderauwera, Ria. "The Brabant Mystic Hadewijch." *Medieval Women Writers*, edited by Katharina M. Wilson, U of Georgia P, 1984, pp. 186–203.

Verdet, Jean-Pierre. *The Sky: Mystery, Magic and Myth*. Translated by Anthony Zielonka, Harry N. Abrams, 1992.

Verhoeven, March. "Ritual and Ideology in the Pre-Pottery Neolithic B of the Levant and Southeast Anatolia." *Cambridge Archaeological Journal*, vol. 12, no. 2, 2002, pp. 233–58.

Vijaisri, Priyadarshini. "Invoking the Erotic Mother: The Outcaste Priestess and the Heroic Men." *"Yogini" in South Asia: Interdisciplinary Approaches*, edited by István Keul, Routledge, 2013, pp. 163–76.

Vitebsky, Piers. *The Shaman: Voyages of the Soul, Trance, Ecstasy and Healing from Siberia to the Amazon*. Macmillan, 1995.

Voyatzis, Mary E. "From Athena to Zeus." *Ancient Goddesses: The Myths and the Evidence*, edited by Lucy Goodison and Christine Morris, U of Wisconsin P, 1998, pp. 133–47.

Vries, Jan de. *Altergermanische Religionsgeschichte*. 2 vols. W. De Gruyter, 1935–1937.

Waida, Manabu. "Birds." *EOR*, vol. 2, 1987, pp. 224–27.

Waller, James C. "Shape-Shifting." *EOW*, vol. 2, 1998, pp. 895–97.

Walraven, Boudewijn. "Shamans and Popular Religion Around 1900." *Religions in Traditional Korea, Proceedings of the 1992 AKSE/SBS Symposium*, edited by H. H. Sorensen, Seminar for Buddhist Studies, 1995, pp. 107–130.

Walters, Barbara R. "Women Religious Virtuosae from the Middle Ages: A Case Pattern and Analytic Model of Types." *Sociology of Religion*, vol. 63, no. 1, 2002, pp. 69–89.

Walton, Francis Redding. "Aphrodite." *OCD*, 1970, pp. 80–81.

Ware, James R., translator. *Alchemy, Medicine, Religion in the China of A.D. 320: The Nei P'ien of Ko Hung*. M.I.T. Press, 1966

Ware, Susan. *Still Missing: Amelia Earhart and the Search for Modern Feminism*. Norton, 1993.

Ware, Timothy. *The Orthodox Church: New Edition*. 1963. Reprint, Penguin, 1997.

Warner, Marina. *Alone of All Her Sex: The Myth and the Cult of the Virgin Mary*. Knopf, 1976.

Warner, Marina. *Joan of Arc: Reality and Myth*. Verloren, 1994.

Warner, Marina. *Monuments and Maidens: The Allegory of the Female Form*. U of California P, 1985.

Waterbury, Florence. *Bird Deities in China*. Artibus Asiae, 1952.

Watson, James L. "Of Flesh and Bones: The Management of Death Pollution in Cantonese Society." *Death and the Regeneration of Life*, edited by Maurice Bloch and Jonathan Parry, Cambridge UP, 1982, pp. 155–86.

Watson, James L., and Evelyn S. Rawski, editors. *Death Ritual in Late Imperial and Modern China*. U of California P, 1988.

Waugh, Earle H. "Religious Levitation and the Muslim Experience: A Study in the Flight Symbolism of Intermediary Figures and Other Images in Medieval Islam." Dissertation, University of Chicago, 1972.

Weber, Bruce. "Jerrie Mock Dies at 88, First Solo Female Pilot to Circumnavigate Globe." *New York Times*, Oct. 5, 2014.

Weinstein, Donald, and Rudolph M. Bell. *Saints and Society: The Two Worlds of Western Christendom, 1000–1700*. U of Chicago P, 1982.

Weinstock, Stefan. "Victor and Invictus." *The Harvard Theological Review*, vol. 50, no. 3, July 1957, pp. 211–47.

Welch, Holmes. *Taoism: The Parting of the Way*. Beacon Press, 1965.

Westenholz, Joan Goodnick. "Goddesses of the Ancient Near East 3000–1000 BC." *Ancient Goddesses: The Myths and the Evidence*, edited by Lucy Goodison and Christine Morris, U of Wisconsin P, 1999, pp. 63–82.

White, David Gordon. *The Alchemical Body: Siddha Traditions in Medieval India*. U of Chicago P, 1996.

White, David Gordon. *Kiss of the Yogini: "Tantric Sex" in its South Asian Contexts*. U of Chicago P, 2003.

White, David Gordon, editor. *Tantra in Practice*. Princeton UP, 2000.

Whitfield, Roderick. *The Art of Central Asia: The Stein Collection in the British Museum*. 3 vols. Kodansha International in co-operation with the Trustees of the British Museum, 1982–1985.

Whittell, Giles. *Spitfire Women of World War Two*. HarperPress, 2007.

Wiley, Roland John. *Tchaikovsky's Ballets: Swan Lake, Sleeping Beauty, Nutcracker*. Clarendon P, 1985.

Williams, Joanna. "Construction of Gender in the Paintings and Graffiti of Sigiriya." *Representing the Body: Gender Issues in Indian Art*, edited by Vidya Dehejia, Kali for Women, 1997, 56–67.

Williams, Walter L. *The Spirit and the Flesh: Sexual Diversity in American Indian Culture*. Beacon P, 1992.

Willis, Janice D. "Dākinī: Some Comments on Its Nature and Meaning." *Feminine Ground: Essays on Women and Tibet*, edited by Janice D. Willis, Snow Lion Publications, 1989, pp. 57–75.

Willis, Janice D., editor. *Feminine Ground: Essays on Women and Tibet*. Snow Lion Publications, 1989.

Wilson, David M., and Ole Klindt-Jensen. *Viking Art*. George Allen and Unwin, 1966.

Wilson, Liz. *Charming Cadavers: Horrific Figurations of the Feminine in Indian Buddhist Hagiograhic Literature*. U of Chicago P, 1996.

Winkler, John. J. *The Constraints of Desire: The Anthropology of Sex and Gender in Ancient Greece*. Routledge, 1990.

Winternitz, Maurice. *A History of Indian Literature*. 3 vols. 1927. Reprint, Oriental Books Reprint, 1977.

Wohl, Victoria. *Intimate Commerce: Exchange, Gender, and Subjectivity in Greek Tragedy*. U of Texas P, 1998.

Wolf, Virginia. *Virginia Woolf: Women and Writing*, edited by Michèle Barrett, The Women's Press, 1979.

Woodward, Kenneth L. *The Book of Miracles: The Meaning of the Miracle Stories in Christianity, Judaism, Buddhism, Hinduism, and Islam*. Touchstone, 2000.

Wright, M. R. *Cosmology in Antiquity*. Routledge, 1995.

Young, Iris Marion. "Humanism, Gynocentrism and Feminist Politics." *Hypatia Reborn: Essays in Feminist Philosophy*, edited by Azizah Y. al-Hibri and Margaret A. Simons, Indiana UP, 1990, pp. 231–48.

Young, Serinity. *An Anthology of Sacred Texts By and About Women*. Crossroad, 1993.

Young, Serinity. *Courtesans and Tantric Consorts: Buddhist Sexualities in Narrative, Iconography and Ritual*. Routledge, 2004.

Young, Serinity. *Dreaming in the Lotus: Buddhist Dream Narrative, Imagery, and Practice*. Wisdom Publications, 1999.

Young, Serinity. "Dreams." *EOW*, vol. 1, 1998, pp. 271–73.

Young, Serinity. "Stars." *EOR*, vol. 14, 1987, pp. 42–46.

Young, Serinity. "Tantra." *EOW*, vol. 2, 1998, pp. 956–59.

Yü, Ying-Shih. "'O Soul, Come Back!' A Study in the Changing Conceptions of the Soul and Afterlife in Pre-Buddhist China." *Harvard Journal of Asiatic Studies*, vol. 47, no. 2, 1987, pp. 363–95.

Zimmer, Heinrich Robert. *Art of Indian Asia, Its Mythology and Transformations*. Pantheon, 1955.

Žornickaja, M. Ja. "Dances of Yakut Shamans." *Shamanism in Siberia*, edited by Vilmos Diószegi and Mihály Hoppál. Translated by S. Simon, Akadémiai Kiadó, 1996, pp. 127–45.

WEBSITES

Egan, Gregory K. *The Earhart Project*. The International Group for Historic Aircraft Recovery, http://tighar.org/Projects/Earhart/AEdescr.html.

Egan, Gregory K., editor. *The Pioneers: Aviation Pioneers: An Anthology*. The Lawrence Hargrave Collection, http://www.ctie.monash.edu.au/hargrave/pioneers.html.

Egan, Gregory K., editor. "Hanna Reitsch (1912–1979)." The Lawrence Hargrave Collection, *The Pioneers: Aviation Pioneers: An Anthology*, http://www.ctie.monash.edu.au/hargrave/reitsch.html.

Hamiaux, Marianne, and Sophie Marmois. "A Closer Look at the Victory of Samothrace." Translated by Susan Pickford and John Tittensor, http://musee.louvre.fr/oal/victoiredesamothrace/victoiredesamothrace_acc_en.html.

Mees, Bernard. "Völkische Altnordistik: The Politics of Nordic Studies in the German-Speaking Countries, 1926–45." Eleventh International Saga Conference, Sydney, 2000, http://www.sydney.edu.au/arts/medieval/saga/pdf/316-mees.pdf.

Poncelet, Albert A. "St. Ursula and the Eleven Thousand Virgins." *The Catholic Encyclopedia*, http://www.newadvent.org/cathen/15225d.htm.

Rabe, Michael. "Sexual Imagery on the 'Phantasmagorical Castles' at Khajuraho." *International Journal of Tantric Studies*, vol. 2, no. 2, Nov. 1996, http://asiatica.org/ijts/vol2_no2/sexual-imagery-phantasmagorical-castles-khajuraho/.

Samaha, John M., S.M. "Our Lady of the Pillar." https://udayton.edu/imri/mary/o/our-lady-of-the-pillar.php.

St. Clare, Lisa. "As the Crone Flies: The Imagery of Women as Flying Witches in Early Modern Europe." Dissertation, University of Oklahoma, 2016, https://shareok.org/handle/11244/34591.

Wescoat, Bonna, Vicki Herzberg, Elizabeth Hornor, and Michael Page. "Samothrace: Framing the Mysteries in the Sanctuary of the Great Gods." Emory University. http://www.samothrace.emory.edu.

WVradioman. "Hanna Reitsch—Test-pilot Interview." 1976. https://www.youtube.com/watch?v=ykre9XCoXac.

INDEX

Note: Page numbers in *italics* refer to illustrations.

adept/s 16, 19, 133, 135, 136, 139, 140, 142, 145, 146, 147, 149, 186, 214, 224

Aeschylus 44, 46, 250

afterlife 16, 30, 31, 53, 60, 61, 63, 196

altar/s 12, 13, 52, 53

Amazons 42, 229, 231

ambivalence 126, 150

ambivalent 24, 33, 62, 99, 117, 123, 126

amulet/s 18, 32, 35, 48, 60, 62, 159

ancestor/s 11, 12, 14, 22, 33, 35, 104, 178, 182, 261n78

Angel Calming Joseph's Suspicion 97

Angel of Death and the Sculptor 101

angel of the house 95, 101–03

angels 9, 15, 20, 55, 78, 95–104, 118, 158, 161, 189, 190, 191, 193, 194, 196, 198, 200, 201, 206, 207, 211, 233

animal/s 8, 14, 20, 22, 25, 40, 41, 60, 75, 80, 83, 112, 117, 122, 127, 136, 138, 141, 144, 146, 149, 156, 157, 162, 166, 167, 171, 174, 175, 187, 257n4, 268n27, 270n2, 285n91, 294n58, 295n67

head/ed 136, 144. *See also under* bird/s

helper 22, 179, 181, 188, 236. *See also* bird/s; horse/s

Ankarloo, Bengt 164

apotheosis 15, 16, 20–22, 94

apotheosis of Empress Sabina *21*

Aphrodite 26, 41, 49–50, 76, 97, 229, 231, 233

Aphrodite Riding a Goose 23

apsarā/s 3, 4, 7, 15, 35, 38, 51, 74, 78, 79, 85, 90, 93, 112, 115, 117–32, 137, 141, 159, 225, 229, 235, 250, 252, 253, 267n2, 270n4, 271n13

and 31, 278n1, 279n25

as swans 74, 271n13, 278n1

Valkyries, and 305

See also Menakā; Pramloca; Tilottamā; Urvaśī

apsarā, netsuke of *128*

apsarā from Borobudur *119*

Apuleius 157, 158, 167

Artemis 26, 41, 50, 77, 162, 233, 256n8

winged 26

ascension 15–16, 22, 79, 100, 177, 180, 196, 200, 211, 220, 225, 227

ascetic/s 22, 79, 121, 125, 129, 130, 132, 141, 179, 188, 194, 208, 212, 221, 222

asceticism 15, 122, 125, 142, 204

assumption 15–16, 100, 196, 200–01, 203

347